WEHALI:
THE FEMALE LAND

TRADITIONS OF A TIMORESE RITUAL CENTRE

WEHALI:
THE FEMALE LAND

TRADITIONS OF A TIMORESE RITUAL CENTRE

TOM THERIK

Australian
National
University

ANU PRESS

Australian
National
University

ANU PRESS

Published by ANU Press
The Australian National University
Canberra ACT 2600, Australia
Email: anupress@anu.edu.au

Available to download for free at press.anu.edu.au

ISBN (print): 9781760464844
ISBN (online): 9781760464851

WorldCat (print): 1366228075
WorldCat (online): 1366227897

DOI: 10.22459/WFL.2022

Cover design and layout by ANU Press

Cover photograph: Senior woman Bei Ho'ar Keke' in her house in Wehali.

Contents

List of Figures

List of Maps

List of Photographs

List of Tables

WEHALI

Table 8.1: Vicarious death of Liurai Brehi   223

Table 8.2: Liver omen categories   252

Table 8.3: Distribution of *fukun* named houses   259

Preface to the 2023 Edition

Tom Therik's *Wehali: The Female Land* is an ethnography essential to an understanding of the cultural history of Timor. Wehali, on the south-central coast of Timor, is a ritual centre and an origin source acknowledged by societies in both West and East Timor. This study is the most detailed, historically focused ethnography of Wehali and its traditions.

This book was originally published by the Research School of Pacific and Asian Studies' Pandanus Books, but that edition is now out of print. This republication by ANU Press, as a volume in the Comparative Austronesian series, makes it readily available to an international audience.

In Timor's traditions, Wehali is the immobile female source of vitality. Symbolically, it is the empty silent centre—'the enveloping sheath'—that has dispensed its vitality to the rest of Timor. It is the female land opposed to the male lands to its east and west.

My foreword to the original publication of *Wehali* sets forth Wehali's historical significance and cultural importance within Timor. Wehali is a Tetun-speaking centre and its influence extended eastward as far as the once historically important domain of Luca in East Timor, but its influence also extended westward to the Atoni-speaking domains under the authority of Sonbai. As an outward-oriented centre, Wehali is also, internally, a complex social formation: Wesei Wehali, a union of 'Heaven' and 'Earth'. This volume examines Wehali's complex internal social organisation as well as its all-important historical and ritual traditions.

Since the initial publication of this volume, its author, Tom Therik, has died. He was a skilled ethnographer, a fluent speaker of Tetun and a sympathetic investigator of Wehali's rich oral traditions. Memories of his gentle, always interested, caring, careful approach to ethnographic research are still fresh in the minds of those who knew him. His contribution to our understanding of Timor is immense. His work is a landmark in the study of Timor.

It is important to note that fieldwork for this study was carried out in the early 1990s when East Timor was part of Indonesia. For Tom Therik, Wehali provided a crucial bridge between the two halves of the island. Tom's premature and unexpected death precluded any updating of his original manuscript to acknowledge the creation of Timor-Leste. Regrettably several photographs in the earlier edition of *Wehali* have gone missing and are not therefore included. As an addition to this new edition, however, two new photographs have been added: one a photograph of three of Tom's closest Tetun supporters: Piet Tahu Nahak, Gabriel Bria and Ferdy Seran; and the other, a separate photograph of Piet Tahu Nahak who was one of Tom's chief collaborators.

James J. Fox
17 January 2023

Foreword

This book offers a fundamental understanding of Timor. Its focus is on a small settlement, Wehali, that defines itself as the 'centre' (Laran) of the island of Timor and indeed, conceptionally, of the rest of the world. As a 'centre', Wehali continues to be the residence of a figure of traditional authority on whom, in the 18th century, the Dutch conferred the title of Kaiser (Keizer) and the Portuguese, the title of Emperor (Imperador) of Timor. Known locally as the Nai Boot, 'Great Lord', or as the Maromak Oan, 'Child of the Luminous', this spiritual figure was the source of life from whom surrounding domains derived their prosperity. Thus, historically, Wehali was the ritual centre of a network of tributary states, which both the Dutch and the Portuguese regarded as paramount to the political organisation of the island.

Despite colonial assertions of its critical importance, Wehali's traditional role on Timor seems to have remained a mystery to both the Portuguese and the Dutch. As glimpsed from the outside, there was always only a fragmentary imagining of Wehali. When, in the first half of the 17th century, the Portuguese-speaking Topasses decided to establish a permanent settlement and trading outpost at Lifao on the north coast of Timor, Wehali was seen as a principal threat to their control of the sandalwood trade. Thus, in 1642, the fidalgo Francisco Fernandez is reported to have led a small troop of men across the island, from north to south, in a raid that burnt Wehali. This daring sortie was supposed to end Wehali's authority and thereby redirect the allegiance of Timorese states to Lifao. Clearly, however, Wehali's authority—whatever it may have been then—was not based on political power that could be wrested from its source. In time, its authority revived and by the 18th century both the Dutch and Portuguese were vying with each other in claiming a relationship to Wehali.

Thus, in 1756, the Dutch East India Company sent a distinguished envoy by the name of Paravicini to set in order its relations on Timor and on the nearby islands. In the end, Commissaris Paravicini produced a contract treaty signed by all of the rulers of Timor and those of the neighbouring islands with whom the Dutch claimed a political relationship. The treaty was a lengthy document with 30 clauses attested to by some 48 signatories. In the treaty, Wehali was referred to by its dual name, Wewiku-Wehali (Wywiko-Bahale). Its ruler was named as the 'great king' of Belo (*groot-koning Belo*), under whom were listed the names of the rulers of 21 'obedient states' (*gehoorsaemeheyt staende regenten*), with an additional seven allied neighbouring states. This treaty laid the basis for all subsequent Dutch claims to a connection with Wehali.

The Portuguese, too, continued to claim a close relationship. Although they never concluded treaties like those of the Dutch, their assertions were no less emphatic. In 1777, the Portuguese in Dili produced an account of the island as divided into two provinces: a western province called Serviâo, inhabited by the Vaiquenos (Dawan or Atoni) and consisting of 16 local kingdoms (*reinos*), and an eastern province called Bellum (or Bellos), inhabited and dominated by the Belu (or Tetun) and comprising no less than 46 small kingdoms. The Portuguese referred to this ruler of the Belos as Emperor. Although the Portuguese never specifically named this ruler, the name of Wehali's ruler recorded on the Treaty of Paravicini was distinctly Portuguese in origin: Hiacijntoe Corea. Clearly, in the 18th century, the influence of the Portuguese on Wehali was greater than that of the Dutch.

Early in the 19th century, provoked by recurrent territorial disputes, the Dutch and Portuguese began intermittent negotiations, which continued until 1916, to demarcate the borders between the colonial powers. In 1851, through a local agreement with the Portuguese Governor in Dili and the payment of 200,000 florin, the Dutch were able to effect a partial delimitation of territories, which was later ratified by a Treaty of Demarcation in 1859. By these agreements, the territory of Wehali was formally assigned to the Dutch but many of its closest aligned domains, such as Suai, were separated and assigned to Portuguese control.

Having gained official jurisdiction over Wehali, the Dutch made no attempt to exercise their authority until the 20th century. With an armed guard of native soldiers, the Dutch controleur, Mathijsen, was able to gain an audience with the ruler of Wehali in 1904, at which the Great

Lord would hardly speak, leaving his deputy to address the Dutchman on his behalf. Eventually Mathijsen's expedition was forced to retreat. Two years later, a military expedition was mounted to 'pacify' the area. This contingent fought its way into Wehali's territory and eventually established a military post at a nearby site, Besikama.

By any historical estimation, Wehali is no ordinary land. Located on a broad alluvial plain (*fehan*) on the south coast of central Timor, Wehali stands opposed to the mountains (*foho*) where most Tetun live. It has no walls, no fortifications, no unassailable redoubts. In this sense, it is totally indefensible as a political entity. A European misapprehension was that the ritual figure who resided in Wehali held some kind of formidable political power. Instead, Wehali is considered *rai feto*, 'female land', as opposed to *rai mane*, 'male land'. On its southern border is the *tasi mane*, the turbulent 'male sea'. As such, Wehali is protected only by the male lands and sea that surround it.

The 'Great Lord' of Wehali has many attributes, but none of these is associated with the exercise of power. Thus the Lord of Wehali is also known as the 'Dark Lord' (*Nai Kukun*). As Dark Lord, he represents the earth. He is described as 'the one who eats reclining, who drinks reclining' (*mahaa toba/mahemu toba*)—the opposite attributes of an active leader. He is also known as 'the Female Lord' and as a representative of the female attributes of the earth, he is—as is everything in Wehali—'feminised'. Embodied in his person is the fundamental Timorese idea that ultimate authority is defined as female.

As a consequence, Wehali is a totally female-centred area: all land, all property, all houses belong to women and are passed from one generation of women to the next. In contrast, most other Timorese societies (including other Tetun groups) are organised along male lines, with a strong bias to inheritance from father to son. In Wehali, men are exchanged as husbands in marriage, never women. And in legend as in reality, Wehali is the 'husband-giver' to other areas of Timor. Thus, whereas Wehali traces its origins within its sphere exclusively through women, all surrounding realms that look to Wehali as their source trace their relations of origin through males who have come from Wehali. Historically, tribute was paid to Wehali by other Tetun and by many of the Atoni population for the performance of the rituals of life. And just as Wehali did not defend itself but left all defence to its surrounding male-oriented domains, so, too,

Wehali had all the attributes of a 'silent' centre. As the Dutch controleur discovered but did not understand, the ruler of Wehali spoke only through his deputy.

Given the levels of political, social and ritual complexity that a study of Wehali poses, this book, *Wehali* by Dr G. Tom Therik, is revelatory. The research on which it is based represents a stunning achievement. To comprehend Wehali as a ritual centre, one must understand the special dyadic language of its rituals, grasp its metaphoric subtleties, decipher the implications of its expressions, and then communicate this understanding intelligently and poetically. Even for a fluent native speaker of Tetun, this is a formidable task, as Tom Therik indicates, but it is one that he has carried out admirably. It is on this firm foundation of linguistic competence that we now have a book that opens the door to an understanding of some of the most important ideas of Timorese life.

Therik begins his book with a view of Wehali from the outside, but this serves only as the prelude to an examination of Wehali from within— an exploration of its origin structures: the internal ideas and narratives on which Wehali is founded. Crucial dual categories—male/female, outside/inside, periphery/centre—serve as key 'operators' that recursively structure a coherent conceptual system that can be replicated in dependent domains that look to Wehali as their source. In line with the ideas that give authority to Wehali as a female centre is an exchange system that reverses the common order of marriage in most of Timor. Instead of exchanging women among related 'male' houses (*uma mane*), Wehali exchanges men among 'female houses' (*uma feto*) and bestows men on other domains, thus sending forth its sons as 'in-marrying' males who give rise to ruling houses elsewhere on Timor.

Tom Therik's book is a subtle exploration of poetry and practice that allows one to appreciate the persistence of ideas that have been vital in the history of Timor. It is hard to imagine a better starting point for the study of Timor than this study of Wehali as its centre. From Wehali, there are many tracks, many paths that lead to the rest of the island.

James J. Fox

Summary

This study examines the historical and cultural dimensions of the territory of 'the four-corner land' (Wehali) in the southern plains of Wehali-Wewiku, West Timor. Within the political structure of the domain of Wehali, the hamlet of Laran is the seat of its supreme ruler, entitled Maromak Oan. His authority is indisputably acknowledged by people of this higher order origin group ('the four-corner land').

Tetun living in this lowland describe themselves as the 'plains people'. Economically speaking, the majority of these people are subsistence agriculturalists who rely on the cultivation of maize, rice and sorghum, and on the extract of the *gebang* palm as an alternative source of food. In terms of social organisation, they live attached to their named houses (*uma maho naran*), which function as primary lineages. Every person identifies himself/herself with a named house as his/her 'trunk house' (*uma hun*). This is the social unit to which a south Tetun traces his/her derivation. For ritual purposes, these named houses are grouped into *le'un*. The grouping of more than one *le'un* composes a larger entity called *leo*. To distinguish a hamlet where a man resides after marriage from the hamlet where his named house is situated, he refers to the latter as his 'trunk hamlet'.

As an ethnographic work, this study explores dual symbolic classifications as expressed in a variety of local categories. Social relations among people at the domain, hamlet and house levels are expressed in 'metaphors for living' such as female/male, inside/outside and centre/periphery. Unlike other societies where the botanical 'trunk' and 'tips' are used as prominent categories to reflect the continuity of life within the societies concerned, the south Tetun botanical idiom rests mainly on the notion of 'trunk'. As for 'tips', south Tetun has 'flower', 'fruit' and other categories expressed in house symbolisms. Wehali is conceived of as the inner house while other domains are its platforms, corner posts, ladders and gates. Wehali is also a dwelling space while others are cultivation spaces. In life-giving rituals, central Wehali is acknowledged as the source of life while its peripheral domains are its source of wealth.

Like other societies of 'unwritten' culture, south Tetun society preserves the knowledge of the past, which we term 'history', in various forms of oral tradition. These narratives provide a legitimate ground for the people to claim their present superior social and political situations. These narratives are associated with a particular origin group at the level of domain, clan or even house (lineage). The corpus of narratives recorded in this study (Reference Texts 2 to 8) represent these three levels. Myths recorded as Reference Texts 2, 3, 4 and 7 were narrated by *adat* historians and represent the higher order origin groups of Wehali and Wewiku. Myths presented in Reference Texts 5 and 6 represent the hamlet of Kateri. The myth in Reference Text 8 is a story associated particularly with the house of Umanen.

From the time of the first contact with Europeans who came to the island of Timor until the present Indonesian government, the domain of Wehali and the hamlet of Laran have experienced dramatic changes. Wehali, which was once considered politically a 'superpower' among domains in Timor, has been reduced to a hamlet of only ritual significance. The historical and cultural dimensions of the 'great empire' which is the focus of this study are reflected by the order of chapters as outlined in Chapter 1.

1

Introduction

Opening Remarks

This book is based on field research on the island of Timor, in eastern Indonesia, from August 1992 to August 1993. I went to Timor to investigate matrilineal societies located in the southern plain[1] of the south Tetun division, and more specifically the people of the old 'empire' of Wehali. In the course of my research, I gradually came to understand how the notion of the 'flow of life', emphasised by eastern Indonesian anthropologists, is also central to south Tetun discourse. This notion is expressed in different sets of lexical terms or dual categories based on different symbolic 'operators'. To explore this basic notion of life, I examine Wehali social organisation and rituals designed to maintain the continuation of their society, the fertility of human beings and crops as sources of livelihood. Thus this work examines expressions of dual categories used by the south Tetun in general and the Wehali in particular to organise their society.

To study dual symbolic classifications in a society such as Wehali, whose history can be traced over several centuries, one is forced to begin with the historical account of their first encounter with 'outside' traders. However, my aim is not to reconstruct their past history. Rather, I attempt

---

1   This plain is known by several names. The Wewiku people favour the term 'Besikama plain' because it is associated with one of the ritual centres in the domain of Wewiku. Some take a neutral stand by calling it the 'Benain plain'. This term refers to the name of the river of Benenai, which divides this plain into two halves. The first half is occupied by the Wehali and the second half by the Haitimuk and the Wewiku. Throughout the book I use the term the 'plain of Wehali-Wewiku', a phrase commonly heard in Wehali.

to highlight how outsiders (in this case European traders, missionaries and colonial government officials) viewed Wehali and how the Wehali perceived themselves based on their own origin myths. Thus the study starts with the presumption that there is a contrast in perspective between those whom I refer to as 'outsiders' on the one hand and 'insiders' on the other. Historical documents written by outsiders are taken to represent their own point of view, while oral histories narrated by ritual specialists represent the insiders, the subjects of my research.

This book began as a thesis. People often compare the process of writing a thesis with the idea of making a journey. My Tetun friends also portrayed my endeavour to learn their cultural life as an attempt to seek the true knowledge inherited from their ancestors. It is not a coincidence that this notion of journey, an important element of Austronesian heritage, is also preserved by the Tetun people. In seeking the true knowledge (of something), the south Tetun delineate it as a journey 'tracing the old path, the old track' (*tuir dalan tuan//tuir inuk tuan*).

Using this notion of journey as an analogy, my endeavour began in Canberra. As part of my preparation for fieldwork, my supervisor, Professor James J. Fox, urged me to translate a collection of invocations published by Vroklage (1953) in Tetun and German. In translating a few hundred lines from Tetun to English, I took the opportunity not only to translate lines of parallel verse and dyadic phrases into English, but also to familiarise myself again with Tetun, a language that was part of my childhood.

I was born and grew up in Atambua, the capital of the regency of Belu. Although the location of my fieldwork was only about 60 kilometres from my home town, during my childhood the difficulty and danger of travelling discouraged people from visiting the fertile plains of south Tetun. In taking up my fieldwork, I went to Betun believing it to be still a remote village, 'isolated geographically, historically and culturally from the rest of Timor societies', as Francillon (1967) phrased it. The rugged mountains enclosing the northern part of Wehali-Wewiku and the rough 'male sea' on the south isolate three ancient domains (Wehali, Wewiku and Haitimuk) from the rest of the world. With its inadequate infrastructure (road and transportation systems), I imagined Betun to be still in the middle of nowhere.

The earlier perception of isolation of south Tetun was further strengthened by its location between two 'unfriendly' groups of people—Halikelen and Mande'u. Travellers who went to Betun or came from Betun to Atambua had to pass through these two places. Halikelen was well known as a place where travellers (on horseback or even by car) would be stopped and forcibly robbed. Mande'u was well known as a place where skilful head-hunters lived.[2]

For the most part, the geographical isolation of south Tetun as described by Father Jansen in 1892, by Father Mathijsen in 1904 and even by Francillon in 1962 to 1964 fitted with my past experience. But to my surprise, by the time of my field research the situation had changed dramatically. Now commuters can use public transport to travel conveniently between Atambua and Betun. It took only two to three hours (because of frequent stops) for me to travel between these two capitals. Electricity is no longer strange for the villagers, although only a small number of people have the privilege of enjoying this luxury. In accordance with the spirit of development stressed by the Indonesian government, a TV relay station has been built in Betun. A few weeks after I left the region, this TV station was officially to begin operating. Whether these new developments, promoted to reach isolated areas, will have any impact on so-called 'cultural isolationism' remains a topic that will need further study.

In its present form, this study reflects my own experience in the field coupled with my endeavour to capture issues that are central to south Tetun social life. These issues range from politics to marriage and kinship to ritual obligations.

A number of ethnographic writings focus on political systems in this region, reflecting the importance of this theme. For the people themselves, the important thing is not so much the system, but the people who exercise its power. This was reflected in my first encounter with the 'deputy head' (*wakil camat*) of the district of Malaka Tengah. After reporting to him,

---

2   Father Jansen in his first field trip to Wehali in 1892 saw four human heads hung on a stick of wood. In his report, he mentioned this experience under the title 'The tough *adat* in Belu' (Laan 1969: 302). In one of my trips outside Wehali, I visited the neighbouring domain of Mande'u (Dirma), a place called Maibiku. One of the *ksadan* (ritual centres) there was set up specifically for head-hunting rituals. People in this place still remember well the songs the head-hunters sang when they proceeded to the hamlet and what type of dance the women performed to praise their heroes and to humble the dead.

he straightaway mentioned a political problem that the south Tetun were (and still are) facing concerning the appointment of a new Maromak Oan, the supreme ruler of the domain of Wehali.

Government and other *adat* elders have endorsed Agustinus Nahak of Haitimuk to be the Maromak Oan. This decision was rejected by the Laran nobles from the hamlet of Maromak Oan. Instead, they proposed their own Maromak Oan by the name of Agustinus Muti (Na'i Muti).

For the first few months, heads of villages, nobles and other *adat* elders voluntarily kept me informed about this 'political turmoil', as they called it, seeing it as the most important thing an anthropologist should know.

Ritual language occupies a special place in people's perceptions because it reveals 'the path of the ancestors' and is therefore considered the language or words of the ancestors. To emphasise this, a ritual specialist would often conclude his explanation of something with the phrase 'these are the words ancestors left for us'. Ritual language is different from ordinary speech in its use of images and metaphors and its distinctive rhythm of expression. But the most significant difference is the consequence the speaker bears if he 're-tells' the words of the ancestors falsely. When a ritual specialist uses ritual language, he is risking death for himself and misfortune for the community if he deliberately alters the words of the ancestors. Another characteristic of this type of language is the heavy use of paired couplets and paired words—or 'the open-closed formula', as it is phrased by the Tetun. Concerning this type of parallelism, my 'instructors' said that like a basket, every expression has to have a lid (*tatakan*). Because of the ethical obligations and language skill necessary to be able to speak in ritual language, I considered myself a slow learner. The idea of 'studying' this type of language is also quite peculiar because one does not learn to be a ritual specialist but is, rather, endowed with this art of speech by the ancestors themselves. This perception influenced the progress of my endeavour to learn ritual language.

But, for others, my endeavour was appreciated because it was also in accord with the cultural concept that to be a respected *adat* elder a man must be able to explain things in various forms of ritual language. On several occasions during my fieldwork I pointed out that I intended to learn ritual language simply 'to be able to offer betel-nut properly'[3]

---

3   'Offering betel-nut' is a phrase used in ritual language to mean 'greetings'.

to my brothers and sisters, but not to become a ritual specialist myself. But when I asked the cultural significance of a place or a personal name, I was often flooded with parallel verses, dyadic sets and other formulaic lines in response to my questions. My knowledge of the dual symbolic classification for organising the social order was built from my learning of the social categories expressed in many forms of ritual language.

Another personal experience worthy of note concerns the cultural ability of the Wehali to receive an outsider into their community of insiders. Working with people who believe that their domain was the first 'to grow' when the earth started to emerge and is therefore the origin place of humans, nobody is made to feel that he or she is totally an outsider. Every outsider is potentially a returning insider. Seven months after I began living among the Wehali, nobles from the houses of Leko and Mako'a Rai in the hamlet of Laran (the hamlet of Maromak Oan) escorted me to pay my respects to the nobles living in the hamlet of Liurai in Builaran. Upon our arrival, the 73-year-old *adat* historian (*mako'an*) named Bau Fahik La Rosi, who claims to be the ninth *mako'an* of the house of the Liurai, greeted me with 198 lines of ritual poetry. As an outsider who came to seek the 'true knowledge of the words of the ancestors', I was greeted as a Chinese dove, a Malay (foreign) duck:

lakateu sina oan	a small Chinese dove
krade malae oan	a small wild duck
no'i nafofek onan	is rowing (toward here)
no'i naknanik onan	is swimming (toward here)

But as an ethnic Rotinese, born and raised in another part of the Tetun-speaking area, I was not totally an outsider. Therefore, toward the end of the poem, this 'Chinese dove, Malay duck' was considered as having returned to 'the grand granary', 'the grand hut', 'the navel land', 'the umbilical cord land' and 'the lap of *ina no ama* (mother and father)'. Unmistakably, it was the journey of a returning insider.

Earlier Writings

There are a number of published ethnographies devoted to the study of the eastern and western Tetun societies. By eastern Tetun, I refer to the ethnic Tetun in the former Portuguese colony that was then the 27th province of Indonesia. It has now become the independent nation of

Timor Leste. The western Tetun are further divided into two groups: the north Tetun and the south Tetun. The north–south division is attributed to administrative, geographical and, to some degree, ethnic boundaries. In terms of culture, however, the Tetun living in the northern part of the southern administrative division are more closely related to the north Tetun than to the south Tetun. To mark the cultural boundary between the north and south Tetun, people employ terms such as the 'mountain people' (*ema foho*) or the 'hill people' (*ema taruik*) for those in the north and the 'plains people' (*ema fehan*) for those in the south. In this account, I refer to the three divisions of ethnic Tetun as east Tetun, north Tetun and south Tetun.

The majority of published works is devoted to east Tetun societies. David Hicks (1971: 17–18) lists these authors and their focus: Forbes (1883), Sá (1961) and Duarte (1964) collected data on the Samora, Fatuberliu and the Barique Tetun; and a few linguists produced grammars, including Fernandes (1937), das Dores (1907), Manuel da Silva (1900) and S.M. Silva (1889). These valuable works were written in Portuguese. My inability to read Portuguese fluently, coupled with my focus on the south Tetun, has meant that I have not examined these east Tetun materials as thoroughly as I would have liked. This language barrier was to some extent overcome, however, with the publication of a few papers on east Tetun in Indonesian and English (L.F.F.R. Thomaz 1981; A.B. Lapian 1980; Parsudi Suparlan 1980; Masinambouw 1980), as well as a monograph written by Capell (1943), whose main interest was linguistic classification; a work by J.K. Metzner (1977) on environmental issues; and a report on a socio-anthropological survey by Mubiyarto (1990, English edition 1991). More importantly, two books written by David Hicks (1984, 1990) and a number of his papers published as chapters in books and as articles in various journals have in many ways overcome the complaint made by Hicks himself about the inferior quality of ethnographic writings on the area (1971: 13, 14).

For the north Tetun, there are also some publications worthy of note. The most frequently cited are a monograph written by Grijsen (1904) and three volumes by Vroklage (1953). The conflicting accounts given by these two authors, which became a focus for critical analysis in Graham (1985) and Hicks (1990), are also a subject I address in the following discussion.

As far as social organisation is concerned, Grijsen and Vroklage gave different accounts on how to characterise the north Tetun societies. Both used the terms *kanoea* (*knua*) and *kotta* (*kota*),[4] which they glossed as 'village' (Grijsen 1904: 43; Vroklage 1953: 473). The same terms are also used by the south Tetun but they imply different meanings. In south Tetun *knua(n)* means 'rind' or 'sheath'. This term is also used as a metaphor for 'house' and 'domain'. So, for example, the phrase *knua as* (high sheath) metaphorically refers to the house of Maromak Oan. In contrast, the phrase *knua kraik* (low sheath) refers to the house of Liurai. It should be stated, in this regard, that the south Tetun do not employ this term for the notion of 'hamlet'. Instead they use the word *leo*. Folk exegesis relates this term to the Tetun word *leon*, meaning 'the shade of a tree'. In Grijsen's description, *knua* or *kota* denotes a conglomeration of 6 to 20 households. This compound of households is enclosed by 2-metre walls of stone, tree trunks or tree branches.

Grijsen claimed that every person in north Tetun associated himself/herself with three patrilineal descent groups. The first group was called the *alin-maun* (yB, eB) group. A man, his brothers, father, father's brothers, grandfather and great-grandfather, with their children and his unmarried sisters, belong to this *alin-maun* group. The *alin-maun* relationship could also be established either by a blood oath or without a blood oath. A relationship established by blood oath was unalterable and therefore passed on to future generations. The *alin-maun* relationship without a blood oath was not inherited (Grijsen 1904: 39–40). The second group was called the *fetosawa* (the wife-taking house). This was the patrilineal group where women of the *alin-maun* group married and resided. The third group was the *uma mane* (wife-giving house), the group from which men of the *alin-maun* group choose their wives. The marriage between a man from the *fetosawa* house to a woman from the *uma mane* house was described by Grijsen (1904: 41–42) as a 'contract' between the two houses establishing the obligatory nature of the marriage. Any man who married outside his wife-giving house had to pay a fine to this latter group. The status and role of the wife-takers were clearly distinguished from the wife-givers. The latter were the source of water, the root of origin and the trunk of life (Brandewie and Asten 1976: 21) and therefore superior to the former. The seating arrangements during marriage ceremonies also

---

4   The Tetun word *kota* means 'fortress' or 'city'.

reflected the asymmetry between *uma mane* and *fetosawa*. Members of the *uma mane* occupied the 'true house' while the *fetosawa* sat on the 'verandah', which was constructed lower than the 'true house'.

Vroklage (1953: 254) acknowledged the importance of the *fetosawa–uma mane* marriage for understanding the north Tetun social network. On average, a man had the option of finding a woman to become his wife in five to six *uma mane*. The most influential *fetosawa* house had no more than 10 *uma mane*, but always endeavoured to have more wife-taking houses. In contrast to the patrilocal marriage and patrilateral affiliation mentioned by Grijsen, Vroklage's account suggests uxorilocal marriage and matrilateral affiliation to be common cultural features in many north Tetun societies. He estimated that in Lahurus up to 99 per cent of marriages were uxorilocal and that descent was reckoned matrilineally (1953: 254–258).

Vroklage's accounts were supported by a later ethnographic note on marriage and kinship by Brandewie and Asten (1976: 19–30). Translating the meaning of *uma mane* as 'the house where the husband resides' (1976: 21), these authors suggested that either uxorilocal or matrilocal residence was a common practice in some north Tetun societies. Concerning the affiliation of children, Brandewie and Asten point out that in the four types of marriage recognised in the region,[5] the children belonged to the mother's lineage (1976: 24–25). Finally, based on this ethnographic note and Vroklage's monograph, Hicks (1990: 56) concludes:

> Regardless of their differences, our two ethnographic sources thus demonstrate that the relationship terminology of the matrilineal Northern Tetum is symmetrically prescriptive and thus diverges from the asymmetric contraction of affinal alliances.

Regarding written ethnography of the south Tetun, the only reliable sources are those from Gerard Francillon's hand. He conducted systematic research in the region for 16–18 months. Based on his fieldwork, he wrote a PhD thesis at The Australian National University (1967), a paper on

---

5   Brandewie and Asten mention four types of marriage: (1) *fetosawa–uma mane* marriage; (2) *uma laran* marriage; (3) *matak no let* marriage; and (4) *husar oan* (*binan*) marriage. In the first three types the children automatically become members of the wife's house. In the last type of marriage, the children are also members of their mother's house until an amount of bridewealth is paid to transfer them to their father's house.

indigenous musicology (1974) and one on systems of brother exchange (1989), and an article on the political organisation of the Wehali published as a chapter in a book (Fox 1980: 248–265).

After the publication of van Wouden's doctoral dissertation (1968), the matrilineal societies of south Tetun in Timor, the Kodi of Sumba and the Wemale of western Seram attracted the interest of later anthropologists such as Rodney Needham. The coming of Francillon to Timor was also driven by the advice given by Needham to study one of these 'matrilineal islands'. Francillon appropriately commenced his thesis according to the local custom by discussing ideas about 'origins' as recapitulated by the south Tetun in their myths of origin.

The myth copied by Francillon from a notebook owned by a school boy (Francillon 1967: 78) noted two main points: 'the main theme is that one class of the present lords descends from the first occupiers of the soil and that another descends from a second more recent wave of immigrants' (1967: 89). The first point was related to the story concerning the coming to the region of Bui Kiak and her brother Mau Kiak from 'the great land' (*rai bot*). Eventually Bui Kiak married a mysterious man and gave birth to a girl called Ho'ar Na'i Daholek. The second point related to the coming of Taek Rai Malaka together with his subjects from Malacca, on the Malay peninsula. They came to Wehali following the path of the sun. Eventually Taek Rai Malaka married Ho'ar Na'i Daholek. Their children ruled the domains of Timor. Two sons ruled domains toward the rising of the sun; the next two sons ruled areas toward the setting of the sun. The last two sons became the immediate protectors of their youngest sister and the three of them were designated to reside in Wehali. The analysis of the myth revealed that the issue concerning the coming of outsiders to rule Wehali was a pre-eminent theme of the myth. The first group of rulers were descendants from a female outsider who came to the region and somehow married an indigenous man. The second group of rulers came from a definite outside place, namely the land of Malacca. Thus, according to this myth, the name of the district (Malaka), where the domain of Wehali is now situated, has its origin in myth. The old Malaka (Malaka *tuan*) is on the Malay peninsula, while the new Malaka (Malaka *foun*) is the present district of Malaka. The present nobles of Wehali and other domains under Wehali sovereignty are descended from these two groups of outsiders.

Despite the differing detail between the myths collected by Francillon and those recorded by Grijsen (1904: 18–20) and Vroklage (1953: 148–149), these myths reveal the same pattern concerning incoming outsiders who established a political structure and ruled domains in Timor.

The origin myths appended as Reference Texts 2 to 6 deal with the same pattern, so common in Austronesian societies—that is, the influence of outsiders in structuring the political communities in Timor (Fox 1994: 1). The myth cited in Reference Text 4 is an example of outsiders who were responsible for founding the three domains in the southern plain, namely the domains of Wehali, Wewiku and Haitimuk.[6] However, myths that I recorded in Wehali (Reference Texts 2, 3, 5 and 6) show another variety of 'outsider origin'. The myths were constructed based on the gender categories of male/female and the spatial categories of inside/outside. In these myths, a man referred to as either descending from the 'sun above' (*loro leten*) or originating from areas toward the 'rising sun' (*loro sa'en*) eventually marries a Wehali woman. The cultural themes of male outsiders coming to Wehali and marrying female insiders persist throughout the myths.

There are at least two key terms used in the myth. The first is the Tetun word *tur* (to sit, reside) and the second the phrase *fo ba* (to give away). In accordance with the uxorilocal pattern of residence, after marriage a man resided (*tur*) at his wife's house. Their offspring were members of their mother's house and so became the first rulers of the land. This metaphor (*tur*) is maintained in my recorded myths. Using the analogy of uxorilocal residence in which a husband is only a 'new man' in his wife's house, the myths always highlight the superior status of the insiders because it was the outsiders who resided (*tur*) in the houses of the insiders. The second phrase, *fo ba*, deals with the story concerning the dispersal of Wehali's sons to sit and rule domains outside Wehali. In this phrase, the superior status of the female insider is unfolded explicitly. It was the female insiders who gave away their relatives (in this case their 'sons', Tetun: *oan*) to outside domains in order to rule those domains and protect their 'mother and father' (*ina no ama*) who sent them. Thus, extending myths recorded by previous researchers in which outsiders directly influence the political

6   This myth was recorded in Wewiku and was regarded by my Wehali informants as Wewiku's version of the origin myth.

structure of the region, the myths I present in this study represent another variant of the Austronesian outsider origin. In this case, the authority of the outsiders was endorsed by the female insiders.

The notion of exchange in marriage is also crucial in Francillon's thesis (1967) and a later article published in *L'homme* (1989). Based on the same presumption proposed by van Wouden that marriage is the 'pivot' for the organisation of society, Francillon brilliantly explained the ideology and practice of returning a woman to her father's natal house upon the death of her father. This practice is called the returning of the *mata musan*.[7] When the *mata musan* has 'fertilised' her father's house, this recipient house has to return a woman offspring to the *mata musan*'s mother's house. Francillon informs us that the returned woman, called 'banana head' (*hudi ulun*), is expected 'to water the root' (*ramas abut*) of her mother's mother's house (1967: 365). Francillon used the expression *tate rai halo we*, which can be glossed as 'making the canal to drive water', as a metaphor for the marriage alliance between two houses. The husband-receiving house is the source of water. The sending of the *mata musan* from the husband-receiving house to the husband-giving house is seen as driving water from the former to the latter. The return of the *hudi ulun* is then considered to refill the source of water.

Marriage alliance expressed in the metaphor of 'driving water' is quite common among the north Tetun. The ethnographic note published by Brandewie and Asten (1976) based on data from Lahurus also discusses the same expression. The Lahurus used the phrase *su kanu foun, baki foun* (to dig a new ditch, a new canal) to describe the alliance between *uma mane* (the wife-giver) and *fetosawa* (the wife-taker). The asymmetric alliance between these two houses is explained in the expression *mota la bele suli sa'e* (water never flows upstream). The interpretation of this phrase is given by the authors: 'as water always flows downstream from its source, never upstream, brides also should come from the *uma mane*, never from the *fetosawa*' (1976: 21). Undoubtedly, this phrase and its interpretation suited the notion of asymmetric alliance as understood by Dutch ethnographers, to prohibit the symmetric exchange of women.

In contrast, the south Tetun understand the terms *uma mane* and *fetosawa* differently. In marriage negotiations, the woman's house (the house where the husband resides) is simply referred to as *uma feto* not *fetosawa*, since the

---

7   Francillon translated this phrase as 'the pupil of the eye'.

latter is a term of reference for 'sisters'. The man's natal house is referred to as *uma mane*. The *uma mane–uma feto* relationship is reciprocal. One house can potentially be a husband-taking group and at the same time a husband-giving group to the same house. Consistent with this pattern of marriage, the metaphors used by the north Tetun to imply asymmetric alliance are unheard of in south Tetun. Following the uxorilocal patterns of residence, land inheritance and succession as custodian of a named house, the south Tetun constitute what Fox describes as a 'house-based' matriliny (1988b: xiii). But the symmetric exchange of women between the husband-giving house and the husband-taking house is not forbidden.

Theoretical Orientation

The analysis of dual symbolic categories to examine the social order of a particular society has a relatively long history in anthropology. Scholars such as E. Evans-Pritchard and Rodney Needham introduced this system of analysis to the English-speaking world, tracing its origin to the French sociological tradition, particularly to the works of Robert Hertz. Evans-Pritchard in his Foreword to Needham's *Right and left* praised Hertz's two important papers as 'the finest essays ever written in the history of sociological thought' (1973: ix). Needham particularly praised Hertz's work on 'The pre-eminence of the right hand: a study in religious polarity' as a 'work of an unmistakable excellence' (1973: xi). Despite Hertz's excellent ideas, it remained hidden until 1933, when Marcel Granet delivered his paper in Paris on 'Right and left in central China' (1973: 43–58).

According to Granet, the concern with human anatomy discussed by Hertz was meant to be a starting point in understanding the notion of religious polarity. Thus, it was not anatomy per se that attracted Hertz but the notion of pure and impure, analogous to the absolute opposition of left and right as the most essential categories in religious polarity. This conclusion was also shared by Needham in his statement that 'Hertz's essay is not about anatomy: it is about values, and in this case, strikingly unequal values' (1973: 124). Hertz's classic essay directly or indirectly inspired the theoretical concern about primitive classification elaborated by Durkheim and Mauss.

Among Dutch anthropologists, a concern with primitive classification evolved in a limited teacher–student network. This subject was prominent in anthropology, one of the most important courses designed to train civil servants who were going to take up positions in Indonesia. One of the instructors of that training course was F.D.E. van Ossenbruggen, who introduced the works of Durkheim and Mauss to these civil servants for the first time. When van Ossenbruggen himself had the opportunity to work as a judge in Indonesia, his knowledge of primitive classification helped him to analyse Javanese culture. It was through van Ossenbruggen's publications that later Dutch structuralists such as W.H. Rassers and J.P.B. de Josselin de Jong, the two co-founders of the Leiden school of anthropology, and F.A.E. van Wouden, a pupil of de Josselin de Jong, became acquainted with the works of Durkheim and Mauss.

The years 1935 to 1940 should be noted as the most important period in the history of Indonesian studies carried out in the Netherlands. In 1935, the framework of Indonesia as a 'field of ethnological study' was pronounced by J.P.B. de Josselin de Jong in his inaugural address to the chair of Indonesian and general anthropology. In the same year, van Wouden successfully defended his dissertation promoted by J.P.B. de Josselin de Jong, who was his supervisor. In 1940, the works of Dutch scholar W.H. Rassers were translated into English. P.E. de Josselin de Jong welcomed this publication as an important piece of work on the reconstruction of the Javanese belief and classification system, a subject of importance for J.P.B. de Josselin de Jong and van Wouden (1983: 9–10). The quotations from Rassers's analysis on socio-cosmic dualism in J.P.B. de Josselin de Jong's inaugural address (1983: 175–177) show the degree of influence Rassers had on this great scholar. It is worthwhile to note in this regard that within J.P.B. de Josselin de Jong's framework, socio-cosmic dualism is considered an element that belongs to the 'structural core' of Indonesian societies.

In his inaugural address for the chair of anthropology at the University of Leiden, J.P.B. de Josselin de Jong stated that ethnological research has to be based on the study of the *sociale struktuur* of a particular culture. Under his direction, students were sent to study the *sociale struktuur* of various societies in Indonesia. This was an effort to identify the common cultural features making up the Indonesian societies as a 'field of ethnological study'. Reasons given by J.P.B. de Josselin de Jong for establishing Indonesia as a whole as a 'field of ethnological study' are summarised by Koentjaraningrat in 14 points (1958: 399–402). In line with the emphasis given in this study, I highlight a few points elaborated by J.P.B. de Josselin de Jong that were considered to reflect features of Indonesian social organisation: 1. Indonesian societies consist of descent groups that trace their origin matrilineally or patrilineally; 2. These descent groups are organised into wife-giving clans and wife-taking clans; 3. The wife-giving clans occupy a higher social status than the wife-taking clans; 4. Marriages of people between clans are regulated by a system of asymmetrical connubium. These four points represent only two elements within J.P.B. de Josselin de Jong's arguments on 'structural core', namely the clan system and the marriage system. What is lacking in Koentjaraningrat's summary is the emphasis on sociocosmic dualism, an important theme within the French tradition that was carried on by Rassers in relation to Indonesia.

With regard to eastern Indonesian societies, de Josselin de Jong's thesis was supported initially by extensive library research conducted by his student, F.A.E. van Wouden. The region considered by van Wouden extends from the 'Timor archipelago in the west to the Southern Islands in the east, and is bordered to the north by the islands of Seram and Buru' (van Wouden 1968: 1), an area of diverse culture and language. These areas were selected because they were believed to form a cultural region and share a common structural core of marriage system, clan system and socio-cosmic dualism. At the time when van Wouden wrote his dissertation, ethnographic sources on these areas were inadequate both quantitatively and qualitatively. Therefore, he relied primarily on scanty information, which ranged from official documents and travellers' accounts to missionary reports.

One strength of van Wouden's work for eastern Indonesia that attracted anthropologists working in this region was his emphasis on cross-cousin marriage. This focus alone has led commentators such as Cunningham and Fox to designate him 'a precursor of Lévi-Strauss' (Cunningham 1971: 844; Fox 1989b: 426; cf. Locher 1968: vii). This designation was based on van Wouden's arguments as summarised below:

> (1) cross-cousin marriage is the 'logical expression of a systematic communication of women among larger descent groups'; (2) the 'lineality' of the descent groups is theoretically immaterial to the forms of connubium; (3) 'ordinary' [symmetric: MBD/ FZD] marriage and 'exclusive' [asymmetric: MBD] marriage are 'representatives of two opposed systems of affinal relationships between groups'; (4) exclusive marriage with the FZD would make a 'systematic ordering of affinal relationship between groups

impossible'; and (5) an 'integral system of affinal relationships based on exclusive or asymmetric marriage would number at least three clans but could also be composed of any larger number of clans linked in a 'closed chain of marriage connexions' (Fox 1989b: 426).

Around 20 years or more after van Wouden's dissertation, islands that compose the present Nusa Tenggara Timur province and the southern part of Maluku province began to attract a growing number of ethnographers. However, unlike the pre–Second World War approach to ethnographic investigation, this second wave of interest in eastern Indonesian studies marks a shift from an overemphasis on model to a more thematic approach. This shift of emphasis promises future comparative analyses within a broader framework for two reasons. First, the region taken as a field of study is not limited only to the societies that structure their alliance on the basis of asymmetrical connubium, but it extends to eastern Indonesian societies that do not have such a system (Fox 1980: 330). Second, it allows study of each society to be based not on a predefined model of a clan system, marriage system and socio-cosmic dualism but on local categories as expressed by the people themselves. This approach focuses on the study of what Fox has termed *'metaphors for living* which are encoded primarily in a pervasive dyadic form' (Fox 1980: 333, my emphasis). My endeavour in this present work, as I see it, is an effort to analyse metaphors for living articulated by the south Tetun of West Timor.

Book Outline

Following this introduction, Chapter 2 contains three sections. First it attempts to situate the study area in the regional administrative system. The emphasis in this part is on highlighting the influence of the Dutch colonial administrative system in reducing the domain of Wehali to a single subdistrict, a policy continued by the Indonesian government. Using the slogan of *anti feodalisme*, the domain of Wehali and other domains have practically ceased to exist within the present administrative scheme. The second section documents the economic life of the south Tetun. The third section focuses on the many oral traditions used in daily life.

In Chapter 3, I present the history of the domain of Wehali in the pre-European period as observed from an outsider's point of view. This chapter serves as the 'threshold' of my study. Subsequent chapters explore how the

Wehali and the south Tetun in general perceive themselves. A number of social categories recurring throughout the following chapters include centre/periphery, inside/outside, female/male (following the Tetun sequence of expression), trunk/edge and first to dry/last to dry. When the Tetun speak about territorial alliances and political systems, the same dominant categories are used in the following order: centre/periphery, female/male and first to dry/last to dry. Therefore, the discussion in Chapter 4 is titled, 'Giving Away the Centre to the Periphery'. When kinship and affinity are in focus, such as in Chapters 5 and 6, the south Tetun emphasis is on the notions of female/male and inside/outside more than on the categories of centre/periphery. These social categories can only be fully understood if the Tetun concept of 'house' (*uma*) is appreciated. This concept is explored in Chapter 7. In that chapter, I claim that the south Tetun house, like the majority of 'houses' in this region, is associated with the 'female'. Thus, again, the dominant categories of female/male and inside/outside are evident in this chapter. To recapitulate, Chapters 4 to 7 emphasise the direction of the flow of life from centre to periphery, inside to outside and female to male. Chapter 8 elaborates on two kinds of rituals: 'life-giving' rituals for humans and for edible crops. In the latter rituals, the south Tetun celebrate the flow of wealth running from periphery to centre, outside to inside, male to female and cultivation space to dwelling space. In a comparative exploration, Chapter 9 highlights the common cultural heritage the Tetun share with their Austronesian relatives, particularly the Dawan-speaking people.

2
The Ethnographic Setting

Introduction

Timor is one of the largest islands in the outer arc of those that classical accounts have grouped in the Lesser Sundas. Due to its recent uplift and turbulent geological past, the island is dominated by rugged and dissected mountains. As a result, topographical differences prevail even within short distances. The geographer Ormeling shows in his study the geological complexity of the island such that 'marine sediments chiefly limestone and marls are especially wide-spread on Timor' (1957: 31). Despite its rugged terrain, there are a few areas that have been classified as lowlands, such as the south plains of Wehali-Wewiku in the Belu regency, the plains of Bena, and the plains of Oesao-Pariti at the head of Kupang Bay. Ormeling identifies the common features of these plains as typical delta zones built up by flooding rivers that brought mud down from the range of mountains surrounding them. Thus, young alluvial plains, below spring tide level and enclosed by hills and mountain ranges, are characteristic of these lowlands. The diversity of vegetation growing in this island also attests to its geological complexity. This vegetation ranges from evergreen monsoon forests to white eucalypt (*Eucalyptus alba*) stands, widespread savanna areas, dense gebang palm (*Corypha utan*) and varieties of mangroves along the coastlines.

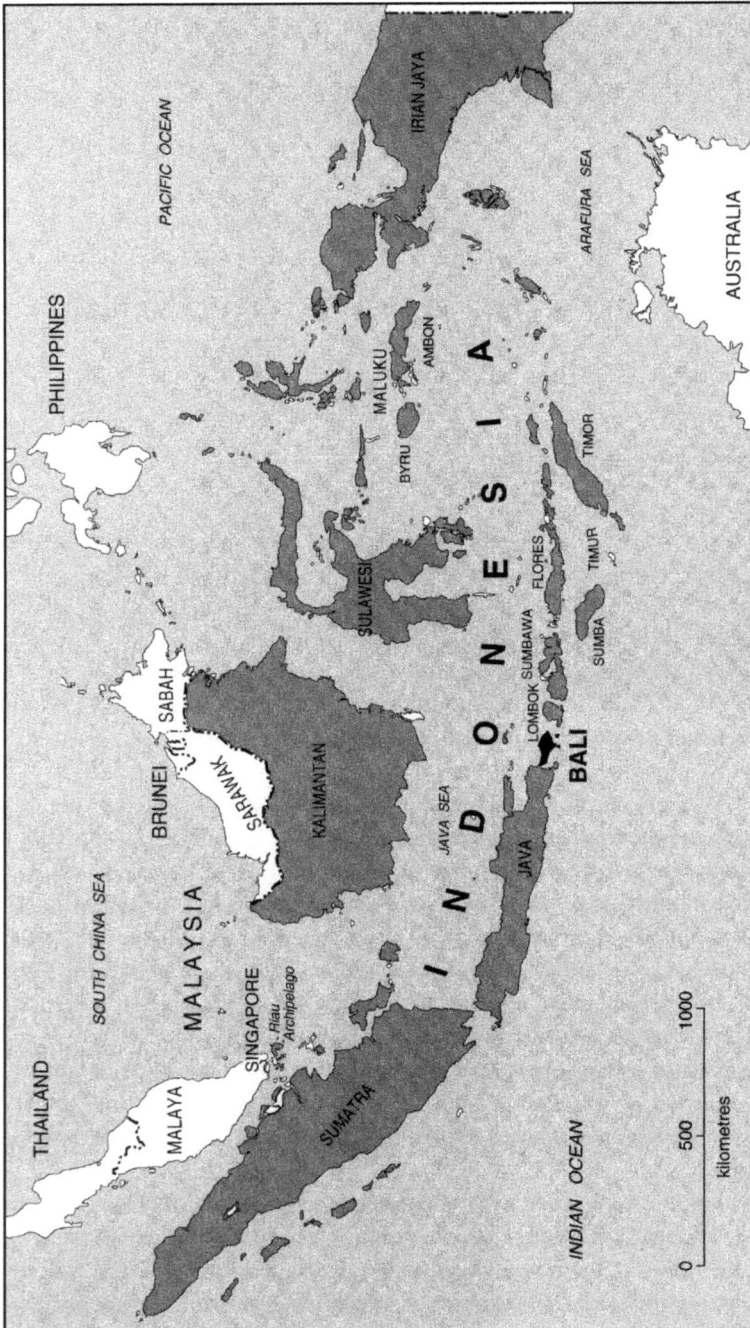

Map 1: Indonesia

Timor's location in between the humid isles of Indonesia and the dry Australian continent affects the climatic pattern of the island (see Map 1). During the dry season, the daily temperature range is quite high, which makes working unpleasant. The movement of air masses between the Asian and Australian continents also affects the distribution of rainfall. The east monsoon brings a dry season for most of the island, but brings a second rainy season for the southern plains. The west monsoon brings the annual rainy season for the whole island. Due to this air movement, Timor and its surrounding islands also suffer from an 'annual windy season', as it is phrased by most people. Thus, in addition to the common division of dry and rainy seasons, people also talk about the so-called 'windy season'. Agricultural activities on Timor are regulated to suit these three sorts of seasons prevailing through the year.

No wonder the people of this island equate their agricultural activities with the naming of rain and wind. There are various names given to identify the blowing of the wind and the onset of the rains, which will be elaborated further in this chapter. To some extent, temperature also regulates the working rhythm of the people. The highest daily temperature is recorded towards the end of every dry season. Travelling along the trunk road of Timor at night during this part of the season, we come across groups of farmers working in their gardens by the light of kerosene lamps. During the day, when the temperature reaches its climax, is a rest period for them. Working at night, besides avoiding the heat of the day, is also to catch up with the work undone.

Ethnic diversity is another aspect of Timor's identity. Studies concerning physical anthropology done by Bijlmer (1929) and Lammers (1948), based on data provided by Vroklage (1948) and von Bork-Feltkamp (1951) in the western part of the island and by other Portuguese anthropologists in the eastern part, do not provide a conclusive answer as to how to group people on the island. Generally speaking, Lammers (1948: 283) distinguished two groups of people in the western part. The predominantly Melanesoid Atoni (or Dawan, as termed by the south Tetun) inhabit areas in the west of this region and the predominantly Malay Belunese inhabit areas in its eastern sector. Areas between the Dawan in the west and the Belu in the east are inhabited by three groups of people, whom Vroklage designated the Noemuti group, the Beboki group and the Insana group (Lammers 1948: 276). These three groups are mixed, having a Melanesoid (Papuan) element, a Weddid element and perhaps even a Negroid element. Lammers describes these mixed populations as having a mosaic of characteristics (1948: 283). Lammers also suggested that further studies are needed in order to reach a more definite conclusion.

An adequate linguistic classification is also needed to delineate the mosaic of this multilingual island. The linguist Capell (1943: 313–314) classified the Timorese languages into Malayo-Polynesian (Indonesian) and Papuan (non-Indonesian). For him, Tetun, Mambai, Tukudade, Galoli, Idate and Dawan belong to the former group, while the latter consists of Bunak, Makasai, Waimaha and Kairui. The range of languages cited is, however, based on the number of informants available at the time of his linguistic research, which does not therefore represent all the languages spoken on Timor. Even concerning the number itself, there is not yet a conclusive answer as to how many mutually unintelligible languages are spoken in Timor. Earlier writers such as H.O. Forbes suggested that there were 40 languages, while Martinho reckoned 16 languages (Capell 1943: 313). Among more recent writers the same uncertainty prevails. Thomaz, a linguist who worked in East Timor during the Portuguese era, listed 19 mutually unintelligible languages spoken in East Timor alone. Not much linguistic research has been done by Indonesian scholars to date, apart from repeating studies carried out by former Portuguese linguists (Masinambouw 1980; Suparlan 1980).

Nowadays, the languages of Timor are classified into two groups, recognised as Austronesian and non-Austronesian languages, respectively. In the best overview to date, Fox and Wurm (1981) compiled a list of Austronesian and non-Austronesian languages spoken in the Lesser Sundas, with notes on the estimation of numbers of speakers and the affinity of the languages concerned (see Map 2). As far as Tetun is concerned, it was estimated that the Tetun speakers (in both East and West Timor) numbered about 300,000.

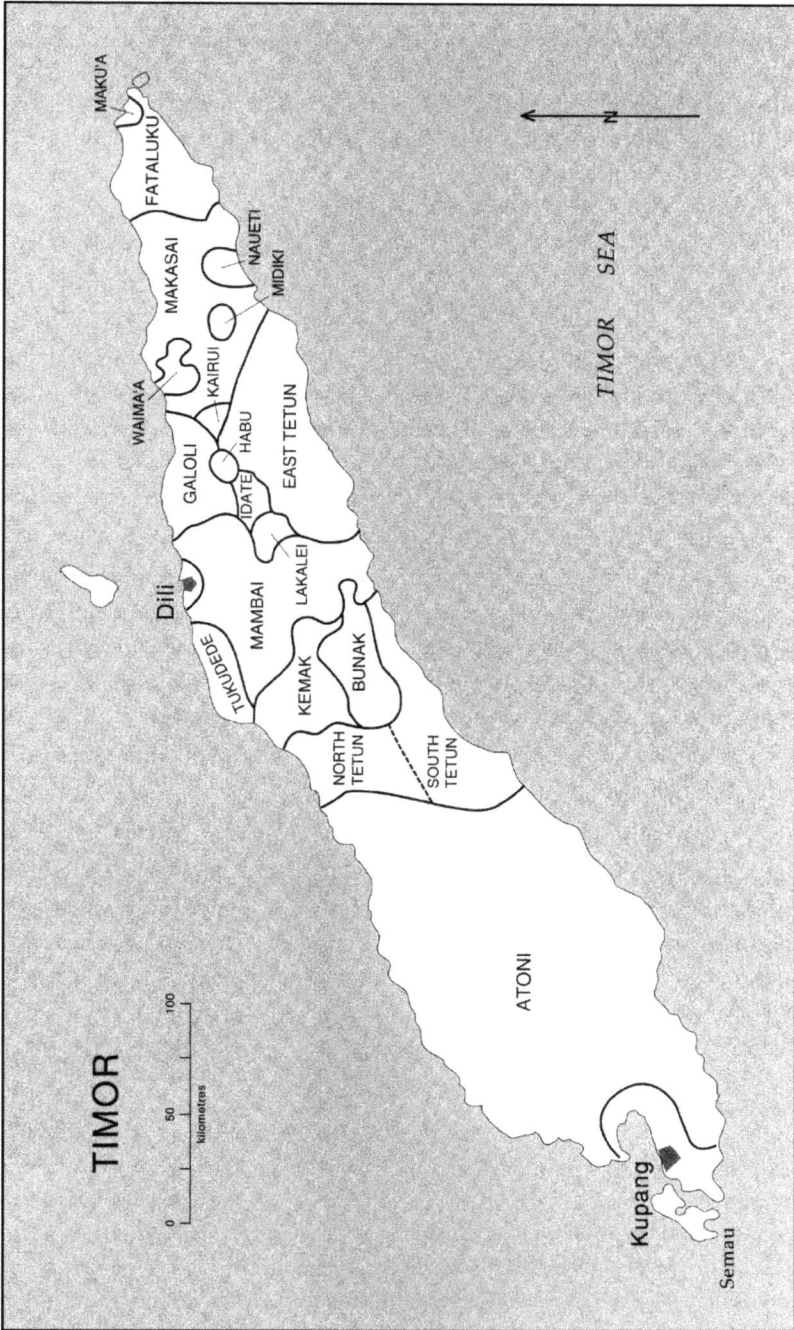

Map 2: Languages spoken in Timor

Based on the 1991 census, I would estimate that in West Timor alone about 190,000 people speak Tetun as their first language. In this relatively recent census, the population of the Belu regency is 216,252. They live in 72 villages (*desa*) that are divided into seven districts (*kecamatan*). Within these 72 villages, there are small clusters of non-Tetun speakers, namely the Ema (*atmas* Ema) who speak *to'ek* Ema and the non-Austronesian Bunak-speaking people. The Ema live in the hamlets of Fatukmetan, Tenu Bot, Sadi, Leo Lima, Leo Hitu and a few more locations in the villages of Tohe and Manumutin. The Bunak are more or less concentrated in 10 out of 12 villages in the district of Lamaknen. A small number of Bunak also live in the hamlet of Labarai, in the village of Kamanasa in the district of Malaka Tengah. Included in these non-Tetun speakers are people from other ethnic groups, either from Timor or from outside Timor (categorised as 'newcomers', or *pendatang*). These non-Tetun speakers then make up 10 per cent of the total Belu population.

The focus of this study is the Wehali, who occupy a narrow strip in the middle of the 300,000-hectare Wehali-Wewiku plains.[1] This huge plain is also occupied by people of the former domains of Wewiku, Haitimuk and Lakekun. They identify themselves as the 'plains people' (*ema fehan*). According to their origin myths, the people of the three domains known as Wewiku, Haitimuk and Wehali originated from three sisters (see Reference Text 4). For this reason, my research extended beyond Wehali to include these other two domains.

A Brief Account of the Regency of Belu

With the introduction of a law regulating the administrative zone incorporating Bali along with western and eastern Lesser Sundas (known as *Undang Undang* no. 69/1958) and a later law on *Pemerintahan Desa* (known as *Undang Undang* no. 5/1979), the so-called 'feudal domains' of eastern Indonesia ceased to exist administratively. The former great domain of Wehali was thus integrated as one area within the six districts of the Belu regency. The border of this once mighty 'empire' was reduced

---

1　There are also other names given to this extensive plain, such as the Besikama plain and the Benain plain.

to the limit of a small hamlet, Laran, the seat of its former supreme ruler, popularly known as Maromak Oan. This section gives an account of its historical irony.[2]

Under the Dutch administration, Timor was part of the province of Lesser Sundas known as *Residentie Timor en onderhorigheden* (Timor and its dependencies). It consisted of three divisions (*afdeeling*), 15 subdivisions (*onderafdeeling*) and 48 self-governing domains (*swapraja*).[3] Over time, the Dutch possessions on the island of Timor were divided into four administrative districts: Kupang, South-central Timor, North-central Timor and Belu.

In the district of Belu, when Grijsen was its controleur (1904), the Dutch government registered 20 *swapraja* as part of the Belu subdivision. Most of the *swapraja* listed in Table 2.1 are shown in Map 3.

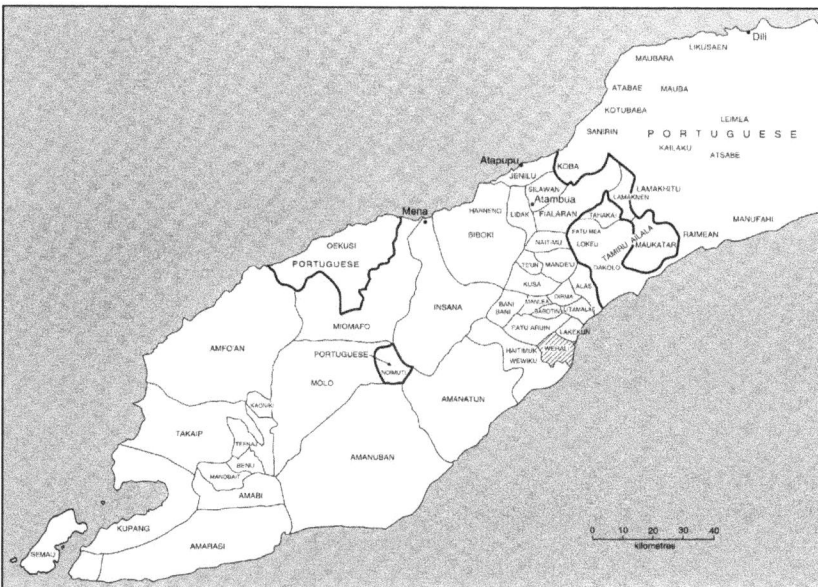

Map 3: *Swapraja* of Belu, after a Dutch map dated 1911

2   Since Francillon (1967: 19–31, 123–135; 1980: 248–265) has already considered the earlier history of this regency, I concentrate more on the administrative history of domains that make up the contemporary regency of Belu. Besides reports written by Dutch officials, the following 'administrative history' of the regency relied on three unpublished monographs: 1. Bere Tallo, *Pandangan Umum Wilayah Belu*, written as a government report in 1957; 2. A.D.M. Parera, *Sedjarah Politik Pemerintahan Asli di Timor* (1971); and 3. A typescript of *Monografi Kabupaten Belu* (date unknown).
3   The names of the districts, subdistricts and *swapraja* are given in the statute book 1916 no. 331 and 372. Mededeelingen, part A no. 3. 1929: 665–686.

Table 2.1: *Swapraja* of Belu in 1904

1. Wehali	6. Lakekun	11. Harneno	16. Naitimu
2. Wewiku	7. Dirma	12. Maukatar	17. Lidak
3. Fatuaruin	8. Mande'u	13. Fialaran	18. Lamaknen
4. Haitimuk	9. Insana	14. Jenilu	19. Makir
5. Nenometa	10. Biboki	15. Silawan	20. Lamaksanulu

A.A. Bere Tallo, the first head of Belu regency in the Indonesian administration, noted that the list merely showed Dutch ignorance of the political structure and alliances prevailing among these domains of Belu and therefore its institution was a terrible blunder made by the Dutch (1957: 18). Unfortunately, Bere Tallo did not elaborate, despite his claim that the contemporary dispute among domains was the result of the publication of the Dutch list. I assume the failure to list the domain of Bauho was one reason for Bere Tallo's disappointment. Considering that this domain is the seat of *Astanara*, the supreme ruler of Fialaran, its exclusion from the 1904 list really was a blunder.

Domains listed in Table 2.1 consist mainly of people from three language-speaking areas: the Bunak (of Lamaknen, Makir and Lamaksanulu), the Dawan (of Nenometa, Insana, Biboki and Harneno) and the remainder, who are the Tetun. In 1910, the domain of Nenometa (also known as Anas) was ceded to the subdivision of south-central Timor, under the Amanatun domain where it originally belonged. Following the establishment of the subdivision of north-central Timor in 1915, the three Dawan-speaking domains of Insana, Biboki and Harneno were included in this newly formed district.

In an attempt to control various petty domains in the Belu subdivision, the Dutch, in collaboration with native rulers, then began their scheme to reduce the number of domains. Among native rulers in the area, the Dutch government favoured the ruling dynasty of da Costa, which headed the domains of Jenilu, Lidak and Naitimu (see *Militaire Memorie van Timor* 1932: 74). The initial opportunity for amalgamation came when civil war broke out in the region in 1913. The people of Naitimu, under their leader, Kau Besin fought against the people of Lidak, whose ruler was a woman named Dona Petronella da Costa. In this civil war, Lidak was assisted by the people from Jenilu, under the leadership of Jozef da Costa, Dona Petronella's brother. Having won the battle, Jozef replaced Dona Petronella and became the ruler of both domains

(Jenilu and Lidak). Eventually, these two domains became one domain under the name Jenilu. Meanwhile, Don Basenti da Costa was appointed the ruler of Naitimu. Following his death in 1914, Jozef, his brother, also incorporated this domain into a confederation of three domains called *Kakuluk mesak* (literally 'the only pillar') in which Jozef was the supreme ruler. This newly established *swapraja* of Kakuluk Mesak was ratified by the Dutch government in their decree no. 13, 7/10/1914.

Then, in 1916, the *swapraja* of Kakuluk Mesak was abolished. Its three domains (Lidak, Jenilu and Naitimu), together with the domains of Fialaran, Lamaknen, Makir and Lamaksanulu, were combined into a single *swapraja* called Belu Tasifeto. So the eight domains in the north had become two *swapraja*, namely *swapraja* Belu Tasifeto and *swapraja* Maukatar. Under the 1904 agreement between the Dutch and the Portuguese concerning the international border of East and West Timor, ratified in 1909 and carried into effect in 1916, there were further changes in the number of domains in Belu. In article 1 of the 1909 tract, the domain of Maukatar was ceded to the Portuguese. In return, the Portuguese ceded Noemuti, Tahakae and Tamiru Ailala to the Dutch (article 2 *Staatsblad* 1909 No. 214). Noemuti was included in the *swapraja* of Miomafo (north-central Timor), Tahakae in the district of Nualain (Lamaknen) and Tamiru Ailala in the district of Lakekun. With the transference of the *swapraja* of Maukatar to the Portuguese, only one *swapraja* was left in north Belu, namely *swapraja* Belu Tasifeto. In the list of districts that made up the *swapraja* Belu Tasifeto, the name Fialaran was replaced by Bauho. In addition, the district of Lasiolat, which was not included in the 1904 list, was now included as part of *swapraja* Belu Tasifeto. The composition of this *swapraja* is shown in Table 2.2.

Table 2.2: Composition of the *swapraja* of Belu Tasifeto in 1916

District	Subdistrict	Name of ruler
Naitimu	–	Hale Kin
Lidak	–	Asa Nesin
Jenilu	–	Josef Faericianus Parera
Silawan	–	Koli Atok
Bauho (Fialaran)	Bauho	Atok Samara
Takirin		Siku Suri
	Dafala	W. Ati
	Manleten	Sili Saka

District	Subdistrict	Name of ruler
	Umaklaran	Seran Kehik
Lasiolat		Don Cajetanus da Costa
	Tohe	Manek Siku (Mau Siki)
	Asumanu	Atok Moruk
	Maumutin	Lau Besin
	Aitoun	Suri Wilik
Lamaknen	Kewar	Bau Liku
	Lakmaras	Bere Tae
	Nualain	Lesu Bere
	Leowalu	Bere Taek
	Fulur	Mau Asa
	Ekin	Fahik Taek
	Lo'onuna	Luan Bau (Mau Loko)
	Dirun	B. Dato Manu
Makir	–	Tes Bau (Leo Bele)
Lamaksanulu	–	Leto Asa

Source: Overakker (1926: 37–44, 1927: 37–39); Militaire Memorie van Timor (1932: 80–83, 119–123).

Their success in amalgamating these domains led the Dutch to take further steps. In order to amalgamate the southern domains, the troublesome Nahak Maroe Rai, the ruler of Besikama, had to be subdued. In an unequal 'battle', Nahak was captured and forced to acknowledge Dutch authority over the area. This 'heroic battle' of Nahak Maroe Rai in We Liman (1908) is still commemorated by the Besikama people in the form of poems, songs and 'battle stories' (*lia hatuda*). With the fall of Nahak Maroe Rai, Wehali and most of the southern domains came under Dutch authority. In a meeting held in Besikama on 29 May 1915, chaired by Grambeg, the *Keser* of Wehali (Bria Nahak), the *liurai* of Fatuaruin (Tei Seran) and the head of the *swapraja* of Wehali, Wewiku, Haitimuk, Fatuaruin, Lakekun, Dirma and Mande'u agreed to amalgamate their domains into the *swapraja* of Malaka. Perhaps the name Malaka was chosen to suit the origin myth recorded by Grijsen (1904) that the ancestors of these people were originally the *Sina mutin Malaka* (literally, 'the white Chinese of Malaka'). The composition of the *swapraja* of Malaka is listed in Table 2.3.

Table 2.3: Composition of the *swapraja* of Malaka in 1916

District	Subdistrict	Name of ruler
Wewiku		Bere Nahak
	Umalor	Bere Klau
	Rabasa	Bere Seran
	Wederok	Klau Fahik
Haitimuk	–	Klau Kloit
Wehali	–	Edmundus Bria Taek
Fatuaruin		Seran Asit Fatin
	Manlea	?
	Bani Bani	?
Lakekun		Loro Tahu Leki
	Litamali	Atok Luan
	Alas	Wilhelmus Leki
Dirma		Fatin Nekin
	Mande'u	Nino Besi Bara
	Kusa	Tuna Berek

Source: Overakker (1926: 37–44, 1927: 37–39); Militaire Memorie van Timor (1932: 80–83, 119–123).

Reflecting on the amalgamation policies outlined here, the 20 domains acknowledged by the Dutch as constituting Belu in 1904 had been reorganised by 1916 such that Belu consisted of only two *swapraja*. Of these, *swapraja* Belu Tasifeto was headed by Jozef da Costa and *swapraja* Malaka was headed by Liurai Tei Seran. This division was ratified on 22 February 1917 with the signing of a short declaration (*korte verklaring*) by the two rulers (Bere Tallo 1957: 19).

Eight years later, the Dutch government issued another decree (*Beslit Gubernemen* no. 39, 28/11/1924), which abolished this system of bi-partition and replaced the two *swapraja* by a single one, namely the *swapraja* of Belu. This *swapraja* consisted of 37 districts. All the domains registered in Tables 2.2 and 2.3 were given equal ranking with the status of district. In this newly established *swapraja*, however, the former subdistricts of Fulur and Ekin were not included in the list of autonomous districts. The Dutch then appointed Hendrikus Seran Nahak, the Maromak Oan of Wehali, to be the ruler of *swapraja* Belu, giving him the title *Keser* of Belu. He took an oath to this effect on 10 May 1926 in Atambua. As his assistant, Seran Asit Farin was appointed by the government to the rank of

Liurai (Overakker 1927: 37, 38). Both were paid according to their rank. The Maromak Oan, entitled *Keser*, was paid an annual wage of 1,200 guilder, while his deputy received 480 guilder per annum (Overakker 1926: 34–35).

The crowning of Seran Nahak as the sole *Keser* of Belu did not benefit the policy of amalgamation initiated by the Dutch. On the contrary, as noted by Francillon (1980: 254–255), various resentments arose both from the north Tetun domains and the Lamaknen area of the Bunak-speaking people. To appease these groups, the Dutch proposed a re-division of the Belu regency into three self-governing political domains (*swapraja*). In a letter dated 12 February 1941, the Resident of Timor, Nieboer, sent a letter to the governor of the *groote-Oost* in Makassar asking his agreement to abolish the single *swapraja* of Belu and re-establish the three former *swapraja* of Tasifeto, Malaka and Lamaknen (de Haan 1947: 17). In this letter, Nieboer also listed the domains that represented the Belu regency (Bere Tallo 1957: 21). Unfortunately, the Japanese took over the government in 1942 before this plan could be implemented.

During the three years of Japanese occupation, the regency of Belu was re-divided into two halves, and each part had its own ruler. One half was called Tasifeto. Its area covered the former Tasifeto *swapraja* and also Harneno, which in preceding Dutch times had belonged to the north-central Timor subdivision. Its first ruler was Nikolas Manek, who shortly afterwards was replaced by Hendrikus Besin Siri, known as Manek da Costa (de Haan 1947: 17). The other half was called Tasimane and covered the former *swapraja* of Malaka in the Dutch period. Its first ruler was Arnoldus Klau, the son of Bere Nahak, the great ruler of Wewiku. He was, however, soon replaced by Edmundus Tei Seran, the ruler of Fatuaruin, a petty domain within Wehali's jurisdiction.

In this short period of Japanese occupation, two significant things can be noted. First, the inclusion of one Dawan-speaking area, Harneno, under the *swapraja* of Tasifeto. Second, the renaming of the former *swapraja* of Malaka as Tasimane. The name Malaka had presumably been chosen to concur with the origin myth recorded by Grijsen. However, the Japanese did not replace that historical name with a strange and unknown name. *Tasi mane* (male sea) physically refers to the rough southern sea of Timor. Culturally, the south Tetun look to this sea as the place from which people and wealth came to the area, so many taboos are associated with it. The name Tasimane also signifies its contrast to the *tasi feto* (female sea) of the northern part of the regency. My Tetun Indonesian–speaking friends were pleased with this contrast, as they repeatedly told me that 'the patriarchal region is demarcated by the female sea, while the matriarchal region is demarcated by the male sea' (*daerah hak bapak dibatasi oleh laut perempuan sedangkan daerah hak ibu dibatasi oleh laut lelaki*).

Just before the Japanese surrendered, a public meeting was held in Kewar, on 5 August 1945. The meeting was chaired by the ruler of Bauho, Hendrikus Besin Siri da Costa. In that meeting it was decided that the domain of Lamaknen, predominantly occupied by Bunak-speaking people, had to be 'freed' from Tasifeto and its Tetun-speakers and become an independent *swapraja*. It was also decided that the ruler of Kewar (A.A. Bere Tallo) be appointed as the supreme ruler of Lamaknen to replace the old Bau Liku. He would rule eight domains: 1. Kewar, 2. Lakmaras, 3. Nualain, 4. Makir, 5. Leowalu, 6. Lamaksanulu, 7. Dirun, 8. Lo'o Nuna (Bere Tallo 1957: 21).

Thus the scheme for tri-partition of *swapraja* (Lamaknen, Tasifeto and Malaka) proposed by the Dutch at the end of colonial era was revived under the Indonesian government. This tri-partition was hailed by the first Regent of Belu as 'a system of government native to Belu' (*sistem pemerintahan asli di Belu*). This 'system' comprised three ethnic groups: Lamaknen, with *Bein Hot* (literally, 'respected sun') as its supreme ruler; Tasifeto, with *Astanara* (literally, 'high anvil') as its supreme ruler; and Malaka, with the *Maromak Oan* (literally, 'small bright one') as its supreme ruler.

At present there are seven administrative districts (*kecamatan*) constituting the Belu regency (*kabupaten*) as shown in Map 4: 1. Lamaknen, 2. Tasifeto Timur, 3. Tasifeto Barat, 4. Malaka Timur, 5. Malaka Tengah, 6. Malaka Barat and 7. Koba Lima. This last district (*koba lima* = five betel-nut containers) was established at the end of 1992. The structure of the regency of Belu was previously composed of six districts. Formerly, what is now the *kecamatan* of Koba Lima was part of the *kecamatan* of Malaka Timur. This new arrangement was considered suited to the ethnic composition of the area because people of this newly founded district are related to the Suai-Kova Lima who are part of the East Timor province.

What is missing in this so-called 'indigenous system of government' described by A.A. Bere Tallo is any acknowledgment of the Ema people (*Atmas Ema*) as an autonomous political unit. Although the Dutch government mentioned in their reports the existence of this particular ethnic group, they were never included in political discourse on the region. Even in the recent reshuffle of districts in the Belu regency, the Ema were not recognised as a separate district.

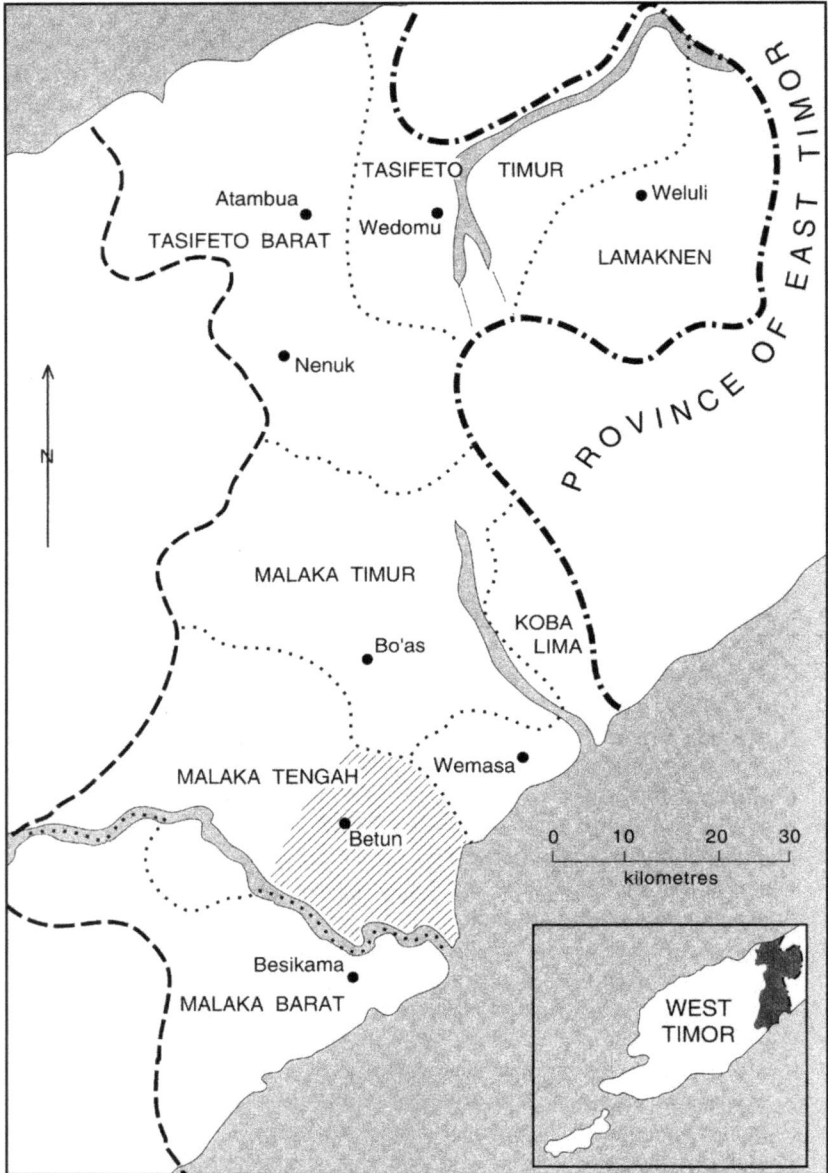

Map 4: Districts (*kecamatan*) in the regency of Belu

The District (*Kecamatan*) of Malaka Tengah

1. Demographic Aspects

The capital of the district of Malaka Tengah is Betun. This district was established in 1964 with Luis Sanaka Tei Seran as its head officer. It represents an amalgam of four domains known as *kena'ian*, namely Wehali, Kakaniuk, Manulea and Bani Bani. According to Bere Tallo, the hamlet of Laran, the traditional centre of Wehali, was initially chosen to be the capital of the newly established district. However, since this hamlet could not accommodate the standard necessities needed for a district capital, the government preferred Betun, which is located less than a kilometre from Laran.[4]

Under the new system of administration (see the decree issued by the head of the regency no. 6/Pem/1966), the district is made up of 11 *desa* (villages). The delineation of the 11 villages was based on the extent of territory and the relative density of population within the territory, with some adjustment for traditional divisions of society based on common derivation. Current population figures for the district and the size of each village are represented in Table 2.4.

Table 2.4: Village size and population

Village	Households	Size in sq. km	Population
1. Kakaniuk	410	36.8	2,225
2. Kareri	709	49.3	3,431
3. Umakatahan	1,142	19.2	6,592
4. Fahiluka	655	29.9	3,549
5. Kamanasa	344	14.6	1,768
6. Naimana	389	9.25	2,068
7. Kletek	474	17.65	2,547
8. Manulea	1,329	50.1	6,488
9. Bani Bani	1,107	50.2	5,555
10. Fatuaruin	609	24.1	2,940
11. Kereana	283	33.9	1,475

---

4   This remark is quoted from a minute held in Betun (1958) regarding an *adat* court case to settle a dispute between Edmundus Tei Seran and Luis Sanaka Tei Seran.

The villages mentioned in Table 2.4 are called *desa gaya baru* (the new-style villages). This form of village was promoted by the government to create an administrative homogeneity and at the same time to avoid the influence of *adat* in the new system of bureaucracy. The main difference between *desa gaya baru* and the traditional village is that the former constitutes a primary unit of administration while the latter is an 'origin unit'—that is, a group of people who claim to have some sort of common origin. This origin unit is called *leo*. The amalgamation of *leo* into new-style villages is represented in Table 2.5.

Table 2.5: Hamlets in Wehali

Village	Hamlet	Village	Hamlet
Naimana	Manumutin	Kateri	Bi'uduk Fehan
	Koba Di'in		Basadebu
	Natra'en		Kateri
	Na'i Lera		Lolobot
Fahiluka	Bolan	Kamanasa	Sukabihanawa
	Umakatahan Ain Tasi		Labarai
	Fahiluka		Fatisin
	Lo'o Sina		Leklaran
	Natra'en Fahiluka		Liurai
	Naekasak		Fohoterin
	Tete Bani		Manliman
	Manekin	Kletek	Kletek Suai
Umakatahan	Umakatahan Foho Hun		Kletek Rai Na'in
	Brama		Toolaran
	Batane	Kakaniuk	Kakaniuk
	Bakateu		Boni
	Matai		Lalu'an
	Tabene		Hali Oan
	Laran		Benahe
	Manumutin Banai		Ninu
	Toohun	Fatuaruin	Builaran
			Wekfau
			Koka

Ironically, in this amalgamation, Laran, the centre of the traditional domain of Wehali, has been grouped within Desa Umakatahan, a village that in Terun's ideology symbolically represents only a 'trunk of the house step//trunk of the garden ladder' (*tetek hun//knuba hun*) of Wehali. With this new arrangement, the village chief is located in the hamlet of Brama, a hamlet that represents a 'female door' (*odamatan rae*) in Wehali's ideology.

In contrast to the general physical morphology of Timor island, most of the people whom I worked with occupy a part of the southern plains of Belu. This plain, which constitutes one-sixth of the Belu regency, is also known as Wehali-Wewiku plains. Five out of the 11 villages listed in Table 2.4 (Umakatahan, Fahiluka, Kamanasa, Naimana and Kletek) are located in this plain. Statistically, more than half of the population (19,871 out of 38,665 people) live in this plain, which constitutes considerably less than half of the territory of the district (133 out of 341 sq. km). By Timor standards, or even Belu standards, this plain is densely populated.[5]

2. Environmental Aspects

a. Climate

Rainfall is the most important factor in the climate of the Lesser Sunda islands because it determines the cycle of agricultural activity. Generally speaking, the district of Malaka Tengah follows the climatic pattern of the Lesser Sunda islands as a typical monsoon area. However, being surrounded by a range of hills and mountains located in the south of Timor, the plains of Wehali-Wewiku and the district of Malaka Tengah in particular experience minor climatic variations.

To give some picture of the climatic variations, I deliberately chose the earliest available data sets as reported by Dutch officers and the latest official reports available at regency level. As far as I know, the earliest report that contains such data is a *Memorie van overgave* written by J.R. Agerbeek in 1916, recording data for 1914 and 1915, while the latest is official data for 1991. Using these three sets of data (see Figure 2.1) as a general guide, we have a picture of the uneven distribution of rainfall between the northern and the southern parts of the regency.

---

5   NTT 70/sq. km; Belu 83/sq. km. The plains region within the district of Malaka Tengah is 147/sq. km.

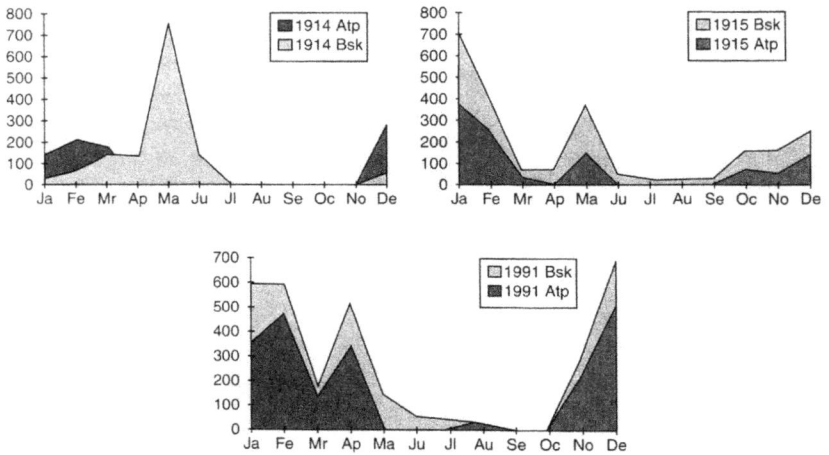

Figure 2.1: Rainfall data recorded in Besikama and Atapupu

In 1915 and 1991, the heaviest rains were recorded during the wet monsoon in both parts of the regency. Both north and south Tetun people call this period of rain 'annual rain' (*udan tinan*). This phrase indicates that it is a 'regular' period of rain. The first heavy fall of *udan tinan* marks the commencement of the planting season. Agricultural rituals concerning the activity of planting begin at that very moment. In 1915 these rains ended at about the same time in February and started again quite early (October). In 1991 these rains set in October–November in both parts of the regency, but the rain had not terminated at the same time earlier in the year. The 1914 report of rainfall shows an exceptional character in which both parts of the regency experienced a rainy season of longer duration. This suggests the possibility of considerable variation in rainfall from year to year.

Using Schmidt and Fergusen's classification of rainfall, in which 60–100 mm of rain in a month is considered 'moist' (as quoted in Metzner 1977: 37), we can delineate a variation in rainfall between the two parts of the regency. Data available in the years concerned reveal that the rainless period occurs between April and October in most parts of the north Belu region. During this period, the east monsoon brings a dry season, which is not further distinguished by the Tetun people. On the other hand, during the same period of time, the east monsoon brings rain to the southern plains of Wehali-Wewiku. This period of rain is called 'the seaside rain' (*udan lor*) by the plains people and 'the pig's rain' (*udan fahi*) by the hill people. Thus there are two principal rainy seasons in the district of

Malaka Tengah, namely *udan tinan* (west monsoon) and *udan lor* (east monsoon). These seasons are further classified by the Tetun following the names of rain and wind as described in Table 2.6.

Table 2.6: Agricultural cycle

Season	Name of rain	Name of wind	Ritual affiliated
The first fall in December	*udan narodan ai tahan* (rain to set off leaves)	*anin dadurus* (hurricane)	*husu udan* (rain making)
Annual rain (*udan tinan*)	*udan namate ahu kresan* (rain to kill hot ashes) *udan kokor botu* (rain with thunder) *udan kakait* (light drizzle)	*anin dadurus* (hurricane)	*husu udan* (rain making)
Transitional period in April	*udan menas* (hot rain)	*anin Bere Bauk* (Bere Bauk wind)	*soe at* (to discard misfortune) *hamiis* (first harvest) *koto to'os etu kukun* (harvest the sacred sorghum)
Second rainy season	*udanlor* (rain from the seaside) *udan kakait* (light drizzle)	*anin Bei Kati* (Bei Kati wind)	*tei fore Wehali* (trampling mung-bean) *hanematan loro* (the We Oe's delivery gift of homage)
Dry season (*rai nalaha*)			*hatama batar mana'i* (delivery gift of homage to the Maromak Oan)

The heavy rain that sets in during October, such as that recorded in 1915, is not considered as the beginning of the planting season. This type of rain is called *udan narodan ai tahan* ('rain to shed leaves') and is said only to last for three days. Therefore, it is described accordingly as *udan we toluk* (literally, rain water three). The period after this rain is marked by the coming out of new tamarind leaves. For the Tetun people, this is a sign that the beginning of the planting season is near.

The commencement of the planting season is indicated by the setting in of subsequent heavy rain about the middle of December. This type of rain is called *udan namate ahu kresan* (literally, rain that kills the hot ashes). The average of 111 mm of rain recorded in Figure 2.1 is considered to bring sufficient moisture to the land to encourage seeds to grow. Now the 'cooked' soil (*tasak*) has become 'raw' (*matak*), a favourable condition for growing. Like the soil, seeds must also be ritually cooled, through a ritual called *hisik fini* (sprinkle the seeds). In ritual terms, the ritual cooling of the earth and the seeds guarantees successful crops. In March, the rain is expected to decrease markedly. Any unexpected rain that sets in during this month will be harmful for the ripening crops. Such unexpected rain is called *udan menas*. *Menas* is probably a disguised form of *manas* ('hot'). This type of rain can be stopped by presenting betel-nut offerings (*haksera mama*) to the ancestors. The harvesting of the first crops is done after executing a particular ritual to make the crops have a 'plain taste' (*miis*). This ritual is called *hamiis*—that is, to make something *miis*.

The second planting season begins in April. Rains blown by the east monsoon are considered sufficient for cultivating the 'second maize' (*batar knau*) and mung beans (*fore Wehali*). This rain is called *udan lor* (rain that sets in from the seaside). The coming of the rain is indicated by the beating of the surf on the coast. Ormeling, in his short visit to Betun, the capital district of Malaka Tengah, which is located about 14 km from the coastline, for some unknown reason noted that he actually heard the beating of the surf from his bivouac (1957: 42, n.1). For the Wehali, the beating of the surf heard by Ormeling is imagined as the male voice of the sea calling for women of the hill.

The south Tetun also recognise two types of drizzle that must be avoided because they are believed to bring diseases. Drizzle by itself is called *udan kakait*, whereas a drizzle that sets in together with the appearance of a rainbow is called *udan baur* (the rainbow rain).

b. Soil

This 30,000 ha of plain has been the subject of various studies. Soil scientists such as Mohr and van Baren identified the margalitic soils found in Timor's hills and plains as vulnerable to erosion. During the rainy season, these soils are carried down from the hills to the plains. Thus the river of Benenai that divides the plain into two halves is responsible for the accumulation of fertile soil in the plains. This study was later confirmed by Hondius (as quoted in Ormeling 1957: 49–51) who examined the varied composition of deposited materials originating in the mountains of central Timor. This variability in type of soil, as well as in its structure, encourages yields from a variety of crops in the plains. Ormeling reported that the south Belu plain had a greater variety of crops than elsewhere in Timor (1957: 49).

c. Trees and Crops in the Hillside

It is true that there is no 'school competition' held in this area to test the children's knowledge of the diversity of local trees and shrubs (and animals) as was conducted by Schulte Nordholt in 1947 in north central Timor (1971: 33). But from market observations, daily conversations and origin myths one can detect the intimacy of the south Belu with the variety of trees and crops in their area. As a district whose territory covers part of both the hills and the plains, Malaka Tengah is the home for trees, shrubs and crops suited to each of these environments.

In the origin myth narrated by an *adat* historian from Kateri, a village situated in the hills part of the district, he refers to two types of shrubs growing in the area, namely *ktuik* and *kleik*. These belong to vine tree species that in the origin myth are described as a 'ladder' that linked the sky to the earth. These species mostly grow in the hills part of the area. The strength, length and straight nature of their vines make these trees suitable for part of the roof construction of south Tetun houses. The elasticity of the vines is useful for joining the 'chest' part of the house to its 'ribs'. In addition to its vines, the *kleik*'s fruits are collected for various purposes. The ripe fruits are boiled to be eaten as snacks. Women and children sell them on market days for extra cash. Candle-nut trees (*kmii*) also grow abundantly in the hills. The main posts of the Wehali house are chosen from the strong branches of the candle-nut tree.

The hills region is suitable for various species of root crops. While root crops are classified as *ubi-ubian* in Indonesia (tuber plants), this translation often causes confusion among the Tetun who recognise two kinds of *ubi-ubian*—that is, *uhi* and *fehuk*. The annual official report published by the government deals only with root crops that are inter-planted in conjunction with maize, rice or sorghum such as cassava (*ai fehuk*) and sweet potatoes (*fehuk malae*). In reality, however, there are other root crops inter-planted with different cultigens. For documentation's sake, I list in Table 2.7 the root crops not mentioned in the official reports, but nevertheless available during market days.

Thus, the difference between *uhi* and *fehuk* is in the nature of cultivation. The newer introduced root crops (such as cassava and sweet potatoes) and the root crops that are inter-planted in conjunction with other staples are called *fehuk*, while 'the native tubers' are called *uhi*.

Table 2.7: Root crops

Cultivated root	Translation	Uncultivated root	Translation
fehuk ema	people tuber	*uhi rama*	bow (for shooting) root
fehuk samea	snake tuber	*uhi laku*	charming root
fehuk nona metan	black woman tuber	*maek*	itchy yam
fehuk nona muti	white woman tuber	*fia*	yam with small leaves
fehuk fafiur	quail tuber		
fehuk lambo	lambo tuber		

In association with the root crops mentioned above, a number of subsidiary plants that have been classified as *kacang-kacangan* (beans) are also known to the area. Again, this category causes some confusion. The Tetun use two words to describe *kacang-kacangan*. Beans that grow wild in jungles are called *ahan*, while cultivated beans are called *fore*. However, there are not many bean varieties growing in the area. Under the category of *ahan* two types are still important for people's diet: *ahan alas* (the forest bean) and *iskoma*. Various types of *fore* grown in the area are *fore rai* (peanut), *fore tali* (kidney bean) and *fore Wehali* (mung bean).

It is also interesting to note that no *uhi* and *fehuk* are mentioned in the origin myths, nor are they included in the agricultural rituals. In response to my query about this evidence, *adat* historians stated that when the first people were born onto the earth, these *uhi* already existed. The *uhi* that grew in the first dry land that emerged out of the sea was called *fia kalo raek*, a small type of yam. Like other 'native' plants mentioned above, this yam also has ritual importance. When a leper dies, the mourners cover their faces with the leaves of this plant to avoid being infected by that disease.

Other crops that are associated with the hills region are fox-tail millet (*tora*), sometimes called *asu ikun* (the dog-tail) and *lena* (sesame). Every market day, the hills people bring various kinds of *uhi*, *tora* and *lena* to market and on their return they bring back products of the plains such as sago powder, wet rice and mung bean, as well as products of the sea villages, such as salt and fish. Although fox-tail millet and sesame are regarded as products of the hills, this does not necessarily mean that the plains people are not accustomed to these species. These crops still occupy an important place in the south Tetun culture. A few kinds of minor diseases such as flu, fever and cough are said to be cured by drinking water mixed with fox-tail millet powder. In certain agricultural rituals, farmers prepare small buckets of these seeds to be ritually cooled. For these reasons, both fox-tail millet and Job's tears are also planted in the plains, although in small quantities. There are various kinds of millet recognised in the area according to their physical appearance. Some millets produce one tail, others produce two or three tails. So they name them accordingly as *asu ikun* (dog-tail millet), *asu ikun knasak rua* (two dog-tailed millet) and *asu ikun knasak tolu* (three dog-tailed millet).

Another inter-planted cultigen that still has ritual and economic importance is a variety of bean commonly known throughout the region as *turis* (cow pea). Maize boiled with *turis* is a delicacy for the people. In 'war ritual', a man will be offered *turis* powder to drink in order to conceal him from his enemies.

d. Trees and Crops in the Plains Region

The springs located on the hillsides make the plains suitable for irrigated wet rice cultivation. Yet a recent survey conducted by the Agricultural Department of the Belu Regency indicates that only about 58 per cent of the potentially irrigated land is cultivated (see Ketaren 1991: 33).

Historical data available on the area reveal that wet rice cultivation was first introduced by the Dutch nearly 80 years ago. *Gezaghebber* Agerbeek in his *Memorie van overgave* reports that wet rice cultivation was introduced to the plains of Wehali-Wewiku in 1916. At that time a complex of 100 ha was irrigated from the spring of We Liman. In 1927, another experiment was conducted during the period of the *Controleur* Seijne Kok, when 18 blocks (*bouw*) of land were cultivated, particularly in the village of Kamanasa. In the same year, under *Gezaghebber* Agerbeek (who was later promoted to *Controleur*, 1916), another 20 blocks of land were developed for cultivation. Francillon (1967: 168) noted that land under wet rice cultivation increased by roughly 300 per cent in a period of 49 years (1914–1963), while over the same period average yields decreased by 150 per cent (from 2.5 t/ha to 1 t/ha). Francillon related the evident lack of interest in developing wet rice cultivation to the Japanese policy of using the plains of Wehali-Wewiku as the food store for the Japanese army. From it the Wehali people were forced to feed some 5,000 Japanese troops. Since then, wet rice cultivation has been considered to be forced labour (Francillon 1967: 168).

Nowadays, it is not lack of interest from the farmers in developing wet rice cultivation so much as the decreasing amount of water available for irrigation that is a major hindrance. Some government officers hesitantly pointed at the erosion due to new road constructions alongside natural springs and the conversion of 415 ha of natural forest into teak or tamarind plantations since 1950 as factors contributing to a decreasing supply of water for irrigation. Table 2.8 documents the conversion of natural forest in the district of Malaka Tengah into stands of so-called 'economic trees' or plantation.

When asked the reasons for lack of success in wet rice cultivation, however, some elders related the problem only to the *adat*. I was told that according to the *adat* of Wesei Wehali, it is forbidden to include wet rice in planting and harvesting rituals. Those rituals are only concerned with dry rice. Thus, the failure of water distribution through a newly built canal from the spring of We Liman is seen by the ruler of Le'un Klot, A. Klau, as due to this *adat* stipulation. He simply said, 'Wet rice cultivation is not the way of our ancestors'. This opinion is also shared by many of his nobles in the domain of Wewiku. Their long acquaintance with dry upland rice (*hare leten*) cultivation can be deduced from the mention of dry rice in myths and the varieties of rice known to them as listed in Table 2.9.

Table 2.8: The conversion of natural forest

Year	Size in ha	Name of tree
1950	4.85	teak
1951	6.5	teak
1952	1	teak
1953	10	teak
1956	25	teak
1958	28.25	teak
1959	40	teak
1987/88	100	teak
1991/92	100	teak
1992/93	100	tamarind

Table 2.9: Names of dry rice varieties

Name of rice paddy	Translation
hare sukabi	the oak (tree) rice
hare kwa metan	the black crow rice
hare Bauk Morin	the fragrant Bauk rice
hare busa ni'an	the dog teeth rice
hare marahuk	the furry rice
hare ekekero	the taily rice
hare babelik	the sticky rice

The other principal crops of the plains area are maize and sorghum. The term for maize in Tetun is *batar malae* (the foreign maize), while sorghum is called *batar ai naruk* (the long stalk maize) in daily speech and *batar na'an tasi* (maize that derives from a fish) in ritual language. It is also called *batar tasi* (maize that came from the sea).

A myth well known in the area describes how the first seed of sorghum was discovered in the head of a *knase* fish. This seed was then planted in a sacred garden called *to'os etu kukun*, which is situated in the eastern part of the village of Laran. Sorghum cultivated in the area is regarded as originating from this particular seed. In rituals, people treat sorghum as higher than maize and therefore the *to'os etu kukun* is planted with sorghum only. Locally, there are various kinds of sorghum named according to the size of its seed, colour, taste and mythical origin. I recorded the varieties of sorghum known to the south Tetun (Table 2.10).

Table 2.10: Varieties of sorghum

Name of sorghum	Translation
batar mean lakulot	red charming sorghum
batar bua funan	areca-nut blossom sorghum
batar na'i katuas	respected man's sorghum
batar laka bela	flat flame sorghum
batar mean	red sorghum
batar na'an tasi	fish sorghum

Maize (*batar malae*) is planted twice a year in most of the plains area and three times a year by the river bank. Maize planted during the west monsoon is called *batar tinan* (annual maize). This kind of maize is planted along with other crops in the annual planting season. The rainy season caused by the east monsoon is the second planting season for the south Tetun. In this season, farmers grow mung bean (*fore Wehali*) and the 'second' crop of maize (*batar knau*). The 'third' crop of maize (*batar au kale'an*) is deliberately planted by the river bank.

Two other kinds of trees that are ritually and economically important for the south Tetun are coconut and palm trees. There are four varieties of palm trees known to the people: *akar bone* (Indonesian: *enau*), *akar lisa* (*Corypha Utan*; Indonesian: *gebang* or *gewang*), *akaria* (sago palm) and *tuak* (*Borassus Sundaica*). The palm most used for house construction and food is *akar lisa* (gebang palm), simply known as *akar*. Compared with other varieties of palm trees, *akar bone* has less economic importance for the people. It does, however, suit ritual purposes. The toxic nature of its leaves is regarded as potentially useful in warfare. Every warrior once carried a small tip of its leaf in his pouch (*kakaluk*) to intoxicate (*halanu*) his enemies. Since the gebang palm is used by the majority of people for building construction and alternative food during famine, it was regarded as the commoners' palm. On the contrary, the small number of sago palms still preserved in the sacred forest of the hamlet of Umakatahan are considered to be the food of nobles. Like other native crops, these varieties of palm are not cited in the origin myths.

In the myth that narrates the origin of edible crops (see Reference Text 7), coconut is cited as deriving from the head of a ruler called Liurai Barehi. Among the kinds of tribute delivered by people as gifts of homage to their supreme ruler at the end of the harvest ritual, coconuts occupy the highest status. The association of the coconut with 'noble products' was strengthened by the economic policy of the Dutch period, which indirectly created differential ownership of coconut trees. On discovering that the plains of Wehali-Wewiku was suitable for coconut plantations, the colonial government regulated the growing of large numbers of coconut trees. Those who wanted to cultivate more than 1,000 coconut trees had to have a concession from the government. Consequently, only a small number of nobles and wealthy Chinese were able to run small plantations.[6] The south Tetun themselves only plant a small number of coconut trees to mark a garden's border, a practice continued up until now. Government efforts to help people run their own coconut plantations to generate cash income also ended unsuccessfully.

Most poor farmers' cash income and alternative food supply during periods of famine derives from the gebang palm. The dependency upon gebang palm for house construction, household utensils, alternative food and the rearing of pigs meant that the cutting down of 200 ha of dense gebang palm in the district of Malaka Tengah in 1993 for a cocoa plantation gave rise to serious protest from the people.

The Language

It took me a few months living with the south Tetun to realise that they have inherited a rich oral poetry and elevated speech in various forms. My endeavour to learn these forms of speech was kindly received by the people. Once I indicated that I wanted to know more about this 'rich culture', I was literally flooded with oral compositions in a binary mode. Almost every single thing that I asked was answered with either couplet(s) of parallel lines or dyadic words. The more I heard this mode of speech, the more confused I became. For the people themselves, my confusion was amusing, because it proved that they possess a language that is difficult for an outsider to learn. For those who travel to the northern part of Belu, this type of language becomes a 'secret' language for communication among themselves. As I slowly mastered this elevated speech, I was considered an insider (*ema itak*—our people) in contrast to those who could not master it, who are referred to as *ema matak* (raw people). Rumours soon spread around the villages that studying *adat* equals learning elevated speech, which makes sense for them. The description of oral tradition in this section then corresponds to local perceptions of learning *adat*. Fox in his *To speak in pairs* emphasises the importance of understanding oral

6   *Gezagheber* Overakker (1926) in his 'Explanatory notes for the annual report on Belu territory' mentions the names of Chinese traders who received such concessions:

Name of owner	Location	Number of trees
Lay DjinPoh	Tobaki	2,800
Leong Eng Djoen	Sali	1,700
Tan Kang Long	WeFatuk	1,500
Lay Djin Pong	Kletek	4,000

poetry and elevated speech because in many eastern Indonesian societies this dyadic language has become 'the primary vehicle for the preservation and transmission of cultural knowledge' (1988a: 2).

The south Tetun in general are well known for their elegant and rhythmic language. This is evident not only in formal communal and ceremonial meetings, but also in their daily life. So heavy is the emphasis on this elevated language that they value others in terms of how someone expresses his/her feelings and opinions in 'beautiful language'. When a young man courts a young woman (*hanimak*), he has to display his ability to attract the woman using oral poetry (*knanuk*) and elevated language (*lia na'in*). Even parents included this factor (to express oneself in poetic language and in a proper manner) in considering every marriage proposal. Many city dwellers know that those who master this language will have the advantage of marrying south Tetun women. For the south Tetun, politeness, good behaviour and good manners are reflected through language. Obviously, by 'language' they mean the using of the right words in the right place at the right time.

The Tetun word for 'language' is *lia*, which also means 'word', 'phrase' or 'news' (Morris 1984: 130). It can also denote 'some serious business'. A person engaged in a court case is said to *kona lia* (in colloquial Indonesian: *kena perkara*), while the actual court or *adat* meeting is called *tuur lia* (colloquial Indonesian: *duduk perkara*). The citing of a story, poetry or a myth is called *de'an lia*. It is interesting to note that the word *de'an* also means 'to swear' or 'be angry'. The compound word *lia fuan* (*fuan* = fruit) refers 'to a definite conversation', 'a message' or 'a mandate'. So there is a kind of moral obligation attached to the word *lia*. Like the word *dedea* in Rotinese, *lia* is not just chatting to pass the time (for which the Tetun employ the term *dale*), it contains messages to be learned or something worthwhile to be considered.

Some of my Indonesian friends suggested that there are three *dialek* in south Tetun: Wehali, Wewiku and Kamanasa. Asking a Tetun opinion on this matter, they would reply that a south Tetun can differentiate the way a Kamanasa person speaks from language users in the other two domains. Apart from the use of particular words or kin terms by the Kamanasa, there are also phonological and rhythmic differences in a small number of words, phrases and sentences pronounced by people of those three domains. The Tetun word for 'rhythm' is *sasere*. (*Tasi sere* = the beating of surf on the beach.)

Table 2.11: Types of oral language

Speech form	Genre	Gloss translation
Everyday speech	*ai knoik* *ai ksaszk (ai laknaik)* *ai kbabelek* *lia tete bai* *soe lia*	folk tale riddle heroic stories proverb cynicism, critique, slander
Ceremonial speech	*rai lian* *lia tebes* *hasee hawaka* *tanis nodi sura*	origin myth true tale greetings lament
Taboo language	*lia na'in* *lia tasi*	respect register sea language
Poetry (*knanuk*)	*knanuk aka belu* *knanuk makerek* *knanuk rai lian* *knanuk tatean* *knanuk ai tahan* *knanuk bermalu* *knanuk fa'e malu*	songs (while pounding sago) cynical poems poems (concerning myths of origin) advice humour love poems farewell songs/poems

As far as oral poetry and elevated language are concerned, there is one main principle underlying them, that is the use of *lia sasaluk*. The word *sasaluk* refers to a shroud obscuring or disguising the conditions of something. *Lia sasaluk* is then translated into Indonesian as *bahasa bungkus* (language which wraps up or enfolds). The expression 'language which wraps up' immediately suggests that the oral poetry and elevated speech consist of many metaphors. These metaphors are expressed in dyadic language, known in Tetun as *knanuk*. The word *knanuk* is related to the verb *hananu* (to sing). So a fine *knanuk* can be chanted and sung by a poet. Table 2.11 is an attempt to classify the varieties of Tetun oral poetry and elevated speech based on the person who recites them, the occasions or events suitable for their recitation and the degree of dyadic language within a narration.

There are difficulties in classifying oral poetry on the basis of status of the narrator or chanter because there is no fixed rule about this. For example, *knanuk aka belu*, usually chanted by young women and men, may also be sung by old women. This relative nature of classification also prevails in respect to elevated speech. An *ai knoik* or a *rai lian* can also be cited as *lia tebes*. When I asked Johanis Seran Kehik, a famous chanter of the Manumutin clan, to narrate an account of the founder of his clan, Ho'ar Nahak Samane Oan, he told me that this constituted a *lia tebes* (true story), while other Manumutin who narrated the same story classified it as *an ai knoik* (folk tale). Similarly, noble women from the village of Besikama sang (*hananu*) a heroic account of fighting between their hero (Nahak Maroe Rai) and the Dutch as an *ai knoik*, while their *adat* historian narrated it as a *lia tebes*. In the domain of *rai lian*, there are also divergent classifications. When I recorded an origin myth in the village of Builaran, the official *adat* historian of Liurai, Bau Fahik, included a folk tale about the seven princesses (*feto hitus*), which his audience claimed was a *rai lian*. Then again, the *adat* historian of Wehali, Piet Tahuk, narrated the coming of the first retainers (Mau Leki and Mau Mauk) to the earth as *lia tebes* and not *rai lian*.

I suggest that the relative nature of this classification is closely connected with the degree of responsibility someone has to bear when reciting particular stories. As a rule, a *rai lian*, narrating the origin of human beings and the earth, can only be recited by an *adat* historian (*mako'an*). But saying this does not necessarily mean that only the *mako'an* possess the knowledge of *rai lian*. As a matter of fact, this origin myth was frequently narrated in front of many people on formal occasions. Very often some couplets and dyadic words cited in this myth are a well-known piece of poetry that can be sung or chanted in other genres of the oral tradition. What makes an origin myth *lulik* (forbidden) to be narrated by common people is the consequence of narrating it. People believe that an origin myth is a sacred history told by their ancestors. It is therefore recognised as their ancestor's path (*bein dalan*). Failing to narrate the ancestor's path correctly will bring disaster for the chanter and the community at large. A *mako'an* is believed to gain the knowledge of the ancestor's path in dreams and therefore he alone has the right to narrate it. Perhaps for this reason, well-known stories such as 'the seven princesses' (*feto hitus*) and the story concerning the first retainers (Mau Leki and Mau Mauk) are regarded only as *lia tebes* and *ai knoik* by famous *mako'an* such as Bau Fahik and Piet Tahuk, but for other elders they are sacred myths.

Hakse hawaka ('greetings', literally 'to salute//to counsel') or *lia riik* (literally, the stand up language) are often chanted by *adat* historians (*mako'an*). These performative speeches are marked by their extended pairing of couplets and dyadic words (see Reference Text 1). In the actual performance of these speeches, a chanter is expected to display his ability by reciting the poem in musical beat as smoothly and fluently as he can. Certainly, a *mako'an*, as an expert in this field, is recommended to execute the task. On many occasions, however, other skilful chanters are also asked to perform it. Not surprisingly, the art of chanting these speeches is desired by many people as it increases their social status. School teachers and village heads are particularly fond of learning it. Names such as Ferdy Seran (the school teacher in Kletek), Sam Kehik (the school teacher in Besikama) and village head of Uma To'os and Julius Bria Seran[7] (a government civil servant) are well known as skilful chanters throughout the region. People often consider them (and they even consider themselves) more skilful than the *adat* historians.

Compared with the varieties of elevated speech and oral poetry, 'taboo language' belongs to a different genre. The Tetun word for 'taboo' in this context is *lulik*. By 'taboo language' I mean the use of a number of euphemistic words and phrases in front of respectable persons and in particular places. Linguists label this as 'taboo wording' (Grimes and Maryott 1991: 5). There are two types of taboo language recognised in south Tetun. First, *lia na'in* (the main, the respectable, the noble language) sometimes called *lia hun* (the trunk language) and, second, *lia tasi* (language of the sea).

Lia na'in or *lia hun* is frequently used to narrate an origin myth, to translate the Christian Bible, to preach in church, for discourses in formal meetings or even in daily conversations with a respected person (nobles) or a loved one. To show their love and respect for others, a number of words are rephrased in certain ways so that the speakers place themselves in a 'humble' or 'lower' position compared to the addressees. Very often, for instance, 'house idioms' are used to describe some actions. The verandah of a house consists of two levels, the higher level (*labis leten*) and the lower level (*labis kraik*). The polite way of moving down the levels is by crawling like a baby (*nakdobos*). So, an order or speech from nobles to the people is imaged as *nakdobos* to the people. In the same manner, asking permission 'to go home', which is normally '*fila*', becomes *hakraik* (lower oneself down from the raised verandah to the lower ground) or *hola tehen* (to take the roof off the house). There are also a number of phrases that are common in Indonesia including 'to walk' as 'to enlighten one self' (*hamaan*), 'to sit' as 'to make oneself heavy' (*hatodan*), 'to sleep' as 'to stretch one's body' (*haknotak*). The Wehali people insist that their domain is the centre of all petty domains. Therefore, they have to speak in a manner suited to nobles. There is no special 'punishment' for those who fail to observe

---

7   Julius Bria published a collection of *knanuk* under the title *Pantun Bahasa Tetun Timor* (1985).

this *lia na'in* except social disparagement as *adat lalek* (literally, having no *adat*). For the Tetun people and elsewhere in Indonesia, to refer to someone as without *adat* (*tak punya adat*) is regarded as a serious insult or even a curse. I often heard parents warn their children, if they happened to pronounce something 'wrong' that 'it is *lulik* (forbidden, taboo) to say such a word'.

Compared with *lia na'in*, there are special words or phrases that have to be used when someone is on the seashore. The use of special vocabularies by anyone who is fishing, gathering seafood, or simply travelling on the seashore is called *lia tasi* (sea language). This type of 'language' is carefully observed by both women and men, young and old, to avoid any unanticipated or unintended result such as the sudden rising of waves, attack by sharks, being 'speared' by mangrove spikes or merely having a poor catch of fish.

Ideally, women are not permitted to come to the seashore because it is the domain of men. The rough south sea of Timor, known as the male sea (*tasi mane*), is believed to be threatening to women. In order to go safely to the shore, women should cover themselves down to the toes. If their thighs are exposed to the 'male sea', they are thought to be in danger of being drawn into the sea by the 'male wave' (*mane lor*). This expectation then becomes a favourite game for the young women. When they approach the sea, they deliberately raise their sarongs up to their thighs to seduce the 'male sea', saying:

Kelen mutin kelen mutin	white thigh, white thigh
se ma at modi mai	who will come to take us
na'i mane lor	the handsome male sea
Mai modi ami	Come and take us away

When I attempted to pursue a deeper analysis of *lia tasi*, I was urged to visit the village nearest to the south Timor Sea (*tasi mane* = male sea), the hamlet of Lo'o Sina. There are few named houses in this village, but the most sacred and therefore uninhabited is called *Uma Tasi* (the Sea House). In Wehali cosmology, this hamlet is considered the first harbour through which people and wealth came to the area. According to a myth narrated in this hamlet, a man named Seran Di'ak was once carried away by a dove from Marlilu Haholek (the first dry land in Wehali) to China. On his return, he brought back a water buffalo called *mane lor* (the man of the seaside). One day when a boy was herding, the buffalo went down toward the sea. The boy, accompanied by his dog, followed the buffalo until the three of them were drawn into the middle of the sea. A few days afterwards they returned to the village. To the villagers' surprise, the fur of the buffalo had turned into gold. Every time the buffalo shook himself, gold fell to the ground. To show their appreciation to the sea, the villagers built a house called *Uma Tasi* (the Sea House).

Because the sea is the source of wealth, those who come to the sea ought to wear 'old used sarongs' (*tais at*: literally, 'ugly sarongs'). Jewellery should be left at home. In this way, people indicate to 'the source of wealth' that they are poor. All the fishing activities are then symbolised as an act of praying for prosperity. Based on this, the south Tetun use the same word for 'to go fishing', 'to gather seafood' and 'to pray' or 'to plea'—that is, *haloon//hakmasin* (literally, to make straight//to salinise). The word for 'to go home' after fishing is *hakraik*, which literally means 'to lower oneself' or 'to humble oneself'. By using this word in this context, the image of descending from a house is also obvious. In Table 2.12, I provide some words that are frequently used on the seashore.[8]

Most Austronesian societies evince some sort of taboo language. This type of language is used to disguise reference to the items mentioned. The likely purpose of 'disguising things' here is to deceive the spirit of the sea. The Tetun words listed in Table 2.12 may also be considered as deception language used to trick the source of wealth in the sea.

From the Wehali people's perspective, both *lia na'in* (the noble language) and *lia tasi* evoke the same 'force'. In dealing with the noble language, they broach the *mahaa toba mahemu toba* (one who eats reclining, drinks reclining), their source of life and fertility. In the case of *lia tasi* they are facing *mane lor* (the man of the wave), the source of wealth and property. Linguistic avoidances relating to these two languages can then be considered as efforts to maintain the flow of wealth from outside into the community.

---

8   Thanks to Catharina van Klinken who allowed me to use much of her data in producing this table.

Table 2.12: Taboo wording[9]

Sea term	Everyday meaning	Sea meaning	Normal term
1. General things			
ai maran abut	root of dry plant	cassava	*fehuk ai*
Katar	itches	tobacco	*tabako*
taha lotuk	narrow knife	betel fruit	*furuk*
Badut	wick lamp	sun, moon	*loro, fulan*
fukun bua	joint of areca nut	young coconut	*nunak*
funa meak	red flower	maize	*batar malae*
Tilun	ear	sea	*tasi*
2. Fishing			
kesak na'in	lord of the fish trap	crocodile	*lafaek*
Klelek	to float	boat	*ro, bidu*
Asu	dog	fish trap	*kesak*
knase rahun	small fish	fish, eels	*na'an tasi, tuna*
biku tahan	the Biku leaves	prawn, shrimp	*boek*
3. People/animals			
Kabuar	watermelon	horse	*kabau malae*
Kbelak	flat	buffalo	*kebau metan* (timur)
knaban oan	basket for liquids	child	*oan*
Metan	dark colour	woman	*feto*
4. Actions			
hadi'a kbonan sia	to firm the sarong	pack up to go home	*fila, fali*
kbonan tali sia kotu	belt is broken	there are lots of fish	*na'an tasi wa'in*
Hakmoo	to gargle	wash	*fase*
Ooe	call to cow	call to women	
Booe	call to buffalo	call to men	
Hakraik	to lower oneself	to go home	*fila hikar uma*
Kuda	to sow	walk, go	*la'o*

---

9   This table is offered as a contribution to future comparative studies of Austronesian-speaking peoples. Further research by specialists is needed to understand the linguistic features of this taboo register. What interests me here is the existence of taboo language as a social phenomena.

3
Two Perspectives on Wehali

Introduction

In this chapter I endeavour to view Wehali from two angles: as perceived through historical documents and as perceived by the people themselves in various forms of oral tradition.

These approaches correspond with two levels of analysis. In accordance with historical accounts, in the pre-European era the many domains in Timor (62 according to one Portuguese source) were ruled by just two or three 'emperors'. An impression one might gain in reading the historical documents is that these emperors, or at least the emperor of Wehali, ruled the realm with coercive power. Therefore, when the subjects' opportunity came to free themselves from the grip of Wehali, 'it was seized with festivity' (Leitao 1948: 207). In this interpretation a number of terms repeatedly occur, such as 'coercion', 'subdue' and 'hegemony' in the sense of 'dominance'. By contrast, in the latter part of the chapter I move to a mode of analysis in which I rely on various cultural categories used by the south Tetun in general and the Wehali in particular for describing their notion of centrality and superiority.

To provide some background on the coming of the earliest Asian and European traders, I begin by highlighting the importance of the sandalwood trade in Asia at that time.

An Historical Account of Wehali's Hegemony

Little is known of Timor's history prior to the arrival of European traders. The Chinese traders who had for centuries made voyages to Timor, where they could obtain sandalwood (*Santalum album* L.) for preparing perfumes and incense, left scant information concerning names for the kings of their trading partners' domains or the nature of any alliances prevailing among those domains.

One of the earliest sources, dated 1436 (Groeneveldt 1960: 116), only informs us that the island of Timor, which was pronounced as *Ti-mun* by the Chinese traders, 'was covered with sandalwood trees'. These traders brought gold, silver, iron, porcelain, textiles and coloured silks to exchange for the products of the island. The same source reveals that there were 12 trading ports throughout the island, without explicitly naming them. A later source, dated 1618, gives more information particularly concerning people's subjection by their rulers. It was noted that 'the natives continually bring sandalwood for bartering with the merchants, but they may not come when the king is not present, for fear of disturbances. Therefore the king is always requested to come first' (Groeneveldt 1960: 117).

There are controversies, however, concerning whether the Chinese traders did come to fetch sandalwood in Timor or whether they obtained it from elsewhere. Meilink-Roelofsz (1962: 102), drawing on a Chinese source from the mid-fourteenth century (Wang Ta Yuan, compiled by Rockhill), suggests that the Chinese traders obtained their sandalwood from the Malacca market and not directly from Timor. This suggestion seems peculiar in the light of data elaborated by many other writers, including the prominent historian, Boxer (1948: 175) and, later, Schulte Nordholt (1971: 165), who wrote brilliantly on the pre-colonial history of domains in Timor based on Portuguese and Dutch archives. The coming of these traders to Timor is also a theme that can be discerned in the Wehali myth concerning *Sina Mutin Malaka* (the white Chinese of Malacca).

1. Antonio Pigafetta's Account

Mentions of the abundance of sandalwood trees on the island of Timor led Europeans to involve themselves in sandalwood trading. With a monopoly on sandalwood, a commodity most needed in China and India, the Europeans expected to enter lucrative markets in the so-called 'Asiatic network' trading areas. The importance of sandalwood trading at that time is indicated in Portuguese and Dutch figures. Van Leur (1955: 209) estimates that in 1614, around 3,000 *picul* of sandalwood were brought onto the market each year. Three months after their conquest of Malacca (1511), the Portuguese began to prepare their way to Timor.

In November 1511, Albuquerque dispatched an expedition of three ships to seek the spice islands in eastern Indonesia under his captain, Antonio d'Abreau. D'Abreau himself was the commandant of the ship *Santa Catarina*, Francisco Serrao was the commandant of the ship *Sabaia*, while the third vessel, a caravel, was commanded by Simao Alfonso Bisagudo, with Francisco Rodrigues as pilot. Concerning Francisco Rodrigues, Albuquerque mentioned his name several times in a letter to the king of Portugal (Manuel), praising him as 'a young man who has always been here, with very good knowledge and able to make maps' (Cortesao 1967, vol. I: lxxix). Obviously, one reason for Albuquerque sending this talented cartographer was to make maps of the spice islands. Upon their arrival in Timor, Rodrigues drew a map of the island and wrote above it 'the island of Timor where the sandalwood grows' (Cortesao 1967, vol. I: 203). A report made by the commander of this expedition was summarised by Cortesao (1967, vol. I: 204) as follows:

> The island of Timor has heathen kings. There is a great deal of white sandalwood in these two islands (Timor and Sumba). It is very cheap because there is no other wood in the forests. The Malay merchants say that God made Timor for sandalwood and Banda for mace and the Moluccas for cloves, and that this merchandise is not known anywhere else in the world except in these places.

Here, not much is said about the existence of domains in Timor, except that they were *cafres*, a Portuguese term for 'heathens'. Based on this exaggerated information, Rui de Brito Patalim, captain of Malacca, wrote a letter dated 6 January 1514 to the king of the Portuguese asking for ships to fetch sandalwood, honey, wax and priests to baptise those heathens.

Just short of a decade afterwards, on Sunday, 26 January 1522, Magellan's men, including Antonio Pigafetta, on their voyage around the world landed on the north coast of Timor, in Batugade (Nowell 1962: 243–246). In his report, Pigafetta gave further information concerning the nature of inter-domain alliances in Timor. He wrote:

> On the other side of the island are four brothers, who are the
> kings of that island. Where we were, there were cities and some of
> their chiefs. The names of the four settlements of the kings are as
> follows: Oibich, Lichsana, Suai, and Cabanaza. Oibich is the
> largest (Nowell 1962: 245).

The domain of Oibich mentioned in that account clearly refers to the
domain of Wewiku (see Schulte Nordholt 1971: 233), ritually one
of Wehali's 'posts' whose ruler therefore has a right to hold the title of
Liurai. In the myth narrated in Wewiku (see Reference Text 4), the
three domains in the plain of Wehali-Wewiku (Wewiku, Haitimuk and
Wehali) originated from three sisters. Thus, when Pigafetta's informants
mentioned the four 'brothers' who ruled Timor, they must have thought
the sibling relation applied between Wewiku and Wehali.

The names Suai and Cabanaza without doubt refer to the domain of
Suai-Kamanasa, part of the present East Timor province. Myths narrated
in south Tetun depict the Suai-Kamanasa as descendants from one Liurai,
Suri Nurak, who left Wehali. The myth owned by the people of the hamlet
of Fatisin, an origin group in the village of Kamanasa, relates how a long
time ago their ruler, known as Loro Akar Lau Da'ok, lived in Wehali.
He lived in a 'fortress' called Fatisin *Kota*.[1] This site is located on the peak
of a rocky hill next to Marlilu Haholek, the first site of Maromak Oan of
Wehali. Due to the tension between those two rulers,[2] the ruler of Fatisin
escaped to Suai-Kamanasa. The return of these people to Wehali around
1910 was then represented as returning to the laps of 'Wehali the mother
and father' (*ina no ama Wehali*).

Concerning the name Lichsana in Pigafetta's account, there are two
possible explanations. According to Schulte Nordholt (1971: 160, n.5a),
etymologically Lichsana derives from Likusaen,[3] a region 30 km west of
Dili, the present provincial capital of East Timor. This region was named
by the Portuguese as Liquiça. This suggestion fits the Wehali system of
government where one of its executive rulers, entitled *liurai*, resides in
Likusaen. He is then known as Liurai Likusaen, the ruler of Wehali's
domains toward the sunrise (*Liurai loro sa'e*). However, the difficulty with

---

1   The term *kota* is a Portuguese loan word meaning 'fortress'.
2   According to myth, Maromak Oan of Wehali was displeased with the ruler of Fatisin for two
reasons: 1. Loro Fatisin had proved that his 'knowledge' of cultivating and harvesting a particular rice
known as *hare kake* (literally, the cockatoo rice) was superior to that of the Maromak Oan. 2. A proposal
by one of the Wehali rulers to marry the daughter of the *loro* of Fatisin was rejected.
3   The word *likusaen* in Tetun means 'python'.

this association (Lichsana as Likusaen or Liquiça) is the location involved. Pigafetta clearly pointed out that this particular domain was located on the south coast, while Likusaen is on the north coast. Pigafetta, who landed at Batugade some 30 km west of Likusaen, must have learned from his informants that Lichsana (in the sense of Likusaen) is on the north coast. Therefore, the association of Lichsana with Likusaen is doubtful.

The second possibility is that the domain of Lichsana mentioned by Pigafetta refers to the present domain of Insana. Regarding this second suggestion, Schulte Nordholt warns that although linguistically it is improbable to confuse Lichsana with Insana, this association is a possible one. Le Roux, who was also puzzled by the exact location of Lichsana, mentioned that in V.O.C. sources 'the names Lixsan, Loksa and Lioksang recur sometimes in connection with Insana; normally this is situated on the north coast of Portuguese Timor between Dili and Maubara. Here indeed is found Liquiça' (Francillon 1967: 68). Although the central hamlet of Insana is located in the interior of Timor, this quotation refers to Insana's important port (Mena), which is located on the north coast. Perhaps based on the same sources, Middlekoop (1960: 20) associated Lichsana with the present domain of Insana.

With reference to 'brotherly domains' as mentioned by Pigafetta in his account, both historical documents and oral history in the region depict these domains as related in some way or another. Whether *Lichsana* is Likusaen or Insana, for the Wehali both domains are ritually considered as Wehali's protectors. The domain of Likusaen in origin myths narrated in south Tetun is ruled by *Liurai loro sa'e*, the ruler of the domains toward the sunrise. He is the guardian from the eastern part of the realm of Wesei Wehali. In contrast, domains toward the sunset (*loro toba*) are ruled by Liurai Sonba'i, *Liurai loro toba*. Here, the domains of Insana and Amanuban, Amanatun, Amarasi and Biboki were founded by Wehali men, respectively Sana Taek, Nuba Taek, Natu Taek and Rasi Taek and Boki Taek. In the Wehali view, the Insana are the Wehali's children and therefore ritually they are also immediate protectors of the *ina no ama Wehali* (the mother and father of Wehali). So far, then, we recognise that Pigafetta's information concerning the 'brotherhood' within the political communities prevailing in 1522 is acceptable as far as it goes.

The omission of the name Wehali from the list provided by Pigafetta, however, is crucial for students of Wehali since, in many later documents and origin myths recorded in the region, Wehali is the greatest 'empire', whose dependents cover most of the domains in Timor. Francillon (1967: 70) proposes two alternatives regarding the omission of the name of Wehali: either 'Wehali had not come into existence yet' or Wehali did not exist in political terms, seeing it as 'more an ideal than an effectively political state'. Thus, in his view, 'Wehali belongs to a different sphere, a mystical and occult one'. Regarding the first proposal, it is hard to determine whether, in 1522, Wehali had already come to exist or not. In my opinion, this is a most ambiguous proposal, questioning Wehali's existence based on a single account of one traveller. Although the second proposal offers the more likely solution, the distinction involved between an 'effectively political state and a mystical state' tends to be an outsider's paradigm that distinguishes domains as either spiritual or secular states. Unlike the Tetun of East Timor, who have a word for 'secular' (*saun*) in contrast to 'sacred' (*lulik*) (Hicks 1984: 3, 6), and therefore distinguish *rai lulik* (sacred land or domain) and *rai saun* (secular land or domain), the south Tetun only recognise the term *lulik*, which in many instances can be translated as 'forbidden'. To articulate the relations between domains, the south Tetun prefer the categories of male/female, inside/outside, centre/periphery or parent/children. So, with regard to the information received from Pigafetta, the four brotherly domains mentioned in his list can be seen as male domains, who ritually functioned as protectors of Wehali, the female domain. They are outsiders, compared to Wehali the insiders, and perhaps more likely to come to Pigafetta's attention for that reason.

2. Sarzedas Document

Another document that can be treated as informative in shedding light on the political communities in Timor prior to the arrival of Europeans is the so-called *documento Sarzedas*. This document is the reference most cited by Portuguese historians such as Alfonso de Castro (1867), Faria de Morais (1944), Leitao (1948) and Helio A. Esteves Felgas (1956). As noted in article 52 of the text, this document reveals the situation of domains in Timor from 1722 to 1725 and as it was still found in 1777 (Schulte Nordholt 1971: 162; de Castro 1867: 202). The document covers extensive areas of interest, from religion and administrations to civil, military and political matters. Regarding the latter, the document reveals that prior to the arrival of Europeans, Timor was inhabited by the Bellas and the Vaiquenos:

who differ a great deal from each other, making up as it were two provinces and two peoples, the eastern part being inhabited by the Bellos, who live in the province dominated by the Bellos, and the western part by the Vaiquenos in the province called Serviao (Schulte Nordholt 1971: 161).

Schulte Nordholt regards the name Serviao as derived from Sorbian, an important trading port situated in north-east Amfoang. In the Paravicini contract discussed below, Sousale was named as ruler of Sorbian. Undoubtedly, Serviao or Sorbian designates the realm of Sonba'i. Vaiquenos is a term used widely in East Timor even until now to designate both the people and the language of the Dawan (de Castro 1867: 328; Thomaz 1981: 57). Thus, as stated in the Sarzedas document, the province located in the western part of the island was ruled by Sonba'i as the supreme ruler, who bore the title *imperator*. This province was said to consist of 16 *reinos* (domains). Of these 16 domains, at least three lie in Belu, namely Drima (Dirma), Vaibico (Wewiku) and Ocany (Akani). Ascambeloe, an unknown domain, probably also lies in Belu. There are four domains mentioned in the list that Schulte Nordholt (1971: 163) could not locate: Mossy, Vaigame, Sacunoba and Amassuax. However, by looking at the domains listed as under Wehali authority in the great contract of Paravicini in which Sucunaba was mentioned together with Baybohie (Sakoenaba Baybohie), I would locate this domain together with Biboki under the regent of north-central Timor in the present system of government.

In the Sarzedas document, the so-called Bellos province, which covered the eastern part of the island, was said to be made up of 46 domains. These domains of varying power were reported to be all free and independent of each other prior to their submission to the Portuguese Crown. The most important among their rulers was Suray de Uzalle. Like Sonba'i, he was also entitled 'emperor'.

The names Bellos, Belos or Belo in other Portuguese sources refer to both people and language in areas where Tetun is spoken outside the Portuguese territory. Luis Filipe F.R. Thomaz, in his paper on the formation of the Tetun language, suggests that prior to the coming of the Europeans, in the 'whole eastern half of the island people speak the lingua dos Belos-Belo being the name of the second Tetunspeaking region—that is, the zone stretching from coast to coast near the frontier' (1981: 55). Obviously

Bellos here refers to Belu, then and now part of West Timor, while its supreme ruler, described as Suray de Uzalle, unmistakably refers to the Liurai of Wehali.

As listed in the Sarzedas document par. 52, the 46 domains making up the Bellos province that was under Portuguese sovereignty were as follows: Sarau, Mattarufa, Faturo, Bibiluto, Vimasse, Viqueque, Laga, Manattuto, Lacluta, Layloa, Luca, Lado, Locury Ayfoam, Somoro, Calacodo, Lacloddott, Alay, Barcola, Titulur Mouves, Mutael, Lequica, Manufai, Lityluli, Sanir, Codaco, Maubara, Laquero, Fatuburo, Boibau, Nassudilly, Girivat, Cutubaba, Balibo, Lamacana, Moguery, Boraramia, Aratassava, Lamiao, Ficlara, Cova, Suailamanaca, Tulufar, Tamiao, Doculo, Luqueo Tafaquy and Juvanilho (de Castro 1867: 202). The names of these 46 domains can be found in a map attached to de Castro's book. However, the accuracy of that map is doubtful, since the 46 domains mentioned above were literally fitted into the available space as part of Bellos province. In that map, Wehali, which is located to the west of the domain of Lakekun, was situated to its east. It seems to me this misplacement was meant to emphasise that Wehali was logically part of the *Provincia dos Bellos* and, therefore, it was placed among these domains.

Despite the mapping inaccuracy and a few unidentifiable names, the Sarzedas document provides invaluable information concerning the political communities in the pre-colonial period, suggesting there was once a degree of unity. Based on the same document, Thomaz (1981: 58) goes further, claiming that before the coming of the Europeans, Tetun, *lingua dos Belos*, had become the 'vehicular' language of most of the eastern part of the island:

> In my opinion, the use of Tetun as a vehicular language is related to the conquest of the eastern half of the island by a military Tetun-speaking aristocracy, the *datos Belos*—*dato* meaning 'noble' and *Belo*, as we have seen, a Tetun-speaking people. The predominance of this nobility was probably a cause—or a consequence—of the hegemony of two Tetun-speaking kingdoms over the whole eastern part of the island (called Provincia dos Belos in Portuguese sources): Luca, near Viqueque and Be-hali ...

This later information suggests that prior to the coming of the Europeans there was a degree of unity amongst the 62 domains in Timor. These domains were mutually 'free and independent' (as phrased in the document), but at the same time they all recognised particular supreme rulers in their regions. Domains in the eastern part of the island were under the 'emperor' of Luca, domains to the west were under the 'emperor' of Sonba'i and those in the middle part were under the 'emperor' of Wehali.

Unfortunately, the Sarzedas document does not specify the names of domains considered to be under the 'emperor' of Wehali. For that reason, the following account of the 'hegemony', to use the term applied by Thomaz, relies solely on oral traditions. Luna de Oliveira (1949: 35–36) in his *History of Timor* quoted a myth concerning the first coming of 'the four tribes' (*hutun rai hat*), known as *Sina Mutin Malaka* (literally, 'the white Chinese of Malacca') (Grijsen 1904: 18–19). On their arrival in Tae Berek (part of Wewiku domain), they planted a banyan tree (*ai hali*), which produced three branches, representing three domains. The trunk of the tree was the *hali* tree, which represents the domain of Wehali (see Reference Text 4). After chasing away the aborigines of the island (the Melus), the domain of Wehali expanded its power to the western and to the eastern parts of the island. Myths concerning the expansion of Wehali hegemony to the western half of the island have been recorded primarily by Middlekoop (Schulte Nordholt 1971: 162). Accounts of the expansion of Wehali to the east were also recorded by de Oliveira. He mentioned the names of domains claimed to be under Wehali as follows: Suai and Camenasse (Suai-Kamanasa), Derma (Dirma), Laguecon (Lakekun), Voho Tehem (Fohoterin), Beboque (Biboki), Insana, Vohorem (Fohoren), Fatumean, Atsabe, Cassa Bank (Kasa Bauk), Leimean, Diruate (Diribate), Marobo, Leten Talo (Leten-teloe), Boebau (Boibau), Balibo and Maubara. Of this list of 17 domains, four lie in West Timor while the rest are located in the western part of the present East Timor province, mainly within at the present regencies of Kova Lima and Liquiça.

The hegemony of Wehali in West Timor, particularly among petty domains (see Chapter 2) spread throughout the present Belu regency, cannot be established with certainty. A.A. Bere Tallo (1957: 4–5) depicts the spread of Wehali's power through marriage alliance. The 'four tribes' mentioned above, according to myths narrated in north Tetun and Lamaknen, having landed in Tae Berek, continued their journey to Halileon Lumamar. From there they moved to Lasiolat. The head of these 'four tribes' was later married to a princess who resided on the peak of Laka'an. The first alliance between Laka'an as *umamane* (wife-giving house) and Wehali as *fetosawa* (wife-taking house) was established with this marriage. This Wehali man was then entitled *loro foho leten//loro tauk dikin* (literally, sun mountain peak//sun rock edge). He resided with his wife and became 'the owner of the rocky mountain'. This marriage produced two children, a boy and a girl. Later the boy took his sister as his wife and she gave birth to two boys (Atok Laka'an and Taek Laka'an) and two girls (Balok Loa Loro and Elok Loa Loro). Like their parents, Atok took his sister Elok as his wife and became genitor of the people of Naitimu. Taek took his sister Balok as his wife and she later gave birth to 10 children: five of them went to the western part of the island, while four went to the eastern part of the island and later founded the domain of Maukatar or Okes Foho Rua, which is situated in the present East Timor. The youngest child, named Dasi Mauk, who remained in Laka'an (Lamaknen) and married Maromak Oan of Wehali's daughter, was thereafter entitled *loro* (Grijsen 1904: 26, 27). With this marriage alliance, Wehali had some sort of relations with most domains in Belu regency, but a special study would be needed to focus on patterns of relations among domains in the Belu regency alone, which cannot be covered in the present work.

Based on mythic material summarised above, the north Belu, particularly the Lamaknen, claim their superiority over Wehali because they are the wife-giving house (Bere Talia 1957: 4). Parera (1971: 36)[4] states that when Grijsen wrote his monograph, Bauho was under the sovereignty of Wehali; therefore the Bauho could not inform Grijsen that their ancestors also came from Sina Mutin Malaka, just as Wehali's ancestors did, although they came via different routes. The ancestors of Wehali came to Timor via Kusu, Kae, Api, Loe and Larantuka Bauboin (Grijsen 1904: 19). The ancestors of Bauho came to Laka'an via Titaborok, Tiborok, Lakaderu, Sinaderu, Budibais, Badabais, Danileo and Tarmutu (Bere Talia 1957: 3). Not only the Tetun, but two of the six origin groups that make up the Lamaknen (the Bunak-speaking area) also claim that their ancestors came from Sina Mutin Malaka (Bere Tallo 1957: 4). 'Now the political climate has changed. Bauho and Wehali are equal and therefore the Bauho can relate that their ancestors also came from Sina Mutin Malaka' (Parera 1971: 36).

From Wehali's perspective, however, their region was the first to dry when the earth emerged from the primordial sea and, therefore, the domain of Wehali takes precedence over other domains. Thus, although non-Wehali

---

4   Parera's unpublished monograph has been edited by Gregor Neonbasu and published under the title 'Sejarah Pemerintahan Raja-Raja di Timor: Suatu kajian atas peta politik pemerintahan kerajaan-kerajaan di Timor sebelum kemerdekaan Republik Indonesia'. Jakarta: Pustaka Sinar Harapan clan Yanense Mitra Sejati, 1994.

and Wehali claim their origin from 'outside', the Wehali notion of 'inside' derives from this piece of origin myth where their area was 'the first to dry' (*maran uluk*). There are various ways of explaining this centrality and these form the focus of the coming chapters.

Using the myth of Sina Mutin Malaka as a basis for explaining Wehali's hegemony, Parera (1971: 94) divides the domains under Wehali into three categories: 1. territories where Maromak Oan allegedly ruled or had direct power; namely, the domains of Wehali, Wewiku, Haitimuk, Fatuaruin, Suai, Kamanasa, Dirma, Lakekun and Fohoterin (to which can be added the domain of Likusaen); 2. domains where Maromak Oan is regarded as the supreme though not necessarily direct ruler; namely, Fialaran, Jenilu, Lidak, Silawan, Naitimu, Mande'u, Biboki, Harneno, Insana, Nenometan, Lamaknen, Lamaksanulu, Makir, Maukatar, Tahakay, Foltafaik, Fatumea, Dakolo, Fohren, Kasabauk, Kawa, Balibo, Maubara and a few more petty domains as listed by Luna de Oliveira (1949); and 3. domains ruled by his brother, Sonba'i, as listed by Schulte Nordholt (1971: 162, 163).

Relying on these oral traditions as a source of information, one gets only a vague idea of how far the hegemony of Wehali extended. For that reason, I now turn to a historical document dated 1756, known as the contract of Paravicini.

3. The General Contract of Paravicini

By the beginning of the eighteenth century, the Portuguese had been ousted from the entire archipelago with the exception of Timor. Relations between the Portuguese and the Dutch on the island were always tense. In collaboration with native rulers and the Larantuqueiros, whom the Dutch called Black Portuguese, a term to put down the latter impolitely (Boxer 1948: 185), the Portuguese endeavoured to expel the Dutch from Timor. Realising the need to consolidate Dutch authority on the island and its vicinity, the Dutch East India Company sent an official, named Paravicini, 'to conclude fresh treaties with the principal chiefs of Timor, Rori, Solor and Sumba' (de Klerck 1938: 318).

Compared with the earliest contracts or 'one-sided commitments' demanded by the Company from native rulers, the contract of Paravicini dated 9 June 1756 (Corpus Diplomaticum CMXCVII) contained a mutual obligation from both sides (see Fox 1977: 71, 72). In that contract, 'Hiacijntoe Corea, the supreme ruler of the Belunese kingdom, the sovereign king of Wywiko Bahale' signed on behalf of the local populations who occupied 29 domains as follows: Bahale, Wywiko, Bany Bany, Dirman, Lakeko, Loabaly, Tehalara, Lamakne, Maubara, Lakoeloe, Samoro, Satoletie, Letitoely, Botoboroo, Lankero, Samayottasabe, Layonea, Diroewaty, Maboro, Lidacdoaliloe, Sakoenaba Baybohie, Junysama, Laymea, Mamefay, Soeway, Reymea, Thieris, Alasluca and Corora. I shall endeavour to plot where these domains are situated.

However, before that can be done, there are basic questions that need to be considered. Who is Hiacijntoe Corea? Do the 29 domains listed above all fall within 'the kingdom of the Belonese'? Regarding the first question, Rogge (1865: 2) in his *Memorie van overgave* explained that the Tetun name of Hiacijntoe Corea was Tee Serang or Tei Seran in more recent spelling.[5] According to the political ideology prevailing in the Wehali-Sonba'i empire, a political community is ruled by two men. The first is a man who is ritually regarded as an 'old woman' (*ferik*). He is the supreme ruler of that community. The second is an 'old man' (*katuas*) who executes the orders of the 'old woman'. Thus, before the coming of Europeans, according to *adat* historians (*mako'an*), this great 'kingdom' of Wehali was ruled by two men, *Liurai feto* (a man who is ritually regarded as female *Liurai*) and *Liurai mane* (male *Liurai*). The office of the male *Liurai* was held by the house of Tei Seran. Thus, without doubt we can ascertain that Hiacijntoe Corea was a *Liurai mane*, more simply known as *Liurai*. Whether Hiacijntoe Corea signed the contract by order of his 'superior 'is impossible to determine. But one thing is clear: according to the ritual function of those rulers, Hiacijntoe Corea had every right to sign the contract on behalf of his domain and other domains 'directly' under his rule.

As regards the second question concerning his right to represent the 29 domains, it is hard to answer with any certainty. As has been mentioned before, we can categorise domains under Wehali's hegemony into three groups. The first group are regions where the female *Liurai* (later known as Maromak Oan) is believed to rule directly. Within the Tetun-speaking areas, before the separation of the island into two halves, this group would consist of the domains of Wehali, Wewiku, Haitimuk, Fatuaruin, Dirma, Lakekun, Likusaen, Suai, Kamanasa and Fohoterin. The last four are

---

5   Dominikus Tei Seran (commonly known as Na'i Kloit), direct descendant of Hiacijntoe Corea, mentioned that prior to the last *Liurai* Tei Seran, all Tei Seran used the spelling Tere Seran. Unfortunately, there is no further explanation of this change.

part of the present East Timor province. Beside this group, there are also two other groups in which the authority of Maromak Oan is recognised. The second group consists mostly of other Tetun-speaking areas, most of the domains that lie in the present Belu regency as well as some located in the present East Timor territory. The third group consists of some domains that lie in Sonba'i's empire, excluding Insana, Manulea, Harneno and Biboki, which are politically closer to Maromak Oan than to Sonba'i (Schulte Nordholt 1971: 232ff). Furthermore, the principal domains in the realm of Sonba'i (such as Amabi, Amfoa'n, Amanatun, Amarasi) were represented in that contract by their own rulers.

The evidence would suggest that Hiacijntoe Corea can be regarded as fully representing the 10 domains of the first group. We can not say with certainty concerning these other domains that are not part of this group whether Hiacijntoe was justified in formally acting on their behalf. With a few amendments to suit present spelling, I list again the names and locations of the 29 domains (Table 3.1).

Table 3.1: Domains under Wehali as listed in Paravicini's contract

Domains	Recent spelling	Present location
1. Bahale	Wehali	district of Malaka Tengah (WestTimor)
2. Bany Bany	Bani Bani	district of Malaka Tengah (West Timor)
3. Wywiko	Wewiku	district of Malaka Barat (West Timor)
4. Dirman	Dirma	district of Malaka Timur (West Timor)
5. Lakeko	Lakekun	district of Koba Lima (West Timor)
6. Tehalara	Fehanlaran (Fialaran)	district of Tasifeto Timur (West Timor)
7. Lidacdoalilu	Lidak, Jenilu	district of Tasifeto Tengah (West Timor)
8. Lamkne	Lamaknen	district of Lamaknen (West Timor)
9. Sakoenaba Baybohie	Biboki	regency of North Central Timor (West Timor)
10. Maubara	Maubara	regency of Liquiça (East Timor)
11. Satoletie	Daro Lete	regency of Liquiça (East Timor)
12. Letitoely	Leten Telu[a]	regency of Liquiça (East Timor)
13. Botoboroo	Boibau[a]	regency of Liquiça (East Timor)
14. Lakoeloe	Lado (Lakulo)	regency of Manatuto (East Timor)
15. Samoro	Samoro	regency of Manatuto (East Timor)
16. Lankero	Laicore,[b] Loceu	regency of Kova Lima (East Timor)
17. Soeway	Suai	regency of Kova Lima (East Timor)
18. Reymea	Raimean	regency of Kova Lima (East Timor)

Domains	Recent spelling	Present location
19. Samayottasabe	Same Atsabe	regency of Same (East Timor)
20. Alasluca	Alas Luca	regency of Same (East Timor)
21. Corora	Kowa	regency of Bobonaro (EastTimor)
22. Maboro	Marobo[c]	regency of Bobonaro (East Timor)
23. Layonea	Ailomea	regency of Bobonaro (East Timor)
24. Laymea	Leimea	regency of Ermera (East Timor)
25. Diroewaty	Deribate[d]	unknown (East Timor)
26. Loabaly	Loa Bali	unknown
27. Junysaa	unknown	unknown
28. Mamefay	unknown	unknown
29. Tueries	unknown	unknown

Note:

[a] Grijsen (1904: 23) considered these two domains (Leten Telu and Boibau) as under Maubara, but he was not sure of their exact locations. At present Maubara is part of Liquiça.

[b] Laicore is a name listed in the Sarzedas document.

[c] See Grijsen (1904); Clamagirand (1980: 140).

[d] As listed in the Sarzedas document (see de Castro 1867: map 1).

The Decline of Wehali Power

With many traditional domains, we may not know when the domain rises to power, but we do know when its power declines. In the case of most eastern Indonesian domains, their appearance in European history also marks the beginning of their decline.

As far as the history of Wehali is concerned, the gradual decline of its unity and therefore the authority of its supreme ruler over other domains has something to do with the involvement of these domains in trading activities with the Portuguese. Schulte Nordholt (1971: 165) sees this hypothesis as an acceptable one. It starts from a presumption that at the height of its power, Wehali controlled trading activities that made it rich and powerful. When its former dependents engaged in trading separate from Wehali, the central authority, however, they also become richer and more powerful. This encouraged them to be more politically independent from the central power. This hypothesis fits the information given to me that in olden times, when annual tributes of homage were still observed by Wehali's dependents, the far-away domains brought silver and gold to the hamlet of Laran. The present material poverty, which can be seen by even a casual observer, was, according to the same source of information, related to two things. First, there was a Liurai named Don Beur,[6] who escaped from Wehali with much gold and silver. Second, there were thieves who stole the valuables stored in the sacred house of Ai Lotuk. The above claims, however, are difficult to verify historically. If the trading hypothesis is an acceptable one, I propose that the competition in trade between the Portuguese, the Topasses, the Makassar and later with the Dutch East India Company was only the prime cause of the gradual decline in unity among the domains. This declining unity went even faster once 'religion' was raised as an issue within this trading competition. The Portuguese (and the Topasses) were associated with Catholicism, the Makassar with Islam and the Dutch with Calvinism, a term commonly employed by Dutch Catholic missionary sources for Protestantism, while Timor was only 'a big island of *cafres* (heathen)' (Teixeira 1961, vol. II: 82). Thus, the competition not only in trade but also in promoting faith must be considered.

1. Trading Strategies

When the Portuguese began their trading mission in Southeast Asia, they began mainly as a maritime enterprise, focusing on the dominance of shipping lanes that link islands within this vast archipelago and not as a power that sought controls over areas of land and their populations. In islands where their presence was based, they began to establish 'trading posts' (*feitorias*)[7] by negotiating with the natives and, as far as possible, avoiding any forceful engagement. With the purpose of protecting their trade and the people involved, 'fortified strongholds' (*fortalezas*) were also built in every trading post that was considered vulnerable from either their trading rivals outside the island or the disputing rulers within the island. Their first *feitoria* in South or Southeast Asia was set up in Calcutta, India, in 1500 (Villiers 1986: 38). As a maritime enterprise, initially the Portuguese were more interested in making profit by

---

6   Father Mathijsen in his first trip to Wehali (1892) was informed that the name of that *Liurai* was Don Pedro (Laan 1969, translated by Embuiru 1993: 313).

7   The Portuguese word *feitoria* was frequently translated as 'factory', which could lead one to associate it with the modern sense of 'manufactory'. In Portuguese, this word refers to an enclosed trading post in which there is also a parish church and a burial place. Every *feitoria* is headed by a *feitor* (factor), which in this case can be understood as a royal business agent or commercial liaison officer (see Diffie and Winius 1977, vol. 1: 311–317).

expanding their commercial networks rather than becoming involved in domestic political affairs. The main precondition for this approach was to establish friendships with indigenous populations and co-operate with native rulers. It is clear from the history of the Lesser Sunda, for example, that initially the Portuguese not only maintained good relations, but actually went further by intermarrying with native women. Apparently, the Portuguese adopted the practice of commercial expansion without territorial dominance from their contemporary trading rivals, the Makassarese and the Javanese.

The practice of establishing *feitorias* and *fortalezas*, originally meant to provide protection for their enterprises in certain areas, turned out, however, to amount to establishing a ghetto within an island consisting of the Portuguese traders, the missionaries who accompanied the traders, the Christian converts and other segments within the society who admitted their loyalty to the Portuguese.

This situation changed when the Portuguese began to play a role in eastern Indonesian trade. At the time they had to confront the Dutch, who in their commercial activities began unlike the Portuguese and soon built up their power to control land and populations. A Makassarese ruler who lost in trading competition due to the territorial claims made by the Dutch, was once reported as protesting to the Dutch that God created the land in order that all could share the benefit of it without claiming ownership over it. Similarly, with the practice of establishing *feitorias-fortalezas*, the Portuguese also shifted from the idea of maritime dominance to territorial occupation. The Lesser Sunda islands were claimed as the first and only area outside the *estado* of India where their trading ports were developed to accommodate the idea of territorial dominance (Villiers 1986: 57). This change in their trading policy suited the contemporary spirit of territorial dominance promoted by their rivals. The Portuguese were encouraged by their claim of precedence in the area since 1511, and the continuing presence of missionaries since that time.

2. Trading and Religious Competition

Although the Portuguese frequented Timor for years following the initial sandalwood shipping in 1515, their first proper settlement (*feitoria-fortaleza*) in the area was not founded on Timor but rather on Solor, the island called on by Albuquerque's men when they were sent to look at Timor in 1511. The choosing of Solor as the first harbour relates to its strategic location and later to the success in the evangelistic mission conducted there by Catholic Dominicans. Being protected by the calm Solor Strait, its harbour provided safe anchorage for their vessels.

Following the report that Timor was covered not only with sandalwood trees but also occupied by heathens, 'who worship nothing nor have any idols' (Teixeira 1961, vol. I: 390), the Catholic Dominicans began their evangelical missions. On Solor island, by the year 1559 there were already 200 Christians converted by João Soares. In 1562, as a refuge against outside intruders, a palisade of lontar palms was built around the dwelling area that was burnt down by Javanese Muslims a year after its construction (Barnes 1987: 209). With help from Goa and alms from Malacca, the Dominican friar Antonio da Cruz, in the year 1566, built a more permanent fort of lime and stone.

This Dominican stronghold was plundered and partly burnt by the natives in 1598 (Boxer 1948: 176), and later attacked by the Dutch, the Makassar and Javanese traders. Dominican sources reveal that more than 200 Javanese Muslims went to destroy the mission, which at the time of attack contained only eight Portuguese, including priests. The raiders, who laid siege to the fort, asked the Portuguese to surrender the priests if they wanted the attackers to withdraw. This condition was resisted by the Portuguese, who said they would not even give them a dog but the sword. Assistance soon came from Banda with a junk of 30 men. These men gave battle to the Javanese, who fled leaving many dead:

> When the Christians and pagans saw such a big victory, they understood that God was on the side of the Portuguese and so those whom we converted were confirmed in their faith and many thousands of pagans asked to be baptized. And not only these but also the people of the neighbouring islands, hearing of the victory asked to be baptized and thus a great door for Christianity was opened there (Teixeira 1961, vol. I: 392, 393).

But the establishment of the mission fort in Solor and later two more churches, by the name of the *Madre de Deus* (Mother of God) and the *Casa da Misericordia* (House of Mercy), provoked more 'religious' conflicts that claimed the lives of at least three Dominican friars between 1581 and 1590.

With the arrival of Appolonius Scotte in 1613, the Portuguese were not only confronted with the Muslims from Makassar and Java, but also with the Dutch, the majority of whom were Protestants. On 18 April 1613, Scotte besieged the fort of Solor when most of its residents were in Timor collecting sandalwood. Scotte then appointed van de Velde as captain of the fort, which was renamed 'Henricus'. Van de Velde razed the main church (*Madre de Deus*) to the ground and also the major part of the other church (*Casa da Misericordia*). These holy places were reported to have been converted into stables for animals.

The attack by the Makassarese on Solar fort (1602) and the occupations of the Solar fort by the Dutch (first in 1613, then in 1618 and later in February 1646) forced the Portuguese to Larantuka and later to settle more permanently in Timor. On Timor, the Portuguese initially established a temporary post in Lifau. One of the reasons for choosing Lifau as a trading and religious post was the warm reception displayed by the native rulers of the area towards the traders, officials and clergy. Unmistakably, this warm reception was connected with the long association between Dominicans and the native rulers of the island. Fr Manuel Teixeira (Teixeira 1961, vol. II: 88, 89) wrote:

> In 1590 Fr. Melchior da Luz or de Antas converted the son of the king of Timor, heir apparent to the throne. He took him to Malacca, where he was welcomed by the Captain of the Fortress, the Bishop Baio and the people; he was baptized by the Bishop and returned to Timor with Fr. Melchior; he was well received by his father, who revered Fr. Melchior very much.

With the re-appointment of Father Miguel da Crus Rangel along with his 12 friars to Solar in 1630, he intended to continue winning the hearts of the Timorese rulers. He sent Father Antonio de S. Jacinto there, and he tried to convert the queen of Mena, but without success (Teixeira 1961, vol. II: 95). Another friar named Cristovao Rangel succeeded in baptising the king of Silabao, who received the name Cristavo. Father Rafael da Veiga baptised the rulers of Amabi and Amarasi.

The conversion of the Timorese rulers was seen as a threat to the long-standing and frequent trade with Makassar, which considered the Lesser Sunda within its sphere of hegemony (Reid 1981: 17). In January 1641, Kraeng of Tello, perhaps with the consent of the Dutch, in a single blow, reduced Mena to ashes and took captives as slaves to Makassar.[8] The rulers of this domain escaped to the mountains for safety. The defeat of Mena was then used by the Portuguese as a pretext to establish themselves in Timor. In June 1641, Father Antonio de S. Jacinto was sent back to Mena, together with two other Dominican friars and 70 musketeers. The Portuguese offered their protection against the Makassarese. On 24 June 1941, on the feast of St John the Baptist, Father Jacinto baptised the queen, the nobles and many people (Teixeira 1961, vol. II: 97). Thus, the defeat of the rulers of Mena opened the door for the Portuguese to extend their hegemony inland. In July 1641, Captain-Major Ambrosio Dias, with 150 musketeers and Fr Bento Serrao and Fr Pedro de St Jose as chaplains, and with the help of the rulers of Mena, Lifau and Amanuban, defeated Liurai Sonba'i. The defeat of Sonba'i was followed by his baptism by Fr Bento Serrao.

3. The Attack on Wehali

The news of the defeat of Liurai Sonba'i must have been heard by his brother, the Liurai of Wehali. The more staggering news heard in Wehali, perhaps, was that of the conversion of rulers of its former domains to Christianity and their subjugation to the Portuguese. The king of Wehali reacted by embracing Islam, 'as the Makassarese and the Buginese were the powerful opponents of the Portuguese' (Schulte Nordholt 1971: 164). News spread in Larantuka on Flores that the king had already accepted a 'hat' (Indonesian, *kopiah*) granted by the Kraeng of Makassar. The acceptance of the hat indicated that the king had promised to become a Moslem (Muskens 1973: 394). As a consequence, a punitive expedition was prepared by the Portuguese to strike Wehali. They set out on 20 May 1642. This expedition was led by Captain-Major Francisco Fernandez. Accompanying this expedition were Father Lucas da Cruz, another three Dominican friars (Antonio Cabral, Bento Serrao and Pedro Manso) and 90 musketeers. On their way to Wehali, the Dominicans baptised the widowed queen of Batimao (Timau, Amfoa'n) and a new king, who was still a boy, with the name D. Pedro. The convoy also baptised nobles of Amarasi. This expedition was then assisted by warriors of these newly

---

8   There is uncertainty as to whether the Makassar took along slaves from Timor. Two European sources contradict each other. In *Daghregister*, 13 May 1649, there is no mention of the capture of people, whereas Biermann mentions 4,000 slaves (Schulte Nordholt 1971: 164). Dominican sources give the same figure as Biermann (Teixeira 1961, vol. II: 97).

converted domains. Leitao (1948: 207) noted that 'after reducing everything to ashes there (in Wehali), he (Francisco Fernandez) withdrew to Batimao'.

The defeat of the great empire of Wehali-Sonba'i marks the end of a hegemony with Wehali as its central power. Leitao thus describes the defeat of Wehali as freedom for other domains:

> The news of the destruction of the mighty potentate of Belos spread rapidly through the other kingdoms in the neighbourhood; the people of these kingdoms seized the opportunity to indulge in festive manifestations, and the kings of the other realms also asked the priests to instruct them in the teachings of Christianity (translated by Schulte Nordholt 1971: 164).

The Centrality of Wehali as Revealed in Oral Tradition

Using elevated speech (*lia na'in*), Wehali ritualists like to present the authoritative 'words of the ancestors', which they call 'the old path, the old track' (*inuk tuan, dalan tuan*) concerning the emergence of dry land from primordial sea, the birth of their first ancestors and the founding of the 'land', 'domain' (*rai*) of Wehali. Asking an *adat* historian to reveal the 'history' of Wehali, he definitely begins with the narration concerning the emergence of the first dry land. The Wehali firmly believe that their domain is the centre of all domains because in primordial time, when the earth was still covered with water, their land was first to appear. Thus, the centrality and hence the superiority of Wehali, as told in origin myths, is based on the notions of 'the first to dry' (*maran uluk*) and 'the last to dry' (*maran ikus*). Wehali was the first land to appear and therefore it is the centre of the 'lands'.[9] In oral tradition, the centrality of Wehali is described in various metaphors. In botanical idiom, Wehali is the 'trunk, root' (*hun, abut*) of all the land; it is the place of 'the first garden, the first palm tree' (*to'os ai fatik//tua ai fatik*). In corporeal metaphors, it is 'the navel land', 'the umbilical cord land' (*rai husar//rai binan*). In house metaphors, Wehali is the inner part of the house while others are its platforms, posts, ladders or simply huts in gardens.

---

9   Bauho and Lamaknen believe that the mountain of Laka'an, which is located in their area, was the first dry land to appear. This claim, as mentioned before, relates to their view that their domains are equally as great as Wehali.

The centrality of Wehali as analysed in oral tradition in this present work is based on four types of elevated language material (as cited in Reference Texts 1 to 8 in the Appendix). Following the Wehali way of classification, Reference Text 1 is a form of 'greeting' (*hasee hawaka*), which is classified as 'honour language' (*lia riik*); Texts 2 to 6 are regarded as 'language of the earth' (*rai lian*); Text 7 is 'the true language' (*lia tebes*) concerning the path of Liurai; and Text 8 is a 'story to be remembered' (*ai knanoik or ai knoik*).

In the following chapters, those eight texts will be considered in conjunction with separate themes discussed in successive chapters. Therefore it is not the purpose of this section to discuss in detail the substance of each individual text but rather to highlight different cultural categories used in different texts in addressing the notion of Wehali's centrality.

Reference Text 2 is an origin myth often referred to throughout this work and therefore deserving of further comment. One reason to quote this myth is that it claims to represent the territory of Wehali as a whole. As a comparison, the myth recorded in the hamlet of Fatuaruin, known as the hamlet of Liurai (Reference Text 3), emphasises more the role of Liurai who rules the land toward the rising sun and the setting sun. The myth narrated in Wewiku (Reference Text 4) emphasises the founding of the three 'sisterly' domains (Wehali, Wewiku and Haitimuk). Narrators of the two myths cited in Reference Texts 5 and 6 clearly stated that their narratives concern the founding of the land of Bakiruk, the other name for the village of Kateri, whose people are culturally considered as the guardians of Marlilu Haholek, the first dry land.

The myth cited in Reference Text 2 was narrated by Petrus Tahu Nahak, who is regarded as the *adat* historian (*mako'an*) of Wehali. Like most origin myths narrated in the region, this myth also starts with the primordial condition, when the earth was still dark and covered with water, the emergence of the first dry land, followed by the expanding of the dry land to cover territories considered as under Wehali's authority. The distinctive features of this myth lie in its detailed elaboration of the order of precedence of *leo* (clans, hamlets) that make up the inner Wehali territory, the narrative of the spread of the sons of Wehali, the 'male Liurai' (*liurai mane*), who occupy and rule the land toward the rising sun and the land toward the setting sun. It concludes with the story concerning the last-born woman, named Ho'ar, who stayed in Wehali. It was she (Ho'ar) who had the right to appoint those Liurai to rule land(s) to the east and west. Due to this function, she was entitled *Ho'ar Makbalin, Balin Liurai,* which can be glossed as Ho'ar the Liurai adviser. Despite this title, she was not the supreme ruler of the realm of Wehali. It was her husband who ruled on behalf of his wife and, therefore, ritually he was considered as the 'female Liurai' (*Liurai feto*). Another significant aspect of this myth lies in its description of the division in the political system between male and female rulers, a common political feature that can be discovered in other parts of the island, particularly in Tetun's immediate neighbour, the Dawan.

Beside the emphasis on the 'first to dry'/'last to dry' and 'trunk root'/'edge foot' categories to communicate the centrality and hence the superiority of Wehali, the myth in Reference Text 2 also employs the idiom of a tree. Accordingly, once Ho'ar was born and her umbilical cord turned into the first dry land, a banyan tree (*ai hali*) grew on this 'first dry land'. Drawing on the analogy of a tree, the myth depicts how the whole empire of Wesei Wehali is just like a tree. Thus, the trunk was planted in the domain of Wehali, while its leaves expanded to cover the surrounding territories. The dense leaves of this tree provided shade (*leon*) for people who were grouped into *leo feto* (female clans, hamlets) and *leo mane* (male clans, hamlets). Wehali's relations with other domains then developed, based on the order of precedence of trunk and leaves. In this scheme, Wehali is the trunk and therefore superior, while others are the leaves and therefore the inferior.

Other categories used in the oral tradition to describe the centrality of Wehali are 'first-born/last-born', 'male/female' and 'inside/outside'. In Reference Text 4, the domains of Wewiku, Haitimuk and Wehali are described as being founded by three sisters. In Reference Text 2, the founders of the land are always depicted as the last-born women, who determine to stay behind in the land of their birth. The last-born, the insider and the female are considered physically vulnerable and susceptible to outside intrusion. Therefore, those who are in the categories of first-born, outsider and male are ritually regarded as their protectors. Various metaphors applied to the protectors, such as 'door', 'fence' and 'post' reveal this function explicitly. What is interesting to note in regard to the traditional notion of superiority is that Wehali was female, the last-born and the weak who needed to be protected by the first-born and the outsider men. As Fox remarks, it is 'a kind of receptive powerlessness that left it open to protection and vulnerable to intrusion' (1982: 23).

Reference Text 1 deals with a form of ritual speech called *hasee hawaka* (to greet, to counsel). It is a custom in the region to receive a distinguished guest who is officially visiting the area, with welcoming greetings. In Dawan, this type of greeting is called *natoni*. There is a saying that to be an Atoni (Dawan) one needs to be skilful in *natoni*. In *natoni* and *hasee hawaka*, speakers use parallelistic poetic forms to narrate the journey of their guests as a mythical journey from 'outside' (the origin places of the guests) to 'inside' (those who accept the guests). When the Catholic bishop officially visited Wehali, he was also received with *hasee hawaka* (Reference Text 1). In this ritual poem, the bishop was described as having crossed mountains, rivers, gardens, forests, huts, granaries, eating wild fruits, climbing every fence in order to get into Wehali, the place to live and rest, the source of heat and flame. What is significant in this 'greeting' is that the speaker clearly distinguishes the 'outside' domains from Wehali, the 'inside' domain. The 'outside' domains are places to work and to accumulate wealth. This 'inside' domain is the place to live and rest, a place where knowledge can be found. The superiority of Wehali lies in the fact that, as 'insider', Wehali is categorised as a 'resting' place, while 'outsider' places are associated with places to work. Thus the cultural category of 'rest/work' articulates the superiority of the domain.

Reference Text 8 recounts how the weak and vulnerable Wehali must rely for their authority not on physical strength, but on their cunning and their spiritual knowledge. Various tricks displayed by Ho'ar Samanek Oan to free her brothers from their opponent, Lakuleik, a nobleman from the sunrise land prove the superiority of cleverness (Indonesian, *akal*) and spiritual knowledge (*matenek*) over physical strength. Wehali cleverness, which is represented by Ho'ar Samanek Oan, proves to be superior due to cunning, nous and knowledge.

The last corpus of categories that need to be highlighted are 'heat' (*manas*), 'cooked' (*tasak*) and 'forbidden' and 'sacred' (*lulik*). In Chapter 8, I discuss in detail the contexts where these categories are fully expressed, namely in the rituals that follow the trajectory of human life and the cycle of agriculture. These categories are also beneficial for comprehending the pattern of relations between Wehali and other domains, since these categories are used to identify the domain of Wehali as a whole, the hamlet of Laran in particular, and the 'female Liurai', as the supreme ruler of Wehali. Take, for example, the childbirth ritual. Following the birth of a child, the baby's mother is expected to observe a seclusion rite, where she and the baby are separated from the rest of the community. For a certain period of time, the mother has to 'roast' her back over the fire (*hatuka ha'i*). The 'heat' that she acquires from the roasting, like the 'heat' that she has accumulated in her body during the pregnancy, is potentially life-threatening. In this condition, she is depicted as culturally to be cooked, a danger and forbidden. The association between femininity, heat, danger and forbidden is explicitly revealed in ritual language in regard to the betel-nut offering, where betel-nut prepared by a woman in front of the hearth is called:

fuik tolu, bua tolu	the three betel leaves, the three areca nuts
haa tasan, hemu tasan	the cooked food, the cooked drink

In contrast, when this 'cooked', 'heated' and 'forbidden' offering prepared by the woman is received by a man, the ritual designation of the offering is changed, as follows:

fuik hitu, bua hitu	the seven betel leaves, the seven areca nuts
haa matak, hemu matak	the raw food, the raw drink

By analogy with a woman, Wehali (the hamlet of Laran and the supreme ruler of the realm of Wehali) is categorically a 'heated', 'cooked' and 'forbidden' domain. These qualities are not something to be avoided. On the contrary, these are the qualities that every person wants to achieve because they are associated with superiority. Thus, Wehali is superior among other domains because she is female, heated, cooked and forbidden. In this condition, Wehali is vulnerable. She is life-threatening, not only for others but also for herself. Her 'safety' depends on the outside man, who is able to change 'the cooked food, the cooked drink' into 'the raw food, the raw drink'. Raw (*matak*) and cool (*malirin*) are the two words used to translate the Christian notion of 'blessing'. Thus, Wehali's superiority is measured by her dependence on 'blessings' shown by other domains.

Concluding Remarks

Both historical documents and oral traditions discussed here reveal that Wehali was once, and still is, a great empire. Yet the two kinds of sources start from different paradigms and, therefore, articulate different forms of discourse. While the historical sources speak about the concentration of power and mode of production associated with it, the oral traditions are based on cultural categories that speak about the superiority of the weak.

European traders and colonial governments learned that Wehali was a great empire, whose power subordinated most domains in the middle part of Timor. Efforts to separate other powerful domains from Wehali, to subdue or to incorporate it culminated in the physical attack on Wehali in 1642. These efforts represent a coercive approach to control the mode of production.

Beside this coercive approach, foreign forces also applied a model of hegemony in the Gramscian sense of political and cultural leadership in transforming local customs and culture.[10] This model was particularly developed by the Dutch, but only at a later stage of the colonial era. Intensive studies of the society and political administrative arrangements of the Belu regency began when the Dutch established their first post in Atapupu in 1862, followed by the founding of the Catholic Mission.[11] In Chapter 2, I discussed how the Belu regency in which the Dutch registered 20 *swapraja* in 1904 was reduced to a single 'kingdom' of Belu in 1924.

Another achievement of the Dutch colonialists was the publishing of a much-cited monograph written by Grijsen, the *controleur* of Belu. This excellent piece of work covered social and political issues in detail and was, therefore, presumably used by the government in their socio-political transformations of the time. It was in this monograph that the phrase Maromak Oan was recorded and introduced as an alternative for the colonial title *Keser*. The status and function of the Maromak Oan were described in that monograph as follows:

> The highest authority was in the hand of Maromak Oan ... He is the son of God who is too high to involve in political matters; he only sits, drinks and sleeps. His faithful subjects (servants) will take care of other matters. The highest servant was the Liurai ... (Grijsen 1904: 22).

---

10   The concept of hegemony was the central idea in Gramsci's social theory. In his 'Selections from the Prison Notebooks' (1971), he developed three models of hegemony. One of these models is hegemony in the sense of political and cultural leadership. The key term used in this model is 'reform' with a strong meaning of 'a transformation of customs and culture' (Bobbio 1979: 39; Bocock 1986: 28, 29).

11   In the early stage of the Catholic mission, the colonial government made it a 'rule' that a mission could only be established in a place where there was already a military post.

As clearly highlighted in this quotation, Maromak Oan was not only a supreme ruler, he had been understood in Christian terminology as the son of God.[12] The culmination of this arbitrary conclusion comes when Seran Nahak, the Maromak Oan of Wehali, was installed as *Keser* of the kingdom of Belu on 10 May 1926. The transformation that was started in 1862 finally achieved its result: all of the domains in Belu had been united under a single power. But following his installation, Seran Nahak could not resist the pressure brought to bear on him by rulers of other domains. In 1930 Seran Nahak was officially dismissed from his new role in disgrace. He went back to his hamlet (Laran) and resumed his traditional office as Maromak Oan of Wehali, a title that he carried to the end of his life.

---

12   The Bible in the Tetun language maintained this translation of Maromak Oan as the son of God. Otherwise, the Tetun *maromak oan* can be translated as the 'small bright one'. Francillon translates it as the 'luminous one' (1967: 24). Literally, the word *ma-roma-k* derives from *roman* or *kroman* meaning 'bright', while *oan* means 'small' and 'child'.

4

Social Relations: Giving Away the Centre to the Periphery

Introduction

This chapter deals with the Wehali's use of dual categories to organise social relations at the house, hamlet and domain levels.

Since the inspiring work of van Wouden, dual symbolic classification has been recognised as an important conceptual mechanism in eastern Indonesian societies. The accumulated ethnographic studies of this vast region reveal similarities and differences in its cultural application as well as its social implications. For some time, Canberra-based anthropologists have been concerned with dual categories that inform the ethnic identity of people within the eastern Indonesian region. Fox, Lewis, Traube, McWilliam, Vischer, Graham and Grimes, to name but a few, have explored a theory of precedence in analysing various patterns of relations that result from the application of dual categories among the people of the region in defining the nature of their social relations. Fox (1990, 1993b) argues that a system of precedence is found not only in eastern Indonesian societies but can also be detected in most Austronesian societies.

In an effort to explore this in the Wehali situation, I focus on the notion of 'centre-periphery' that Wehali use continually to describe their differences from others. To do so, I begin with origin myths and other kinds of oral tradition that describe Wehali as the centre of all societies. My aim is to discover other cultural categories built around this key contrast. These cultural categories in turn become a stepping stone to understanding the nature of Wehali relations at the levels of domain, village, hamlet and house.

The phrase 'giving away' (*fo baa*) in this chapter's title is taken from an origin myth that narrates the dispersal of Wehali men to neighbouring regions where they established new communities. This phrase is used by the Wehali to argue that they are the origin of all societies. Thus the notion of 'centre-periphery' begins at this point.

Ideological Construction of Centre-Periphery

1. Centre

The Wehali people elaborate the concepts of centre and periphery in various idiomatic expressions. Underlying these idioms is a core network of terms that imply the notions of centre and inside. These include the botanical *hun* (source, trunk, origin), the anthropomorphic *husar binan* (umbilical cord) and the house idioms of *laran* (inside) and *klaran* (interior, inner side, centre).

According to their origin myths, the first dry land was located in the region of Wehali. At that time the size of this land was only as small as 'a chicken's eye, a slice of areca nut' (*rai manu matan//rai bua klaras*). Since this small piece of land was the first to emerge from the primordial sea, it gained the names *rai hun* (the original land) and *rai husar//rai binan* (the navel land, the umbilical cord land). Out of the primordial sea grew a banyan tree (*ai hali*). It was in this primordial sea that 'the Only Woman on Earth' (*Ferik Ha'in Raikklaran*) gave birth to a daughter called Ho'ar Na'i Haholek (literally, 'the squirming Ho'ar'). Her umbilical cord was twisted within the roots of the banyan tree and eventually 'grew' (*tubu*), or turned into that first dry land. So, according to folk interpretation, the name Wehali (or in ritual language 'Wesei Wehali') derives from this portion of the origin myth. It implies the notion of the primeval land.

As time went by, Ho'ar Na'i Haholek produced more *funan* (literal meaning: 'flowers'; metaphorical meaning: 'daughters') and more *klaut* (literal meaning: 'fruits'; metaphorical meaning: 'sons'). As more people were born, the dry land spread further and so did the banyan tree. The shade (*leon*) of the banyan tree provided shelter for the 'sons' and 'daughters' of Ho'ar Na'i Haholek. The folk etymology of the word for 'hamlet' (*leo*) also draws on lines in this portion of the origin myth. The Tetun word *leon* means 'the shade of a tree'. My informants insist that the word for 'hamlet' (*leo*) came from this botanical idiom: *leon*. Thus, in Reference Text 2, there are the following lines:

ka'an ne'e tubu ti'an baa hali aa	the umbilical cord grew into a banyan tree
foin ha'ak:	and so the saying goes:
'Maromak nahonu hali leon di'ak	The Bright One has provided a good dense banyan tree
soe nahon la sar, karas hat ne'e	its shade provides shelter to the four 'chests' (of the house)
soe nahon la sar, kbelan hat ne'e	its shade provides shelter to the four 'ribs' (of the house)
sei Bere Lelo Babesi hali leon di'ak	this banyan tree is called the strong Bere Lelo
sorin balu leo feto, balu leo mane	one half of the shade is called 'female' shade, the other half is 'male' shade
leo feto leo mane, balu la sasin'.	the female hamlet (clan) and the male hamlet (clan) were both in the shade.

This portion of the narrative provides the Wehali people with an ideology, based on the imagery of a tree, that they are the trunk (*hun*) of all societies. The tree produces shade (*leon*) to provide shelter. Such shelters take the form of a hamlet (*leo*). Wehali is the trunk, while other hamlets (*leo*) make up its shade (*leon*). As stated in the origin myth, the shade (*leon*) produced by the 'Wehali tree' is of two kinds: female shade (*leon feto*) and male shade (*leon mane*). It is a cultural premise in Wehali that women belong to the inner part of a dwelling, while men belong to the outer part. So, considering the *leon* produced by 'Wehali's tree' divides into female hamlets (*leo feto*) and male hamlets (*leo mane*), the female can be designated inner hamlets (*leo laran*), while the male become contrasting outer hamlets (*leo molin*).

Beside these botanical idioms, the Wehali people also employ anthropomorphic terms to elaborate their 'originality' and 'centrality'. There are two ways of expressing this notion of centrality, as illustrated in Figure 4.1. The first is by linking their land as the centre of the earth to the vertical axis of north–south. This mode of expression is used to mark the difference between the central and the peripheral clans of inner Wehali. The second method of expressing centrality is by linking their land to the horizontal axis of east–west. This mode of expression is used to indicate the difference between the inner Wehali and other domains or societies.

To designate the status differences between hamlets within Wehali, the Wehali people constantly use the dyadic terms 'navel', 'umbilical cord' (*husar*, *binan*) /'edge' (*tehen*), and 'trunk' (*hun*) /'foot' (*ain*). So, hamlets that are classified as 'navel' are categorically female, centre and trunk of Wehali society. In contrast, hamlets that are classified as 'foot' are categorically male and outside. To contrast Wehali with societies outside Wehali, they employ a different terminology, namely 'head' (*ulun*) and 'tail' (*ikun*). In this case, Wehali is put at the centre as the 'trunk land' (*rai hun*) and the 'navel of the earth' (*rai husar binan*). In this spatial orientation, areas spreading to the east are labelled as the 'head land' or 'the sunrise land' (*rai ulun* or *rai loro sa'e*), while areas lying toward the west are called the 'tail land' or 'the sunset land' (*rai ikun* or *rai loro toba*) (see Figure 4.1).

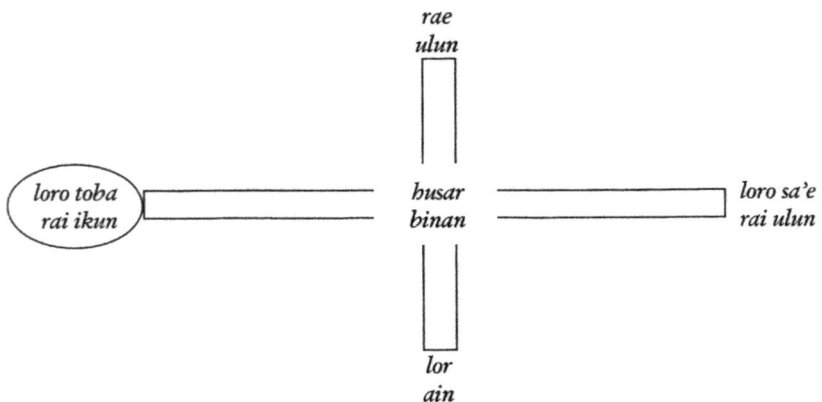

Figure 4.1: Timor as seen from Wehali

Thus far I have dealt with the notion of origin as based on the argument of the birth order of the world, which is developed from Wehali's own explanation of how the world came into existence. Asked why they claim that their region is the centre of all societies, *adat* elders will respond: 'because the earth was first born here' (*tan rai ne'e moris uluk iha ne'e*). The phrase 'first born' (*moris uluk*) is contrasted to 'last born' (*moris ikus*). According to Wehali cosmogeny, before the earth came into being, water covered the land. In turn, this statement provides a basis on which to contrast the 'first dry' (*maran uluk*) and the 'last dry' (*maran ikus*) or, simply, to contrast the 'dry land' (*rai maran*) and the 'land still covered with water' (*rai sei we*). Consequently, 'first born' and 'dry' are categorised as being in the centre (trunk), as opposed to 'last born' and 'wet' (water), which are classified as periphery.

But the tracing of 'centre' draws further on birth order terms expressed through the cognate forms: *ulun* and *uluk* in contrast to *ikun* and *ikus*. Here I want to emphasise the multi-dimensionality of these categories. Although the form *ikun* (noun) is cognate with *ikus* (adjective, 'last') they are valued differently in contrasting applications, for while *ikus* may be classified with 'periphery' as in the 'last dry land', *ikun* may be classified with 'centre' when it refers to the last-born daughter (*ikun*) who stayed and minded Wehali, while her older brothers (*ulun*) left the area. Thus, *ikun* here is valued as centre, while *ikus* is associated with periphery. So, on the one hand, 'last-born' may be associated with the 'trunk' or 'centre', while on the other hand it is related to the notion of 'periphery'. The bi-function of terms like 'last-born' should not be construed as an inconsistency in the symbolism of dual classification since, for the Wehali, it is the result of a logical analogy. In the context of creation history, the Wehali region was the first dry land to appear. They phrase this as 'first to dry' (*maran uluk*). Within this context 'first' (*uluk*) is valued 'higher' than 'last' (*ikus*): it occupies a privileged status because it has existed 'longer'. In the context of birth order, where *ulun* = first born, *ikun* = last born, it is *ikun* that attracts a more privileged status than the 'head' (*ulun*). The valuation of this 'privilege' is, however, based on the same logic: the last born, remains 'longer' in Wehali. Therefore the last born deserves a higher status.

2. Periphery

In comparison to the variety of terms used to denote the notion of 'centre', terms associated with the notion of 'periphery' are limited. The terms most commonly used are *molin* and *tehen*. The word *molin* denotes space outside a house, village or domain. Given the structure of a village, a farmer's gardens are located 'outside' the village, in the realm of *molin*. So when a person speaks about *molin*, the connotation is the outside, peripheral space used for cultivation or animal husbandry. Based on this usage I take 'outside' and 'periphery' as the appropriate English translations for the Tetun word *molin*.

The word *tehen* is mostly found in the compound form *tasi tehen*, which means 'the edge of the sea'. The words *molin* and *tehen* are applied in different contexts. As mentioned earlier, the word *tehen* is used in conjunction with the division of clans or hamlets within the Wehali. So, in Wehali, one encounters clans that are designated as the 'trunk hill clans' (*leo foho hun*) and 'the sea edge clans' (*leo tasi tehen*) or the 'sea feet clans' (*leo ain tasi*). To differentiate between the society of Wehali and societies outside Wehali, however, the word *molin* is used.

The most distinctive imagery applied to describe societies outside Wehali incorporates what I call garden idioms. The Wehali imagine that their domain is a residential realm. Areas outside this realm belong to *molin* (cultivation space). This idiom finds elaboration in a kind of ritual language termed *hasee hawaka* (greeting poems). To examine one instance, I draw on that from a procession held in October each year in which the statue of the Virgin Mary is carried from one village to another and finally to the cave of Lourdes, a place on a hill that, according to the origin myth, was the location of the first dry land. In Indonesia, this activity is called Perarakan Bunda Maria (the procession of Mother Mary). Prior to this annual procession, the Catholic bishop who resides in Atambua is invited to lead the ceremony. It is customary in the region to welcome a distinguished guest with a *hasee hawaka* ritual poem. At this particular welcoming ceremony, the bishop is greeted by an *adat* historian entitled *mako'an* (literally the one who cuts (*ko'a*) the words). What is of interest in this context are the cultural labels used by the *adat* historian (Petrus Tahu Nahak) to designate various domains and regions outside Wehali territory.

In the greeting poem, he describes the bishop's trip from Atambua (the capital of the regency) to Betun (the capital of the district) as a mythical journey from the main harbour (*namon matan*) to the spring of the Bright One (*we matan Maromak*), the owner of fire, the owner of heat (*malaka na'in//amanas na'in*), the place to lie down, the place to dwell (*hoku fatik// natar fatik*), the place to sit, the place to strengthen oneself (*hatodan fatik// habesi fatik*). What appears unusual in this formulation is the description of Atambua as 'the main harbour', when, for the Wehali, Atambua is only a 'garden', a cultivation space. This is, however, due to the status of the bishop as the Catholic leader in the regency, so that Atambua as his place of residence is referred to as 'the main harbour'. The bishop's status may be understood through the titles given to Catholic clergy. In Tetun a priest is called Na'i Lulik (master of the forbidden), while the bishop in the greeting poem is described as holder of the great taboo, holder of the mighty heat (*makaer lulik bot//makaer manas bot*). This title refers to the Wehali political structure in which the function of the ritual ruler is delineated as constituting the source of all heat and taboo. In Chapter 2 I mentioned that in Wehali ritual language the first dry land is called 'the old harbour' (*namon tuan*). Both the terms *tuan* and *matan* denote notions of primacy. The shift in the designation afforded Atambua (from the notion of 'garden' to the notion of 'centre') should not then be interpreted as introducing a new or unusual concept. Rather, it reflects the norm that every periphery is potentially a centre in itself. In this sense, the 'periphery' is a dynamic category, while the 'centre' is a relatively static category.

In his journey from 'the main harbour' to 'the old harbour' the bishop was described as having crossed rivers and forests, climbed every fence, and stopped over in granaries of various gardens so as to reach the central area conceptualised as the Wehali's residential territory. This 'journey' was described in ritual poetry of strict parallelism. In order to elucidate the notion of 'periphery', in Table 4.1 I have summarised the cultural labels given to people and places mentioned in that part of the poem depicting how the bishop makes his way through Wehali's periphery.

Table 4.1: Wehali's periphery as cultivation space

People and places	Cultural labels
Wesei Wehali	the source of the flame, the source of the heat (*malaka na'in//mamanas na'in*)
Virgin Mary	mother Mary, suckling Mary (*ina Maria//susu Maria*)
Jesus Christ	the Only Son (*Oan Mane Kmesak*)
Bishop	the holder of the great taboo, the holder of the great heat (*makaer lulik bot//makaer manas bot*)
Church	the black bright house, the red (gold) bright house (*uma metan Maromak//uma mean Maromak*)
Atambua	the main harbour, the main spring (*namon matan//we matan*)
Tukuneno	the rooster (*manu aman*)
Dafala	the stony fort of Dafala, the black house of Dafala (*fatuk baki Dafala//uma metan Dafala*)
Lelowai	the ladder of the granary, the supporting step of the post (*klobor matetek//hisa riin matetek*)
Halikelen	the granary of Halikelen, the hut of Halikelen (*klobor Halikelen//laen Halikelen*)
Halilulik	the boiling water, the strong post (*we laka//riin besi*)
Mande'u	the younger *dato*, the elder *dato* — the younger *loro*, the elder *loro* (*dato alin ida//dato maun ida* — *loro alin ida//loro maun ida*)
Eturafoun	the granary of the tame rooster, the hut of the tame rooster (*klobor manu maus//laen manu maus*)
	the small black rope, the big black rope (*tali metan ki'ik//tali metan kwa'ik*)
Seon	the junction of the river, the black stone (*mota sorun/ /fatuk metan*) the *ahan* fruit, civet-cat dog, civet-cat pig (*bua ahan//asu kmeda/ /fahi kmeda*)

As the bishop came closer to the centre that is conceptualised as Wehali residential territory, the idiom changes from 'garden' to 'stable' or 'fence'. In the old stronghold of Maibiku, which is located in the domain of Dirma, he was greeted by 'the children of the four enclosures, the children of the four stables' (*oa natar hat//oa lalu'an hat*) who escorted him to the hamlet of Sulit Anemeta, the border of Wehali's inner territory. Being considered as the outer border, this hamlet is referred to as 'guardian of Liurai's stable' (*makdakar knokar Liuran*). When he entered this hamlet (Sulit Anemeta), the bishop was depicted in the poem as being on the edge of Wehali

residential space. Therefore he was regarded as having already entered via
'the four posts' that separate the centre of Wehali from her periphery.
These four posts are guarded by the four male rulers entitled *loro* (literally
meaning 'sun'). In their status as guardians of Wehali they are referred to
as 'the strong posts, the valuable posts' (*riin besi hat//riin kmurak hat*).
These rulers are Loro Wewiku, Loro Haitimuk, Loro Lakekun and Loro
Dirma. Only by passing through these guardians is one eligible to meet
'the mother, the father' who rest at the centre.

In summary, this mythical journey is delineated as a trip from:

molin	to	*Laran*
periphery	to	centre
cultivation space	to	dwelling space

3. Sociological Implications of 'Centre-Periphery'

The foregoing discussion of the notions of 'centre' and 'periphery' focused
on their contrast. At this level of analysis every dual symbolic classification
entails categories opposed to each other: centre/periphery, trunk/tips,
flower/fruit, navel/foot, head/tail, first-born/last-born, elder/younger,
and so on.

These opposed categories certainly provide a basis for asymmetrical
relations between persons and groups both within and outside Wehali.
However, no single opposition (e.g. first-born/last-born) can be taken
as a 'ready-made recipe' for the construction of social hierarchy. I have
indicated earlier the diverse applications and polyvalency of 'last-born'
within the whole corpus of oppositional terms. Perhaps this polyvalency
of particular oppositions is another reason to conclude with Fox that
'there is no one privileged opposition, but rather a complex of interactions
of valent oppositions' (1990: 8). In the context of Wehali, both *ikun* and
ikus belong with different valencies in the corpus of centre and periphery
classifications. Thus, the discussion of the sociological implications of
the notions of 'centre' and 'periphery' must be put in the framework
of the interaction of 'valent oppositions' in all their complexity.

The Wehali claim that their domain is the centre of all societies. This
claim is based on the origin myth that the first dry land was situated in
their area. The same origin myth also narrates that the elder brothers left
Wehali to occupy land to the east and west, while the younger brothers

and the youngest daughter stayed 'to look after' (*makdakar*) the navel land. Quite clearly, this narrative is based on a set of complementary categories that includes first-born/last-born, elder/younger, male/female and centre/periphery. To pursue the notion of complementarity involved here, I must analyse further the distinction between centre and periphery as a contrast between residential space and cultivation space.

In the origin myth, the elder brothers were sent away (*foo ba*) to found new communities outside Wehali. Thus, according to Wehali's cosmic symbolism, they are depicted as living in Wehali's gardens. Their (cultural) functions were to till the land in order to produce food to feed their 'mother and father' living in the centre, whom they also protect. In their capacity as 'farmers', the elder brothers have the status of a male child in the family. However, in their function as protectors (*makdakar*) they have the status of executive rulers of the central authority, therefore deserving of the titles *loro* (literally, sun) or *liurai* (literally, above the earth). In this way the division of spiritual and temporal authorities suggested by van Wouden (1968: 114–115) and later elaborated by Cunningham (1962: 63–67) and Schulte Nordholt (1971: 236–239) may also apply in Wehali. The Wehali attest that they are the source of life and, therefore, life flows from the centre to the periphery. On the other hand, the periphery, which is delineated as a 'garden', is the source of wealth. By giving away their elder sons to the periphery, the Wehali expect wealth to return to the centre. So the flow of life runs in the opposite direction to the flow of wealth (see Table 4.2). In relation to the origin of life, the periphery becomes the life-taker and the wealth-giver.

Table 4.2: Flow of life and flow of wealth

	Life-giver	Life-taker
Basic dyadic set	centre (*laran*)	periphery (*molin*)
	trunk (*hun*)	edge (*tehen*)
	hill (*foho*)	sea (*tasi*)
	sheath, rind (*kakun*)	content (*isin*)
Gender category	female	male
Associated meaning	poverty	wealth
	static	dynamic
	inside	outside
	Inside	**Outside**
Life-giver	life and authority	>>>>>>>>>>>>>>
	<<<<<<<<<<<<	wealth and power

The function of 'protector' in turn gives the outside societies some source of power. Being masculine in this society means having every right to talk in public. So it is the male Liurai (known as Liurai) who is authorised by the female Liurai (known as Maromak Oan) to do the speaking. According to the south Tetun political concept, then, the power of the Liurai to speak stems from Maromak Oan, in the silent ritual centre.

The Wehali dual conceptual categories cited in Table 4.2 are not simply static in nature. Rather, these categories become guiding principles or, in Fox's term, 'operators' for building up different relations and even creating new categories (Fox 1989a: 45). Using the imagery of a sword, by giving away their men to the periphery, the Wehali picture themselves as retaining the sheath (*knua*) and giving away the blade (*isin* = inwards). Using the imagery of a nut, Wehali is the shell (*knua*) while the periphery is the content (*isin*), implying that Wehali becomes poor and the periphery becomes rich, Wehali becomes weak and the periphery becomes strong.

Centre-Periphery in Inter-Domain Relationship

The idea that the present order of domain and clanship was founded in myth occurs in most eastern Indonesian societies and has been examined by anthropologists for the island of Timor and islands immediately surrounding it. Among these, Fox, Kana, Lewis, Traube, McWilliam and Graham especially also explore the use of botanical idioms in describing the nature of domain and clan relations.

The Tetun have no specific term for 'domain' or 'kingdom'. Rather, Tetun use a generic term *rai*, which covers the meanings of earth, island, land, region, domain and dirt. So, the earth is designated *rai klaran* (the middle, inside world), heaven is *rai leten* (the above world), the island of Timor is *rai Timor* and the domain of Wehali is *rai Wehali*. They believe that the centre of the earth, or at least of Timor, is located in their region. Areas or regions surrounding it are regarded as 'peripheral'. These 'outside lands', or to use the Tetun phrase *molin*, are divided into two halves: sunrise land (*rai loro sa'e*) and sunset land (*rai loro toba* = land of the setting sun) or land of the falling sun (*rai loro monu*). This cultural concept of spatial orientation can be observed in many forms of oral composition, such as the two forms cited below. From these, my aim is to delineate a set of symbolic co-ordinates that are the bases for social classification of land and clanship.

Text 1: *Ho'ar Nahak Samane Oan* (The Manlike Ho'ar Nahak)

The following is a summary of this well-known myth as recorded in the hamlet of Umanen (the whole narration of the myth is provided in Reference Text 8).

An old respected mother (*ferik*) gave birth first to six sons and then to a daughter. They lived in the hamlet of Umanen, in the region of Wehali. The name of the only daughter was Ati Batik. As a farming family, the six brothers had the responsibility 'to feed' the whole family. One day they thought that their gardens were not producing enough to feed them and therefore they needed additional income to support the family. They then decided to raise income by betting on cock fights. With that decision in mind, they left Wehali and went to 'the land of the flaming sun, the land of the glowing sun' (*rai loro lakan//rai loro len*). This land was called 'the head land' (*rai ulun*). Unfortunately, the six brothers lost in the matches and therefore became slaves in that land.

When the six brothers left their hamlet, their young sister was still a baby. One day when she came of age, she asked her mother if she had brothers. Her curiosity led her mother to reveal the truth that she actually had six brothers who were in slavery in 'the head land'. Knowing the reason for her brothers' slavery, she then decided to go and free them by engaging in the same activity of cock fights. Disguising herself as a prince, she set off to the head land accompanied by her men (*hutun no renu* = commoners). When they arrived at their destination, she found out that her brothers were tied in a pen at the back of a house. She then invited their 'owner' named Lakuleik to bet on cock fights. This time her opponent lost all the matches and so all his property. As a last bet, she asked her opponent to bet the six bound slaves in the backyard. From the very beginning her opponent had suspected that Ati Batik was not a man. Now he was even more convinced that she was his slaves' sister. With these convictions in mind Lakuleik invited Ati Batik to compete in other contests that would likely require Ati Batik to expose her body and so reveal that she was a woman. The first contest was to measure how far one could urinate and the second was to measure how long one could stand the cold water of the river while bathing nude. Ati Batik passed the first contest successfully by using a piece of bamboo.[1] For the second contest, Ati Batik successfully evaded participating in the 'impossible' competition with another trick. Ati Batik arranged for her people to set fire to their huts immediately before the competition started. So when both contenders were in the water, Lakuleik started to take off his sarong. Ati Batik also did the same thing. However, since she wore more than one sarong, it took a while before her body was completely exposed. In the meantime her hut was consumed by fire. She took the opportunity to break from the contest and rescue her hut. This golden opportunity enabled her, along with her brothers and her men, to escape from the head land (*rai ulun*) and return to her family. Soon after their arrival, according to the myth, 'she promoted the six brothers to become heads of the regions' (*nia nasa'e nikar niakan naan mane nen sia nalo ba ulun*), 'so the land could have rulers' (*ne'e be rai ne'e no nikar ulun*). Their promotion to rulers is recounted in the following lines of the oral poetry:

Manu aman malae nadu be nadu	The foreign roosters have come (appeared)
nadu na'ak nia heti ren sia monu	come and say that their head-cloths have already fallen
nadu na'ak nia so'e ren sia monu	appear and say that their head accessories have already fallen
so'e ren sia monu kain Maubesi	their head accessories fall on the stalk of Maubesi
heti ren sia monu tenan Maubesi	their head-cloths fall on the land of Maubesi
foin atu ba foti le'u rei ulu	then the head accessories are rescued and have re-encircled their heads
foin atu ba foti kaku rei ulu	then the head-cloths were rescued and have been re-installed
mane alin mane maun na'ak atu natetu nikar ba fatin	the younger brothers and the elder brothers have resumed their positions

---

1   It is not the custom of the people to discuss sexual organs publicly. When this narrator came to this part of the trick, he explained and re-enacted how cunningly Ati Batik put a bamboo under her sarong. His audience, which consisted of men and women, young and old, laughed and at the same time were 'proud' of his ability to describe the trickiest part of the story.

mane alin mane maun na'ak atu nasa'e nikar ba fatin	the younger brothers and the elder brothers were restored back to their places
sa'e nikar ba dato na'in dato Umanen Lawalu	restored to the position of *dato* of the clans of Umanen Lawalu
tetu nikar ba fatik Loro na'in Loro Umanen Lawalu.	re-enthroned in their positions of *loro* of the clans of Umanen Lawalu.

The final episode of the myth narrates the coming of her opponent to Wehali. He came to propose marriage to Ati Batik, with the intention of taking her back to his own domain. Again another trick was performed to prevent her being taken away. A subsequent visit of her opponent was intended as revenge on Wehali, in the form of cock fights. In this match, both the land of Wehali (the navel land) and the land of the sunrise (the head land) were placed as bets. Ati Batik bet the navel land; Lakuleik, her opponent, bet 'the head of the land' (*rai ulun*). After hanging up the sheath of her sword in a tree that produced three branches (*ai sorun tolu*) she was ready to enter the contest. In this contest, Lakuleik lost his land. He said to Ati Batik, 'Friend, I have lost everything. The land of the flaming sun is yours, the navel land is also yours. Wherever I go, I go on your land. Therefore allow me to stay here.' His plea was accepted and so Lakuleik was 'taken into Wehali' (*hatama baa Wehali*) and was charged with 'looking after the young areca nuts of Wehali, the young betel leaves of Wehali' (*dakar bua kau Wehali//takan kau Wehali*). Ati Batik was then called Ho'ar Nahak Samane Oan to mark her diligent performance as a man.

How do we interpret this myth? Hicks (1984: 2) suggests that there are various ways of interpreting Tetun myths as a sacred charter, as a structural tract, as history or as an imaginative creation of oral art. In order to do justice to the text itself, and the literary context from which this text comes, I would begin with a note on Wehali's classification of oral poetry. This piece of literary art is classified by some as *ai knoik* (a folk tale) and by others as *lia tebes* (a true tale). This may be because, according to the Wehali system of classification, it is not a sacred charter or *rai lian* (language of the earth), but neither is it simply an entertaining story or an aetiological myth. Rather, the story of Ho'ar Nahak Samane Oan contains all three elements and therefore it can only be narrated by a particular person. In the case of this text, it was narrated by Yohannes Seran Kehik, the head of Uma Katuas lineage in the hamlet of Umanen. Among the members of the hamlet, he is considered to be an *adat* spokesman (*mako'an*).

This story was narrated in front of many members of the hamlet. At the beginning the audience was very calm and quiet. But when the story reached its climax they started to giggle and laugh, even jumping in and persuading the narrator to retell 'the amusing' part of the story, as when the narrator used his body language to re-enact the tricks displayed by Ho'ar Nahak Samane Oan. When it came to the urination trick, he jokingly said 'do not ask me how Ho'ar managed to install the bamboo so that she could appear to urinate further than Lakuleik'.

The point is that the 'cleverness', 'tricks' and 'out-smarting' (*matenek*)[2] of Ho'ar are the entertaining parts of the myth. Ho'ar, even though she is a younger woman, can *mengakali* (out-smart) such an important man as Lakuleik. Furthermore, the man's name, Lakuleik, when related to the word 'foolish' (*beik*) can produce a rhyme ending with the same sound -*eik*, such as *Lakuleik beik* (the foolish Lakuleik). The opposition between clever and foolish in this part of the myth shows a resemblance to the Rotinese opposition of *lela* and *nggoa* as discussed by Fox. So, as with the Rotinese, the opposition between clever and foolish 'provides a categorical basis for the glorification of the cunning and acumen of the trickster' (1990: 8). The other interesting part of the myth lies in the heroic efforts performed by a younger woman to rescue her elder brothers. These are the elements (that is, cunning and bravery) most enjoyed by the audience. For the nobles of Umanen, the importance of the myth lies in the political aspect of it: it is the house of Umanen Lawalu that bravely rescued and re-appointed the rulers in the Wesei Wehali territory. To highlight this, the narrator of the myth felt it necessary to add a concluding statement: *tan lia ne'e, rai ne'e foin halo no ukur* (based on this story, now we have government in our land). For most Wehali audiences, this story proves the superiority of the Wehali insiders over her inferior outsiders. But the audience that came to hear the myth found the acumen and amusing tricks of Ho'ar of most interest.

Linguistically, this myth is organised around basic oppositional categories of centre/periphery, inside/outside and female/male. These fundamental categories are then used as 'operators' to define a set of related categories as shown in Table 4.3.

---

2   The word *matenek* in Tetun also implies know-how in magic.

Table 4.3: Basic oppositional categories

inside	*laran*	*molin*		outside	
⇓	⇓	⇓		⇓	
umbilical cord	*husar binan*	*ulun*	*ain*	head	tail
		⇓	⇓	⇓	⇓
		loro sa'e	*loro toba*	sunrise	sunset
mother-father	*ina-ama*	*oan mane*		son	
⇓	⇓	⇓		⇓	
female	*feto*	*mane*		male	
⇓	⇓	⇓		⇓	
last-born	*ikun*	*ulun*		first-born	
clever	*matenek*	*beik*		foolish	

Taking these linguistic categories together, we can build up a set of cultural oppositional categories based on gender contrast, age contrast, spatial contrast and ranking contrast:

Gender contrast:	female/male
Age contrast:	elder/younger
Generation contrast:	parents/children
Spatial contrast:	inside/outside, centre/periphery, navel/head
Rank contrast:	superior/inferior

In Wehali, and in many parts of eastern Indonesia, cock fights and garden work typically belong in the world of men. In the text of Ho'ar Nahak Samane Oan, these two types of work are performed outside the village. This emphasis indicates that areas outside Wehali are considered as 'working places'. In the myth concerning Ho'ar Nahak Samane Oan, the journey from the centre to the peripheral societies is described as a journey 'to search for wealth'. The Tetun phrase used in this context is *buka sotir no ua*, which can be translated literally as 'to search for luck and money'. In that story, this idea applies to the six brothers who engage in cock fights to search for wealth. Since this is man's work, Ho'ar Nahak Samane Oan later has to disguise herself in order to engage in such work.[3] In this myth, Ho'ar leaving the 'mother' at the 'centre' manifests the knowledgeable

---

3   As a disguised person she is not an anomaly sexually. It is true that Ho'ar is a common woman's name, but the prefix *sa-* in *samanek* indicates that she is a woman pretending to be a man. There is no indication in the text that would lead to any conclusion that the fight between Ho'ar and Lakuleik is a fight between an unambiguous male versus an ambiguous female. Here Ho'ar simply had to disguise herself in the form of a prince so she could engage in a male activity (see Viqueque text elaborated by Hicks 1984: 12).

inside compared to the foolish outside. So, the myth permits not only the contrasts between female inside and male outside, but also the wealth outside and the source of life and knowledge inside.

This myth further reveals notions of female 'superordination' and male 'subordination'. These terms can easily mislead people into developing a notion of coercive power in the sense of the physical superiority of the inside and the inferiority of the outside. Nowhere in the myth is there an indication of this type of relation. The text speaks about the superiority of the inside, not based on coercion, but on ritual rights. As is stated in the final episode of the text, before commencing the cock fight: 'Ho'ar hangs up the sheath of her sword in a tree which has three branches'. This sentence is concerned with ritual symbols. Being the centre, Wehali is metaphorically considered to be the 'sheath of the sword' (*knua*). According to the Wehali, the sword has been given away to the outside people who act as Wehali's protectors. In this analogy, the sheath is the mother and the sword is the son. Thus, in the myth Lakuleik represents the son and Ho'ar the mother. The defeat of Lakuleik can then be interpreted as the obligation of a son to surrender to his mother.

Text 2. The Giving Away of Men

In Reference Text 2, the story concerning the departure of the Wehali's men 'to sit' in territories toward the sunrise and sunset began when the marriage of Ho'ar Na'i Haholek gave birth to six boys and one girl.

N a'i taek Malaka nola ti'an Ho'ar Na'i Haholek, foin te baa mane na'in nen, feto na'in ida.	Na'i Taek Malaka married Ho'ar Na'i Haholek and had six boys and one girl.
Mane ulun Na'i Saku Mataus, Na'i Bara Mataus, Na'i Ura Mataus, Na'i Meti Mataus, Na'i Neno Mataus, Na'i Leki Mataus.	The first born was Na'i Saku Mataus, then Na'i Bara Mataus, Na'i Ura Mataus, Na'i Meti Mataus, Na'i Neno Mataus, Na'i Leki Mataus.
Ikun aa feto naran Ho'ar Mataus, Ho'ar Makbalin Balin Liurai	The last born was a girl named Ho'ar Mataus, entitled Ho'ar Makbalin Balin Liurai (lit. Ho'ar, the one who was in charge of appointing Liurai)

The narrator then went on to describe the marriage between Ho'ar Mataus, the youngest daughter and a man from the seaside without commenting on the remaining six sons. In response to my query, he explained:

Na'i Saku Matatts no Na'i Bara Mataus ami fo ba tuur iha rai loro sa'e	Na'i Saku Mataus and Na'i Bara Mataus were given away to sit in the land of the rising sun
Na'i Ura Mataus no Meti Mataus ami fo ba tuur iha rai loro monu	Na'i Ura Mataus and Meri Mataus were given away to sit in the land of the setting sun
Na'i Leki Mataus no Na'i Neno Mataus hela ba Wehali	Na'i Leki Mataus and Na'i Neno Mataus were left in Wehali
Ho'ar Mataus, Ho'ar makbalin balin Liurai ne'e nia maktuur iha Uma rai lale'an nodi titu ba Wesei Wehali	Ho'ar Mataus, the one who appointed the *liurai* sits in the house of earth and sky to look after Wesei Wehali

This origin myth is regarded as 'the trunk language' (*lia hun*) shared by all members of Wesei Wehali. Being the trunk narrative, this myth provides a sacred charter that establishes the order of creation of the earth and human beings. As a 'sacred history', this myth can only be told by an *adat* historian (*mako'an*). Francillon, during his research in Wehali, was given a copy of a similar kind of origin myth.[4] The text of his myth, as he noted, was taken from the notebook of a schoolboy in Suai. Comparing the myth that I recorded and the one reported by Francillon, it seems to me that this 'sacred charter' has been preserved by the Wehali in such a manner that its structure has not changed. The names of the six sons written in Francillon's text are the same as those in my text but in a different order. What is significant for Wehali is who goes where and who stays where. This 'ordered structure' is maintained by the Wehali. Both Francillon's and my texts reveal that the elder brothers were given away 'to sit' (*tur*) in the land towards the sunrise and the land toward the sunset. The youngest stayed in Wehali.

Although the word 'to sit' does not explicitly relate to notions of 'centre' and periphery, it must be considered in this light because it denotes a political aspect, a theme that is built into the entire discourse. In Tetun, the term 'palace' is translated as 'a sitting place' (*tuur fatik*). So, according to Wehali ideology, the four brothers were not only sent to dwell: they were sent to rule the eastern and western regions on either side of Wehali. Since they were sent from the centre to the periphery, the sender occupies the position with superior status. In this case, the notion of superiority is not based on the pattern of relations between bride-giver and bride-taker

---

4   Francillon (1967: 78) mentions that his text of the origin myth was copied from the notebook of a schoolboy who was instructed by his maternal grandfather to preserve this 'sacred language'.

clans, as is common throughout eastern Indonesian societies. Rather, their asymmetrical relation is based on the notion of origin (*hun*). Wehali is the trunk and other societies are its 'flower' (*funan*) and 'fruit' (*klaut*). As the trunk, Wehali is the source of life and therefore deserves to be called 'mother and father' (*ina no ama*) while other peripheral societies are its daughters (*funan* = flower) and sons (*klaut* = fruit).[5]

Text 3: The Departure of the Rulers (*loro*)

The myth narrated in the village of Builaran also concerns the departure of men (in this case the Liurai of Wehali) to the 'outside' domains. According to this myth, when the earth had completely dried, a group of 10 men (*mane sanulu*) came from the sun above to Wehali:

Hat tuur iha Wehali nen la'o	Four of them remained in Wehali, six went on.
Loro mane kwaik aa baa iha Likusaen Baboen, ida baa iha Biboki, ida baa iha Insana, ida baa iha Amnuban, ida baa iha Amnatun, ida baa iha Amarasi	The elder *loro* went to Likusaen Baboen, one went to Biboki, one went to Insana, one went to Amanuban, one went to Amanatun and one went to Amarasi
hat hela baa Haitimuk, Wewiku, Dirma, Lakekun	four men were left in Haitimuk, Wewiku, Dirma and Lakekun

This myth has a slightly different emphasis. Unlike the myth from the inner Wehali region, which focuses on the founding of Laran as the centre and the trunk of society and as a seat for the *ina no ama* (mother and father of Wehali), the myth preserved by the hamlet of Builaran concerns the ordering of the 'border' between the centre and the peripheral domains. Builaran, which is known as the hamlet of the Liurai (*leo* Liurai) naturally engages in 'outside' affairs. One of the ceremonial functions of 'outside' rulers is to protect the centre. In line with this function, the

---

5   This issue arises in respect to Schulte Nordholt's argument concerning the superiority of Maromak Oan over the As Tanara of the Fialaran domain as based on the myth cited in Grijsen (1904: 129). In this myth it was said that a daughter of Maromak Oan married a prince of Fialaran. Schulte Nordholt then concluded that 'the Maromak Oan is recognized as superior ruler because he is the *bride giver*' (1971: 256, my emphasis). The superiority claimed is, however, based on the view that the mountain of Laka'an in the Fialaran territory was the first dry land to emerge and therefore constitutes the trunk (*hun*) of all societies. The Wehali, on the contrary, believe that the sacred hill of Marhlu was the first to dry and therefore that they are the trunk of all societies. Thus, the notion of origin (*hun*) plays a pre-eminent role in the claim to superiority.

myth preserved in this hamlet concerns the drawing of borders between the inner protectors and the outer protectors. Based on an order of precedence, the domains of Wewiku, Haitimuk, Lakekun and Dirma are regarded as inner protectors, while other domains toward the sunrise and sunset are regarded as outer protectors. It is also interesting to note that *adat* historians who are in charge of narrating the inner Wehali history usually limit themselves to narrating only the central 'evidence', such as the emergence of the first dry land and the birth of the first human beings. The Liurai *adat* historian's emphasis, however, is more on the 'distribution' of Wehali's men to peripheral societies and less on the notion of 'the beginnings'.

Like the narrative cited in Text 2, the Builaran myth is also regarded as a *lia hun* (trunk language). This myth reveals that the '10 men' (*mane sanulu*) of Wehali were called *loro* (literally 'sun').[6] Six *loro* were sent to rule domains in the west and east. The first-born ruled the areas towards the sunrise (Likusaen Baboen), while the rest ruled the areas toward the sunset (Biboki, Insana, Amanuban, Amanatun and Amarasi). The four youngest men stayed and ruled the four domains surrounding Wehali. Like the first six rulers, they were also called *loro*. In relation to the notion of protecting the centre, these *loro* play different roles. The first six *loro* are considered 'outside or peripheral rulers' (*loro molin*). In this capacity they are referred to as 'the lord of granaries, the lord of huts' (*klobor na'in//laen na'in*). The second four *loro* are called 'the inside rulers' (*loro laran*). In house and garden imagery, these inside rulers are regarded as the guardians of four valuable posts, four iron posts (*rin kmurak hat//rin besi hat*).

The pattern of inter-domain relations, as depicted in the three examples of oral tradition discussed above, evinces a principle of precedence. Both the second and the third myths, narrated in the hamlets of Laran and Builaran, indicate that domains outside Wehali originated from Wehali. The new communities built up outside Wehali are the 'fruit' of Wehali's tree. In other words, their origin groups based on a genitor in each case have their derivation in a source in the progenetrix line of Wehali. Here we are faced with the reckoning of genitor lines emanating from a progenetrix line. The five sons who married women from outer domains in the second myth would refer to their origin house as *uma hun* (the trunk house) and the house they lived in as *uma tuur fatik* (the sitting place house).

---

6   The title *loro* refers to a male ruler, the second rank of nobility in the structure of the Liurai's government.

According to the marriage customs, the five sons could take up residence only in their wives' houses. So, the descendant of the five sons who lived in peripheral domains trace their origin group to five different genitors. The asymmetrical relations between the origin groups based on genitor lines and the 'trunk' progenetrix line are defined as relations between tree trunk/fruit, parents/children, life-giver/life-taker, centre/periphery and female/male.

The pattern of relation based on these criteria of precedence are further replicated at the levels of village, hamlet and house. However, at the hamlet and house levels, the role of these criteria is significantly reduced. They are replaced to some extent by other criteria of precedence: namely, first-born/last-born or elder/younger. To say this does not necessarily mean that criteria used for the inter-domain level are irrelevant at the village, hamlet and house levels. Rather, the lower the level (e.g. house), the more important the age category becomes. Conversely, the broader the level (e.g. inter-domain), the more important the spatial and rank categories remain. These assumptions are manifest also in the first and third myths quoted above, with slightly different emphases in each. In the first myth, the emphases are on the knowledgeable inside compared to the foolish outside; the superiority of inside compared to the inferiority of the outside; and the outside as the place to accumulate wealth, but the inside as the source of life. The emphasis in the third myth is on the rank of rulers who act as protectors of the ritual centre.

Centre-Periphery at the Village and Hamlet Levels

The distinction between centre and periphery, inside and outside can be observed further in village structure. To demonstrate this distinction, I have chosen to describe a grouping of hamlets which, culturally, belong to outer Wehali and a grouping of hamlets of the inner Wehali. The former will be represented by the village (*desa*) of Kamanasa, and the latter by the villages of Kateri, Umakatahan, Kletek and Fahiluka. These villages are situated in the district of Malaka Tengah.

1. Outer Wehali

The present village (*desa*) of Kamanasa consists of seven hamlets (*leo*). With the aim of consolidating diverse hamlets into larger administrative units called *desa*, the present Indonesian government encompassed the seven hamlets into what is known as *desa* Kamanasa. The seven hamlets are: Fatisin (derives from *fatu isin*, literally 'flesh of the stone'), Liurai (derives from *liu* = to surpass and *rai* = land; Liurai = to rule the land), Manliman (derives from *mane liman*, literally 'men's arms'), Leklaran (derives from *leo klaran*, literally 'middle clan or hamlet'), Sukabi (Australian oak tree), Sukabihanawa (Sukabi + *hanawa* = to rest) and Labarai (the hamlet of Bunak-speaking people).

According to oral history narrated in the area, the people of these hamlets were originally refugees from a Portuguese colony in the eastern part of Timor. Indeed, the name of the village is often mentioned as Suai Kamanasa. The term Suai denotes a domain of origin in as much as the Kamanasa people claim that originally they came from Suai, a Tetun-speaking area across the former international border between East and West Timor. This identification of Kamanasa with the Tetun people of Suai goes against the complex structure of the present-day village because included within this single administrative unit are people of a different ethnic origin, namely the Bunak, who migrated to the area along with the Suai Kamanasa people some 90 years ago.[7] Although administratively the hamlet of Labarai is part of the village of Kamanasa, it is ritually distinct as they do not participate in an important agricultural rite, called 'delivering the head maize' (*hatama batar ulun*), celebrated annually by the former Suai people. From among the six hamlets of the former Suai people, the hamlets of Fatisin, Manliman, Leklaran and Liurai claim to come from the same place in Suai-Kamanasa and to constitute a single origin group. This origin group, on which I focus my analysis, is called Kamanasa. As a symbol of unity, these four hamlets treat one sacred

---

7   As noted by Francillon, these people fled from East Timor during the battle of Manufahi (*hatuda Manufahi*), in which the local people fought against the Portuguese. My estimate of some 90 years derives from information provided by the clan head of Labarai, who told me that his own father was among those young refugees. I gathered the same information as Francillon concerning this battle and I am not aware of any written documents concerning it. However, information given to me describing the people's refusal to pay tax to the Portuguese as one reason for their escaping from their homeland provides a clue to the historical dating of their migration. The introduction of tax came alongside establishment between 1885 and 1914 of the international border separating the then Portuguese Timor and Dutch Timor. This migration must have occurred during that period.

house located at the ritual centre of the village as their ancestral house. This house is then regarded as the most sacred house of the people of Kamanasa. Reflecting the physical appearance of this sacred house, they refer to it as *uma* Ai As (the high posts house) or *uma* Ro Malae (the foreign ship house).

The overall layout of the village shows a clear distinction between areas used for dwellings and areas used for cultivation (see Figure 4.2). In this figure, the dwelling space is termed 'inside', 'interior' (*laran*), which I gloss as 'centre', and the cultivation space is termed 'outside', 'periphery' (*molin*). In the cultivation space, each household has its own gardens. Some gardens have a permanent hut (*laen*); others have only a temporary hut for ritual purposes during harvest. According to folk etymology, the word *laen* (hut) is related to the word *la'en* (husband). One of my informants said that the 'hut is the garden's husband' (*to'os ne'e nala'en baa laen*). In any case, *laen*, which are located in the cultivation space, are without doubt male domains. (There are, for example, various restrictions on unmarried women entering someone's garden hut.) In contrast, a residential house (*uma*), which is located in the dwelling space, is associated with females. The phrase *uma na'in* (literally, the lord of the house) is a term that refers to a man's wife. Thus the categories of inside, female, dwelling place and source of life as against outside, male, cultivation space and source of wealth are also used in describing the physical structure of the village.

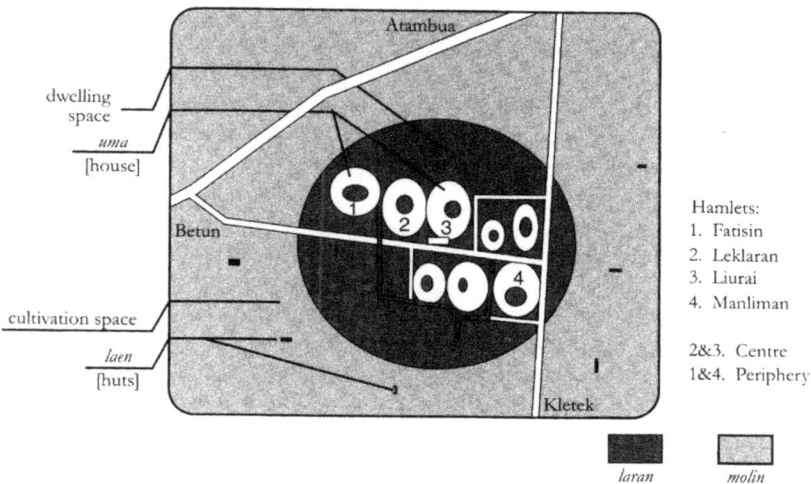

Figure 4.2: The four hamlets related as a single origin group in Kamanasa

The pattern of relations among hamlets reveals its similarity to the pattern of relations among domains. Being a ritual community, the form of relations among these four hamlets of Kamanasa is understood as that between parents and male children and between females and males. Based on the origin myth of Kamanasa, the hamlet of Liurai (see Figure 4.2, hamlet 3) is regarded as the seat of Liurai Suri Nurak. The hamlet of Leklaran (literally 'inner side hamlet'—see Figure 4.2, hamlet 2) is the seat of the Liurai's sister. In the house symbolism, the hamlet of Leklaran represents the inner house while the hamlet of Liurai is the platform. In rituals, people of the hamlets of Fatisin and Manliman refer to people of the hamlets of Leklaran and Liurai as 'mother' (*ina*) and 'father' (*ama*) respectively. Reciprocally, the latter two designate the former two hamlets as their sons (*oan*). So, within this origin group, the hamlets of Liurai and Leklaran are depicted as located at the centre of the Kamanasa and therefore deserving of being called the central hamlets. By contrast, the hamlet of Manliman (Figure 4.2, hamlet 4), which is located to the east of the centre, is considered to be a male first-born child; and the hamlet of Fatisin (Figure 4.2, hamlet 1), located to the west of the centre, is considered to be a male last-born child. In an indication of how categorical distinctions are replicated at different levels, in respect of Liurai and Leklaran both Fatisin and Manliman (hamlets 1 and 4) are now depicted as located 'outside' the residential space and so, categorically, they are peripheral (*molin*). Culturally, they are considered to be male children who have an obligation to till the land in order to feed their mother and father, who rest in the centre. During the harvest ritual, members of these two hamlets (1 and 4) give a tribute of seven cobs of corn to the centre hamlet to symbolise the feeding of the centre by the periphery. This offering of tribute also acts as an acknowledgement that the descendants of these two hamlets recognise the hamlets of Liurai and Leklaran as their origin hamlets. Thus, the pattern of relations among this origin group is also regulated by the dual category of centre/periphery. This opposition is further developed in botanical terms of trunk/tips. The hamlets of Leklaran and Liurai are the trunk, while the hamlets of Fatisin and Manliman are their tips.

The distinction between centre and periphery is further replicated down to the level of relations between houses within a hamlet. In order to explore further the dual symbolic classification, I concentrate here on two hamlets, namely Fatisin and Liurai. A common feature of hamlets in south Tetun, including these two hamlets, is the importance of the orientation of the houses, which may be toward empty spaces or more often toward the sacred houses of the hamlets. In the origin group of Kamanasa, a sacred house is called *uma metan* (the black house) and is uninhabited. While in Wehali in general, a sacred house is called *uma lulik* and is uninhabited. Named houses within a hamlet are arranged to face this sacred house. The exact genealogical relations between the members of named houses with the ancestors of the sacred house is never clear. Asking about these genealogical ties, informants would only refer to the sacred house as the founder of the hamlet. So, the identity of people within a hamlet is bound to the original founding ancestor of the hamlet.

Structurally speaking, every hamlet has its own identity in respect of its history and ritual function within a larger entity. This is evidenced by the layout of the hamlets as shown in the examples of Fatisin and Liurai (Figures 4.3 and 4.4). Houses in the hamlet of Fatisin (and also in the hamlet of Manliman) are organised in a concentric pattern, mostly facing inwards. These two hamlets are categorically male children. By contrast, the hamlets of 'mother and father' (Leklaran and Liurai) are likewise organised in a circular pattern but most of the houses exhibit a parallel orientation (see Figure 4.4). While this distinction may be observed to be typical, my Tetun informants saw these arrangements as different realisations of a single principle. Thus, comparing the orientation of houses in the so-called 'central hamlets' with the orientation of houses in hamlets ritually considered as peripheral throughout the plains of south Tetun, one can deduce that houses in the former exhibit parallel orientation while those in the latter show a concentric arrangement. When this fact was pointed out, the Tetun explained that basically every named house must be oriented towards the house that represents the founder of the clan. Consequently, houses of every clan are organised in a concentric pattern. However, there is also another way of meeting this requirement in respect of sacred houses in which the front half is built oriented towards the direction of the coming of their mythical male ancestor, while the back half is oriented towards the direction of the coming of their mythical female ancestor. These houses, which represent the houses of 'mother and father', constitute the trunk houses in an origin group. In a higher order origin group, such as the cluster of four hamlets discussed above, the hamlets ritually considered as 'trunk hamlets' are therefore set out with houses in parallel orientation. With this arrangement, according to native considerations, every hamlet or clan that constitutes an origin group 'supports' the trunk hamlet, the hamlet of the mother and father.

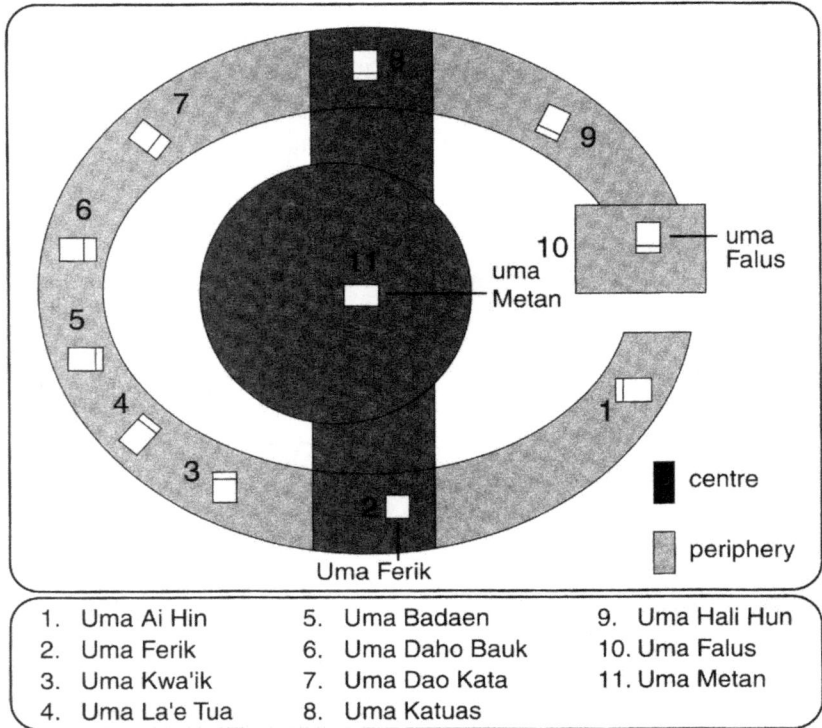

1.	Uma Ai Hin	5.	Uma Badaen	9.	Uma Hali Hun
2.	Uma Ferik	6.	Uma Daho Bauk	10.	Uma Falus
3.	Uma Kwa'ik	7.	Uma Dao Kata	11.	Uma Metan
4.	Uma La'e Tua	8.	Uma Katuas		

Figure 4.3: The origin group of Fatisin

In the hamlet of Fatisin (see Figure 4.3), the front doors (*oda matan lor*) of every house are built 'to face' the sacred 'black house' (*uma metan*) in the middle (House 11).[8] Facing the southern sea, and located in the northern part of the hamlet (House 8) is *uma* Katuas (the house of the respectable man or the old man's house). As its name suggests, this house is categorically male. Decisions regarding agricultural activities, the ritual obligations of each house within the hamlet or matters concerning the welfare of the hamlet in general have to be discussed in this house. The front verandah of a house is usually covered by mat-walls. These mats are called the 'female mats' (*kleni feto*). During the day, these mats are removed to give the impression of an open space. The front verandah, which is the space of men, is thus characterised by its 'openness'. Consistent with this notion of openness, the front verandah of *uma* Katuas has no such wall.

---

8   The word used for 'to face' is *tane*, which literally means 'to hold up from underneath', 'to support'. So these houses are delineated as supporting the 'important house' in the centre.

On the opposite side of the hamlet is located the *uma* Ferik (the house of the respectable woman or the old woman's house) (House 2). Its name suggests that this house is female and therefore, in many senses, a contrast to the *uma* Katuas. Most houses have a front platform or verandah that is the sleeping space of the male members of the household. Thus, the platform is associated with maleness. In contrast, the lack of a platform in the *uma* Ferik denotes its status as a female house. The most important function of women in rituals is to prepare sacrificial betel-nut. Based on this analogy, the house functions as a place to prepare betel-nut during certain rituals held in the hamlet.

These three, *uma* Metan (11), *uma* Katuas (8) and *uma* Ferik (2), make up the centre of the hamlet. They are surrounded by named houses, namely, *uma* Kwa'ik (3), *uma* La'e Tua (4), *uma* Badaen (5), *uma* Daho Bauk (6), *uma* Dao Kata (7) to the west and *uma* Hali Hun (9) and *uma* Ai Hun (1) to the east. This group of houses constitutes a 'mother elder–younger sister' (*inan bi alin*) bond. Within this bond, every house has its ritual function. At the hamlet or origin group level, these houses occupy the realm of the periphery (*molin*). They are regarded as the male protectors of *ina no ama* (mother and father) who rest in the centre. *Uma* Falus (10) deserves special explanation. The word *falus* in Tetun means 'widower'. My informants described the house as 'like a man without a wife or a woman without a husband' (*nu'u mane la no fen, feto la no la'en*). In ritual language, this house is called the 'house to dry one's sweat' (*uma hanawa kosar*) or as expressed in a ritual poem:

Uma dala oi sia	The house at the front of the road
uma tur tuli	the house to sit and to call upon
tur tuli hamara kosar	to sit, to call on and to dry one's sweat
hamara kosar foin fiu	dry sweat before continuing (the journey).

Its name suggests that this house is sexually indeterminate. Every outsider is called *ema matak no let* (literally translated as 'the raw and gap person') and is expected to 'dry his sweat' in this house before proceeding into the centre of the hamlet, which is regarded as 'the origin of heat and origin of sacredness' (*manas hun//lulik hun*). So this house plays the role of front gate or front house of the hamlet. In this front house, one is conceptually prepared to face 'the source of heat' (*manas hun*), which can harm 'the raw people'. To avoid this danger, one needs to rest in a 'liminal space' located in between the inside (conceptually 'residence') and the outside (conceptually 'gardens'). This is the place of *uma* Falus.

By contrast, houses in the hamlets of Liurai (see Figure 4.4) and Leklaran are organised in a more parallel pattern, in the sense that the named houses are oriented in one direction, namely towards the seaside (*lor*). The only exception is the orientation of the *uma* Amanas (the heat house). It is oriented toward the *ksadan*, the ritual centre of every hamlet or conglomeration of hamlets. In Kamanasa, this ritual empty space is located at the centre of the hamlet, while in inner Wehali territory, it is situated outside the hamlet.

With the exception of *uma* Amanas, every house mentioned in this figure is delineated as facing the most sacred house, namely the *uma* Ro Malae (the house of the foreign ship). According to the myth of origin of the Kamanasa people, the first ruler who came from Suai Kamanasa (in the present East Timor region) was called Liurai Suri Nurak. He arrived with his followers who became founders of the four hamlets that at present are part of the village of Kamanasa. To commemorate the coming of Liurai Suri Nurak as the founder of the Kamanasa, a sacred house was built at the ritual centre of Kamanasa, located in the hamlet of Liurai. This house is called *uma* Ro Malae. Compared to other sacred houses (*uma* Metan), each of which represents the founder of an origin group at the hamlet level, the *uma* Ro Malae is built distinctively on higher posts. Thus, people call this house the 'high post house' (*uma* Ai As). As the most sacred house in Kamanasa, this house becomes the centre of the annual maize harvest ritual.

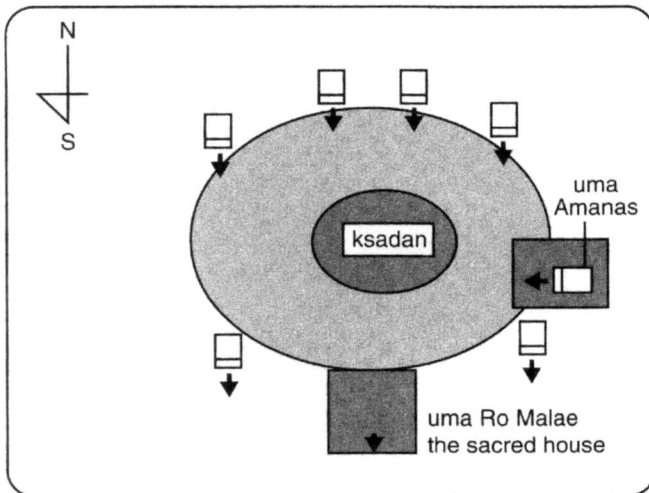

Figure 4.4: The origin group of the Liurai of Kamanasa

Compared to the hamlet of Fatisin, for example, in which one can observe the difference in construction between a male house (*uma* Katuas), which has a platform, and a female house (*uma* Ferik), which has no platform, within the hamlet of Liurai (Figure 4.4) all houses have platforms. Here, even the most sacred houses in Kamanasa have platforms. This unusual aspect of their construction follows the myth concerning the founding of Kamanasa, where it is narrated that these hamlets of refugees were founded by a man called Liurai Suri Nurak, and are therefore considered male. Within this cluster of named male houses there is a female house called *uma* Amanas (heat house). This is the place to prepare sacrificial betel-nut. The orientation of this Amanas house is somewhat surprising. In a parallel pattern one expects every named house to face the same direction as the sacred house. In the case of the Amanas house, however, it faces the *ksadan*, the ritual space at the centre of the hamlet. Unlike *uma* Ferik in Fatisin, this house has a platform. The same construction is observable in the hamlet of Leklaran. Although it is considered to be a 'mother' hamlet, every named house there has a platform. In these instances, the distinction between *uma* Ferik and *uma* Katuas rests on the arrangement of the walls. The platform of the *uma* Ferik is enclosed by plaited screens. By contrast, no screens are hung around the platform of *uma* Katuas.

2. Inner Wehali

The area that I gloss as inner Wehali primarily comprises five hamlets: Kateri, Umakatahan, Kletek, Fahiluka and Laran. At present, these five hamlets still play an important role in ritual, although they are not part of the contemporary administrative centre. In Table 2.5, I listed the names of hamlets that have been amalgamated to compose administrative units designated 'villages' (*desa*). In this amalgamation policy, these five hamlets are included in the present-day villages of Kateri, Umakatahan, Kletek and Fahiluka. In this arrangement the hamlet of Laran is included in the village of Umakatahan. Thus, administratively, the hamlet of Laran is now only one *dusun* (an administrative designation for hamlet) among the nine *dusun* that make up the 'village' of Umakatahan. Ironically, the name of Laran, the ritual centre of Wehali, is not used as the village name.

In ritual language these four-plus-one hamlets compose a single territory called 'the four-corner land, the four-elbow land' (*rai lidun hat, rai sikun hat*), which in this study is referred to as 'the four-corner land'. The 'four' in this phrase refers to the four hamlets of Kateri, Umakatahan, Kletek and Fahiluka. These four hamlets regard the fifth hamlet (Laran), which in Tetun means 'inside' or 'interior', as their central hamlet. This designation is based on origin myths. In the myth cited as Reference Text 2, people of this 'four-corner land' acknowledge their origin from a common genetrix called Ho'ar Na'i Haholek. Her house is called the house of EarthSky (*uma Rai Lale'an*). To symbolise their unity, the people of this 'four-corner land' erected a sacred house in the hamlet of Laran as their common ancestral house. This house is conceptually the house of Earth-Sky. However, since the Earth-Sky is a mythical house, the new house erected in the hamlet of Laran represents that mythical house. This 'new' house is called Ai Lotuk ('slender tree'—see Figure 4.5, House 1).

Given the presence of this sacred house, the hamlet of Laran is categorically considered the most sacred hamlet. Members of the other four hamlets treat the hamlet of Laran as their 'mother' hamlet. Reciprocally, members of the Laran hamlet designate those four hamlets as their children. Thus, an order of precedence based on the categories of parent–child is employed by the Wehali to explain the hierarchical contrast between Laran as the centre hamlet and the others as peripheral hamlets. The botanical idioms of 'trunk of tree' (*hun*) versus 'flower' (*funan*) and 'fruit' (*klaut*) are also important categories used to explain the nature of relations between these hamlets. Since the hamlet of Laran is associated with the genetrix Ho'ar Nai Haholek it is the 'trunk', while the hamlets of Kateri and Umakatahan are the 'flowers' and the hamlets of Kletek and Umakatahan are the 'fruit'. The metaphors 'flower' and 'fruit' designate the gender qualification of 'female' and 'male' children respectively.

The Ai Lotuk was originally fenced in a square shape with mangroves (*ai tasi*) obtained from the seaside. At present one can still observe traces of the old structure. The area inside this fence is called Ai Lotuk Laran (interior of the Ai Lotuk). So, in the hamlet of Laran, which in itself means 'inside' or 'interior', there is also a particular place called 'interior'. I therefore gloss it as the 'centre of the centre'. All sacred houses in each hamlet that comprises the territory of 'the four-corner land' have to be built supporting this particular 'centre'. Literally, it means that these sacred houses are built facing towards the area of Ai Lotuk Laran.

The centrality of the hamlet of Laran within the so-called territory of 'the four-corner land' may be delineated in another way by using idioms of house symbolism. In ritual language, the four hamlets of Kateri, Umakatahan, Kletek and Fahiluka are symbolised as the four corner posts of a house and therefore they are referred to as 'the four iron posts, the four valuable posts' (*rin besi hat//rin kmurak hat*). The two posts at the back of this symbolic house are represented by the hamlets of Kateri and Umakatahan. As these posts are labelled female posts, these two hamlets are also designated female hamlets. In the same way, the hamlets of Kletek and Fahiluka are designated male hamlets. Being labelled 'posts', the four hamlets are conceptually and physically 'supporters' (*maktane*) of the centre hamlet of Laran. The physical orientation of those hamlets reflects the notion of 'support' or *tane* as it is termed.

The centrality of Laran is also commonly described by using the dichotomy of dwelling and cultivation areas. Just like the overall layout of the four hamlets in Kamanasa, 'the four-corner land' may be viewed in terms of this dual division in which the hamlet of Laran is a dwelling space, or rather a resting space, while the four hamlets are categorically a cultivation space or the place to work. Asking people of these four hamlets about their ritual function and obligations as members of this higher order origin group in 'the four-corner land', one would be given a fixed response: 'It is our duty to feed the mother and father who rest in the centre' (cf. Reference Text 8). This response is an application of the concept of 'rest' and 'work'. Laran is a resting place. 'Mother and father' in this hamlet only 'eat reclining, drink reclining' (*mahaa toba//mahemu toba*) and it is the job of their 'children', who occupy the cultivation space, to till gardens in order to feed the reclining parents.

This conceptual division between dwelling and cultivation, reclining and working is said to be replicated in the orientation of the hamlets and named houses within each hamlet. Thus, houses in the cultivation area must support houses in the dwelling area. With this notion in mind, the ancestral house which symbolises the unity of named houses in each hamlet must be erected facing towards the Laran hamlet and, more particularly, facing the centre of the centre (Ai Lotuk Laran). Orienting their named houses in this direction implies that the houses physically 'support' (*tane*) the Ai Lotuk and, therefore, it is an acknowledgement of the superiority of Ai Lotuk over their own ancestral houses. The notion of superiority is encapsulated in the 'working' and 'reclining' categories. It is the superior who reclines and the inferior who works. Thus, ancestral houses in the hamlets of Kateri, Kletek and Fahiluka are built to support the Ai Lotuk. The only exception is the orientation of the named houses in the hamlet of Umakatahan. Its ancestral house is built parallel to the Ai Lotuk. Both of them face the 'seaside' (*lor*). This exception is understandable if one realises that this hamlet has two functions in regard to Laran. Using the same house symbolism, Umakatahan is a 'post'. Being a post, its houses have to support the Ai Lotuk. But the second function of Umakatahan as 'the trunk step, the trunk ladder' (*tetek hun//knuba hun*) of a house restrains it from organising its houses facing the centre of Laran. Because of this function, Umakatahan is no longer a cultivation space. It is part of the dwelling space, even though only as its 'ladder'.

Due to the importance of Laran as the central hamlet, the arrangement of named houses in this hamlet are particularly significant. As shown in Figure 4.5, the named houses in this hamlet are organised in a parallel pattern to face the Ai Lotuk (House 1), the 'sacred jungle' (*alas lulik*)[9] or 'ritual centre' (*ksadan*). These named houses are located in four areas within the hamlet, each called a *le'un*. The Tetun word *le'un* literally means 'a small section of narrow inhabited plain' (cf. Mathijsen 1906: 77); Morris (1984: 130) interprets it as a (populated) plain. The Wehali used these original meanings to designate sub-groups of people who inhabited a section of a *leo*. Each *le'un* contains one or more named houses. Every named house within a le'un is related as a group of *uma inan bin alin* (mother elder sister younger sister houses).

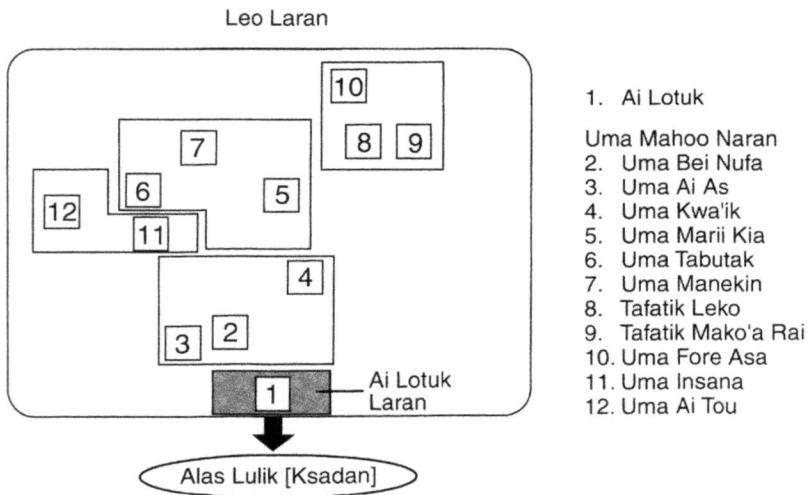

Leo Laran

1. Ai Lotuk

Uma Mahoo Naran
2. Uma Bei Nufa
3. Uma Ai As
4. Uma Kwa'ik
5. Uma Marii Kia
6. Uma Tabutak
7. Uma Manekin
8. Tafatik Leko
9. Tafatik Mako'a Rai
10. Uma Fore Asa
11. Uma Insana
12. Uma Ai Tou

Ai Lotuk Laran

Alas Lulik [Ksadan]

Figure 4.5: Named houses in the hamlet of Laran

---

9   Every 'sacred jungle' is considered a *ksadan* (ritual centre).

With reference to Figure 4.5, *le'un* Klot consists of Houses 2, 3 and 4; *le'un* Tatinis Lolon consists of Houses 5, 6 and 7; *le'un* Akar Laran consists of Houses 8, 9 and 10; and *le'un* Loro Monu consists of Houses 11 and 12. Each *le'un* is headed by a female and a male *fukun*. Since heads of hamlets are also called *fukun*, these heads of hamlets are designated as *fukun bot* (the chief *fukun*). In daily conversation, however, people do not differentiate the *fukun bot* and the *fukun*. Everybody is called *fukun*.

People say that the title *fukun* only applies to the hamlets outside Laran. 'Laran, as the hamlet of nobles, only recognises the title *ferik* (old woman) and *katuas* (old man)' was the most common argument I heard on this point in Laran.

Being the ritual centre of Wehali, where the Maromak Oan resides, the named houses within the hamlet are referred to in two ways. Houses 8 and 9 are referred to as *tafatik*, a compound word of *tur* (to sit) and *fatik* (place). The term *tafatik* is commonly translated into Indonesian as '*istana*' (palace).[10] The rest are simply called 'named houses' (*uma mahoo naran*). Both *tafatik* and named houses are built facing the ancestral House 1.

There are two reasons why those two particular houses (*tafatik* Leko, House 8 and *tafatik* Mako'a Rai, House 9) are called *tafatik*. According to the Haitimuk[11] and other nobles in Wehali, the Leko house is a *tafatik* because it is a place where the Maromak Oan resides. This means that this house supplies a woman as wife to the Maromak Oan. But according to nobles in Laran, the Leko house is a *tafatik* because the Maromak Oan is chosen matrilaterally from among male members of this house. *Tafatik* Leko is therefore the natal house of the Maromak Oan. Since Leko and Mako'a Rai are the houses of two sisters, both are called *tafatik*. Until now it is still contested whether the Leko house is the house that supplies the Maromak Oan, or the house where Maromak Oan resides. The latest contest between the house of Leko in the hamlet of Laran that supports Agustinus Klau and the house of Makbalin in the hamlet of Haitimuk that supports Agustinus Nahak Seran as the proper Maromak Oan of Wehali reflects the constant disputes between nobles of these two hamlets.

---

10   Nobles of Houses 8 and 9 refuse to call House 5 a 'palace' (*tafatik*). One of them told me that members of House 5 are not nobles. They are commoners who have an obligation to serve the nobles who sit in Houses 8 and 9. Therefore, they refer to that house simply as a 'named house'. However, members of the house concerned refer to their name house as a *tafatik*.
11   Haitimuk is a domain located in between Wehali and Wewiku. Traditionally, this hamlet provides the Maromak Oan for Wehali.

Despite this competition, no one disputes the primacy of the hamlet of Laran as the central domain, the Leko as a house is closely associated with the ruler of Wehali, and Ai Lotuk as the centre of the centre. As shown in Figure 4.5, the named houses in this hamlet are organised with a parallel orientation facing outwards.

The named Houses 2 (*uma* Bei Nufa), 3 (*uma* Ai As) and 4 (*uma* Kwa'ik) are located in *le'un* Klot. Founders of these three houses were the sisters: yZ, mZ and eZ, respectively. At present, members of House 3 no longer live in Laran. This house has collapsed, with only its male pillar left (*kakuluk lor*). The name *klot* (narrow) given to this *le'un* is said to be related to a space inside a house referred to as *we klot*. This is the quarter to store water jars, firewood and other household utensils. My Tetun friends explained that just as the *we klot* stores household needs, people who live in *le'un* Klot are obliged to serve the needs of the Maromak Oan, the lord of the 'slender tree house'. Bei Nufa, the male guardian of House 2, pointed to the walls of his house saying: 'My house looks uglier than the "slender tree house". The wall panels in my house are squeezed with three pieces of bamboo slivers, while the "slender tree house" has four bamboo slivers.' In arranging wall panels, the more squeezers used the better the result. There are still more detailed construction differences between the guardians' houses and their master's house, which point to the hierarchical nature of the relation between these two groups of houses. Thus, using the house metaphor of *we klot*, members of Houses 2 and 4 are 'servants'[12] of the Maromak Oan. Houses 2 and 4 provide women who regularly go every night into the Ai Lotuk in order to light the firewood in the hearth and to light the lamp made of candle-nut called *badut*. As an Ai Lotuk servant, Bei Nufa, the male guardian of House 2, also functions as the Maromak Oan's messenger to the people who live in hamlets toward the sunrise, including the hamlets of Umakatahan, Kletek and Fahiluka. Uma Kwa'ik (House 4) is regarded as a 'gate' to the Ai Lotuk Laran. Thus House 4 marks the border of *le'un* Klot. Once we step into this territory, we are at the edge of Ai Lotuk Laran. In former times, there were a number of prohibitions one needed to observe when entering this territory.

---

12   The Tetun terms that I translate as 'servants' are *feto ra* (female 'servant') and *klosan* (male 'servant'). In fact, these terms mean much more than that. The terms go beyond our English word 'servant' to indicate a relationship of confidence. People are proud to be *feto ra* and *klosan* of their masters.

The area where *uma* Marii Lia (House 5), *uma* Tabutak (House 6) and *uma* Manekin (House 7) are situated is called *le'un* Tatinis Lolon (*le'un* at the edge of the river). The name of this *le'un* is claimed to be taken from a *tafatik* in the hamlet of Laran Ain Tasi. The guardians of House 5 (Ho'ar Nahak and Na'i Bo'uk) trace their origin to this hamlet (Laran Ain Tasi). Guardians of Houses 6 and 7 have left Laran and therefore people only count this *le'un* as consisting of one named house (House 5). In the hamlet of Laran, House 5 functions as the last gate that links Laran as a space for humans and Ai Lotuk Laran as an ancestral space. Once this border is crossed, people are already in between the territory of humans and that of the ancestors. Thus *uma* Marii Lia functions as a connecting point. In the annual tribute of homage, for example, when those who deliver the seven cobs of maize are on their way to Ai Lotuk Laran, they cry out as soon as they pass the *uma* Marii Lia.

Tafatik Leko (House 8), *tafatik* Mako'a Rai (House 9) and *uma* Fore Asa (House 9) are located in the *le'un* of Akar Laran. The latter house is called the 'supporting house' (*uma sasi'an tatane*) of the former two sisters' *tafatik*. At present, the office of female guardian of these two *tafatik* are, respectively, in the hands of Theresia Telik Seran, known as Na'i Nis, and Welhelmina Ho'ar Seran, known as Na'i Mea. Whether these two nobles are the rightful guardians of these two most important houses is a delicate matter.

The fourth *le'un* is called Loro Monu (sunset). The most important named house in this *le'un* is *uma* Ai Tou (House 12). Just as *uma* Bei Nufa in the *le'un* Klot serves as the connecting point between hamlets toward the sunrise and the central hamlet of Laran, *uma* Ai Tou is the connecting point between hamlets toward the sunset and the central hamlet of Laran. The hamlets toward the sunset include the four hamlets within the present village of Kateri and other peripheral hamlets.

In fact, the positions of House 2 and House 12 as connecting points between hamlets toward the sunrise and toward the sunset emphasises the hamlet of Laran as a central hamlet. In Figure 8.2, I depict the centrality of the hamlets of Laran by illustrating the passing of a rope of command, called *kbabukar*, from the centre to the periphery.

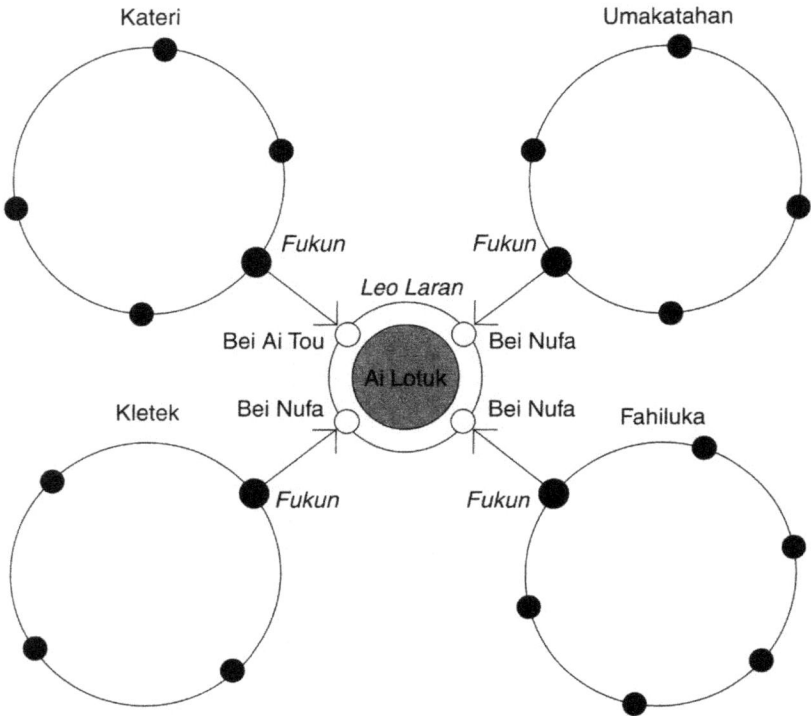

Figure 4.6: Spatial orientation of the inner Wehali—the 'four-corner land'

In regard to the territorial alliances discussed in this chapter, Figure 4.6 helps us to depict schematically the central location of the hamlet of Laran within the organisation of hamlets in this 'four-corner land'.

From the Laran point of view, the four hamlets depicted in Figure 4.6 are cultivation space: the people of these four hamlets are children who till gardens in order to feed 'the one who eats reclining, drinks reclining' (*mahaa toba*/*mahemu toba*) in the centre. But as one moves outward to the hamlet level, it is the *fukun bot* who is the reclining one. They are surrounded by *fukun* as their workers. In turn the *fukun* also becomes the reclining one, surrounded by the 'old women' (*ferik*) and 'old men' (*katuas*) of each named house. At the 'house' level, it is the *ferik* and *katuas* who are the reclining parents, while members of the lineage are the cultivators. The names of the four-plus-one hamlets and their *fukun bot* that are conceptually regarded as surrounding the central hamlet of Laran, are provided in Table 4.4. Every *fukun bot* is identified by the name of his house. Therefore in the column for Fukun there is a list of named houses.

Table 4.4: Assembly of the four *ferik*, four *katuas*

Village (*Desa*)	Hamlet (*Leo*)	Clan head (*Fukun Bot*)
Umakatahan	Umakatahan	Uma Katuas
	Batane	Uma Katuas
	Brama	Uma Mamulak
	Tabene	Uma Kliduk
		Uma Marii Lia
Kateri	Kateri	Uma Bei Rai
		Uma Bei Tema
		Uma La'e Tua Klolok
	Umasukaer	Uma Hanematan Babenik
	Bi'uduk	Uma Foho Bot Manas
Kletek	Kletek	Uma Lo'o
		Uma Mamulak
		Uma Katuas
	Wedare	Uma Lo'o Aknotak
Fahiluka	Fahiluka	Uma Bei Tou
		Uma Mamulak
		Uma Ferik Katuas
	Lo'osina	Uma Katuas
	Natra'en	Uma Katuas
	Manumuti	Uma Katuas

Concluding Remarks

In this chapter I have attempted to show the consistent application in Wehali of notions of centre and periphery from the cosmological level down to the level of the house within a hamlet. Along this continuum, I also pointed out the different patterns of relations based on diverse criteria constitutive of precedence at each level of social organisation. Among other things, these patterns are based on the various oral traditions on which my analysis drew, especially in respect of relations between domains. Within a domain, the higher order origin groups, such as the four hamlets discussed in relation to Kamanasa acknowledge a particular ancestral house as representing their founder. Similarly, at the lower level, members of named houses all acknowledge a particular sacred house as that of a founding ancestor of the hamlet. Yet the pattern of relations among hamlets within a higher order origin group and the pattern of relations among named houses within a hamlet are subject to different characterisations of precedence. The former (within the group of related hamlets) is based on parent–child criteria of precedence, while the latter (within a hamlet) is expressed in terms of elder–younger sibling relations of precedence.

The same pattern of relations prevails also among the higher order origin group of 'the four-corner land'. However, there is a significant difference between Kamanasa, an outer Wehali origin group, and 'the four-corner land', an inner Wehali origin group.

The Kamanasa trace their origin to a genitor named Liurai Suri Nurak. This genitor structure has its implications in the organisation of the hamlets within the higher order origin group. Within this structure, the hamlets of Fatisin and Manliman are the male hamlets. In the generational categories, the central hamlets are the 'parents' while the peripheral hamlets are the 'sons'. In comparison, members of the higher order origin group of 'the four-corner land' trace their origin to the genetrix Ho'ar Na'i Haholek. The genetrix structure of this origin group permits the division of peripheral hamlets into male and female gender. So the hamlets of Kateri and Umakatahan are categorically female while the hamlets of Kletek and Fahiluka are categorically male. If we pursue this further, there is a tendency to feminise gender. Therefore, although in the higher order a *fukun* that represents a hamlet is categorically male, at the hamlet level the *fukun bot* is categorically female, surrounded by male and female *fukun* in the *le'un* level. The changing of cultivation to dwelling space, transforming working categories to reclining categories aligns with this changing of gender.

5

Marriage and Alliance

Introduction

Any discussion of marriage and alliance in Wehali involves at least three topics: (1) the type of marriage, (2) the issue of bridewealth and (3) the nature of marriage arrangements. These three areas are important components within what is termed *adat sabete saladi* (literally, 'the custom of sitting cross-legged'). The Wehali claim that there are marked differences between the plains Tetun of the southern region and the hill Tetun of the northern region in terms of their *adat*. Ask a south Tetun the difference between *adat* of the hill and *adat* of the plains people and he or she will explain that the south Tetun 'eat while sitting, drink while sitting' (*mahaa tur//mahemu tur*); while their hills neighbours 'eat while standing, drink while standing' (*mahaa rik//mahemu rik*).

This chapter elaborates on the distinguishing features of the *adat sabete saladi* of the south Tetun. Rai Dais, a former head of the district of Malaka Barat, in an attempt to describe the distinctiveness of this *adat sebete saladi*, draws an analogy between the expression used to denote what constitutes an *adat sabete saladi* (namely, 'eat while sitting, drink while sitting') and the cultural title given to the Maromak Oan, the central authority of Wehali who 'eats reclining, drinks reclining' (*mahaa toba/ / mahemu toba*). Although Rai Dais does not explore the nature of this analogy, both *adat sabete saladi* and the political structure in Wehali reveal a common 'female focus' within south Tetun culture.

Concerning the ideology of marriage, reports by government officials and accounts by Belunese students describe marriage in Wehali as *kawen tama* (literally, 'entering marriage'), although this expression may be a literal translation from the Indonesian *kawin masuk*, the expression according to the Wehali, suggesting a rule of uxorilocal post-marital residence—that is, the man leaves his natal place after marriage and resides in his wife's house. This *adat sabete saladi*, as they phrase it, stands in contrast to the hills Tetun-speakers, whose post-marital residence is virilocal.

Another difference stressed by the Wehali is the ideology of bridewealth. The Wehali make clear in various levels of discussion that they do not recognise bridewealth. Some of them proudly and philosophically argue that in any practice of bridewealth payments, women are degraded and treated as objects. 'We place a high value on women, so we do not ask for bridewealth' claim most Wehali elders. Other people express a different view by saying that marriage in Wehali is as easy as buying betel-nut: 'Once you have betel-nut to offer, the woman is yours.' Of course both these versions are exaggerated accounts in order to praise or criticise the Wehali system of marriage. Whatever their differential assessments, these expressions reveal that for marriage in Wehali the exchange of bridewealth is not significant. Rather, what is important in this system of marriage is the exchange of a man for a woman. So, in giving a man to take up residence in his wife's house, the man's house expects a woman, entitled *mata musan* (literally, 'source seed'), to be planted in their own house in the next generation. The alliance between these two houses is not completed by this exchange of a man for a woman who is metaphorically symbolised as 'seed', because in the following generation that woman's house, having sent out a 'seed', expects repayment in the form of another woman returned to them as 'banana head' (*hudi ulun*).

More often, we hear the south Tetun talk about marriage as an alliance between *uma* (houses). The husband refers to his wife's house as *uma tur fatik* (literally, 'the sitting place house'), in the sense that he is only a 'guest' in that house, and to his own natal house as his *uma moris fatik* (literally, 'the birth place house') or *uma hun* ('the origin house'). What is important in marriage for the south Tetun is that it establishes alliances that can guarantee the perpetuation of the kinship group—that is, the house and the conglomeration of houses that share the same original sacred ancestral house. In Wehali discourse, without female children the kinship group will perish (*ha'i mate*, literally 'the fire will die'). Whereas by retaining women within their natal house, the woman's own kinship group will always have someone 'to light the fire, boil the water' in their house (*nalaka ha'i, hamanas we*). For the man's kinship group, this form of marital alliance guarantees them someone in return 'to light the fire and boil the water' in their own house in the next generation. Given these intentions, one might expect a symmetrical marriage practice in which houses are reciprocally both husband-taking and husband-giving houses to one another. This type of alliance, however, is not widely practised. Yet marriage is regarded as renewing alliances between two houses. By 'renewing' the alliance the Wehali mean perpetuating an already established alliance by repeating the pattern of previous marriages. This continuation of marriage links is called *kadain talin*,[1] which for convenience can be translated as 'chain marriage'.

Marriage Stages

The first step towards marriage in Wehali is when a young couple express to their parents their intention to marry. The marriage is completed in various stages, the final one being the husband residing in his wife's house. The whole process is regulated in *adat* and, therefore, each stage of marriage has its own name or term. According to Wehali descriptions, there are three stages in the arrangement of marriage: (1) 'the front door betel-nut' (*fuik bua oda matan*), (2) 'the verandah prohibition betel leaves' (*fuik badu labis*), and (3) 'the true betel leaves, the true areca nut' (*fuik tebes, bua tebes*).

1. The Front Door Betel-nut (*Fuik bua oda matan*)

The Wehali marriage process is preceded by a period of courtship, which in Tetun is called *hanimak*, meaning literally 'to play around' and 'to stop for a while'. As the term suggests, a young man is free to choose whichever woman he is going to court or to stop there for a while. During the courtship, a man tries to impress a woman by reciting love poems. In response, the woman must compete with the man's skill in chanting poems. If during 'the playing around' they decide that they have met

---

1   The noun *kadain* in north and east Tetun refers to a kind of net sack (cf. Mathijsen 1906: 57; Morris 1984: 93). In Wehali ritual language, the word *kadain* is paired with *tanasak* (a plaited palm leaf sack). So, the parallel of *tanasak talin//kadain talin* puts emphasis on the links that connect the plaited baskets. Marriage alliances established between two houses are portrayed as ropes or chains (*talin*) that connect the two net sacks (*kadain*). Based on this notion, I translated *kadain talin* marriage as 'chain marriage'.

the right person, then the first stage of marriage begins. However, if one of them decides to the contrary, the relationship may end without any sanctions whatsoever. During the courtship period, a woman can receive more than one young man at a time, and the man also can visit a number of women.

Those who initiate the first stage of the marriage process are the woman's parents. After several instances of his courting, the woman's parents ask their daughter the reason for the young man's visits. Learning of his serious intentions they then choose a close relative (usually a woman) to become their mediator (*ai kletek*: literally 'bridge'). Together with the woman's mother, she makes some cake and sends it to the man's parents. The sending of cake(s) indicates to the man's parents that their son has frequented the home ('played around') with the cakesender's daughter.

Now it is the turn of the young man's parents to act. They then choose their own female mediator. For the purpose of mediating between the man's house and the woman's house it is important to choose a mediator who lives in the same hamlet as the woman. The mediator's function is to take some betel leaves and areca nuts to the woman's house. This betel-nut termed *fuik bua oda matan* ('the front door betel-nut'), is put in a pyramid-shaped basket called *hane matan*. When the mediator is taking the betel-nut to the woman's house, she has to hide under her shoulder cloth (*hafu'ut*). The way she carries it mimics the carrying of a baby under one's arm. It is important for the mediator to take this gift in silence and to hide it from others' attention.

Upon arrival at the girl's house, the mediator offers the gift (*sasolok*) to the mother and mentions that it is a small token from the boy's family. This betel-nut is termed 'front door betel-nut' because it symbolises the official coming of the boy to the house. Some informants mention that the betel-nut also symbolises the man himself, who shows his good intentions in courting by sitting on the open platform of the house. This betel-nut is then distributed to the girl's MB (*tua na'i*) and other members of her house group, as a kind of invitation to discuss the formal 'knocking at the door'. In this discussion, the girl's mother's brother acts as spokesman for the girl's house. If the 'formal visit' of the young man is accepted, the betel-nut is then chewed together. However, if the woman's house rejects the idea of the boy coming into their daughter's house, the mediator will return the gift to the boy's parents. Formulation of these messages varies from person to person. Communicating that an official 'knocking at the door' has been accepted is often phrased as follows:

Oa feto no kida ti'an no kfina ti'an	The daughter already has weaving equipment and rolls of thread
soru natene ti'an te'in natene ti'an	(She) knows how to weave and to cook

Having received this message the boy's house will begin to prepare for the second stage of the marriage process.

2. Betel Leaves to Restrict the Verandah (*Fuik badu labis*)

The second stage is called 'platform prohibition betel leaves'. There are also other terms referring to this stage, such as 'prohibition betel leaves' (*fuik horak*), 'to hang up the prohibition' (*tara horak*) or, in ritual language, the 'named betel leaves, the named areca nuts' (*fuik maho naran//bua maho naran*). These terms all indicate the same thing: that the platform of the house used for 'playing around' has been occupied by a particular man. Now the woman is restricted from receiving other male guests.

As in the first stage, the woman's house takes the initiative in the second stage. The woman's mediator (*ai klete*) goes to the man's house to negotiate the appropriate time for them to come and 'lift the prohibition' (*hasa'e horak*). To lift the prohibition, the man's family must prepare certain necessary items: one silver coin (*murak tomak ida*), one woven cloth made of local cotton (*tais lima rasan*), one knife (*tudik*), two bundles of betel leaves (*fuik sasoka rua*), seven times seven dried and sliced areca nuts (*bua klaras butuk hitu*), one and a half metres of white cloth, one bottle of palm gin (*tua botir ida*) and one chicken (*manu ida*). I have been told that these 'gifts' (*sasolok*) imply certain meanings. The silver coin[2] together with the betel-nut, when placed in the family's forbidden pyramid-shaped plaited basket (*hanematan lulik*), informs the ancestors (*bein*) of the woman's house that their child (*bein oan*) has become engaged to marry. The engagement itself is implied in the offering of the woven sarong and the white cloth.

---

2   Vroklage (1953: 141) once saw a silver bracelet given as part of the gifts brought by the man's house. Based on the presumption that bride price or dowry is the mark of difference between the south and the north Tetun, he suggests that by bringing the silver gift, the south Tetun imitated the 'patriarchal' marriage custom of the north.

The palm gin, chicken and knife are used to communicate the message to the entire hamlet that 'the platform already has its occupant' (*labis no na'in ti'an*). What is important in the arrangement of these gifts is that the gifts for the ancestors, the 'dark people' (*ema kukun*), must be separated from the gifts for human beings, the 'bright people' (*ema roman*).

After all the gifts have been presented, the young woman and the young man are considered to have changed status. The young man is no longer an outsider of the house, even though he has not really become one of the insiders. He is in the stage of becoming a son-in-law. In this 'liminal phase', he is referred to as one who is not yet fully a 'new man' (son-in-law) of the house. The Tetun term for the man in this 'in-between stage' is *balu mane foun*, which translated literally means 'half new man'. It should be noted that the phrase *balu mane foun* is used only as a term of reference, particularly when the addressee is not around. Otherwise, he will be referred to simply as 'child' by the woman's parents. The young woman is also referred to as *balu feto foun* (literally, 'half new woman') to indicate that she is not yet fully a true daughter-in-law of the man's house. According to my informants, to address someone directly as 'half new man' or 'half new woman' is insulting. In this transitional phase, the couple have to go through a 'trying out period' called *sasadin*. The future son-in-law is expected to visit his fiancée more often, working in her garden and, most importantly, showing good manners while talking to members of the house. The future daughter-in-law is expected to show her skill in weaving. A gift of a hand-made sarong for the man is a token that she is capable of doing women's jobs. In contrast to the man, she only comes to the man's house on the man's invitation. Even then, she cannot walk alone to her love's house. During harvest, for example, the man's sister will bring her to help with harvesting in the garden. In Wehali, it has become a custom that only a married woman can go alone to her husband's garden.[3]

During the 'trying out' period, if the man decides that this woman is not suited to him, he can ask his family to 'dismiss the prohibition' (*kasu horak*). The gifts given by the man's house at the first stage of marriage will then be returned. The man cannot be 'prosecuted' for his decision not to marry the woman, and the amount of the gifts he brought in will be fully returned. However, if the woman refuses to marry the man because she has

---

3   The Wehali consider their gardens to be wives' domain and the huts (*laen*) in the gardens to be husbands' (*la'en*).

already found a more suitable partner, the woman's house must return all the man's gifts and pay a fine consisting of a woven cloth (not necessarily made of local cotton) to 'cover the shame' caused by the woman. In every fine, it is also necessary to include the offering of palm gin and a chicken or pig, depending on the size of the wrong-doing.

3. The True Betel, True Areca (*Fuik tebes, bua tebes*)

This stage of marriage is considered, particularly by the churches (both Catholic and Protestant), as *nikah adat* (*adat* marriage). In contrast to the first two stages, in this stage the initiative is taken by the man's house. In principle, the gifts offered by the man are the same as those offered during the second stage. Apart from these compulsory gifts, there are also added gifts in terms of money and *taha tur* (literally, weeding equipment). Regarding the 'money', my Wehali friends emphasise that the amount is not important. In contrast to the practice of bridewealth observed among the north Tetun, they phrase the giving of money in the south Tetun regions as 'to respect and to praise the woman' (*hakneter haktaek oa feto*). People only mention that when it comes to 'money' the Wehali recognise the principle of *tama soil/sai seti* (which I gloss as 'easy to put in, but hard to take out'). This phrase implies that whatever the amount of money the man's house decides to give, the woman's house cannot reject or dispute it. The second implication is that once it is offered, it cannot be taken back. Other non-compulsory gifts usually come in the form of horse(s), cow(s) or buffalo(s). These gifts are termed 'weeding equipment' (*taha tur*) because they are considered to be the man's helpers in the field. It should be noted that these non-compulsory gifts must be returned to the man's natal house on his death.

Apart from those gifts, there is still another gift usually brought by the man's house: rice and pigs needed for the feast. These gifts are also mentioned in the formal discussion between the two houses prior to the marriage ceremony. In that discussion, these gifts are termed as 'gifts that accompany the new woman' (*sasolok hohela feto foun*). The context of this phrase can only be understood if we recall that during the 'trying out period', the woman was expected to help the man's house in the field during harvest time. So these gifts of rice and pigs are reckoned as a return for the woman's work. The implication of the designation is that the material things brought by the man's house (whether they are enough for the feast) are not important, but rather that the helping hands of the bride are most valuable. All of the additional gifts are carried in the sacred baskets by young women (*feto ra*) and young men (*klosan*), but gifts to be offered to the ancestors are carried by a married woman, usually the man's MBW (*ina fetok*).

In the process of delivering the gifts, certain rules must be observed. The man's party should not go straight to the woman's house, but should first visit the mediator's house. In regard to the spatial symbolism of the hamlet, this house is referred to as 'the closest house' (*uma kre'is*) of the bridegroom. This house is considered to be a place 'to sit and rest one's sweat' (*uma tur hanawa kosar*) before the bridegroom's party continues its trip to the bride's house. Due to this function, some people refer to the mediator's house as the 'camp site' (*batane*). Those who are in charge of bringing the obligatory gifts (*mama lulik*) must then walk in silence to the woman's house. Neither those who come nor those who wait for them can greet each other. The hostess pretends that no one is entering the house. Members of the house go on sitting and chatting without interruption. Those who come to the house go straight into the house and lay the gifts beside the hearth next to the female post (*kakuluk feto*) of the house. After laying down the gifts they leave and join their party who are waiting in the 'closest house'. The reason for going in silence is that the women in charge of the gifts for the dark people thereby partake of the 'dark' existence, and consequently are categorically 'hot' and 'dangerous'. Human beings who are categorically 'cold' are endangered if they improperly greet or are greeted by these 'dark, hot' beings. Several hours after the dark people (*ema kukun*) are believed to have entered the woman's house, the entire man's party go together to the woman's house. This time the rule of 'silence' is no longer observed. As is the custom in south Tetun generally, the hosts first greet the guests by saying: *'Haman mai ti'an?'* (literally, 'Are you making light your steps here?'). The guests politely respond: *'He'e. Fafudi hein tian?'* ('Yes. Are you waiting while chatting?'). The greeting is followed by exchanging betel-nut and an informal chat.

Meanwhile, the girl's MBW (*ina fetok*) prepares betel leaves and dried areca nuts to be offered to the ancestors. Betel leaves (*fuik*) brought by the man's family are grouped into seven piles. Each pile consists of seven leaves. Three dried, sliced nuts (*bua klaras*) are then laid in the middle of each of these sacred piles. These seven piles of betel-nut are then laid down at the base of the 'male post' (*kakuluk mane*), which is located at the front part of the inner house. Now it is the girl's MB's turn to offer the betel-nut (*sera mama*) to the dark people. The seven piles of betel-nut prepared by the MBW are rearranged to suit the number of sacred baskets and pouches hanging on a male pillar. Each basket represents a female ancestor and each pouch represents a male ancestor. The baskets are called *koba lulik*, while the pouches are called (*kakaluk lulik*). This ritual offering is accompanied by a short plea to the ancestors. In Tetun the action of 'praying' is called *hakro'an hakmasin* (literally, 'to plead and to make oneself salty').[4]

After a meal is served, the young couple are called forward to receive advice (*sadan*) from the elders of the husband-giver's house and the husband-taker's house. Usually this occasion is when the advisers from both parties demonstrate their ability to use dyadic pairs in speech. Advice given to young couples is called *sadan uma kain foun, ha'i kain foun* (literally, 'to make a place for the new stalk of the house, the new hearth of the house'). The aim of the advice is to prepare the young couple for life as a family. In Wehali this aim is referred to as 'to lay betel-nut in the female child's basket and in the male child's pouch' (*hahida bua baa oan feto no oan mane sia kabinan, sia kakaluk*).[5] The common metaphors used (horse and gardener) explicitly refer to men's jobs. The giving of advice starts after the husband-giver's house formally 'hands over' the young man to the husband-taker's house, saying:

Ami tutur ata hasan mamfatik	We present the slave to you the ruler
Hakabit hola	please accept him
Haliku hola	take care of him

---

4   An example of the plea *halon hakmasin bodik uma kain foun ha'i kain foun* (to bow and to salinise for the new house and the new fire) is as follows:

Aa bei sia	Oh ancestors
tua no nurak, ata no na'in	old and young, commoners and nobles
ohin loron funan no klaut sia at halo uma kain ha'i kain	today the flower and the fruit are going to found a new stalk of house, a new stalk of fire
tan nia bee uma ruas tur ti'an, libur ti'an	for that reason the two houses have gathered together
at husu bei sia iha kukun kalan	to ask (you) ancestors in the dark and night
fo mai matak no malirin	send down the raw and the cool
ne'e be dikin bele fo kmurak	so the tips (of the plant) may produce valuables
ma abut fo matak	and roots produce raw things

5   Judging from the two marriage ceremonies that I attended during my stay in Wehali, and from various discussions on this matter, it seems to me that the advice is directed more toward the 'new man' than toward the 'new woman'.

Kabun fuan ran	(your own) foetus blood
Tan nia emi naha na'in ti'an	because he is already your baggage carrier
Emi klaleban na'in ti'an	he is already your baggage taker
Emi batar musan ti'an	he is already your seed of maize
Batar sasuran ti'an	he is already your own maize
Emi renu onan	your own subject
Emi hutun onan	your own people
Emi tota ba	train him
Emi hanorin ba	teach him

Sometimes the bridegroom's father is also asked to give more advice to his son. Here is an example of the advice given by a father to his son and to the girl's family:

Oan mane, ohin loron ha'u hasei ti'an uma kain baa o	Son, today I entrust a household into your hands
ha'u la solok sa ida tuir o	I do not endow you with (material) things
ha'u no tua na'i ama etuk hosi uma ok	your MB from your house and me
hodi kmukit no susar ha'u latan ti'an baa uma feto	our destitution and poverty are known to the female house
oe kmurak ha'u latan ti'an	a valuable whip has been entrusted (to the female house)
nu'u osak kabau rin di'ak, ha'u latan ti'an baa uma feto	a good horse with fine feet has been entrusted to the female house.
Nahuu baa ohin loron hosi uma feto	You, female house. From now on
nu'u kabau di'ak ida, tula naha ba ona	mount your food supplies on this horse's back
tau sela bee tula naha	When it has a saddle, mount them on his back
la tau sela bee, tula naha baa	when it has no saddle, keep raising them on
kotuk kane bee, tula naha	keep mounting the supplies even though it has blisters on its back
la kotuk kane bee, tula naha baa	keep mounting the supplies when it has no blisters

The advice given by the husband-giver's elder is as follows:

Ohin loron ha'u latan kusin latan fareu	Today I entrust you (the wife) the horse saddle and the string cord
Tula naha sa'en naha ba	(You may) ride and load your baggage on
To'un ida be okan ona kmalar moris be okan ona	Whether it is limp or lively, (the horse) is yours
La'o di'ak be fareu ne'e o tone ti'an la'o di'ak ha'i be fareu ne'e o tone ti'an	If it walks well, the string cord is already in your hand. If it walks badly, the string cord is also in your hand
Atu malolo be nia o ona, atu mabit be nia o ona	To make it run slow is your business. To make it run fast is also your business

The advice given by the husband-taker's elder is as follows:

Ohin loron uma ne'e ami latan ona, to'os mos ami latan ona	Today we entrust you the house and the garden
Atu malolo be nia o ona, atu ma-at be nia o ona	Whether to make them good or bad, they are yours
Atu mafou be nia o ona atu mabusik los be nia o ona	Whether to repair it or to leave it (the house) as it is, it is laid in your hand
Atu sesu teni maluan teni be nia o ona	Whether to enlarge or broaden (the garden), it is laid in your hand

Having received their advice, the bridegroom changes status to become the new man (*mane foun*) and the bride becomes the new woman (*feto foun*).[6] The man is no longer referred to as *oan mane* (as in the first and second stages) by his parents-in-law, for he has become *oa la'en* (child husband). His wife's elder brother will call him *meo*, which literally means 'hero', because by his marrying in, he (the new man) has conceptually forced the brother to leave the house. So, the new man is also referred to as 'man who enters the house' (*mane maktama uma*) while the wife's brothers are referred to as 'men who leave the house' (*mane maksai uma*).

---

6   Unlike virilocal societies where a bride is expected to cry because she has to leave her house and live with her husband, in the marriages that I attended in south Tetun, it was the bridegroom who cried bitterly after receiving advice from both his own MB and his wife's MB, not only because he had to leave his natal house but because in his wife's house he is symbolised as a horse. Another marriage advice session that I recorded dramatically describes how being a horse to his wife's house, the husband has to carry burdens without complaining, even if his back has been wounded because of those burdens.

If during married life there is conflict between husband and wife, it is the task of the MB and FZH of both sides to settle the dispute. The meeting to settle the dispute is called *hamanas hikar ukun badu* (to re-heat the *adat* law). The conflict makes the *adat* law become inactive and cool. 'To re-heat the law', the couple must prepare *tua* (palm juice) and *etu* (food) to be served during the meeting with their elders. The amount of *tua* and *etu* needed depends on the level of the meeting.[7] Many couples whom I interviewed explained that if there is a dispute between them, they always 'lose' and the *tua na'i, ama etuk* (the term for MB and FZH) always 'win' because they have been served with *tua* and *etu*. They also explained that their parents always remind them to maintain a good married life if they do not want *their tua na'i, ama etuk* to eat their 'sweat'. However, the MB and FZH claim their right to eat and drink. One elder in the village of Kamanasa jokingly asked, 'What is the name for, if they do not eat pig's head and drink palm gin?' Perhaps based on this custom of 'eating' and 'drinking' when settling a dispute, the term of reference *tua na'i* for MB and FZH has been extended to become *tua na'i ama etuk*.[8]

The purpose of such a meeting is to settle the marital dispute. However, if the dispute cannot be settled and both sides agree to divorce, then they discuss the possibility of 'lowering the prohibition' (*kasu horak*). Thus the prohibition hung up (*tara horak*) in the second stage of marriage is now lowered. If the wife agrees to divorce because of her husband's wrong-doings, the compulsory gifts and other materials, including the additional gifts called *taha tur* brought by the man's house in the third stage of marriage, cannot be taken back and so the man simply leaves his wife's house empty-handed. In the case where the woman is accused of being unfaithful, and both sides agree to divorce, the woman's house must return all the gifts brought by the man and must pay an amount that the

---

7   If the dispute is settled by MB (*tua na'i*) to reheat the *adat* the couple concerned are obliged to serve those who participated in that meeting with: (1) *tua sangkir ida* (a cup of palm gin), referring to several bottles of palm gin, (2) *kelek ksoik ida* (one chicken drumstick, meaning the couple must prepare either a chicken or a pig, and (3) several bundles of betel leaves and several bunches of areca nuts. If the dispute is settled at the clan head level (*fukun*), the couple concerned are obliged to serve: (1) *tua kusi ida* (one jar of palm gin), (2) *dikur ro'a ida* (a full arm span of buffalo horns) or *nea ksuik ida* (a long boar's tusk) and (3) several bundles of betel leaves and several bunches of areca nuts.

8   The indigenous translation given to this term is 'the lord of palm gin and the father of food', to suit these customs. Linguistically, the lack of the phoneme -*n*, a marker of genitive construction, in the word *na'i* makes the translation 'the lord of the palm gin' misleading. In Tetun the word *tua(n)* also means 'old' and 'respected'. So, the phrase *lia tuan*, for example, means 'an old, highly valued story'. Therefore the kin term *tua na'i* must be translated as 'the most respected person'. The folk interpretation given by the Wehali to articulate the meaning *of tua na'i* has to be treated as an effort to stress the privileged status of the MB and FZH within a house.

man's house feels will compensate for the time and energy that their man spent working to feed the woman's house. Such cases cannot be solved by an overnight meeting.[9]

Idiom and Mediation

The Tetun have no specific term for 'marriage'. The most common words used to describe marriage are *kawen*,[10] *hola malu* (*hola* = to take; *malu* = to reciprocate) and *tur* (to sit). These words are used mainly in daily conversations. But the language used in origin myths, folklore and the poetry of the region relies on the 'betel-chewing' idiom to refer to marriage as well as sexual intercourse.[11] One origin myth (see Reference Text 2) narrates that a man who lived in the world above asked the only woman who lived in the world below to stretch out her hands in order to receive 'betel quids' (*kmusan*) sent down to the earth. At that time she could not catch the *kmusan* sent down to her because there was no dry place for her to rest her feet. The *kmusan* thus fell into the sea and turned into a *knase* (mullet) fish. Another myth regarding the origin of food narrates that the first seed of sorghum was derived from the head of the *knase* fish. It is important in this regard to understand the play on the similar sound of the words *kmusan* (betel quids) and *musan* (seed). Thus, using a word with almost the same sound can suggest a different meaning, as when this myth goes on to narrate that a man from *loro leten* (the sun above) came and 'threw the *kmusan*' to a princess in Wehali with the result that she became pregnant. In this part of the story, the *kmusan* that is mentioned explicitly can also be understood implicitly as a metaphor for male sperm.[12]

The use of betel-nut or betel-chewing language as an idiom is also prominent in Wehali descriptions of the stages of marriage. The betel-nut given by the man during his courtship period is referred to as 'the

---

9   During my stay in Wehali there was no opportunity to attend this sort of meeting. So, my description of divorce is based solely on informants' accounts.

10   According to Wurm and Wilson, the word *kawen* pro ably originated from the ProtoPolynesian *qa(a)wana* meaning 'marriage' (cf. 1975: 128).

11   The 'Betel-chewing traditions in South-East Asia' explored by Rooney (1993) show a variety of practices and symbols manifested in the offering of betel-nut.

12   Hicks mentions that the Tetun of East Timor used the same word (*kuda*) to translate the verbs 'to plant' and 'to copulate'. In Wehali it carries only one meaning: 'to plant'. However, the word most commonly used in Wehali to indicate the meaning of 'to plant' is *taman*, which is probably a corruption or a metathesis from the Indonesian *tanam*.

empty (literally, 'gap') betel leaves, the empty areca nut' (*fuik let// bua let*). The Tetun word *let* (empty) can also be translated as 'gap' or 'space'. Thus gaps between bamboo slats laid down as flooring in the Wehali house are termed *let*. In ritual language the idea of 'gap' (*let*) is always paired with 'raw' (*matak*). So the pairing of 'gap' and 'raw' in ritual language to mean stranger (e.g. *ema matak no let* = the raw and gap people, means 'stranger') provides another clue to translating this stage of marriage as the strange, unmarked betel-nut. In the second stage, the betel-nut offered has changed status from being unmarked to marked. In this stage of marriage the betel-nut is referred to as 'named betel leaves, named areca nuts' (*fuik maho naran, bua maho naran*). In the last stage of the marriage process, the marked betel-nut becomes 'true betel leaves, true areca nuts' (*fuik tebes, bua tebes*).

The changing status of the betel-nut reveals the shifting status of the couple expressed in the changes in the terms used. In the initial stage of the marriage process, both members of the couple are still regarded as 'children' and therefore they are called *oan mane* (male child) and *oan feto* (female child). In the next stage they are no longer 'children', but have become adults. Adulthood, in many societies and in Wehali as well, is associated with marriage. For the young couple, who have become 'engaged' and are waiting to be married, the appropriate terms of reference for the young woman and young man respectively are *balu feto foun* (literally, 'half new woman') and *balu mane foun* (literally, 'half new man'). In the final stage of the marriage process, their status is raised to become 'new man' (*mane foun*) and 'new woman' (*feto foun*) respectively. These changes in status at each stage of the marriage process also bring changes to rules, restrictions and prohibitions that must be observed by the couple.

In this way the marriage rituals and arrangements serve as a gradual process in shaping a young woman and a young man to become mature adults. In Wehali, the concept of 'adulthood' refers to the married status of a person. The analogy of a 'journey' is common in Wehali culture, and the three stages of marriage also delineate a journey of people from childhood to adulthood. Table 5.1 summarises the three stages of marriage by highlighting components whose qualities are transformed from unmarked status to marked status, from a raw and unshaped condition to a shaped condition, and from the stage of childhood to adulthood.

Table 5.1: The stages in the marriage process in Wehali

Component elements	Transformative stages of marriage		
	I	II	III
Betel-nut offered	Empty (gap) betel-nut	named betel-nut	true betel-nut
Couple's status	child	half man/half woman	man/woman
Initiating house	woman's	woman's	man's
Gifts from man and man's house	betel-nut for the woman	betel-nut for the woman's house	betel-nut for the 'dark' and 'bright' people
Gifts from woman and woman's house	betel leaves for the man	none	male sarong (tais mane) for the man
Prohibitions	none	mainly concerning the woman	concern both sides

The critical stage is the second stage of marriage. In this stage, the young man is no longer a lad but neither is he an adult. He is regarded as *balu mane foun* by his potential wife-giver's house. In the same way the woman is considered as *balu feto foun* by her potential husband-giver's house. In these circumstances both the woman and the man are restricted from behaviour commonly observed by an unattached young man or woman and even by married couples. Thus, the *balu feto foun* cannot go unaccompanied even when she is invited to attend some sort of ceremony in her man's house. The man has somewhat more freedom than the woman. When he visits the woman's house, the parents (and other members of the house) always find an excuse to go out and stay overnight in the field. The main restriction on them as a couple is that they cannot go alone together to the man's field, since only a married woman should go to her husband's field.

The distinction between 'silence' and 'speaking' observed during the deposition of the gifts also deserves comment. In Wehali, 'speaking' or 'chatting' is regarded as a measure of good behaviour. The Wehali could not imagine life without 'chatting'. Among everyday greetings commonly heard in Wehali is one for responding to a host's greeting in which the guest will say 'Are you chatting (*fafudi*) while waiting?' In one of the origin myths, it is narrated that 'the only woman on earth' went up to the world above to complain of being left alone without anyone to talk to (*fafudi*). Again, in the story of Liurai Suri Nurak, the hero killing all of his enemies is distressed because there was no longer anyone with whom he can talk (*fafudi an*). However, for certain periods during particular rituals, this talkative society is obliged to observe silent moments. For example, those who bring the gifts to the ancestors (referred to as 'the dark gift') during the third stage of marriage must refrain from *fafudi* in order to avoid danger. For the Wehali, 'dark', 'heat', 'danger' and 'silence' belong to the same category and characterise the feeling of sacredness. Therefore in approaching the woman's house, which is regarded as the source of dark and heat, silence must be observed.

The choice of a mediator between houses is significant not only for practical reasons, but especially for symbolic reasons. It is important that the man's mediator's house be located within the same hamlet as the bride. This house is called *uma tur hanawa kosar* ('the house to rest one's sweat'). To avoid the danger that might befall them, the bridegroom's party must not enter the bride's house directly. They have to prepare themselves in the mediator's house before entering the bride's house, which in this circumstance has become the house of heat and dark.[13] These houses have become the border and liminal space between the outside world of men and the inside world of women. By marriage, a man who is delineated as occupying the peripheral realm is brought into the centre world of women through this 'liminal' house.

The Perpetuation of Alliance

In Wehali one often hears people speak about a form of marriage called *kadain talin*. This phrase is frequently paired with *tanasak talin*. Thus, the dyadic set for this form of marriage is *tanasak talin//kadain talin*. *Tanasak* is a general term for plaited palm-leaf baskets for storing goods, particularly food. Due to its small size, a *tanasak* is usually carried by women on their heads. *Kadain* is a large netbag used for carrying goods, particularly by men. *Talin* literally means 'rope', 'cord' or 'string'. Thus, the terms *tanasak* and *kadain* refer to baskets for storing goods, *tanasak* being associated with women and *kadain* being associated with men. However, when the word *talin* is added, it refers to two or three baskets that have been linked together by cord chains. These baskets are hung above the hearth and are used as a place to store cooked food. These storage baskets provide the Wehali with their imagery for marriage alliances. If two houses contract

---

13 The function of this 'mediating' house can be compared to the function of the mediating house in the hamlet of Fatisin.

a marriage more than once, these houses become linked by a 'cord' just like the *tanasak talin//kadain talin*. The first marriage alliance that takes place between two houses is regarded as having laid down *tanasak* and *kadain*. The second marriage is regarded as linking the first *tanasak* and *kadain* to the second *tanasak* and *kadain*. With this metaphor, the Wehali claim that the alliance between the two houses that was established by the first marriage is perpetuated by the second marriage. The perpetuation of alliance between two houses is expressed as follows:

Ita uma rua nuu tanasak talin kadain talin	These two houses are like those baskets
mate keta la kotu kadain talin	even death cannot set us apart
ita uma rua nuu lilin fui mutu	these two houses are like wax
kamadadak fui mutu lilin fui mutu	that has been melted together to form a wax candle

To elaborate on this practice for the 'perpetuation of alliance', I base the following discussion on genealogical data from the house of Leko (*uma* Leko), in the hamlet of Laran (*leo* Laran) (see Figure 5.1).

There are three noble houses in this hamlet. The first house is *tafatik* Leko,[14] the house of the Maromak Oan. My informants said that when a Maromak Oan is appointed, he will reside (*tur*) in this house. This implies that a Maromak Oan is chosen among those who reside in this house as a new man. The second house is called *tafatik* Mako'a Rai (literally, the one who 'cuts' the matters of the land). This is a house where matters pertaining to *adat* are discussed. The third house is called *uma* Marii Lia. During an *adat* ritual, Wehali nobles must call on this house before proceeding to the most sacred house in the realm of Wehali, called Ai Lotuk (literally, the slender tree), because the guardians of *uma* Marii Lia are considered the gatekeepers for this sacred house.

The founder of the house of Leko was a woman from Insana in the Dawan-speaking region. She was called Na'i Us Bano of 'the respected Insana' (Insana *tuan*). She married a man from the Makbalin house (*uma* Makbalin) in the domain of Haitimuk called Lesu Berek (others called him Seran Berek).

14　The term *tafatik* derives from two words: *tur* = to sit; *fatik* = place. *Tafatik* may then be glossed as 'palace'.

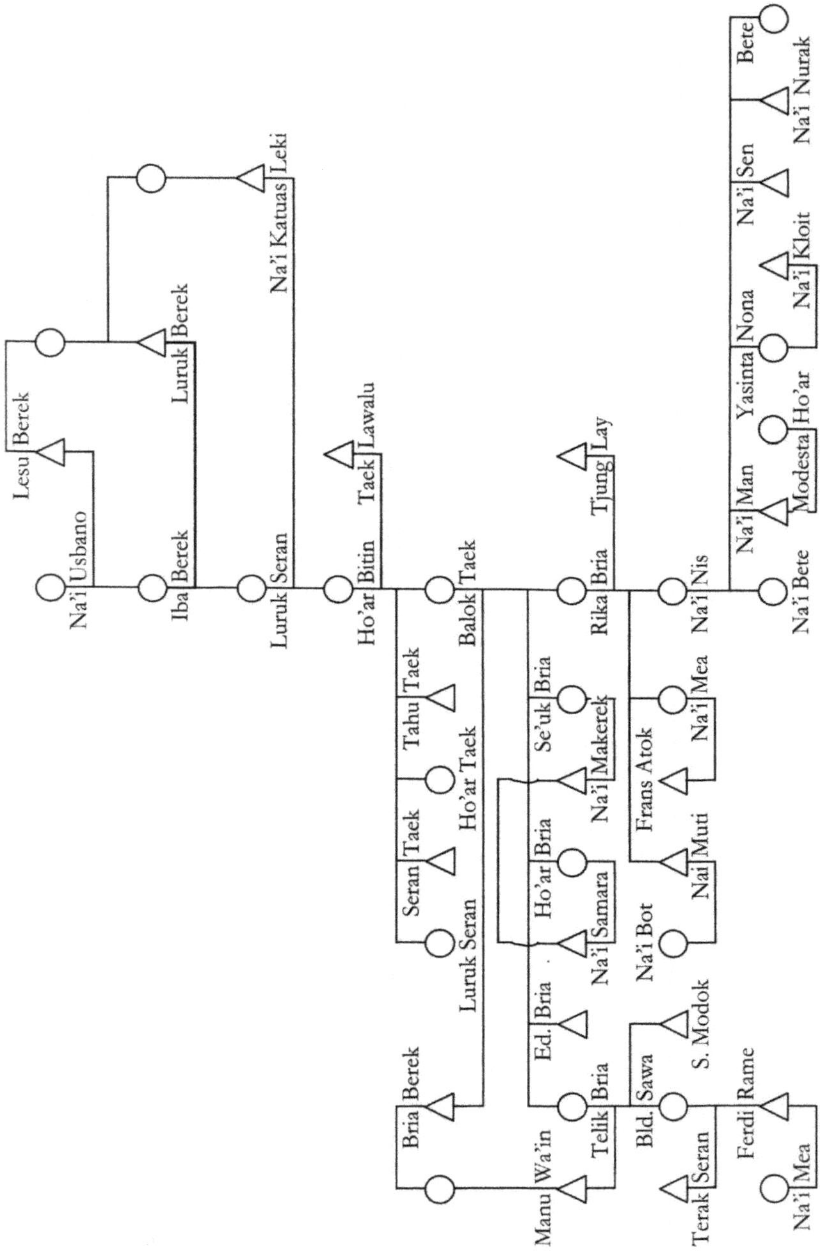

Figure 5.1: Genealogy of the house of Leko (*tafatik* Leko)

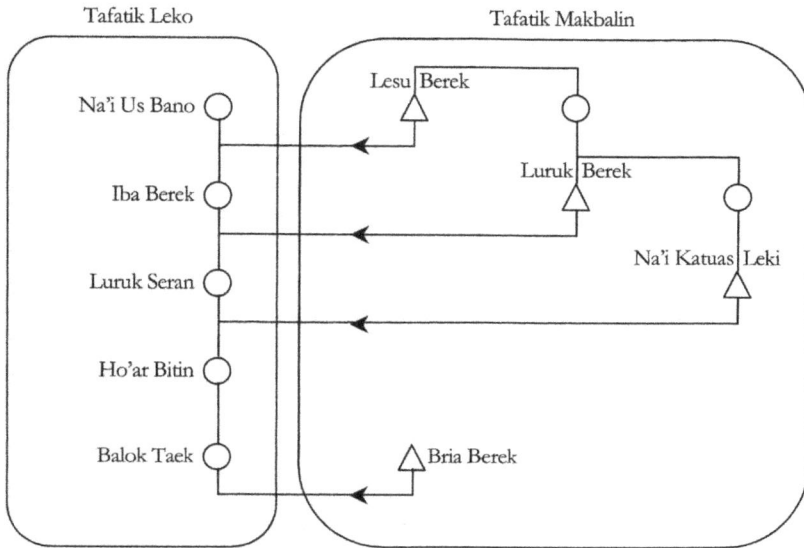

Figure 5.2: Marriage alliance (Leko and Makbalin)

So, from the beginning, the house of Leko in the hamlet of Laran was founded by people from outside Wehali: a woman from Insana and a man from Haitimuk. A daughter of Na'i Us Bano (Iba Berek) married her father's sister's son from the Makbalin house called Luruk Berek. Following the path of his mother's brother, Na'i Katuas Leki from the Makbalin house married Luruk Seran, the daughter of Iba Berek. Later Bria Berek, the *loro* of Haitimuk from the same house of Makbalin married the granddaughter of Luruk Seran of *tafatik* Leko. This pattern of marriage, in which a son follows the path of his mother's brother might represent a case of asymmetric alliance between these two houses as illustrated in Figure 5.2.

In this figure, the house of Makbalin represents a husband-giving group, while the house of Leko is the husband-taking group. It should be added that out of five generations of marriages recorded between these two houses, *uma* Makbalin of Haitimuk always provided the men.

Within the asymmetrical scheme just mentioned, genealogical data from the house of Leko also reveals another category of preferential marriage in which a younger brother follows the path of his elder brother (see Figure 5.3).

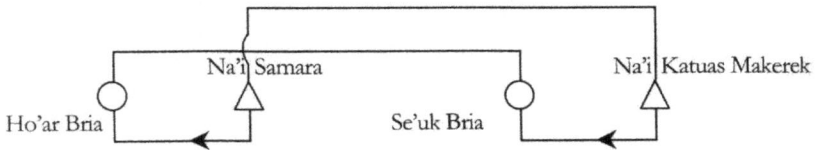

Figure 5.3: Path of brother

In this case, the two brothers Na'i Samara and Na'i Katuas Makerek from *uma* Katuas, in the hamlet of Liurai, Kamanasa, married the two sisters Ho'ar Bria and Se'uk Bria from *uma* Leko. With the marriage of Ho'ar Bria to Na'i Samara, the Katuas house had already laid down their basket (*tanasak*) in the house of Leko. Therefore, the marriage between Se'uk Bria to Na'i Katuas Makerek was no longer considered as the laying down of *tanasak* but rather as linking (*hatalin*) the first *tanasak* brought in the first marriage to the second *tanasak* brought in the later marriage. The purpose of linking the *tanasak* is to perpetuate the alliance between these two houses. The *kadain talin* marriage was also established between *uma* Marii Lia and *tafatik* Fehan Laran. Two brothers from Fehan Laran, Taek Manehat Kwa'ik and Taek Manehat Ki'ik, married Bete Kwa'ik and Bete Ki'ik of Marii Lia, respectively.

A third form of *kadain talin* marriage is bilateral cross-cousin marriage, which I mentioned previously in relation to 'giving back a seed' (*mata musan*) between the houses concerned, and discuss this in more detail below.

Giving Back Seed and Returning the Banana Head

While bridewealth is not important in Wehali marriage arrangements, what is significant is the giving back of a 'seed' in the next generation and the returning of a 'banana head' in the following generation. In accordance with Wehali uxorilocal post-marital residence, a husband is obliged to leave his natal house and reside in his wife's house. But the sending out of a man from a house then generates the coming of a woman into the house in the following generation, for the house that receives the man is then obliged to give back a 'seed' to the husband-giving house. This seed is termed *mata musan*. In south Tetun in general, a *mata musan* can be a male or a female. When the *mata musan* has children in his/her father's sister's house, this house is in turn obliged to return the eldest daughter of the *mata musan* to the initial husband-receiving house. This woman is then termed the banana head (*hudi ulun*).

As in most Austronesian languages (Wurm and Wilson 1975: 71), the word *mata(n)* has several meanings in Tetun. Hicks has listed its meanings as: eye, any eyelike feature, focus, centre, orifice, spring, origin and source (Hicks 1978: 199; cf. Barnes 1977: 300–317). The word *musan* literally means 'seed'.[15] This phrase *mata musan* is translated by Francillon as 'the pupil of the eye' (1967: 351) in the sense of a substitute for the father. Certainly, the Tetun phrase *mata musan* can be translated into Indonesian as *biji mata*, which means the '(father's) beloved'. However, to translate the phrase *mata musan* in this way distorts the botanical idiom communicated in the Tetun expression. In an effort to capture all the nuances of its expression in English, I prefer to translate it as 'source seed'. This translation accommodates the notion of a house exchanging a brother, expressed in botanical idioms as a process of exchanging 'betel-quids' (*kmusan*).

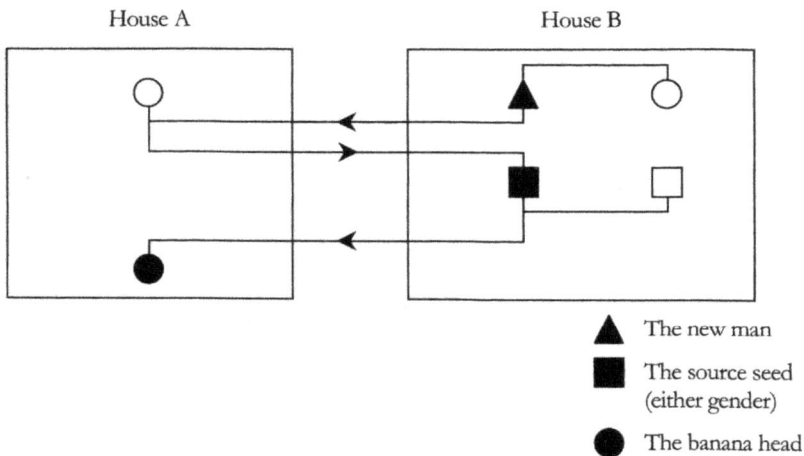

Figure 5.4: Giving back seed and returning the banana head

---

15   Francillon mentions that the word musan is also a euphemism for the 'clitoris' (1967: 433). Unfortunately, various people in Wehali whom I interviewed could not verify this second meaning.

Compared with the term *mata musan*, the term *hudi ulun* does not present such difficulties in translation because it can be rendered literally as the 'banana head'. The schematic Figure 5.4 illustrates the alliance between two houses based on a single marriage.

Here houses, rather than individuals, are the basic contracting units. In Figure 5.4, Houses A and B have engaged in a marriage contract. House B supplies House A with a man. Using the conventional metaphors, this man is symbolised as 'betel-quids' (*kmusan*). As a *kmusan*, he is expected to fertilise House A by marrying a woman of that house, so that she can produce offspring. When House A is fecund enough, the wife's kin give back a child from their house to the husband's natal House B. I have been informed that according to *adat*, in respect of a marriage between people of different clans that have not intermarried previously, the *mata musan* must be appointed from the middle or most often the youngest child. In the case where previous marriages have already occurred between two houses within the same clan, theoretically all children (married and unmarried, male and female) are potential candidates for selection as *mata musan*. However, in order to avoid future difficulties that would arise through choosing an already married person, the husband's kin generally prefer an unmarried *mata musan*. Considering also that a *mata musan* is expected to ensure the continual existence of the recipient house, the husband's natal house prefer to receive a female *mata musan*. In the case where only one daughter has been born into the family and therefore the wife's kin are reluctant to give her up, then the husband's natal house can negotiate with his wife's house to postpone the sending of *mata musan* until this girl marries and has children herself. But what usually happens in the negotiation(s) is that House A tries to keep the female child in their own house and to persuade House B to take a male child instead. The person that has been appointed, or to use the Tetun word *marak* (a Dutch loan word), is then transferred to House B. If the *mata musan* is a male, he is expected to marry his *talain feto* (FZD). In the case of a female *mata musan*, she is expected to marry her *talain mane* (FZS). When this *mata musan* has proved to be fecund enough in House B, his/her eldest daughter has to be returned to House A. This eldest daughter is called the banana head (*hudi ulun*). With the returning of the banana head the obligations on both houses in the marriage contract have been fulfilled.

But this schematic procedure seldom happens in practice. The reality is usually more complex simply because there is no obligation for the *mata musan* to marry his/her own cross-cousin, whom he or she has likely earlier treated as a brother or sister. To elaborate on this marriage exchange as it is practised in Wehali, I offer a description of the process of asking for and giving *mata musan* and the returning of *hudi ulun*.

A formal discussion on *mata musan* starts when the sad news of the death of a husband is conveyed to his natal house. A polite way to convey condolences to the husband's kin is to say: 'We come to let you know that your daughter-in-law suffers from fever and headache' (*Ami mai fo hatene ba emi tan oa feto isin manas ulun moras*). This sad news is then conveyed among the man's kin. Together with other members of the hamlet they form a lamentation group. When this lamentation group comes to pay respects to the dead, they do not go straight to the mourning house. They must wait in a 'closest house' (*uma kre'is*) until a candidate for *mata musan* chosen by the wife's kin comes to pick them up. If the chosen *mata musan* is not suitable, the husband's kin will wait until all the deceased's children are presented to them. This process can take days or even weeks, while in the meantime the corpse becomes rotten. In these circumstances the wife's kin usually surrender to the demands of the husband's kin.

When both parties agree on the appointment of a candidate as *mata musan*, then the husband's kin wrap a cloth around the *mata musan*'s body to indicate that he or she has been transferred from his/her mother's house to his/her father's sister's house. The *mata musan* then leads his/her 'new house' to pay respects to the dead.

This custom (that is, the selection of a *mata musan* prior to the burial ceremony) is regarded by the local government and the church as inhumane and a health risk. The local government has issued a regulation that the duration of a wake is limited to three days only. The impact of this new regulation on the practice of giving back the *mata musan* is that it curtails any extension of the pre-burial period. Consequently, agreement on a *mata musan* may be postponed until the burial ceremony is over. This regulation has certainly helped to solve the health risk of concern to authorities, but it effectively prolongs the period of negotiations over the designation of a *mata musan*.

In the past, the woman's house usually surrendered to the demands of the man's house in order to avoid delaying burial. Now, with the appointment of *mata musan* taking place even after the burial, the wife's kin have a better chance of forcing their decision on the husband's kin. In many cases nowadays, the husband's kin might decide to accept the *mata musan* proposed by the wife's kin rather than take the risk of not receiving any. In a case where the husband and wife have no children, then a *mata musan* can be chosen from among the wife's nearest female kin: her sister's daughters or her classificatory sister's daughters. In the absence of maternal nieces, the husband's kin may ask that the property obtained by the couple during their marriage be divided between the two houses. This division of property is called *hafu'ut kabala*. The noun *hafu'ut* derives from the root verb *fu'ut* meaning 'to twist'. It refers to the way a man 'twisted' his upper cloth around his shoulder. Later this verb became a noun meaning a man's shoulder cloth, or in Indonesian, *selendang*. Concerning the word *kabala*, there are two possible meanings: (1) a wrapping cloth used by men (Indonesian: *sarong*) or (2) a loin cloth (Indonesian: *sabuk*). By *hafu'ut kabala* they mean to divide the man's belongings into two halves: one half for the wife's kin and the other half for the husband's kin.

The returning of the 'banana head' (*hudi ulun*) is a less complex matter than the giving of *mata musan*. As a general rule, a *hudi ulun* is chosen from the eldest daughters of the *mata musan*. However, there are also restrictions on who can become a 'banana head'. In the case where there are no previous marriages between the two houses or clans, then a 'banana head' has to be an eldest daughter of the *mata musan*. If the *mata musan* begets only sons, then the *mata musan*'s natal house has to wait until one of these children begets a female child. If the *mata musan* is childless, however, then there is no obligation for the house to return a 'banana head' at all. In the case where there have been previous marriages between the two houses, then a son is also permitted to become a banana head. However, it must be added that to agree on a decision to return a male banana head, the negotiations very often run for quite some period of time.

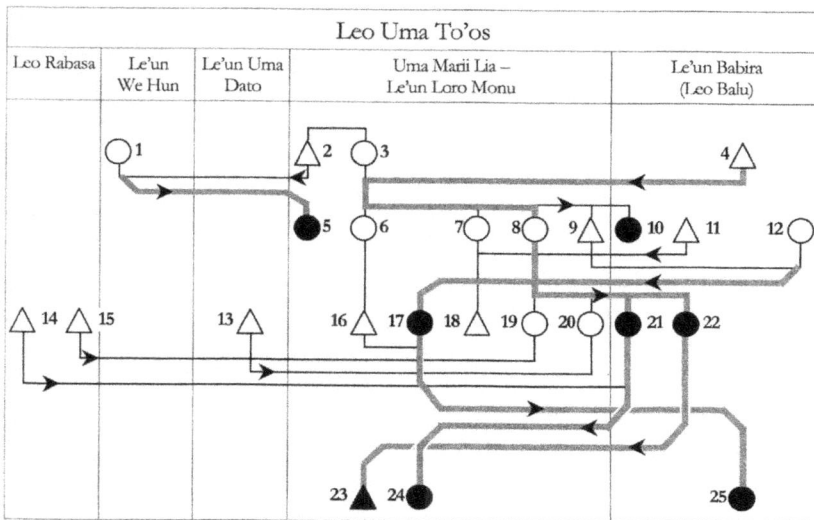

Figure 5.5: Genealogy of the house of Marii Lia

Figure 5.5 illustrates the practices of giving back *mata musan* and returning *hudi ulun* between houses (*uma*) within the same hamlet or clan (*leo*), and between houses of different hamlets or clans (*leo*).[16] The description is based on a named house in the hamlet of Uma To'os (literally, 'the garden house')—that is, Uma Marii Lia.[17]

The hamlet of Uma To'os is divided into five sub-clans (*le'un*[18]), namely *le'un* Babira (Leo Balu), le)un Loro Monu, *le'un* Uma We Hun, *le'un* Uma Dato and *le'un* Uma Klolok. Uma Marii Lia belongs to *le'un* Loro Monu (the sunset *le'un*). The name *marii lia* (literally, to erect words, the house

---

16 Folk etymology relates the Tetun word *leo* to a shady (*leon*) populated place under a tree. Based on this folk etymology, the term *leo* is used to designate a 'settlement' or a 'hamlet'. Those who live under the same shade (*leon*) are members of a name group who are related matrilaterally to the same female ancestor. Therefore, the term *leo* also means 'clan'.

17 In south Tetun, there are two ways of naming a house. In the first, the name of a house follows the name of the male genitor of the house. For example, if the genitor of the house was Bei Kaku the house will be called *uma* Bei Kaku. In the second, the name of a house follows the ceremonial function of the house. So Uma Marii Lia indicates that the function of the house is to settle *adat* matters for the member houses of this origin house; Uma Makbukar denotes its function as mediator between the central named houses and peripheral named houses; Uma Ferik is a place to prepare betel-nut (*halo mama*) to be scarificed for ancestors; Uma Katuas is a place to offer the betel-nut (*sera mama*) to the ancestors.

18 There are various ways of naming a *le'un*. In the hamlet of Uma To'os, the names of its *le'un* are given in accordance with: (1) location: *le'un* Loro Monu means it is located in the eastern part of the hamlet, (2) history of establishment: *le'un* Leo Balu refers to the fact that half of its named houses had moved to another place and had become a separate origin group, and (3) cultural function: *le'un* We Hun denotes that the named houses within this *le'un* are playing roles as female houses of the hamlet.

that has the authority to decide *adat* matters) suggests that this house is ceremonially a male house.[19] Being a male house, men born into this house are potentially heirs to the hamlet head Uma To'os (*fukun*). As shown in Figure 5.5, this house was occupied by Fore Bria (3). She was a female head of the clan, entitled *fukun ferik* (literally, 'old woman *fukun*'). Those born in this house refer to this house as their *uma moris fatik* (the 'birth place house'). Among these people, only women who belong to an *inan bin alin* (literally, mother, elder and younger sisters) group have a right to inherit and become the guardian (*makdakar*) of this ancestral house.

Fore Bria's brother, Leki Bria (2), was her counterpart in the office of clan head, and was entitled *fukun katuas* (literally, 'old man *fukun*') or was referred to simply as *fukun*. He married a woman, Luruk Bei Na'i (1), from the *le'un* of We Hun and therefore he became 'the man that entered the house' (*mane maktama uma*) and was not considered to belong to the house in his wife's *le'un*. In accordance with the rule of post-marital residence, this house was only his 'sitting place house' (*uma tur fatik*). Although he was a clan head within the hamlet, his status as *oan la'en* (daughter's husband) prevented him from holding the title of *katuas* in his wife's house. When he died, the We Hun people sent his daughter to Uma Marii Lia, the natal house of Leki Bria. This girl, Se'u Leki Bria (5), was then called *mata musan*. Fore Bria (3) herself married a man named Tae Lekik (4) from the *le'un* of Babita. They had four daughters and one son. Before Tae Lekik (4) died, the house of Marii Lia managed to send the youngest daughter, Udu Tae Lekik, who was known as Bua Lala (10) to her father's natal house as a *mata musan* in respect of an earlier marriage that had taken place between a man from the *le'un* of Babira and a woman from the *le'un* of Loro Monu. So, Bua Lala (10) was not sent to the *le'un* of Babira to replace her actual father, but rather to replace somebody else there.

When Tae Lekik (4) died, the house of Marii Lia asked the Babira people to postpone the taking of a *mata musan* until the next youngest daughter Udu Tae Lekik, known as Na'i Ki'ik (8),[20] proved to be fecund for their

---

19   The use of 'male house' in this context refers solely to the ritual function of the house concerned. A female house is a place to prepare for offering; a male house is a place where the offering takes place.
20   The Tetun have a naming system in which two sisters or two brothers might share the same name. In Figure 5.3, one name—Udu Tae Lekik—is shared by two people. This name is called *naran mata bian* (ancestral names). To distinguish these two people, they are given another name called *naran babaur* (nickname). So the first Udu Tae Lekik is called Bua Lala, while the second and youngest Udu Tae Lekik is called Na'i Ki'ik.

house. When the time eventually came, the house of Marii Lia sent the youngest daughter of Udu Tae Lekik, named Luruk Bria (22), to replace Udu Tae Lekik's father as a *mata musan* in the *le'un* of Babita. Another of Tae Lekik's daughters, Rika Tae Lekik (7), was married to Tae Nahak Bria (11), a man from the *le'un* of Babira. Even though the genealogical connection between Tae Nahak Bria (11) and Tae Lekik (4) is unknown, the fact that they came from the same *le'un* suffices for the Wehali to categorise them as 'father' and 'son'. So, in their reckonings, two men from the same *le'un* had married into and resided in the house of Marii Lia. At the same time Rika Tae Lekik's (7) brother named Seran Tae Lekik (9) from the house of Marii Lia married a woman, Ho'ar Tae Tetik (12), of the *le'un* of Babira. After this marriage, Seran Tae Lekik (9) was then appointed as the clan head (*fukun*) of the hamlet to replace his MB (Leki Bria).

The fact that three marriages had already occurred between people of the house of Marii Lia and others from a single *le'un* (even without their having definite genealogical ties) is enough for the Wehali to regard these marriages as 'chain marriages' (*kadain talin*). What is important for the people in the Marii Lia house of *le'un* Laro Monu is that those three spouses derive from a single birth place (*le'un* Babira). What binds the three people together is their derivation from the 'place' in which they were born. These three people refer to their natal *le'un* as *le'un moris fatik* (the birth place *le'un*).

When Seran Tae Lekik (9) died, Bano Seran (17) was sent back as a *mata musan* to the house of Marii Lia and eventually married her FZS, Klau Bria (16), who was the male guardian of the Marii Lia house. After the marriage, Klau Bria was appointed to replace his MMB and his MB as the clan head (*fukun*) of the hamlet as well as the head (*fukun*) of the *le'un* Laro Monu. When Klau Bria died, the house of Marii Lia returned Luruk Klau Bria (25) as a banana head (*hudi ulun*) to the *le'un* of Babira. Once the banana head had been returned, the marriage obligations, in terms of the giving back of the seed and the returning of the banana head stemming from the marriage between Seran Tae Lekik (9) and Ho'ar Tae Tetik (12), had been accomplished. Their *mata musan*, Bano Seran Tae Lekik (17), has become the title-holder of the *ferik* (old woman) of the Marii Lia house. As a *ferik*, she is regarded as the female guardian of the house. Coincidentally, the one who acted as the *katuas* (old man) of the house was her husband who was her FZS. Her husband died several years ago, so the office of clan head (*fukun*) as well as the offices of *fukun* in the *le'un* Laro Monu and 'the old man' (*katuas*) in the Marii Lia house was transferred to her sister's son, Seran Tae Nahak (18), the son of Rika Tae Lekik (7). So now, the offices of old man and old woman in the house of Marii Lia are in the hands of Seran Tae Nahak and Bano Seran Tae Lekik.

So far we have been dealing with the marriage of a female mata musan to her FZS. This type of marriage is preferable, but not obligatory. Many *mata musan* that have been living for years with their FZC psychologically treat this 'cross-cousin' as their own 'sibling' and vice versa. In these circumstances, both choose to marry people 'outside' their house. This case is also evident in Figure 5.5. The *mata musan* Ho'ar Tae Nahak (21) married a man, Klau Bria (14), from another hamlet (*leo* Rabasa). With the marriage of Tae Nahak Bria (11) to Udu Tae Lekik (8), and the coming of *mata musan* Ho'ar Tae Nahak into their house, the *le'un* of Babira was obliged to return a banana head to the house of Marii Lia. However, because this *mata musan* Ho'ar Tae Nahak is married to a man who is not her FZS (*talain*), at some time in the future the *le'un* of Babira must give back a *mata musan* to the hamlet of Rabasa, when Ho'ar Tae Nahak's husband dies. The matter becomes even more complicated because there have been no previous marriages between the *le'un* of Babira and the hamlet of Rabasa. Therefore, when it comes to the returning of a banana head, the *le'un* of Babira will definitely insist that the banana head must be chosen from the eldest daughter of their *mata musan*. The same is true for the marriage of Seran Klau of Rabasa (15) to Se'uk Tae Nahak of Marii Lia (19). The house of Marii Lia will insist on having an eldest daughter as their banana head.

Equally important in understanding the matrilineal social organisation of the south Tetun people is a knowledge of the transmission of ritual and political offices. In south Tetun in general, and Wehali in particular, both women and men are entrusted as custodians of named houses. As ritual officers, they are entitled to be called *ferik makaer lulik* (literally, 'the old woman who guards the forbidden objects') and *katuas makaer lulik* (literally, 'the old man who guards the forbidden objects'). For short they are called *ferik* (the old woman) and *katuas* (the old man). In this capacity, as the terms suggest, the safety and continuation of the named house and its sacred objects that symbolise its unity are entrusted to their care. The task of caring for these symbols of unity (house and sacred objects) is transmitted matrilaterally. Due to the prominent status of Uma Marii Lia within the clan of Uma To'os, the offices of ritual leader and clan leader are vested in the same person. As leaders of the clan they are called the male *fukun* (*fukun katuas*) and the female *fukun* (*fukun ferik*).

As a general rule, the office of *ferik* is transmitted through women, that is from mother to daughter. Using Figure 5.5 as an example, this model is represented in the transmission of the title from Fore Bria (3) to her eldest daughter, Udu Tae Lekik (6). A second model is represented in the transmission of office from Udu Tae Lekik (6) to her brother's daughter, Bano Seran (17). Currently, the office of *ferik* within the Marii Lia house is in the hands of Bano Seran. She was charged with the custodianship of her named house simply because she is a *mata musan* to that house. Assuming that she were not a *mata musan*, she would belong to the named house of the *le'un* of Babira and could not receive the *ferik* title in Marii Lia's house. Thus, the title passes through women. However, it can pass through men if the recipient has 'returned' to the natal house of the man concerned. Using these models as guidelines, hypothetically, when the current *ferik* dies, the title could be transmitted in various possible ways. The strongest possibility is that the title for the house will be transferred to Se'u Leki Bria (5), the *mata musan* of Leki Bria (2). Another possibility is that the title will be transferred to Luruk Tae Nahak (19) or her sister (20) the daughters of Se'uk Tae Nahak (8). The third alternative is that the title will go to the banana head (24). If there is no consensus as to whom the title will be entrusted, a shaman (*matdok*) is called upon to perform a spear divination (*afuan*). Like the office of *ferik*, the transmission of the ritual office of *katuas* is also ideally passed through the female line, even though it is held by men. Based on Figure 5.5, this transmission passed to ZS or MZS. Thus, the office of *fukun katuas* held by Leki Bria (2) was not transmitted to his own son but to his matrilineal heir, that is a son of his sister—that is, Seran Tae Lekik (9). When Seran Tae Lekik died, this office was passed to his sister's son, Klau Bria (16). Since Klau Bria did not have a sister, when he died, the office went to his MZS, Seran Tae Nahak (18).

Marriage and Politics

On several occasions I indicated that the Tetun word *tur* meaning 'to sit' is used as an idiom to denote 'marriage'. For example, the sentence *mane aa tur ti'an iha uma nabaa* (the man sits in that house) must be translated as 'the man is married to a woman in that house'. Besides the word *tur*, the Tetun also employ the word *tara kakaluk* ('to hang up the pouch') meaning something similar. These two terms are especially significant in distinguishing a 'legal' wife from an 'illegal' one. When a man marries more than one wife, he 'sits' in one house, but 'hangs up his pouch' in the other house(s). Perhaps the usage of these two expressions originated from the rule of uxorilocal post-marital residence. In marriage a man resides (*tur*) in one house, but he may also 'hang up his pouches' in more than one house. Nowadays, the Tetun Indonesian-speakers translate marriage in terms of *tur* as *kawin syah* (legal marriage) and *tara kakaluk* as *kawin tak syah* (illegal marriage). These translations are relevant only in relation to the transmission of office. According to custom, children from a *tara kakaluk* marriage are not able to hold title as 'old woman' or 'old man' of a named house. But otherwise children from both *tur* and *tara kakaluk* marriages have the same status and any one may be chosen to return 'seed' (*mata musan*) to his or her father's natal house when the latter dies. These terms also do not affect inheritance, given that it is based on matrilateral transmission. But *tur* and *tara kakaluk* marriages are politically significant, because they can determine the validity of a particular person's claim to hold office in a house or clan.

To elaborate on the distinction between *tur* and *tara kakaluk* in the local political sphere, I analyse an *adat* court case dated 9–13 May 1958.[21] This adat court case was chaired by A.A. Bere Tallo, the first regent of Belu, who at that time was acting as Ketua Dewan Pemerintah Daerah Sementara, Swapraja Belu (Chairman, Board of Government for the Interim Territory Swapraja Belu). Present at this meeting were Liurai Malaka (Luis Sanaka Tei Seran), the former Maromak Oan of Wehali (H. Seran Nahak) and seven petty rulers within the realm of Wehali. Each ruler was accompanied by his own *adat* historian (*mako'an*). The purpose of this meeting was, among others, to settle a dispute within the house of Liurai. Edmundus Tei Seran, the ruler of Fatuaruin claimed that his step-grandfather (Luis Sanaka Tei Seran, known as Na'i Bo' uk—see Figure 5.6) was a person who could not inherit the office of Liurai from Edmundus' great-grandparent, Liurai Tei Seran. Edmundus Tei Seran also claimed publicly on several occasions that, according to the custom in Wesei Wehali, he was the rightful Liurai. By 'custom' he meant that the former Liurai *tur* in Edmundus' own house, but *tara kakaluk* in the house of Luis Sanaka.

---

21 I obtained minutes of this meeting from the personal archives of Mr Blasius L. Manek in Atambua.

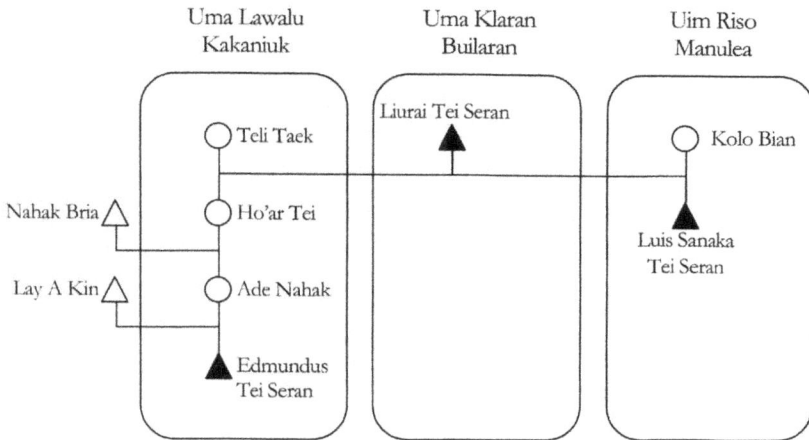

Figure 5.6: Valid and invalid marriage

My discussion of this case here is intended to provide material for, firstly, an understanding of the concept of *tur* and *tara kakaluk* in marriage alliance and, secondly, consideration in the next chapter of how the south Tetun trace their origin.

In order to decide whether Luis Sanaka Tei Seran was the right person for the office of Liurai, *adat* historians (*mako'an*) from both parties were invited to narrate the origin of the two persons concerned. Seran Dasi Bria, the *mako'an* of Wehali, residing in the hamlet of Kletek, commenced his testimony with an origin myth. According to the myth, formerly the land of Timor was governed by two rulers: a man who was categorised as 'female ruler', commonly known as *Liurai feto*, and a 'male ruler' known as *Liurai mane*. Both lived in the hamlet of Laran. The female Liurai lived in a house called 'the high shield' (*knua as*) and the male Liurai lived in the 'low shield' (*knua kraik*). Later, the female Liurai was popularly known as Maromak Oan (literally, 'the small bright one') and the male Liurai was simply known as Liurai. One day people from the domains of Lakekun, Diruma (Dirma), Wewiku and Haitimuk chased the male Liurai away from Laran.[22] The whole house of the male Liurai, including its 'protectors' (Taroi Metan and Taroi Mutin) escaped from Laran to take refuge in Dawan territory. On their way to this destination, they came across Dawan people from the

---

22   The *mako'an* of Wehali from Kletek, Seran Dasi Bria, based his account of how the four peripheral rulers rose in revolt against the central power (*Liurai mane*) on a story concerning two wanderers named Ati and Bere, who were treated badly by the Liurai. The same revolt is also reported by Cunningham based on information given to him by the ruling house of Insana (1962: 59).

domain of Insana. With help from Insana heroes, the Liurai's enemies were driven back. The Liurai house was then built in the hamlet of Builaran. To acknowledge the helping bands of the Insana, the hamlet of Builaran is ritually called 'edge of the gebang palm of Insana, edge of the tuber of Insana' (*akar Insana rohan//maek Insana rohan*). With this nickname, according to the *mako'an*, Insana is considered to have every right to become involved in affairs within the Liurai house.

Not long after their stay in Builaran, people of this hamlet became disappointed with the Liurai's behaviour.[23] Once again the Liurai house was forced to leave the hamlet of Builaran. This time they went up north to Fatubesi in the Dawan domain of Manlea on the border of the regency of Belu. In this domain they built their own houses. One of these houses is called *uim* Riso.[24] It was occupied by Luru Muti Ki'ik, the female ancestor of the future successors to the office of Liurai because a man who married into this house was the first Liurai of Wehali who lived outside Wehali. Therefore, the legitimate Liurai of Wehali can be traced from the origin house—*uim* Riso—in Manlea to the genetrix, Luru Muti Ki'ik.

Luru Muti Ki'ik married the highest ruler of Manlea called Usi Fia Ro. Following a rule of uxorilocal residence, Usi Fia Ro resided in her house. They had three daughters. Kolo Bian married Seran Okneo and lived with her husband in Babotin. Ho'ar Bian lived with her husband in Nintesa (Kusa). The youngest Ae Bian lived in the uim Riso with her husband, Tae Bian of Banhae. Ae Bian gave birth to Usi Fore Tuna, who married Seran Tae, becoming the second wife to the first Liurai of Wehali, entitled Liurai Sasita,[25] which literally means 'Liurai the red calico'. In ritual language he is called Seran Tae *baboto makerek//rui makerek, sui Likusaen//sui Wehali, ro'a Likusaen//ro'a Wehali* (Seran Tae the soft skilful bones, the hard skilful bones, who fought Likusaen with horns, who fought Wehali with horns, who stretched arms to reach Likusaen, who stretched arms to reach Wehali). Kolo Bian gave birth to Dasin Bano Taen, who became the third wife of Liurai Sasita Mean. When the latter died, Usi Fore Tuna married Luis

---

23   According to the myth, the Liurai accused the Builaran people of stealing one of his favourite horses called *ain kalete*.

24   The Manlea are bilingual speakers of both Dawan and Tetun. Schulte Nordholt mentions that half of them speak Tetun and the other half speak Dawan (1971: 240). As a matter of fact, the house built by the Liurai was given a Dawan name—*uim* Riso. *Uem* (pronounced as *uim* by the Tetun) is a metathesis from *ume* meaning 'house'.

25   Sasita is a Portuguese loan word, from *chita*, meaning 'calico', which also gave rise to the Indonesian term *kain cita*.

Ta'olin, the ruler of Insana. Dasi Bano Taen, the third wife of Liurai Sasita Mean had one son, who later replaced his father as Liurai. He was known as Liurai Mane Kmesak (the only son of Liurai). He married seven women. One of these was Abu Lolon. The crucial part in determining the status of Abu Lolon, which created many disputes, is whether Liurai Mane Kmesak actually 'sat' in her house or he simply 'hung up his pouch' there. The present Liurai of Malaka, Luis Sanaka Tei Seran, holds the view, along with many Wehali nobles and other elite in the village, that Abu Lolon was an invalid wife (*tara kakaluk*). As an invalid wife she was known as *maktukun*, literally meaning 'an inedible fruit'. Therefore, any claim to the office of Liurai by members of her house is considered to be invalid.

The point of reckoning to be sought should come from the marriage between Usi Fore Tuna and the Insana ruler, Luis Ta'olin. This marriage produced three daughters and two sons. Kolo Bian lived with her husband in Babotin. Ae Bian lived with her husband Sako Atiut Leu, the ruler of Nunponi. Kahalasi Ta'olin resided with his wife (with the nickname Tai) in the *uma* Klaran in Builaran. The youngest son (Fatin Luis Ta'olin) replaced his father to became the second ruler of Insana in the line of the house of Ta'olin. The youngest daughter, Ho'ar Bian, was returned to Uim Riso to continue this house because her mother lived with her husband in Insana. Ho'ar Bian married Tae Bian from Banhae, her classificatory father's sister's son. Thus, the valid Liurai is traced through the line of Ho'ar Bian. She had one son and three daughters. One of the three daughters, Usi Eno, married Usi Nikin, a Banhae man. She gave birth to Kolo Bian, the third wife of Liurai Tei Seran, the third woman from the house of Riso to marry a Liurai. Liurai Tei Seran's first wife was Kabosu Senu, a commoner from We Tatunu. People regard this marriage as 'hanging up the pouch' and therefore members of her house have no right to the office of Liurai. There is no report of members of the We Tatunu house ever claiming to be a valid successor to the office of Liurai. It can be assumed, then, that the people of Tatunu acknowledge Kabosu Senu as *maktukun*. From this marriage a daughter called Uduk was returned to *uma* Klaran, the natal house of Liurai Tei Seran in Builaran, as *mata musan*. The second wife was Teli Taek of the house of Lawalu, Kakaniuk. The marriage status of the third wife, Kolo Bian, and the second wife, Teli Taek, were the major issues that culminated in the *adat* court case.

To establish whether Kolo Bian or Teli Taek was the valid wife, *adat* historians (*mako'an*) from both parties had to testify as to which one actually 'ascended' (*hasa'e*) to the house of Liurai. With the custom of marriage where a man resides in his wife's house, the Liurai can, in turn, reside in both houses. But when the house of Liurai moved back from Manlea to Builaran, only Kolo Bian, according to these *mako'an*, brought her house's sacred regalia. Following the south Tetun way of arguing, Kolo Bian thus ascended (along with her sacred regalia) to the house of Liurai. In this way, the Liurai is regarded as having conceptually resided in his wife's house.

The three *adat* historians (*mako'an*) from the house of Lawalu, Kakaniuk, could not give a definite answer and evaded the issue by saying that as young *mako'an* they did not know whether or not Teli Taek ascended to the Liurai's house. Mako'an Baria Seran Fahik of Tualaran in the first hearing testified that both Teli Taek and Kolo Bian ascended to the house.[26] However, at the second hearing he changed his mind by saying that only Kolo Bian ascended to the house of Liurai. This testimony that only Kolo Bian was the valid wife of the Liurai supported the claim made by the *mako'an* of Wehali, Seran Dasi Bria, from the hamlet of Kletek and was therefore regarded as conclusive. The implication of this conclusion is that only a member of her house is entitled to the Liurai office. Luis Sanaka Tei Seran listed the sacred regalia that his mother (Kolo Bian) brought from Manlea to Builaran.[27]

---

26   For their historical interest, I must here quote reports written by a Catholic priest, Father Jansen, during his first visit to Wehali in 1892 (Laan 1969: 309–310). At that time, apparently the house of Riso in Manlea had been moved to Builaran. But contrary to the conclusion of the Betun meeting in 1958, Jansen mentioned that he actually visited the Liurai's house in Builaran and was accepted by the Liurai's mother, Teli Taek (Jansen referred to her as Teli Seran). He also mentioned that at that time the young Liurai called Na'i Kin was not home. Since the death of his father Liurai Dominggus, his mother was in charge of the government on behalf of this 10-year-old Liurai. This latter information is rather bizarre since it goes against the political system in Wehali.
27   The sacred regalia cited as brought by Kolo Bian were:
   a. 2 swords (*surik lulik Liurai*).
   b. 1 golden staff (*oe mean*). The name of the original owner of this staff is engraved in its holder: *Don Aleesoe Fernando de Wayhale*.
   c. 1 silver staff.
   d. 1 knife with silver holder (*badi lulik mutin*). This knife was used to divide up the whole of Timor. It is a symbol of the Liurai's power over the Timorese domains. Schulte Nordholt also mentions this knife and its function (1971: 243).
   e. 1 dagger.
   f. 1 bronze betel-nut container, inherited from Liurai Mane Kmesak.
   g. 1 bamboo container inherited from Liurai Tei Seran.
   h. 1 saddle made of Amarasi woven cloth.
Concerning this last item, L.S. Tei Seran explained that the mention of Amarasi cloth is important to prove that Sonba'i, the ruler of the Dawan, originated from the house of Liurai and that he was the younger brother of Liurai. Most of these items were presented to me for inspection by a member of the Abu Lolon house.

The meeting in 1958 came to the conclusion that Kolo Bian was the valid wife and therefore Luis Sanaka Tei Seran was the rightful Liurai. Then, another claim to the office of Liurai was raised by a member of Abu Lolon house (Dominicus Tei Seran—see Figure 5.7). This claim was also based on the *tur* and *tara kakaluk* ideology. It is thus true to say that marriage is a political affair.

The acknowledgment that marriage is a political affair has further implications. As far as alliance between houses is concerned, two forms of alliance are commonly practised. There is, first, asymmetric alliance. The husband-taking house endeavours to maintain its superiority by continuing to provide women for the husband-giving house. There is also symmetric alliance where a house can become both a husband-taking house and husband- giving house at once. The application of these forms of alliance is closely related to the importance and the greatness of a domain in the area. The house of the Liurai has employed both these forms of alliance. In relation to the tiny domains of Manlea and Banhae, the house of Liurai more often plays the superior role by providing women for these domains. However, in relation to the mighty domain of Insana, the house of Liurai provides women for them and, at the same time, takes wives from them.

Concluding Remarks

In this chapter I have attempted to show that the betel-chewing culture common throughout the Southeast Asian region plays a particular role in articulating relations among the Tetun. The concept of *sera mama* (betel-nut offering) reveals that betel-nut served as intermediary between the living and the dead. The various names given to the stages in the arrangement of marriage also reveal that betel-nut is used as a means to establish relations among people. The south Tetun, particularly, measure the degree of a person's good behaviour from his/her conduct in offering betel-nut to others. It is fair to say, therefore, that betel-nut is instrumental in establishing communications not only between the living and the dead, but also among the living themselves. Regarding the latter, sexual relationships between a man and a woman are symbolised by the sending of betel-nut, back and forth, between two individuals and their houses. The importance of betel-nut as an idiom for marriage affects every stage of marriage arrangements, signified by specific names for these betel-nut gifts. The different terms given to the betel-nut gifts indicate the changing stages of marriage and the changing status of the man and woman concerned. What is most significant, however, in the series of marriage stages is that the process of uniting the man and woman in marriage is delineated as a 'path' or 'journey' from the outside man to the inside woman.

The notion of 'path', which is common in many eastern Indonesian societies and in south Tetun in particular is further elaborated in a form of marriage, which the south Tetun call *kadain talin* marriage. Marriage between persons of two houses means establishing a 'path' between these houses. The first path is established when a man resides in his wife's house. The second path occurs when the husband-ta king house returns a 'seed' (*mata musan*) to the man's natal house. This relation is then perpetuated by the sending of a 'banana head' (*hudi ulun*) to the *mata musan*'s house. When it comes to the transmission of offices, the matter becomes even more complicated. In the above discussions I have deliberately chosen two examples: first, from the transmission of office of *fukun* within the hamlet level and, second, from the transmission of office of Liurai, the executive ruler of the domain of Wehali. At the hamlet level, the transmission is through sisters. In the case of the house of Liurai there is a tendency that the transmission is through a man to his own son provided the offspring is from a *tur* marriage. When Liurai Sasita Mean died (see Figure 5.7) he was replaced by his 'adopted' son, Liurai Mane Kmesak. The latter was claimed to be Sasita Mean's sister's son. But when Liurai Tei Seran died he was replaced by his own son, Luis Sanaka Tei Seran. The deviation from the matrilateral transmission of office means that Luis Sanaka Tei Seran is not regarded as Liurai according to custom (Liurai *adat* or Liurai *ukun badu*). He is designated by his opponents only as Liurai promoted by government (Liurai *ukun rai*).

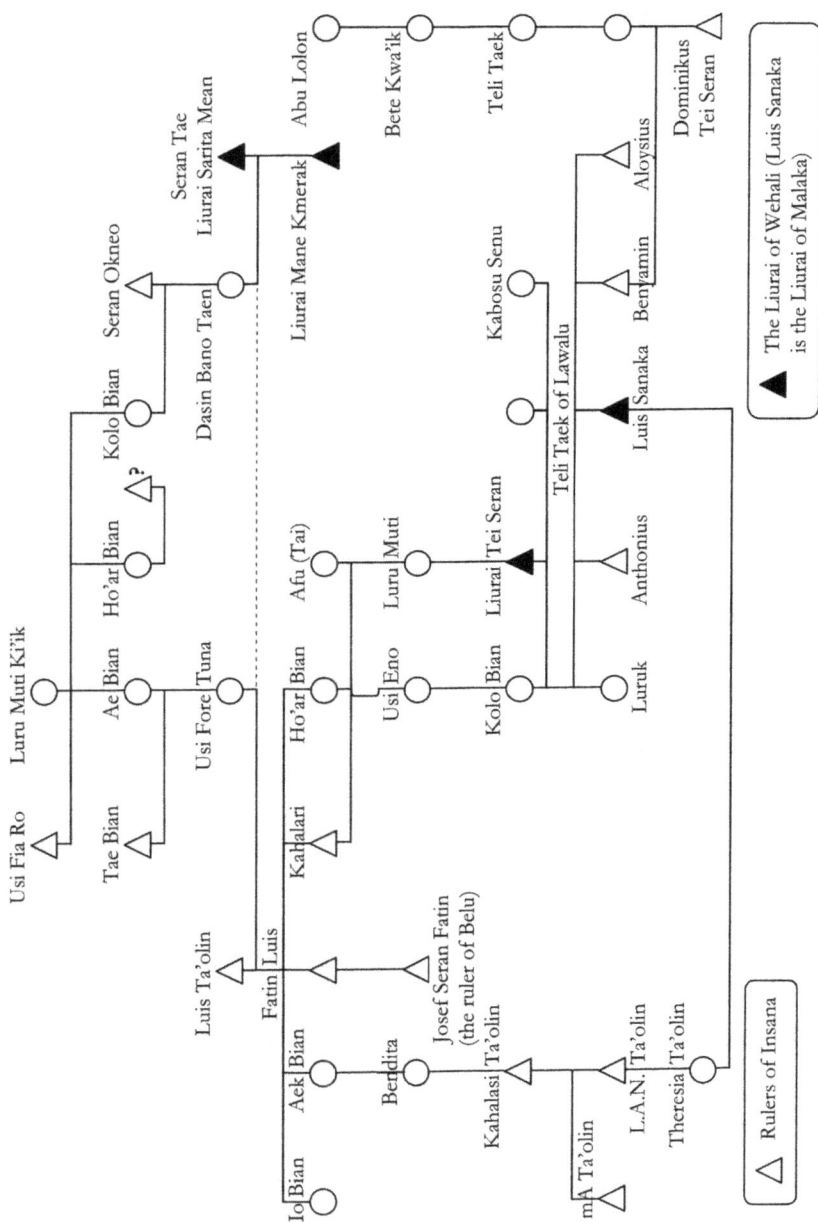

Figure 5.7: Genealogy of the house of Liurai

151

Photograph 1: Agustinus Klau.

A noble from the hamlet of Laran and a claimant to the position of Maromak Oan. Ritually, he holds the position of female ruler, *Liurai feto*.

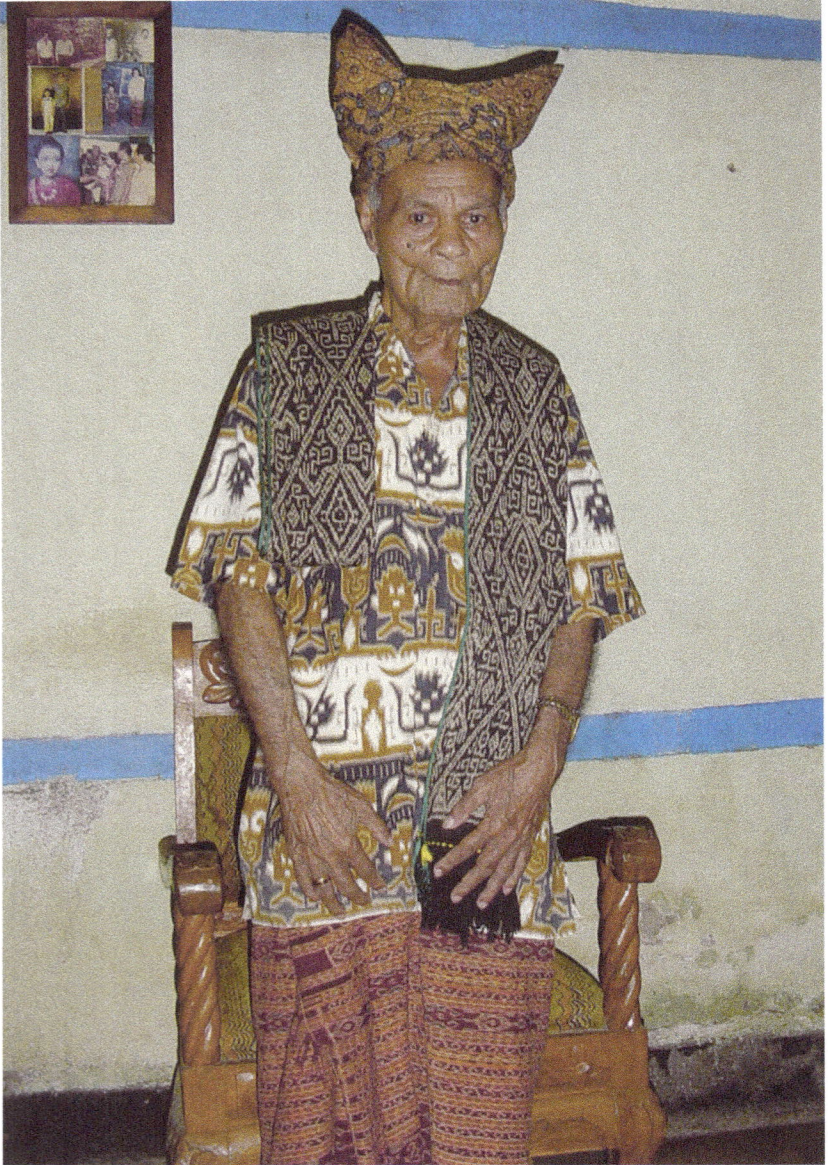

Photograph 2: Luis Sanaka Teiseran holds the position of male ruler, *Liurai mane*.

This picture was taken in July 2003, a week before he passed away.

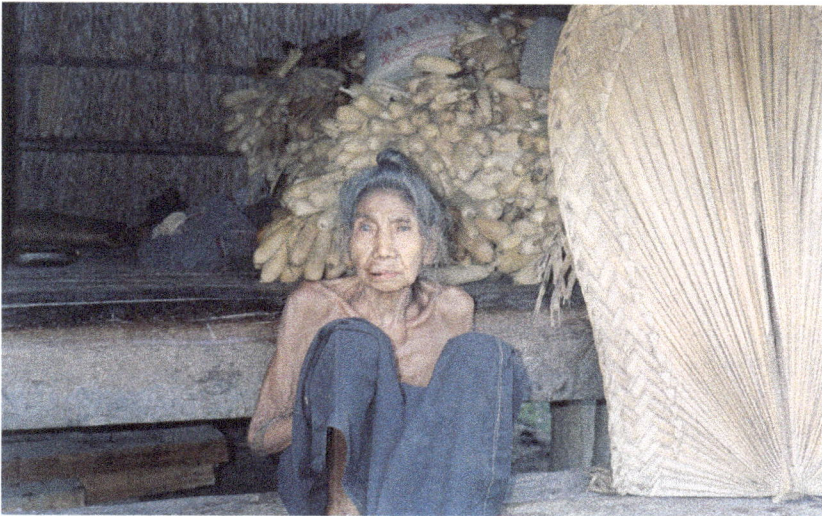

Photograph 3: The woman known as the Ferik Lulik, the 'Forbidden Old Lady', who until her death in 1993 served as the guardian of the Ai Lotuk, the most sacred house in Wehali.

Here she sits on the veranda of her own Uma Lulik.

Photograph 4: Dato Tolus Loro Tolus, the head of the Dirma clan, sits on stones arranged around the great banyan tree in the headhunting compound in Dirma.

Previously enemy heads were hung on the tree's branches as part of the rituals conducted in the compound.

Photograph 5: Men of the hamlet of Leklaran erect a named house.
The two higher posts in the middle are significant. The right one is the 'male post' (*rin mane*) located at the front of the house so that it faces the outside world. The left one is the 'female post' (*rin feto*) located at the back of the house next to the hearth. This post symbolises the women's world. The beam that joins the male and female posts is called *laho dalan* (literally, 'the mouse path'). It represents the protection given by ancestors or 'dark people' (*ema kukun*) to the house dwellers.

Photograph 6: Ai Lotuk, the Origin House of Wehali.
Conceptually this house is also the origin house of all the people of the world.

Photograph 7: These two women are the official guardians of the Origin House, Ai Lotuk. Men are not permitted to enter this house.

Photograph 8: During the maize harvest ceremony people bring offerings of betel-nut and cobs of corn from the new harvest to the burial ground of their immediate families.

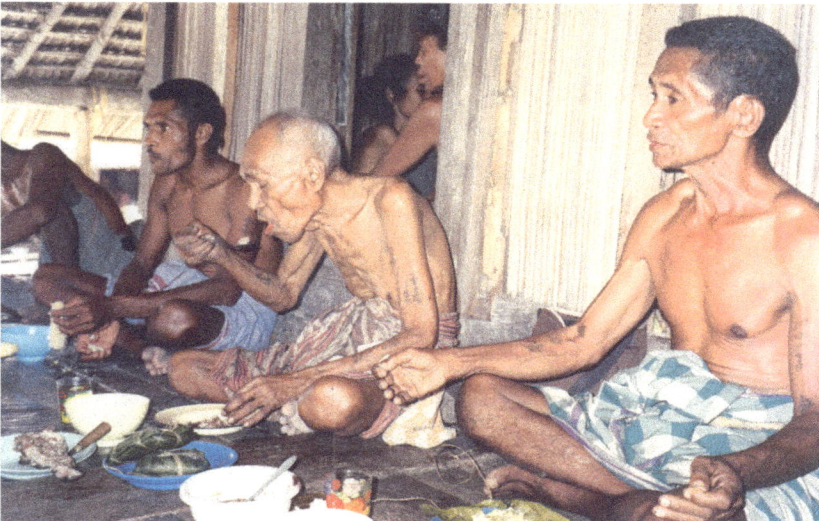

Photograph 9: Eating 'dark food' during the maize harvest ritual.

Photograph 10: Offering betel-nut at a rain ceremony.

Photograph 11: Piet Tahu Nahak, Gabriel Bria and Ferdy Seran.

Photograph 12: Piet Tahu Nahak, Wehali Adat Historian, of the Trunk House of Makaer Lulik.

6

Paths and Borders: Relations of Origin, Consanguinity and Affinity

Introduction

In the preceding chapter I have attempted to show that the notion of 'path' is crucial in understanding south Tetun social relations. The Tetun idiom of marriage as a 'path' is clearly stated in the notion of incest, in which committing incest is understood to be 'walking the wrong path' (*la'o sala dalan*). The idea of a 'path' in turn forms a basis for understanding the south Tetun concept of origin. Between houses, marriage alliances that have been established by a particular ancestor of a named house becomes a 'path' for the later generations.

In this chapter I deal with two related topics: first, how the Wehali conceive of their origins and, second, how people organise their relationships at the house and clan levels.

Relations of Origin

The dispute between the two Tei Seran described in the previous chapter deals with a key issue that turns on the notion of 'origin'. Thus, to settle the dispute, *adat* historians were asked to narrate the origin of the opposed persons. The Tetun word for 'origin' is *hun*. So the *adat* historians were literally asked to reveal the *hun* of Edmundus Tei Seran and Luis Sanaka

Tei Seran.[1] In Tetun, narrating the origin of a clan or a house is phrased as describing 'the path and the track'. With this phrasing, the founding ancestor of a particular clan or house is imagined as having made a lengthy journey, establishing along the way relations with people from other houses and clans. Narrating the origin is meant to reveal the starting point of the journey that led to present conditions, as well as revealing the nature of the relationships established by those ancestors.

The dispute in the Liurai house, then, provides the ideal point of departure for an analysis of what Fox calls 'origin structure' (1988b: 8). It is common for the people to consider that the further a person is from his/her *hun*, the more distant he/she is from the group. These genealogical distances are based on the place of birth of a person. Depending on the purpose of reckoning, a person's origin can be traced to a particular founding ancestor of a named clan or to a named house. These distances are conceived of in three terms—that is, *ten*, *besik* and *uma kain*.

Membership of a person within a named house is distinguished according to whether that person was born from the same 'intestine' (*ten*) or from a different 'intestine'. Those who are born from the same *ten* are regarded as sharing the same blood transferred from their mother. Therefore, marriage among members born of the same *ten* is regarded as incestuous and in south Tetun is called *hakur biti kluni* (literally, 'to cross mat and pillow'). The ideology of 'incest' is also expressed in terms of 'path'. A person who has committed incest is described as one who 'walks the wrong path' (*la'o sala dalan*). With this concept in mind I have translated the phrase *hakur biti kluni* as 'crossing the established path'.

According to the 'path' reckoning, parents refer to their biological children as *oan ten*, while the children refer to their biological father and mother respectively as *aman ten* and *inan ten*. Siblings of both sexes refer to each other as *maun/ bin/ alin ten* (eB/eZ/yB, yZ) by birth. The term *ten* cannot be extended to collateral relations; its usage is limited to people who are born of the same womb.

Those who are born from a different womb are referred to by the terms *besik* and *uma kain*. Thus, a person's MBC and FZC are referred to as *talain besik* (true cousins) and never as *talain ten*. In the same way, a person's FB,

---

1   Although most of the discussion in that meeting took place in Tetun, as an archive the minutes were written in Indonesian. In this context the Tetun word *hun* was translated in the minutes into Indonesian, *asal usul* (origin, derivation).

for example, is referred to as *aman besik* (true father) and not as *aman ten*. Those who are removed by collateral reckoning traced through different genealogical levels are referred to by the term *uma kain*. A person's MZeS and FBeS, for example, are referred to as *maun uma kain*. In the same manner, the person's MMBSC and FFZSC, for example, are referred to as *talain uma kain*. The term *uma kain* (literally, 'stalk of the house') signifies that the people concerned were not born in the same house but are related collaterally. Thus, the Wehali possess a particular term that can be translated as 'classificatory', namely *uma kain*. This term is usually applied to those who are removed by genealogical levels to collateral relationships. In considering marriage the first choice of a man is with a woman who is categorically his 'true cross-cousin' (*talain besik*). An alternative choice is from among those who are categorically his classificatory cross-cousins, *talain uma kain*.

In reckoning the 'path' of a person, there are two central figures with whom this person relates himself/herself, namely the old woman (*ferik*) and the old man (*katuas*) who are chosen from the maternal line to become the guardians of the house's sacred objects. For a son, it means he must relate himself to his mother or mother's sisters and his mother's brother. These two central figures within a named house represent two kinds of relations. Relating oneself to the female figure means tracing the path to the sacred centre of the house. Relating oneself to the male figure means tracing the path to the power who rules the named house. Since the male figure represents this power, he is considered the most respected person in a named house. In a named house, this male figure is represented by the mother's brother, the one that holds the title 'old man' (*katuas*). He is addressed as *tuak*, which literally also means 'the respected one'. Although the father's sister's husband is also referred to as *tua na'i* (and is also addressed as *tuak*), only the mother's brother enjoys the privileged status and the full reference of *tua na'i ama etuk*. In his function as the one who determines the continuation of a named house by appointing someone 'to light the fire in the house', as they phrase it, he is the leading figure of the house. Reference to this principal figure is expressed in the following poem.

Tua tahan ba dedon keta masee	do not greet (someone) when the palm leaves are rustling
tua tahan nakbohar keta masee	do not greet (someone) when the palm leaves make a noise

keta masee na'i baba tuak Lekik	do not greet Lekik[2] the maternal brother[3] and Lekik the mother's brother[4]
na'i loro tuak Lekik, tuak maktun hori leten sia mai	lord, the tuak that comes down from above
na'i baba tua Lekik baba maktun hori as sia maz	the binder, the *baba* that comes down from the heights
tun to'o raiklaran fila naree	descends to the earth, returning to inspect
tun to'o rai tenan falu naree	descends to the wide earth to watch
falu naree ha'i lakan oan ida	returns to inspect the little flame
fila naree ha'i len oan ida	returns to watch the little glow
ha'i laka len ne'e Marlilu haholek leten sia baa	this flame and glow is in the sacred place that was first to dry (Marlilu haholek), the place above
ha'i laka len ne'e Marlilu haholek as sia baa	this flame and glow is in Marlilu haholek, in the heights

The *tua na'i* who has been charged with guarding the house's sacred objects (*lulik*) is addressed by members of the house as *katuas* (old man). His counterpart, the female guardian is called *ferik* (old woman). Both *ferik* and *katuas* from every house within a hamlet constitute an origin group called *leo* (clan). This origin group lives together to comprise a hamlet. Thus the word *leo* can be translated either as 'clan' or 'hamlet'. A *leo* comprises all persons who share the same sacred house, called *uma metan* (black house) in some hamlets or *uma lulik* (sacred house) in others. Usually a senior *katuas*, called *fukun bot*, is chosen to be the head of the *leo*. His counterpart automatically becomes the female *fukun*. Both *fukun ferik* and *fukun katuas* are charged with guarding the clan's sacred objects which are stored in the house of the male *fukun*.

There is a possibility that, in former times, each set of four clans or hamlets constituted a larger origin group. In the domain of Wewiku, for instance, four clans constitute a community of 'four of the plains area' (*Le'un Has*) made up of the clans of Uma Lor, Uma La Wa'in, Rabasa and Le'un Klot. These four clans claim to have originated from a fifth clan, namely *leo* La Sa'en, the clan which provides a leader for this higher order origin group. This leader is referred to as 'the one who eats reclining, drinks reclining'

---

2   Lekik is a common name given to men.
3   Term used only in north Tetun.
4   Term used only in south Tetun.

(*mahaa toba*//*mahemu toba*). Similarly, inner Wehali is composed of four clans, namely Kateri, Umakatahan, Kletek and Fahiluka. These four clans constitute an origin group called 'the four-corner land'. The old men and women from the four clans form a council called *ferik hat, katuas hat* (the four old men, the four old women). However, this is not a permanent council with a governing body. Based on their origin myth, people from these four clans acknowledge that they stem from a fifth clan, namely *leo* Laran and more particularly from one great named house called Ai Lotuk (literally, 'the slender tree'). This is a symbol of their unity as people of one origin. Consequently, the hamlet of Laran is considered a place where the *ina no ama* (mother and father) of the whole four-corner territory resided. This 'mother' and 'father' are the supreme rulers of the realm of Wesei Wehali. The mother is represented by a man called *Liurai feto*, who is categorised as a female ruler. This ruler is referred to as Maromak Oan. The father is represented by a man commonly known as *Liurai mane* or simply as Liurai (literally, 'to surpass the earth'). As mother and father of the whole community, they are referred to as 'those who eat reclining and drink reclining' (*mahaa toba mahemu toba*).

The cluster of four plus one clans also becomes an economic unit, as they share an official who is charged with matters pertaining to the fertility of gardens. This official is called *lalawar*.[5] The *lalawar* of Kamanasa, who resides in the hamlet of Liurai, and the *lalawar* of Wehali, who resides in his wife's house in the hamlet of Lo'o Sina, proudly claim that when it comes to garden work, they are the kings. When gardens are prepared, for example, people only join forces together if the *lalawar* issues an invitation. A notice for villagers not to harvest their coconuts for a certain period of time only becomes effective if it is issued by a *lalawar*. In former times, planting and harvesting could only begin if the *lalawar* had already planted and harvested in a small square garden next to the hamlet of Laran called *to'os etu kukun* (literally, the dark noble garden). Nowadays, the villagers plant their gardens and harvest without waiting until the *lalawar* has performed this duty, even though the *lalawar* still faithfully performs his task.

---

5   In north Tetun the noun *lalawar* means 'orchard'; the associated verb is *knawar* meaning work.

Relationship Terms

Tracing of the 'path' is manifested in Tetun kin terms. Regarding these, however, a few comments are necessary on birth order terms and gender qualifiers that are distinctive features in Wehali, compared to the use of terms in north Tetun. Based on a list of 51 terms published by Vroklage in 1953 and an article published by Brandewie and Asten in 1976, which has kin terms scattered throughout it, Hicks (1990: 49, 55) gathers, rearranges and revises Tetun relationship terms according to a general convention suitable for analysis. In the introduction to his analysis, he quotes Vroklage as saying that among Tetun, the south Tetun have more variations on these kin terms. Vroklage himself noted 19 dialectal variations occurring in the neighbour domains of Lasiolat (the place where Vroklage collected his kin terms), out of which 15 are found in the south Tetun region (1953: 421). Interestingly, most of the variations concern birth order and gender qualifier terms, as well as terms for the third ascending genealogical level upwards.

The terms for birth order are *kwa'ik* (eldest), *klaran* (middle) and *ikun* (youngest) and the gender qualifiers are *mane* (male) and *feto* (female). In general, the north Tetun also recognise these terms. At the same time, some variations can be found in Wehali, particularly regarding the term *kwa'ik*. When a Wehali addresses a first-born male or female person, the term he or she uses is *ulun* (literally, head) not *kwa'ik*. This term in turn becomes the nickname of the person concerned. So, for example, a woman named Fouk who is the eldest sibling would be called Ulu Fouk; or a father who is the eldest in his family would be called *ama ulu*. Fouk would be referred to as *kwa'ik*, but addressed as *ulu*. Unlike the situation in north Tetun, the south Tetun distinguish here between terms of address and reference. Based on this practice, I list terms used for reference separately from terms for address (Table 6.1).

Table 6.1: Birth order terms

Terms of reference	Terms of address	Meaning
Kwa'ik	ulu	head, first-born or eldest
Klaran	klara	middle
Ikun	iku	tail, last-born or youngest

The gender qualifiers of *mane* (male) and *feto* (female) are used to denote the sex of persons at the second ascending and first descending genealogical levels. Thus, the term for someone at the second genealogical level is *bei* and to specify the sexual identity of the person concerned, *mane* or *feto* is attached to that term. So *bei mane* signifies a male PP and *bei feto* denotes a female PP. Similarly, in the first descending genealogical level the gender qualifiers signify the sexual distinction between a female child (*oan feto*) and a male child (*oan mane*). So, too, as gender qualifiers these terms distinguish female cross-cousin (*feto talain*) from male cross-cousin (*mane talain*). In such contexts the words *feto* and *mane* are what I call 'general' qualifying terms. There are, however, instances when the same gender qualifier, *feto*, has different connotations. As listed in Table 6.2, the terms *ina fetok* (MBW, FZ, WM, HM) and *feton oan* (ZC) do not simply denote a person's sexual identity, but act instead as a marker of affinal status. When I asked why a male ego called his FZ and MBW *ina fetok*, the response was that their daughters are in a preferential marriage group. 'You cannot marry someone whose mother you call *ina*', is a standard answer one might hear in the field. So too with the difference between the terms *oan feto* and *feton oan* where the former term literally means a 'female child', such as the speaker's own daughter or brother's daughter, while the latter term designates a marriageable group, that is those who are categorised by a male speaker as sister's children whom his own children might marry. Thus, the qualifier *feto* may mark an affinal category and not merely a gendered individual.

In Table 6.2, I present a list of kin terms used by the south Tetun in general, and more particularly by the Wehali. Within this list I have included certain specifications that may be useful in understanding the south Tetun kinship system.

Consanguineal Relations

Not all social ties between members of a house can be explained based on the meanings carried in these terms. However, to describe the pattern of relations in a house, wherever possible I start with folk interpretations carried by the terms.

Table 6.2: South Tetun kin terms

1.	*bei ut*	PPPPP
	bei kla'ok (bei ala, bei klutis)	PPPP (in the hamlet of Fatu Isin — *bei klutis*)
	bei ubu	PPP
	bei mane	FF, MF
	bei feto	FM, MM
2.	*ama*	F, FB, MZH, WMB, HFZH
3.	*ina*	M, MZ, FBW, HFZ, WMBW
	ina fetok	MBW, FZ, WM (m.s.), HM (w.s.)
4.	*tua na'i*	MB, FZH, WF address: Tuak: MB, FZH, WF, HFZH, HF (w.s.)
	tua na'i ama etuk	MB
5.	*banin mane*	WF, FZH, MB
	banin feto	WM, FZ, MBW
6.	*maun*	eB, FbeS, MZeD address: *manu, ulu*
7.	*bin*	eZ, FbeD, MZeD address: *bi, ulu*
8.	*alin*	yB, yZ, FByC, MZyC address: *ali, iku*
9.	*nan mane (naan)*	B (w.s.)
	nan mane uma kain	FBS, MZS (w.s.)
	mane malun	yB, eB, WZH
10.	*fetosawa*	Z (m.s.)
	feto malun	Z (w.s.)
	feto sawa uma kain	FBD, MZD (m.s.)
11.	*talain mane*	MBS, FZS (w.s.)
	talain feto	FZD, MBD (m.s.)
12.	*la'en*	H
13.	*fen*	W
	ki'i	eBW, WeZ (m.s.)
	tua	WyZ (m.s.)
14.	*rian*	WB (m.s.), HB (w.s.), ZH (m.s.), MBS, FZS address: *ria*: WB, HB address: *meo*: ZH (m.s.) address: *baen*: HZ (w.s.), BW (w.s.), MBD (w.s.), FZD
15.	*nababan*	DH, SW, FZD, MBD, BW, HZ
16.	*oan feto*	D, BD
	oan mane	S, BS
	feton oan	ZC
17.	*bein, oan bein*	CC

Terms for the third, fourth and fifth ascending levels are seldom used in Wehali. In a society in which an accurate genealogical record is not really an important issue, I found that terms used for the third genealogical level up were ambiguous and sometimes used inconsistently. When I asked for the Tetun terms for these genealogical levels, my informant, a woman from the hamlet of Umanen, had to discuss and debate with others regarding not only the terms themselves but also the levels at which these terms apply. The terms for the third genealogical level upwards provided in Table 6.2 are the result of this short 'consultation'. There is also a subsidiary term for the fourth genealogical level, namely *bei ala* (literally, 'an accountable grandparent') or *bei klutis* (literally, 'iguana grandparents') according to the people from the hamlet of Fatu Isin. My informants could not give further explanation or interpretation of these two terms. Similarly, I have no folk interpretations for the term *bei ubu* (PPP), but the terms *bei klaʼok* (PPPP) and *bei ut* (PPPPP) given to these genealogical levels, according to my informant, are related to the physical appearance of people in those generations. The root word of *klaʼok* (= *klalaʼok*) is *laʼo* meaning 'to walk'. As an adjective, the word *klalaʼok* means 'behaviour' or 'conduct'. So this term is said to indicate that those who are in this generation physically can no longer walk upright. Regarding the fifth genealogical level, a short explanation was given to me. The word *ut* according to some informants refers to a kind of insect. So, someone at the fifth genealogical level not only cannot walk upright but crawls like insects do. Based on the second meaning of *ut* as 'powder', 'residue', 'waste' (e.g. *batar ut* = maize powder), other informants explained *bei ut* as the one who is already worn out. It has to be added that many people frankly acknowledge that they do not know the specific terms for the third genealogical level upwards. The most common general term used for those levels is *bei sia* (literally, 'they, the PP'). This term implicitly covers the third genealogical level upwards.

Terms for maternal grandparents are the same as terms for paternal grandparents. The sexual distinction is marked by the terms *mane* for 'male' and *feto* for 'female'. So the term *bei feto* refers to MM and FM while the term *bei mane* refers to FF and MF. When grandparents die, they become ancestors. In invocation sexual distinction is no longer important. The ancestors are addressed by a general term *bei sia*. Thus, every invocation starts with the phrase *ah bei sia* (oh, ancestors).

The relationship between grandparents and grandchildren is marked by affection, intimacy and most of all by familiarity. A grandchild addresses his/her grandparent by the term *bei*. Grandparents also address their grandchildren with the same term *bei*, or *oan bein*. To show their affection, sometimes grandparents address their grandchildren with the term *na'i* which in this context can be translated as 'love'. The familiarity between grandparents and grandchildren is, perhaps, related to the sleeping arrangement in houses. Grandchildren, in their childhood, sleep and spend more time with their grandparents than with their biological parents. In order to give more private time for the mother and father in the house, grandparents often take their grandchildren to the gardens and spend a few nights there. The familiarity between members of these alternate generations make the grandchildren feel closer to their grandparents than to their parents. When grandchildren need something, they first turn to their grandparents for help. When grandchildren make jokes, they feel free to touch and jab their grandparents, behaviour which is uncommon between children and parents.

As a kin term, *ama* refers only to one's father or father's brother. As a polite address, the term *ama* or *ama na'i* is used to greet all male seniors, just like the usage of the term *bapak* in Indonesian. If the family lives in their own home (separated from the wife's parents), both parents and children sleep together in the inner house. This is the time when both the father and mother show their warm affection to their children. Only when the children are 10 to 15 years old do the warm relations gradually change. A son will no longer sleep with his parents. He is expected to sleep on the verandah and spend more time with other men outside the house. For a girl of that age, her father will build a temporary compartment within the house, called *loka laran*, as her sleeping space. From then on relations between a father and his son and daughter are marked by distance. A son gradually builds up a formal relation with his father. He still learns from his father all sorts of things, such as how to make traps for game catching, tools and all sorts of garden work. But in contrast to the relation between a grandfather and a grandson, the relation between a father and son is a kind of instructional relationship, like the relation between a teacher with his pupil. The phrase 'I instruct my son strictly so that he can become a good person' (*ha'u knorin oan kodi kbit ne'e be nia bele dadi ema*) is not an uncommon expression heard from a father.

In contrast to the changing attitude of a father, *ina*, the mother is more constant in her relation with her children. The warm relationship between a mother and her children in their childhood develops into a mutual trust. Children are more open with their mother than their father.

A daughter in particular has more intimate relations with her mother. The skill of weaving, which is considered a rite of passage from childhood to adulthood, is transferred from mother to daughter.

Just as *ama* is the term for FB, *ina* also is the term for MZ. The explanation given for addressing ego's mother and ego's MZ with the same term (*ina*), and ego's father and ego's FB with *ama* is quite simple: '… because our "mothers are sisters" (*inan bin alin*) and our "fathers are brothers" (*aman maun alin*)'. The implication of this expression is that parallel cousins are like true brothers and sisters. Marriage among them is incestuous.[6]

Among persons whose fathers are brothers (*aman maun alin*), the relationship is not always harmonious. Without citing statistics, a member of the district police gave his impression that disputes among sisters are fewer than among brothers.

Since there are few terms used to denote individuals of the same generation who consider themselves as siblings, some clarification is necessary here. The terms of address for eB, yB, eZ, yZ respectively are *maun*, *alin*, *bin* and *alin*. Brothers who were born from the same womb (*maun alin ten*) express their consanguinity as *mane malun*. In the same manner, sisters who are *bin alin ten* express their consanguinity as *feto malun*. The *mane malun* group refer to their sisters as *feto sawa*, while the *feto malun* group refer to their brothers as *naan*. Those who are related as *feto sawa* and *nan mane* express their common consanguinity as feto *nanaan*.

When a south Tetun is asked how he/she would describe the relation between *feto sawa* (sisters) and *nanaan* (brothers), a definite answer would be given: distance. To justify the answer, very often the phrase is quoted:

Taman hudi lua lotuk	(Like) planting the Luan banana garden
nalai kladik	as borders (of the field)
feto sawa ta bafu	sisters are on the one side
nan mane ta bafu	brothers are on the other side

6 Relations between persons whose mothers are sisters is intimate and trusting, even when they share the same husband. The latter statement refers to a sororate marriage, which is not widely practised and therefore this observation is based on only a single example, where the two sisters (Bi Pouk and Bi Bete) were married to the same man. Not only the women themselves, but the children of these two sisters seemed to develop a healthy relationship, just like children of a single mother.

The background of this short saying can be explained in the light of agricultural activities. In this fertile plain of Wehali-Wewiku, bananas are one of the agricultural products and a source of income for the people. Because banana trees consume more space in gardens, they are not planted in the middle of the garden. Instead they are planted (along with coconut trees) around the garden. Therefore, banana trees mark the limit or border of one's own garden. The word used for 'border' is *kladik*. So banana trees are used as *kladik* to separate one garden from the other. Folk interpretation given to this poem was 'just like banana trees mark the separation between gardens, they also mark the separation between siblings of the opposite sex'. Unmistakably, the emphasis given in this phrase relates to marriage alliance in which the rule of incest prohibits marriage between brothers and sisters and therefore every brother and sister must know the limit of their 'path'. 'Crossing the established paths' (*hakur biti kluni*) means committing incest.

Relations between brothers and sisters can be depicted also as the relation between a protector and the protected. This notion of 'protection' is developed in marital, political and economical relations. The emphasis on 'brothers are protectors' in the sense that they provide protection to sisters is manifested in marriage arrangements. Parents seek opinion and approval from the elder brothers concerning the men who want to marry the sisters. In political terms, Maromak Oan, the supreme ruler of Wehali, is categorically female. Being a female he is depicted as resting inside Wehali while his executive, the male Liurai, protects him from outside. Using the pattern of relations between brothers and sisters as an analogy, the Liurai is ritually considered as the Maromak Oan's protector. However, it is not the protector who is the superordinate, but rather the one who is protected who is the superior.

The concept of 'protector' is also applied for economic reasons. In economic terms it means a brother is expected, as far as possible, to help his sisters when they are in economic crisis; more particularly, a brother is obliged to assist his sister's children (*feton oan*). With the increasing number of men working in cities, we increasingly encounter the *feton oan* lodging (freely) in their MB's houses. After all, the brother is the *tuak* (MB) of his sister's children, the most respected person in his sister's house. Therefore, help to his sister's children in this way is regarded as a small token of his responsibility.

The relationship between elder brother (*maun*) and younger brother (*alin*) is marked by an order of precedence. This *maun-alin* group (called *mane malun*) is referred to as *nan mane* by their sister. The relationship among the *maun-alin* is phrased by the people as *hakneter haktaek*. *Kneter* is a small ladder erected at the front gate of a garden used as access to the garden. *Taek* is a small step in front of a house that provides access to the verandah. The concept of 'precedence' can be understood from the notion of *hakneter haktaek* as explained by the Wehali. The terms of address among the *maun-alin* group reveal this notion of *hakneter haktaek* in which the yo unger brother (*alin*) gives precedence to the elder brother (*maun*). The elder brother is addressed as *ulu(n)* literally meaning 'head', while the younger is addressed as *iku(n)* literally meaning 'tail'. When their father dies, the elder son potentially inherits the office of the 'old man' in their named house.

This order of precedence in which the elder brother is superior to the younger brother is reversed among the sisters who constitute a *bin-alin* (eZ-yZ) group (called *feto malun*). They are referred to as *feto sawa* by their brothers. On the death of a woman who was the title-holder 'old woman' in the named house, the elder sister gives precedence to the younger sister to replace the deceased woman as *ferik* (old woman) of their house. In this case, although she is younger than her sister and possibly younger than everybody else within the named house, she is respected as an 'old woman' who is responsible for the continuation of their named house.

Affinal Relations

The notions of 'border' and 'protection' that mark the pattern of relations among people who share the same blood to some extent can be observed in affinal relations.

The term used to communicate the notion of 'border' in affinal relations is *banin*, meaning 'ditch'. In the plains of Wehali-Wewiku, a small amount of rain is enough to make hamlets overflow with water. In order to protect houses from the overflowing water, every household digs ditches (*banin*) around their houses. Thus a ditch marks a border between two houses. Based on this practice, a 'ditch' also becomes a metaphorical border between domains. In ritual language the word *banin* is paired with the word *satan* meaning 'to close' or 'enclosure'. So to delineate the limit of the realm of Wehali from other peripheral domains, a chanter usually employs the dyadic pair of *banin Wehali*//*satan Wehali* which can be translated as 'the border of Wehali, the enclosure of Wehali'. As an affinal term, *banin* denotes affines of the first ascending generation. When a man from House A marries a woman from House B, he refers to members of the older generation in House B as his *banin*. In a narrow sense, *banin* is translated as 'father- or mother-in-law' (Morris 1984: 10). Thus, in the imagery of ditches (*banin*) that demarcate house and domains, the parents-in-law are called *banin* in the sense that they become 'ditches' between the husband and wife. The sex of the *banin* is marked by the gender qualifiers *mane* and *feto*. The mother-in-law and her sisters are referred to as *banin feto* while the father-in-law and his brothers are referred to as *banin mane*. Since the ideal marriage directs the marriage of a man to his MBD or FZD, a *banin mane* is also potentially a *tuak*. In the status as *banin mane* and *tuak*, he is the most respected member in his child's house.

In accordance with the preferential system of bilateral cross-cousin marriage, one's *tua na'i* (MB, FZH) and *ina fetok* (MBW, FZ) are potentially one's *banin* (parents-in-law). Here the Wehali differentiate between the affinal term (*banin*) and the consanguineal terms (*tua na'i* and *ina fetok*). However, since there is no obligation for cross-cousins to marry, a parent-in-law can be a person who is not necessarily one's own *tua na'i* or *ina fetok*. In the case where a person's parent-in-law is his/her *tua na'i* or *ina fetok*, then he/she can use either the affinal or the consanguineal term in reference. Teknonyms are also used for reference.

Affines in the first ascending generation (*banin*) refer to the married-in man and persons in his generation as *nababan*. The Tetun word *baban* literally means 'to attach'. So the *nababan* are those who are attached to the *banin*'s house. The implication is, therefore, that they are not regarded as members of the house. By referring to someone as *nababan*, according to the Wehali, he/she is excluded from membership of the house concerned. Those who are members of a house are those who are born in the house and therefore are called *uma na'in* (literally, the owner of the house). In contrast, *nababan* is someone who is attached to the house. In a narrow sense, a *nababan* also means either son-in-law or daughter-in-law. However, as I noted earlier, this term refers to ego's generation in contrast to *banin* of the preceding generation.

Concerning son-in-law and daughter-in-law, the Tetun populations of West and East Timor use the same terms, *mane foun* and *feto foun* respectively. These terms are also used in many conversations in the south

Tetun regions. But, due to the uxorilocal pattern of residence, the south Tetun commonly refer to the married-in man as *oan la'en* (literally, the child's husband). Many informants insist that the term *mane foun* for the in-married man is appropriate for the 'hill' people of north Tetun, whereas to emphasise their own identity, the south Tetun say: 'we the plains people refer to our sons-in-law as *oan la'en*. Another term commonly used to refer to a son-in-law is *mane maktama uma* (literally, man that enters the house). The opposite term is mane *maksai uma* (literally, men that go out of the house) to denote the wife's brother. Like the term *nababan* mentioned above, these two terms (*oan la'en* and *mane maktama uma*) emphasise that the in-married man is not a member of his wife's house.

These terms of reference imply that an in-married man has no authority within his wife's house. As the 'child's husband', he submits himself to his wife's father's authority, whom in a prescriptive marriage he respects as *tuak*. Even as a husband (*la'en*), he is not permitted to join his wife (*fen*) inside the house. His space is limited to the verandah of the house, where he spends most of his nights. The sexual relationship as husband and wife is limited to the opportunities offered by his parents-in-law. Parents always find excuses to visit families or spend a few nights in the garden in order to give more privacy for the husband and wife alone in the house. An in-married man has more freedom to govern his own household only when his father-in-law dies or if he and his family move to his new house.

In the initial period of marriage, the *banin* avoid as far as possible addressing their *oan la'en* directly. It is common among the Tetun, as well as among other people in the region, to address a married couple by the name of their child. So, for example, a man whose son is called Berek will be addressed as Berek *aman* and his wife as Berek *inan*. For a recently married couple, the husband will be addressed as *rahaman* and the wife as *rahinan*.[7] According to folk interpretation, these compound words derive from the word *rahuk* (body hair), *aman* (father) and *inan* (mother). Addressing a person as *rahaman* or *rahinan* has the connotation of putting the person down because the man and the woman are treated as an 'imperfect' mother and father.

---

7   Francillon (1967: 361) cites the terms *kalisama* and *kalisina*, which, according to my informants, are used mainly by the Kamanasa and the Kletek people.

Between husband and wife, there is also a degree of hesitation in addressing one another. Francillon rightly observed the existence of indirect address, from the husband toward his wife and vice versa by using an available third person as intermediator. In the presence of his wife's brother (*ria*), for example, the husband will ask: '*Ria*, would you tell your sister to give me this' (1967: 430).

The avoidance by the *banin* and the wife of greeting directly the young son-in-law and husband with the alternative teknonym (*rahaman*) is due to their trying to avoid making him feel inferior in the house. From other perspectives, the avoidance is also related to the responsibility of the in-married man within the house. As long as he has the status 'child's husband', he will still be considered as a 'child' regardless of how old he is and how many children and grandchildren he has. When his wife's house conducts a ceremony, a marriage ceremony for example, sons-in-law of the named house cannot even sit on the step of the verandah. The young ones will stand on the ground, while the old ones sit on mats spread out on the ground. The only exception is for the bride's father. As a married-in man his place is outside the house. However, as the bride's father, he is permitted to sit 'quietly' on the upper verandah together with other senior members of the named house. The rest of the in-married men, who are standing and sitting on the ground, are referred to as *mane lais* (literally, quick men, helpers) by members of the named house (*uma na'in*). Orders given by *uma na'in* will be quickly executed by *mane lais*.

Unlike the situation among the north Tetun where only one term of address is used for WZ (*ka'a*), the south Tetun have different terms of address for WyZ from WeZ. The term for WyZ is *tua* and the term for WeZ is *ki'i*. The term of address *tuak* (MB, FZH) denotes a privileged status of a particular person. Related to this term, *tua* is also the term used by an in-married man to address his wife's younger sister. It is said that by addressing the WyZ with this term, the man actually elevates her from his generation level to a parental level, such that a 'border' has been created between the 'new man' and his younger sisters-in-law, so he cannot marry any of these women while his own wife is alive. This changing of genealogical level from ego's generation to the preceding generation also seems to accord with the custom for the transmission of inheritance, in which the youngest daughter potentially will inherit her mother's house and eventually will become the title-holder of *fetik* (old woman) of the house. Being a *fetik* she will also become the central figure for ritual performances within her named house. By the same analogy, with the coming of the 'new man' to reside in the house, the wife's youngest sister becomes the fluid element, moving up to the parental level.

It is said that the different terms applied to the younger and elder sisters derive from the practice of sororate marriage. According to this custom, when a wife dies her husband can choose either to go back to his natal house or to continue to stay in his wife's house and marry one of his late wife's sisters. In the case of the second option, he will choose to marry the younger sister. In order to prevent the marriage taking place before the wife dies, it was said that a term that can be regarded as 'border' must be laid between these two people. This 'border' is signified by the term *tua* addressed to the wife's younger sister. 'By addressing one's wife's younger sister as *tua* one automatically respects her as one's own *tuak* (MB)' was the sort of explanation given to me.

Ria is a term of address applied reciprocally by a person to denote all male affines of the same generation. This reciprocal term suggests that there is an equal relation between male members of the husband-taking house and husband-giving house in the ego's generation. However, the relation between an in-married man and his wife's brothers is asymmetrically marked by the changing of the term of reference. With the entry to the house of the new man, the wife's brothers will be referred to as 'men that leave the house' (*mane maksai uma*), in contrast to the new man who is the 'man that comes into the house' (*mane maktama uma*). The phrase *mane maksai uma* attached to the wife's brothers is regarded as a privileged reference, since the holder of the title 'old man' of a named house is chosen from those who 'leave' the house and not from those who 'enter' the house. The difference between 'leave' and 'come in' is interpreted in political terms as between the one who has the right to rule the house and the one who has no right to rule the house. As *mane maksai uma*, the eldest brother will rule his natal house although residing 'outside' the house. He will then be the title-holder (*katuas*) of the house. Like his youngest sister, he will also become a central figure in all ritual performances of the house.

A change in the term of address also occurs in the cross-cousin (*talain*) group. When a woman marries her own *talain* (MBS or FZS), she will maintain the term of reference for her husband's brothers as *talain mane* and her husband's sisters as *talain feto*. But the term of address is changed from the common usage of teknonym to a new term—*baen*. A woman will address her husband's sisters with this term. She will also address her brother's wife as *baen* if the latter belongs to the *talain* group in addition to all women in the *talain* group (MBD, FZD). The word *baen* in Tetun indicates old age. Hudi *baen*, for example, refers to 'the oldest fruit in a banana bunch' (Morris 1984: 8). By addressing them as *baen*, she reacknowledges their privileged status as their respected *tuak*'s children.

The south Tetun distinguish between the general term 'children' (*oan*) and the marked term 'sister's children' (*feton oan*). Sisters call their brothers' children *oan* (child), but brothers call their sisters' children *feton oan* (sister's child). *Oan* and *feton oan* define preferential marriage groups. Marriage between people who are classified as *oan* and *feton oan*, according to my informants, guarantees a successful marriage because the husband and wife, to quote a popular saying, will *hakneter malu, hakmoe malu* ('mutually respect and honour each other'). This phrase is interpreted as follows: 'because their parents are people who belong to the same natal house, their children cannot easily get divorced'. It is interesting to note that the descendants of brothers and sisters who are separated from their common natal house by marriage to others comprise preferential marriage groups. So, in the initial generation (that is among siblings of opposite sex) marriage is prohibited, but in the subsequent genealogical level (that is among cross-cousins of opposite sex) marriage is preferential. The directed marriage between members of these two groups is expressed in the consanguineal terms *oan* and *feton oan*.

Concluding Remarks

The relationship terms, equivalences and distinctions as observed from Table 6.2 reveal certain key features. In the second to fifth ascending genealogical levels, there is no distinction, for example, between mother's father and father's father. Both are addressed by the same term *bei*. In invocations, the different terms used to denote people of the third, fourth and fifth ascending levels are irrelevant. They are addressed with a general term *bei sia* (*bei* = grandparent; *sia* = they). In the first ascending genealogical level, there is no distinction between the uterine and the affinal groups. The equations in this genealogical level reveal a symmetric terminology, as also reported by Cunningham (1964: 204) among the Dawan and Hicks (1990: 48–56) among the north Tetun. This rule of symmetry is indicated by the following equations: MB = FZH, WF (m.s),

HF (w.s) while FZ = MBW, HM (w.s), WM (m.s). In the ego's generation, brothers refer to their sisters and parallel cousins of the opposite sex as *fetosawa*, and sisters refer to their brothers and parallel cousins of the opposite sex as *naan*. Those who are categorically *fetosawa* and *nan mane* are forbidden to marry one another. Cross-cousins refer to each other as *talain*. The men are *talain mane* and the women are *talain feto*. Marriage between *talain mane* and *talain feto* is preferential.

In the first descending generation, the terms suggest an asymmetrical pattern in which the term for BC (*oan*) is distinguished from SC (*feton oan*). The distinction made between sister's children and brother's children can be understood in relation to affinal alliances. Firstly, the distinction emphasises that the mother and her sisters have primary rights over the children. The continuation of a named house more or less depends on the sisters' children. Secondly, it emphasises also the power of brothers over their named houses. After all, these brothers are the *feton oan*'s MB, the most 'respected' figure (*tuak*) in a named house.

Hicks, based on ethnographies written on north Tetun and his own work in east Tetun, concludes that 'terms used by both Tetum populations are in almost every case identical' (1990: 48) despite a few exceptions used in one area but unheard of in another area. Vroklage, who spent some time in south Tetun, regarded the different kin terms employed by the people mainly as dialectical variations. In my view, however, they are more than simply dialectical variations. The different terms of address and terms of reference relate to the custom of uxorilocal post-marital residence so heavily emphasised by the south Tetun.

The last point that I need to raise here concerns the lack of terms for husband-giving and husband-taking houses in Wehali. The Wehali repeatedly mention the significance of the 'border' (*banin*) metaphor laid between a woman and a man, the woman's house and the man's house. Despite this repetitive emphasis, there are no terms used to distinguish these two affinal groups. There are no terms used to differentiate the husband-taking house from the husband-giving house. This lack of terms supports the fact that both patrilateral and matrilateral cross-cousins (*talain*) are marriageable. This may give some grounds to claim that the asymmetric, circulating connubium suggested by van Wouden based on the north Tetun data simply does not work in Wehali. As a matter of comparison, in north Tetun, the division between these two houses is spelt out as the division between *uma mane* (the wife-giving group) and *feto sawa* (the wife-taking group). A house that has been categorised as *feto sawa* can never provide a woman to her *uma mane*. The asymmetrical alliance between these two houses is correctly expressed by Brandewie and Asten as: 'the flow of the water is always from the source, going downstream, never upstream. Brides should come from the *uma mane* and never from the *feto sawa*' (1976: 21).

The south Tetun do not develop this distinction as the north Tetun do. However, in marriage arrangements, one often hears the husband-taking house identified as the female house (*uma feto*), while the husband-giving house is addressed as the male house (*uma mane*). In marriage arrangements, a moderate number of gifts of 'betel-nut' are transferred from the male house to the female house. During the marriage ceremony, members of the woman's house sit on the upper platform while members of the man's house sit on the lower platform. Advice given to the married couple also recognises that the woman's house has a privileged status. Thus, there is some degree of asymmetry between the husband-taking house and the husband-giving house. But it does not provide enough of a basis for speaking about an asymmetrical alliance. This distinction is important to understand the present organisation of houses in a hamlet where some houses are categorised as male houses and some as female houses. At present this organisation into male and female houses is understood solely in ritual terms. A female house is a place where the offerings are prepared (*halo mama*), while a male house is for the actual offering itself (*sera mama*). The asymmetric relation between these two houses is also expressed in ritual terms. A female house is regarded as more sacred than a male house. Therefore, any discussion or meeting in the hamlet is held in the male house and never in the female house. In this way, the female house will remain superior to the male house, just as the *uma mane* is superior to the *feto sawa* in north Tetun. The lack of fixed terms for the husband-taking and husband-giving houses and the ritual organisation of houses in hamlets into female and male houses suggests that formerly a hamlet (*leo*) was an endogamous unit, in contrast to a house (*uma*) which, still remains a unit of exogamy.

7

Ancestral Path in the Wehali House

Introduction

Analyses of traditional dwellings and settlements are not new in anthropology where the foundation for such studies is traced to the pioneering work of Lewis Henry Morgan in his *Houses and House—Life of the American Aborigines* (Morgan 1881, reprinted 1965). In his Introduction to the 1965 reprint, Bohannan summarises the main aim of this book as follows:

> What does domestic architecture show anthropologists—either ethnologists or archaeologists—about social organization, and how does social organization combine with a system of production technology and ecological adjustment to influence domestic and public architecture? (1965: x)

Despite Bohannan's indications of some weakness and necessary emendations, the theoretical points made in this book are still fascinating and instructive even today.

Marcel Mauss (1970) contributes another perspective to the early study of domestic organisation. His ecological approach is beneficial in understanding not only the structure of the Eskimo house, but also the structure of Eskimo ideas and their mode of gaining a livelihood. Concerning these two pioneering works (Morgan and Mauss), Fox (1993a: 7–8) remarks:

> These two major studies, although developed from differing theoretical perspectives, established the initial foundation for the anthropological study of houses and their relation to social life.

Morgan's and Mauss's studies also constitute the basis of Lévi-Strauss's (1963) often-cited works on 'house societies'. In her monograph *The Living House*, Waterson (1991: xv–xvii) acknowledges that the intermittent interest in the 'house' following the pioneering works of Morgan (and Mauss) was substantially rekindled by Lévi-Strauss. Waterson sees the development of structuralism in the 1960s and 1970s as 'stimulating a new spate' of studies treating the 'house' as a focus. However, the renewed attention to the notion of 'house' cannot be regarded as simply a continuation of a kind of study that had been neglected since the time of Morgan and the era of Mauss. Various new emphases have been put forward by later researchers. Ellen (1986: 4) analysed studies on the 'symbolic organisation of lived-in structure' according to their focus, and found there are studies that emphasise 'rules governing the structure of space', as in the work of Pierre Clement (1982); the 'archeometry of symbolism' as dealt with by Rassers (1982); a focus on the 'symbolic concordance between the house and other collective representations' in the works of Cunningham (1962, 1964), Barnes (1974) and Kana (1978); as well as Forth (1991), who regards the Sumba house as 'a symbolic microcosm', and Fox (1993a), who emphasises the 'symbolic pre-eminence of the house'.

Another issue concerns the terminology and approach appropriate to this topic of study. With their emphasis on the physical structure and the materials used to construct a building, the so-called 'traditional architects' commonly employ terms like 'vernacular', 'indigenous', 'primitive' or 'traditional' houses. None of these terms, however, reveal what Bourdier and Alsayyad (1989: 7) describe as 'the enduring values of their builders and symbols that signify deeper structures of society'. To avoid imposing 'outside' categories onto local knowledge, I prefer to use the term 'house' as the translation of *uma* without adding other attributes such as 'traditional' or 'indigenous'. The same is true of my account of the main structural elements, as well as the metaphors used by Wehali in explaining the symbolic meanings of these elements. My emphasis is on 'what the Wehali say about their house', rather than idealised, formalised exogenous interpretations.

In this respect, I must point out that following intense promotion by government at the regional and district levels of a new style of house based on 'health standards', the Tetun people now classify their own houses in terms of *rumah sehat* (healthier house) and *rumah adat* (*adat* house). The villagers refer to the first type of house as *uma malae*. The word *malae* literally means 'malay', an attribute given to objects and persons introduced to the area from outside. Therefore the word *malae* can be translated as 'foreign'. Thus, *uma malae* means 'foreign house': 'foreign' in terms of its structure, materials, orientation and most of all the lack of any ritual necessary for its construction. By contrast, this chapter deals only with the so-called *rumah adat*. The term *rumah adat* is not, however, the locals' own way of referring to their houses, but rather a designation given by outsiders to mean the opposite of *rumah sehat* (literally, healthy house).[1] The Tetun people in general simply call their own style of house *uma*.

Types of House

There are two types of *uma* recognised in the Tetun area: *uma roman* and *uma kukun*. The *uma roman* (literally, bright house) is designed as a residence and comes in two varieties. On the one hand, a 'named house' (*uma maho naran*) contains ancestral relics passed through the female line and guarded by a woman and a man from that line. Thus, *uma* in this sense can be glossed as an ancestral or a lineage house. On the other hand, there are houses that have no ancestral relics and are, therefore, termed 'unnamed house' (*uma maho naran ha'i*). I also heard owners of this kind of house refer to it as 'an ugly house' (*uma at ida*). The latter houses are residences for other members of the lineage. Thus, a named house is lived in by a female guardian of the lineage, while other members of the lineage reside in unnamed houses.

The *uma kukun* (literally, dark house) is not designed as a residence and also comes in two varieties. First, there is 'the forbidden house' (*uma lulik*) or 'the black house' (*uma metan*) as it is known in south Tetun and among the Kamanasa-Suai people respectively. This kind of house represents the

---

1   It is common knowledge that government officials identify the *rumah adat* with *rumah tidak sehat* (unhealthy house). Confronted with this stereotyped identification, the head of Kamanasa village, Nicolaus Teti, could find only one reason to label the *rumah adat* as 'unhealthy', namely, its lack of ventilation. However, with the typical 'healthy house' having a low corrugated iron roof and walls (made of dried midribs of gebang palm) touching the ground, those who live in this type of 'healthier house' tend to be 'unhealthy' in the dry climate of summer and the annual flooding of rainy seasons.

clan because the clan's ancestral relics are kept inside the house. Second, there is the *uma kakaluk* (amulet house) named for the *kakaluk* pouch carried by a man wherever he goes. Formerly, when a man engaged in tribal warfare, his amulets were stored in this pouch. From this habitual practice, the word *kakaluk* has come to mean 'amulet'. Nowadays, *uma kakaluk* is popularly known as 'the medicine house'. People with broken legs, for example, were taken into the house and stayed there for three, five or some other uneven number of days.[2] As an amulet house, *uma kakaluk* is categorically a male house because originally it was constructed as a place where men came to seek strength and immunity in times of warfare. For this reason, it is said that no women are permitted to enter this particular house. School teachers and other government officials introduce it as a 'house of defence' in the sense that the security of the clan is understood to rely on how well the people preserve the house.

All these houses are built following the same basic design. The difference between the two types of house rests mainly on the fact that *uma roman* is designed as a residential unit while *uma kukun* is not. As a residential unit, a house always has an outer section or verandah 'attached' (*labis*) to the main building. By contrast, the lack of *labis* in house construction suggests that it is not a residential unit. The basic design just mentioned, according to the Wehali, imitates the 'first house' as depicted in their origin myth. Therefore, in the next section I begin with the cultural design of the Wehali house as narrated in this type of myth.

The House of Earth-Sky

The myth concerning the 'first house' cannot be separated from the myth concerning the emergence of the first dry land. Narrated in a figurative way, its meanings are expressed in metaphorical terms. In this sort of myth one cannot expect to find a detailed description of the physical elements of that first house. The most important information the myth reveals is the ordered structure of the house and the living space of the first human being. Accordingly, the first house as narrated in the myth was called *uma Rai Lale'an* (the house of Earth-Sky) occupied by Ho'ar Na'i Haholek. In this myth Ho'ar is delineated not as an ordinary living

---

2   The Wehali relate uneven numbers to *kukun* (ancestral spirits, dark) and even numbers to *roman* (living human beings, bright). So, to ask for *monas* (strength and invulnerability) from ancestors one ought to stay for an odd number of nights inside the house.

human being of the kind Wehali refer to as 'bright people' (*ema roman*), but rather as a 'dark person' (*ema kukun*). Her house is also regarded as a dark house (*uma kukun*) in contrast to those ordinary houses subsequently termed bright houses (*uma roman*). Because the dark house is a sacred house, its existence can only be revealed by means of 'disguised language' (*lia sasaluk*):

uma niak aa, uma Rai Lale'an	her house is called, the house of Earth-Sky
lale'an ne'e hodi knanuk naak ee:	the sky is described in verse as follows:
'Hali ne'e nahako kraik oan basuk	'The banyan tree produces a lot of branches
hali ne'e nataha kraik oan basuk	the banyan tree produces a lot of leaves
morin kodi kato'o rai Malaka	its aromatic flavour reaches the land of Malaka
bosok nola dei na'i Taek Malaka	it tricks the lord of Malaka
beur nola dei na'i Taek Malaka	it deceives the lord of Malaka
mai ee tiha hali hun aa.'	to come and cast his fishing net under the trunk of the tree.'

To understand more of the sacred nature of this house, one must recall the myth of origin (Reference Text 2) that recounts the emergence of the first dry land from the primordial sea. Accordingly the first dry land, which in ritual language is called *rai manu matan, rai bua klaras* (the land as a chicken's eye, the land as a slice of areca nut) formed from the umbilical cord of Ho'ar. It was on this first dry land that the first house of Ho'ar stood. Therefore this house is identical with the first dry land and the navel of the first woman. They are described in the myth as:

na'i husar ne'e nia	the noble's navel is here
loli husar ne'e nia	the entangled navel is here
manu matan ne'e nia	this is the chicken's eye
bua klaras ne'e nia	this is the slice of areca nut

The exegesis I was given of this passage pointed out that in former times there were no 'ordinary' houses because there was no dry land. The earth was still covered with water. Out of this primordial sea grew a banyan tree. Ho'ar, the daughter of the first woman, lived on top of this tree. The living space on top of the tree was called 'sky' (*lale'an*) and constituted her house. At that time, the distance between sky and earth was only as tall as a banyan tree. Therefore, this very first house is called 'the house of Earth-Sky' (*uma Rai Lale'an*).

This name suggests that the first mythical house can be considered as consisting of two parts. The upper part is called *lale'an* and the lower part is called *rai*. However, only the upper part constituted the living space and therefore the 'hearth' as a symbol of the living house was located in this true upper part. The fire that shone from this hearth attracted a man from far away, named Taek Malaka. The myth then goes on to say that after a period of courtship, Taek took Ho'ar as his wife and resided in her house.

Another version of the origin myth (cf. Reference Text 5) does not mention the name of the house as the house of earth-sky, but its description fits the dichotomous structure of the primordial house. In his description, the narrator called this primordial house *natar knese uma rua*. *Natar* in south Tetun refers to an open space in a field or in the middle of a village.[3] *Knese* is a species of tree commonly found at the seaside. *Uma rua* literally means 'two houses'. Both these versions of the origin myth state that the two parts of the house were linked by a ladder-door made of vines from the Ktuhak and Kleik trees. Emphasising the closeness of the upper part and the lower part, a version of the myth recorded in the domain of Wewiku describes these sections as linked by a spider web. So access to the 'earth' section was through this spider web that functioned as a vulnerable ladder:

tobu tuir laliran kaban	step on the spider saliva thread
sama tuir labadain kaban	trample on the spider web
sama nikar ain atu kotu la kotu	trample again without breaking it
tobu nikar ain atu kotu la kotu	step again without breaking it

The dichotomous structure of the house, in terms of sky:earth and upper:lower, such that the upper-sky part was occupied by women and the lower-earth part by men, is a popular theme among story-tellers and can be observed in many forms of oral tradition in Wehali. The story of the 'Seven Princesses' (*feto hitus*) is one of these. In this folk-tale (*ai knoik*), seven princesses who lived in the sky often 'flew' down to earth to pick betel-nut from an orchard guarded by a man. This man noted 'the stealing'

---

3   In east Tetun, *natar* means 'a rice paddy field' (Morris 1984: 152; Metzner 1977: 46, 126).

of the betel-nut, since the beating of the wings worn by these princesses always made a noise. Using a 'classic' tactic, also well known in the story of Retna Nawang Sih of the Babad Tanah Jawi (Fox 1995), to steal the 'wings'[4] of this heavenly nymph, this man finally married the youngest sister of the seven princesses. This folk-tale is more specific in describing the hidden design of that mythical house. As well as the dichotomous structure and the hearth, it mentions the location of a 'female attic' (*kahak rae*) above the hearth (*loka laran*) as the sleeping place of those princesses and also the front platform as a space for their father to sit while chewing his betel-nut. Based on these myths, the Wehali claim that the structure and internal organisation of their houses are copied and further developed from that first mythical house.

Orientation of Houses

When it comes to the 'orientation of Tetun houses', Grijsen (1904: 43–47) is quite ambiguous as to whether the Tetun regard it as an important topic. On the one hand, he indicates that Tetun society does not pay much attention to the orientation of houses, while at the same time he also noted that houses in the domain of Fialaran were built facing the mountain of Laka'an, and houses in the domain of Jenilu were built facing the sea. This apparent contradiction actually indicates that 'orientation' is among many topics discussed by the Tetun when a house is going to be built. The significance of house orientation in Tetun society is emphasised by Cunningham when he says that the houses of the Belunese (the Tetun), like those of the Dawan (Atoni), are directed toward the land of origin of their ancestors (Cunningham 1959: 162). It is this link between house orientation and the paths of ancestors, suggested by Cunningham, that I explore here.

Since the paths of ancestors are narrated in the origin myth, knowledge of the orientation of a house must be sought from this myth. According to the myth, the house of earth-sky was located in the mountain region, which in Tetun is termed *rae*.[5] But the *rae* mentioned in this myth does

---

4   In Babad Tanah Jawi, Jaka Tarub stole the clothes of Retna Nawang Sih when she was swimming in a lake.

5   Vroklage regards the word *rae* as synonymous with *rai* meaning 'land' or 'earth' (1953: 512). The same assumption is made by Francillon, although he acknowledges that the Wehali ignore this translation. Actually, for the Wehali, *rae* refers to a living space in the mountains or, as Morris puts it, 'high regions on the mountains' (Morris 1984: 158).

not refer to a high place generally in the mountain regions. It refers to a particular place that is now situated at the village of Kateri. This place is considered by the Wehali as the first dry land on earth and therefore they named it Marlilu Haholek, which means the first sacred dry land. It was in this sacred region that the first female ancestor called Ho'ar Na'i Haholek lived. So, for the Wehali the word *rae* is associated with 'mountain', 'high' (place), 'sacred', 'dark', 'life' and 'female'.

When Ho'ar reached marriageable age, a nobleman from the 'seaside' (which in Tetun is termed *lor*[6]) came to marry her. Although there are various accounts of this recorded by previous researchers (see Grijsen 1904: 18–20; Vroklage 1953: 148–149; Francillon 1967: 78–82), these versions converge on one ultimate point, namely that a group of outsiders came to Wehali by way of the sea. The origin myth recorded by Grijsen even specifies the names of places that these outsiders call at before reaching Wehali—that is, 'Poeloe Koesoe, Poeloe Kae, Poeloe Api, Poeloe Loe and Larantoeka-Baoeboin' (1904: 19). Francillon noted the way these people came ashore: 'They arrived from the great land suspended by the hands from the branches of a floating Ficus (tree) named Hali Barlele' (1967: 78). The myth that I recorded does not specify which 'land' these outsiders came from nor how they came to Wehali. The most important point for my *adat* historian is that a man from the sea came to Wehali. He came because he was attracted by a light shining from the hills of Marlilu. This man was called Taek Malaka.

Another folk-tale that I recorded in the hamlet of Lo'o Sina (literally, the Chinese garden house) also narrated the coming of a man from the sea. In this tale, when a man and his buffalo called *mane lor* emerged out of the deep sea, the fur of the buffalo was covered with gold. Every time he shook his body, the gold fell to the ground. The storyteller concluded his tale by saying that it was the man from the seaside (*lor*) that brought wealth to Wehali. Thus, for the Wehali, *lor* is associated with low, front, wealth and male.

---

6   Compared to the meaning of *rae*, the translation of the word *lor* is straightforward. Morris translates the noun *lor* as 'low-lying ground', 'the tidal regions', 'seaside'. As an adjective it means 'low, towards the bottom'. Thus, *uma lor* means 'a low house'. Morris also suggests the meaning of *lor* as 'south' (Morris 1984: 133). Francillon gives the translation of *lor* as 'horizon'. Probably this translation comes from the way the Wehali explain the meaning of *lor* by pointing to the large open horizon at the south sea, as they did with me. It is necessary also to add that the reduplication of *lor*, *loloran* means the 'rolling waves'.

The marriage between Ho'ar who lived in *rae* and Taek who came from *lor* produced six sons and one youngest daughter. These seven children were later spread out following the gradual expanding of the dry land. The first two sons lived in the area toward the rising sun and the next two sons lived in the area towards the setting sun, while the last two sons and the youngest daughter remained in Wehali. People now living in these eastern and western territories in the island of Timor are considered by the Wehali as descendants from this 'mountain woman ancestor' and the 'seaside man ancestor'.

To commemorate the mythical house of earth-sky, another house called *Ai Lotuk* (literally, slender tree) was built in the hamlet of Laran as the origin house of the Wesei Wehali people. The front half of the house is oriented towards the seaside (*lor*) and the back part of the house is oriented towards the high region in the mountain (*rae*). As a sacred house, it is also popularly known as Uma Maromak (the house of the Bright One). In ritual language this house is called 'the sheath of Wesei, the sheath of Wehali' (*knua Wesei, knua Wehali*). The ritual name indicates that this sacred house is categorically a female house. Ferdi Seran, a school teacher and a respected *adat* elder in Wehali, explains that using the metaphor of a sword: 'The sheath is the house of the sword. So, the sheath is categorically female, while the sword is male.' By mentioning this ritual name, emphasis is placed on the nature of the 'femininity' of this sacred house. As a female house, this house (and other clan houses) has no front platform (*labis*) of the kind that serves as the men's sleeping verandah. As the most sacred house in the whole realm of Wesei Wehali, the direction or orientation of this sacred house becomes a 'standard direction' for understanding the orientation of other clan houses and lineage houses within the inner Wehali territory.

There are three doors that are located in different segments of the outer walls of the house. The first is *oda matan lor*,[7] often described as the male door. This door is located in the front half of the house. The other two doors are located in the back half of the house. Neither one is directly opposite the front door. One of these two doors is called *oda matan rae*. If we use the sacred Ai Lotuk house as a point of reckoning, this door is

---

7   The common word used for 'door' is *oda matan*. In ritual language, *oda matan* is paired with *heli matan. Heli* means 'to conceal', 'to cover up', but, the word is not commonly used. The word *odan* refers to branches of bamboo. A bamboo with strong branches will make a good ladder. So, *odan* can also be translated as 'ladder'.

located at the right side of the back of the house where it faces the setting sun. In daily conversation this door is referred to as a female door. Water, firewood, food and other daily needs are brought into the house through this door. Women and children also use this door for access into the house. Directly opposite this door is a third door called *oda matan la sa'en* with which no gender category is associated. Regarding the designation of this door (*oda matan la sa'en*), there are different proposals as to how to it should be translated. Some people refer to this door as the 'door of the rising sun' (*oda matan loro sa'en*) since together *oda matan la sa'en* and *oda matan rae* comprise an axis of the path of the sun. Other people simply translate it literally as 'the unclimbed door'[8] because there is no access into the house through this door. It remains closed until a particular ritual event is observed in the house.

The orientation of a Wehali house may be explained in two ways. The first is based on the orientation of the front half and back half of the house. Using the metaphor of the human body, the front half is called *karas* (chest) and the back half is called *kidun* (buttock). The former is facing the seaside (*lor*) while the latter is facing the high place in the mountain (*rae*). Within this human analogy, a Wehali house is depicted as a person facing the south sea with her back turned to the mountain. In this layout, a long axis that runs from 'buttock' to 'chest', from back to front, from north to south is imagined as running from mountain to sea, from the high place (*rae*) to the low place (*lor*). In ritual language this axis is termed *foho hun, ain tasi* in which the mountain (*foho*) is described as the source and origin (*hun*) and the sea (*tasi*) is the 'foot' (*ain*).

In many Austronesian societies, 'trunk' is usually paired with 'tips' and not with 'foot'. However, the pairing of 'trunk' (*hun*) with 'foot' (*ain*) in Wehali, I would argue, cannot be seen as a deviation from the common Austronesian paradigm. In the phrase *foho hun-ain tasi*, we encounter double pairs: 1. *foho-tasi* and 2. *hun-ain*. The first pair (*foho-tasi*) reveals the ancestral path mentioned above. This pair is of paramount importance in explaining the orientation of the house. Concerning the second pair, *hun* usually comes in a pair with *dikin* or *lain* (tips),[9] while *ain* is normally paired with *ulun* (head). However, *dikin* is incompatible with *tasi*. So, one

---

8   *La sa'en* is supposed to be derived from *la* = not (negation) and *sa'en* = to climb. So, *oda matan la sa'en* can be translated as 'the unclimbed door'.

9   There is a marked difference between *dikin* and *lain* which I gloss as 'tips'. *Lain* refers to the tips of a tree as a whole, while *dikin* refers to the pointed end of the crown of the tree.

cannot say, for example, *tasi dikin* but one can say *mota dikin* (tips of a river). On the other hand, *ain* is compatible with *tasi* as well as with *dikin*. Given these associations, the long axis of *foho hun ain tasi* can be translated as 'the trunk of the mountain and the tips (instead of 'foot') of the sea'. With this notion a Wehali house, like most other Austronesian houses, is imagined as growing up like a tree from the trunk to the tips (Ellen 1986: 26; Waterson 1991: 124–129; Fox 1993a: 17).

The second way of looking at the directionality of a house is by observing the orientation of its doors. Although conceptually the notion of *lor* stands in the opposite direction from the notion of *rae*, the actual positioning of these doors within a house is not a direct opposition, since the female door, which is called *oda matan rae*, is not located in the back wall as a contrast to the front male door (*oda matan lor*), but rather merely placed at the rear of the house. Therefore, one cannot speak of an axis of *oda matan lor* and *oda matan rae*. Instead, one can speak of the sunrise and sunset axis represented by *oda matan la sa'en* and *oda matan rae*. As noted above, *oda matan la sa'en* is only opened when certain rituals are observed within the house. So during harvest, birth or burial rituals, when this door is opened, these two doors (*oda matan la sa'en* and *oda matan rae*) conceptually delineate the sunrise–sunset and hence east–west axis. The former is considered the east door, while the latter is the west door. Given the 'ritual' importance of the east door, which is only opened during birth (including first harvest) and death rituals, the east–west axis also implies the path of life–death.

Yet the orientation of a house is only partly accounted for on the basis of these directional and oppositional co-ordinates (mountain–seaside, buttock–chest; sunrise–sunset), for house orientation also expresses the nature of the Wehali social relations. In other words, by seeing a named house one can make a good guess as to the order of precedence of that house within a grouping of houses as illustrated in Figure 7.1.

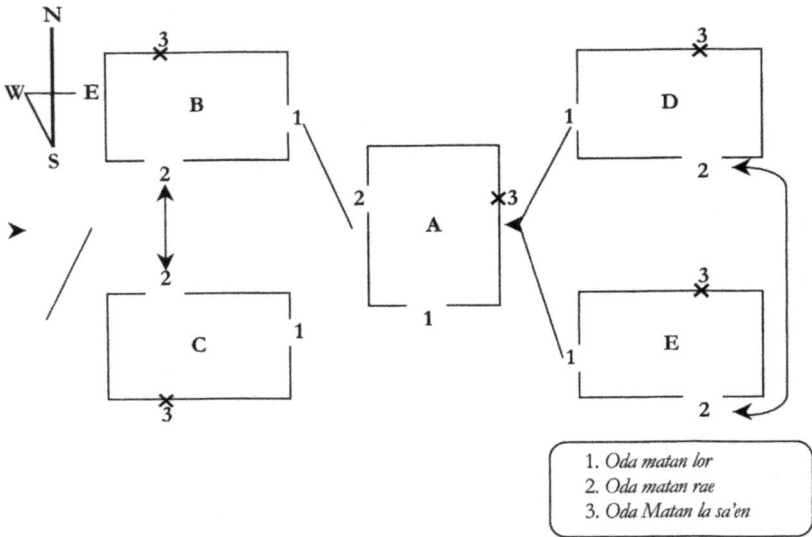

1. *Oda matan lor*
2. *Oda matan rae*
3. *Oda Matan la sa'en*

Figure 7.1: House orientation

With reference to the types of houses outlined above, in this sketch House A represents the dark house (*uma kukun*). It is the forbidden house of the clan. Houses B to E are named houses (*uma mahoo naran*). In this figure, the front half of House A, represented by door 1 is directed towards the southern sea (*lor*). The other lineage houses are arranged differently around the clan house. Within the concentric pattern of a settlement, the front doors of the lineage houses (B to E) must be constructed 'facing' the clan house. The Tetun word for 'facing' is *sasi'an//tatane*, which can be translated as uphold//support.[10] In daily conversations people will say that 'the front door supports the black house' (*oda matan lor si'a baa uma metan*). In the Tetun concept, the supporter is considered as smaller than the one that is supported. Thus, in the expression above, people have acknowledged an order of precedence between the clan house, which is supported by the lineage houses, according to which of the lineage houses (B to E) give precedence to the clan house A.

---

10   Morris translates *sasi'an* as a noun, meaning 'a counsellor', the dignitaries who accompany and support the *liurai* (ruler) (1984: 168). While the noun *tatane* is translated as 'a woven serving tray', the verb *tane* means 'to support', 'to hold up from below' (1984: 180, 181).

With regard to the lateral axis, there are also different arrangements applying to these four lineage houses. From the location of their 'female doors' (*oda matan rae*), it is clear that houses B and C belong to the same mother-sister, *inan bin alin* group (literally, M-eZ-yZ group). As a consequence, the exchange of men in marriage between these two houses is prohibited. Being related as elder-younger sisters (*bin-alin*, eZ-yZ), their female doors have 'to support' each other, as Wehali people phrase it. In accordance with the system of inheritance, the yZ has priority rights over their named house. So, it is the elder sister who 'supports' the youngest sister. In Figure 7.1, the female doors (2) of houses B and C are 'supporting' each other. Conceptually, these two houses are regarded as 'sharing' the same female door.[11] In the case where C is supporting B, then C will be called *uma maksi'an maktane* (the upholding, the supporting house). Although houses B and C are both named houses, the fact that their female doors are 'supporting' each other indicates that one house is a bigger named house than the other. If, for example, house B is supporting house C, then the people of house C will refer to house B as *uma maksi'an maktane*, and so house C has precedence over house B. In most cases, a supporting named house (B) is occupied by an elder sister who conceptually 'supports' her youngest sister who resides in the named house C.

Houses D and E are not related in terms of a mother-sister (*inan bin alin*) group and therefore marriages between these houses are permitted. Men can be circulated not only between these two lineage houses, but also between them and other lineages within the clan because houses D and E do not share a female door with any other lineage houses. In these circumstances, the order of precedence of these houses is not based on relative age, but rather on gender categorisation. A female house gives birth to the male house, so that the latter gives precedence to the former. For these reasons, discussion of the spatial orientation of a house, a hamlet or a domain in Wehali leads us back to their origin myths, since a prior knowledge of the 'paths of the houses' is needed in order to understand the order of precedence of houses within a hamlet or the order of precedence of hamlets at the territory level.

---

11   Celia Ferreira reports that the same concept prevails also in Palauan society. The difference is only in the terms used: the Palauan share the same *biai* (kitchen), while the Wehali share the same *oda matan rae* (female door) (1987: 81, 82).

The Four-Corner House

The south Tetun houses of inner and outer Wehali are a rectangular shape built on slender posts, with the posts supporting the inner section being longer than those supporting the outer section that functions as a platform or verandah. This construction makes the back part of the Wehali house higher than the front part. For the Wehali, the rectangular shape and the higher-lower structure of their houses have cultural significance as encoded in origin myths and various forms of ritual language.

Their rectangular houses are called *uma lidun hat* (the four-corner house). In order to fix the rectangular shape when erecting a new house, those who are 'knowledgeable'[12] in house construction consider in detail where the four corner posts should be situated because the rectangular shape of the house is determined by the precise position of these posts. These 'four corner posts' are called *ri(n) lidun hat*. The strength of a house depends on the strength of its four corner posts. So these posts are symbolised as guardians of the house and in ritual language are called *rin monas rin tos* (literally, the strong post, the hard-durable post).

Using the rectangular shape of the house as an analogy, the inner Wehali people delineate their territory as a 'four-corner land'. Within this 'four-corner land', the four posts of the house are represented by the four hamlets: Kateri, Umakatahan, Kletek and Fahiluka. In their function as 'posts', these four hamlets are ritually regarded as 'the stronghold of Wehali, the fortress of Wehali' (*besi Wehali, baki Wehali*). The first two hamlets are 'the female posts' of the Wehali house, while the latter two hamlets, which are located close to the seaside, are considered to be 'the male posts'. Still drawing on the house ideology, these four hamlets are portrayed as the backbones of the Wehali house. Being classified as posts, these hamlets are reckoned as the immediate protectors of the seat of Maromak Oan (the Bright One) located in the hamlet of Laran. This

---

12 Like the Rotinese (cf. Fox 1993c: 143–145), the south Tetun recognise two forms of knowledgeable person—that is, *makerek* and *badaen*. The latter word refers to a person who is known as skilful in using his hands in creating something. My informant gave examples of these two forms of knowledge as follows. A carpenter is a *badaen* man who uses his hands in carving the house posts. By contrast an *adat* and ritual expert is a *makerek* man because he carves the posts with words (*lia*). Gender categories can also be added: *badaen* denotes a male category, while *makerek* denotes a female category. Those who are experts in planning and constructing, as well as narrating are the *makerek badaen* people. Another thing that needs to be emphasised is that the knowledge of *makerek badaen* is not something that can be acquired. Rather, it is inherited. So, in a clan (*leo*), the knowledgeable persons constitute a lineage, called *uma makerek badaen*.

is the seat of central authority in Wehali. Drawing on the imagery of a 'hearth' located inside a house, the hamlet of Laran (which itself means 'centre') is described in ritual language as manas *ha'in*//*klak ha'in* (the only heat, the only burning charcoal).

This concept of 'house society' can be traced down to the clan and lineage levels. When a clan house is built, its four posts must be provided by particular lineages (*uma*) that ritually play the role of 'guardians' of the clan. Following the same pattern, when a lineage house is constructed its four corner posts are provided by the particular named houses that act as 'guardians' (*makdakar*) of the lineage house. So, when Uma Loro Fulan (literally, the house of the sun and moon) in the hamlet of Le'un Klot was rebuilt, the four posts were provided by the Haitimuk people. According to their myth of origin, the people of Le'un Klot derive from Haitimuk. Therefore, the Le'un Klot people recognise the Haitimuk as their guardians. In ritual language, the Haitimuk are referred to as:

mahein nanokar	the watchers of the stable
mahein dadasan	the watchers of the fence
makdakar inuk tuan	the guardians of the old track
makdakar dalan tuan	the guardians of the old path

These four corner posts were then taken to Le'un Klot by four minor male rulers (*dato*), namely Dato Mota, Dato Tamiru, Dato Kalete and Dato Bulu As. These are the immediate 'protectors' of the Le'un Klot. The same set of arrangements can also be observed in the domain of Wehali. I have been informed that if the most sacred house within the realm of Wesei Wehali, known as Ai Lotuk (literally, a slender tree) and situated in the hamlet of Laran, had to be renovated, then its four posts would have to be gained from the hamlet of Sulit Anemeta, 'the guardians of the stable of Wehali' (*makdakar knokar Wehali*). These posts would be brought down by the four clan heads (*fukun*) who represent the four hamlets in Wehali, namely those of Kateri, Umakatahan, Kletek and Fahiluka.

The rectangular form of the Wehali house, marked by its four corners and other ordered structural elements, is fundamental to Wehali social relations. In summary, this rectangular house is called *uma lidun hat* and the four corner posts are *rin lidun hat*. Based on the imagery of a rectangular house, the Wehali portray their territory as 'the four corner land' (*rai lidun hat*), 'the four-elbow land' (*rai lidun hat*). The four posts can be further distinguished in terms of gender classification: the two front posts are male posts, while the two back posts are female posts. In ritual, the four hamlets mentioned above are also categorised as male and female hamlets. The hamlet of Kateri, located in the mountain region, and the hamlet of Umakatahan, located in the plain but ritually regarded as part of the inner Wehali house, play the role of female hamlets. These hamlets are called *leo foho hun* (hamlets on the trunk of the hill). By contrast, the hamlets of Kletek and Fahiluka, which are located close to the seaside, play the role of male hamlets. These hamlets are called *leo ain tasi* (literally, hamlets on the leg of the sea). Again, the cultural associations of woman:man as mountain:sea is maintained here.

Ritual Posts

There are no fixed rules on how big a named house has to be. On average, the ratio between the longer and the shorter sides of the house is about 5:4 outstretched arms (*ro'a*). In general, the height of the inner house floor is about one metre above the ground, while the front platform is about 10 to 20 cm lower than the inner house. The difference in height between the floor of the inner house and the floor of the highest platform (*labis leten*) depends on the size of the floor beams. The same differences in height can be applied to the floor of the higher platform and that of lower platform (*labis kraik*). The step (*tetek*) to the lower platform is built some 20 cm above the ground. Silt deposited by annual flooding in the area has raised the level of the ground so that it now almost touches the lower platform of many houses. In these circumstances, a *tetek* is not needed for practical purposes. However, the *tetek* serves not only a practical purpose, but primarily it symbolises the different status of those who occupy it during an *adat* gathering. Therefore a *tetek* is considered an integral part of the three layers of the floor. In the house of a clan head (*uma fukun*), the *tetek* is wider than in other named houses. This *tetek* can then be called the lower platform (*labis kraik*). In this case, what serves as the lower platform in most houses becomes the middle platform (*labis klaran*) of the *fukun* house. Thus, the platforms of Wehali houses can be considered as a trichotomy if the ladder is reckoned as the lowest platform. On the other hand, it can also be treated as a dichotomy if the ladder is not treated as a sitting place.

In erecting a house, concentration is focused on where this new house is to be constructed, towards which direction it must be oriented and who is responsible for providing the main building elements that serve as the focus of ritual for the house. So, when Uma Ha'e Bot from the hamlet of Fatu Isin was to be 'reunited'[13] with its mother (Uma Tanani) in the hamlet of Leklaran, the guardians of the Tanani house invited the guardians of two other houses (Uma Bei Fahik Bere Bauk and Uma Bei Kabu) to negotiate on the location and the orientation of this forthcoming house. These latter two houses are the 'supporting' houses of the former one. These were important issues to discuss, particularly the orientation of the forthcoming house, because the house to be 'reunited' was a male house, while the three houses mentioned above (*uma* Tanani, Uma Bei Fahik Bere Bauk and Uma Bei Kabu) were categorically female houses.[14] The aim of the discussion is phrased as 'to tie the trunks together' (*hun beli meti*). Since, according to the myth, those three houses were related in a mother-sister group (*uma inan bin alin*), and therefore conceptually shared the same female door, they had particularly to negotiate the orientation of the relocated house's female door so it would not 'share' the same female door as they themselves do. The second concern of this meeting was to decide who was going to provide the main building elements, namely the posts (*rii* or *rin*). As has been mentioned, the four corner posts and the two main pillars of a house represent different *uma* within a clan. So, in this meeting the guardians of these *uma* were reminded of their ritual requirement to provide these 'ritual' posts, referred to as *riin makerek//riin mean* (literally, the engraved post, the golden post).

---

13   It was said that the guardians of the Uma Ha'e Bot in the hamlet of Fatisin have returned to their domain of origin in Suai (the present East Timor territory) and therefore this house had to be returned to its mother, Uma Leklaran Tanani (or simply Uma Tanani) in the hamlet of Leklaran. This house was then considered to be reunited with its mothers and sisters. In this 'new settlement', Uma Ha'e Bot was designated Uma Makbalin so as to take the place of the named house they had previously 'supported'.

14   The Kamanasa people were originally Suai people of East Timor. They migrated to the Wehali territory (or using their phrase, returned to the lap of Wehali) some 80 to 90 years ago. Among the migrants were members of Uma Makbalin origin group and Uma Tanani origin group. These two houses originated from male and female siblings. The former is the male origin group, while the latter is the female origin group. Uma Ha'e Bot discussed here is a 'supporting house' of Uma Makbalin and therefore is considered as Uma Makbalin's son. Thus, Uma Ha'e Bot is a male house like Uma Makbalin whose name and status it subsequently acquired.

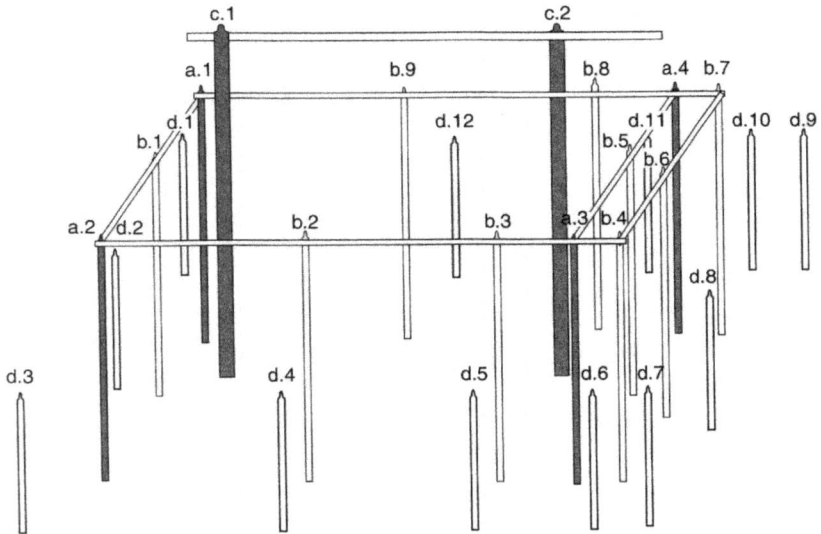

Figure 7.2: House posts

a. *Rin lidun hat*; b. *Ksa'es*; c. *Kakuluk*; d. *Rin kiak*.

In general one can distinguish three kinds of posts (see Figure 7.2): 1. the four corner posts (*rin lidun hat*—a.1 to a.4 and *ksa'es*—b.1 to b.9); 2. the two pillars (*kakuluk lor* and *kakuluk rae*—c.1 and c.2); and 3. the 12 peripheral 'orphan' posts (*rin kiak*—d.1 to d.12). When the first two posts are 'planted',[15] the katuas performs a short ritual.

Sequentially, the four corner posts are the first to be planted. These posts are divided into two categories: the male corner posts and the female corner posts. When these posts are going to be planted, those who are symbolically represented by the posts should be the first to dig[16] the ground. In practice, these people are merely present at the scene. The actual digging is conducted by those who are categorised as *liman lais ain kmaan* (fast arms, light feet), the helpers in house construction. From my

---

15 I participated in the erection of a named house in the hamlet of Leklaran, in the village of Kamanasa. The posts of this house were not 'planted' into the ground, but rather installed on top of stones. Some other houses have even used concrete as the bases of the posts. The villagers informed me that the 'planted' posts easily become rotten in the plains of south Tetun because of the annual flooding. Considering that nowadays the wood used for posts is not easily obtained, many posts of new named houses are no longer planted into the ground. However, for the forbidden house (*uma lulik*), planting the posts is still considered necessary.

16 The common term for 'to dig the ground' is *ke'e rai* (to cut the earth). However, in the context of house construction, the Tetun use the phrase *hakane rai*, which literally means 'to wound the earth'.

observation, there is no definite regulation on the sequence of digging, although some people said that the holes for the two female posts should be prepared first. Once the four corner holes are ready, the living space is considered as having been determined and for a moment everyone is cleared from this site.

In the middle of this rectangular-shaped ground, a female mat (*kleni feto*) is spread out and the preparation for the rite of 'feeding the earth' (*hahaan rai*) is begun. The guardians of the house (*ferik-katuas*) come forward with *mama lulik* (forbidden betel-nut). These *mama lulik*, translated for me as 'offerings', consist of a small bundle of cotton, a silver coin (*kmurak*) or sometimes a golden chest plate (*kbelak*) worn by men, a knife, seven betel leaves, seven dried sliced areca nuts and a mixture of coconut juice and pig's blood. The male guardian (*katuas*) carries the juice and blood in a palm leaf basket called *knaban*. This is a male object and therefore carried by a man. The rest of the items are placed in a square palm-leaf container (*koba*). This *koba* is then put inside a pyramidal-shaped palm leaf basket (*hane matan*) and carried by the female guardian (*ferik*). Again gender categories are applied to these baskets. *Koba* is categorically female, because it is a woman's betel-nut container. On the other hand *bane matan* is categorically male because in the marriage ceremony the male gifts are placed in this type of basket. When this 'sacred betel-nut' has been laid in the middle of the female mat, then work can continue because a guarantee of the safety of the work has been properly installed. A slight variation was observed in the hamlet of Le'un Klot. Prior to the preparation of the corner post holes, a short ritual of 'cooling down the earth' (*halirin rai*) was performed. For this task the title-holder of *katuas* fetched a bucket of water from the sacred spring situated in the eastern part of the village. With this water in hand, he watered the spots that had been marked for 'planting' the four corner posts and the two main pillars.

The second step is erecting the *ksa'es*, of which there are nine in all. Of the *ksa'es* posts, six are located midway between the four corner posts and the remaining three are along the edge of the platform. These posts support structures of the house. The trunk part is 'planted' in the ground, while the tips take the beams that support the middle of the rafters. As intermediate posts, no ritual event is observed when they are erected. Once the four corner posts and the nine rafter supporter posts (*ksa'es*) have been erected, the rectangular shape of the house is complete and so the third step can be commenced.

The third set of posts to be erected are the two main pillars of the house. One is located in the front half of the house, which is conceptually oriented toward the seaside (*lor*), and is therefore known as *kakuluk lor*. This pillar is also given another name, male pillar (*kakuluk mane*), because it is a place where a man invokes his ancestors. The second pillar is located in the back half of the house, which is conceptually seen as oriented toward the high place in the mountain (*rae*). For this reason, the pillar is named *kakuluk rae*. When a woman prepares betel-nut sacrifice, she is delineated as preparing them in front of the *kakuluk rae*. Therefore this pillar is also known as the female pillar (*kakuluk feto*). Both the male and female pillars are described as sacrificial pillars in Figure 7.3 to emphasise the ritual significance of these pillars. They are the most important posts in a Wehali house and this importance is signified firstly by the name *kakuluk* itself and secondly by rituals performed in connection with their erection. Tetun Indonesian speakers translate the Tetun word *kakuluk* as 'grand post' (*tiang agung*). In Tetun, the term *kakuluk* is related to the noun *ulun* ('head'), adjective *ulu* (first born) and adverb *uluk* ('before', 'former' or simply 'first' in time). So, the term *kakuluk* denotes the prior and thus superior existence of these pillars compared to other posts. Physically, one can distinguish a male pillar from a female pillar as shown in Figure 7.3. The top end of the male pillar is carved in a pointed shape. This top end is called *amak*. The top end of the female pillar is cut in a V-shape simply called *hasan*, which means 'junction'. These two pillars are then linked by a ridge pole called *laho dalan* (path of rats). The hole that joined *amak* with the ridge pole is called *inak*.

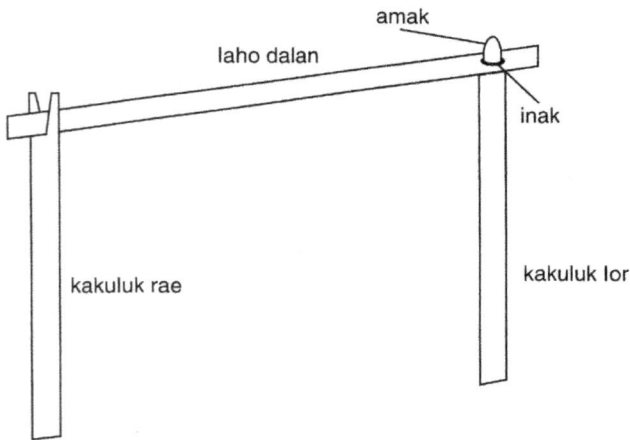

Figure 7.3: Sacrificial pillars

When a named house is no longer safe to be inhabited, all parts of the building can be dismantled except its male pillar. This remains in its place until a new house is erected. If the pillar is considered strong enough, the new house will reuse the old male pillar. The ritual importance of the male pillar is revealed in the following saying:

ita hotu hotu hahina baa nia, hahama baa nia	all of us treat it as our parents
nia mak tane baa maromak	it is the one that supports the bright one
nia mak simu lia simu ibun	it is the one that receives the language and the mouth[17]
nia mak nato'o baa maromak	it is the one that passes (our plea) to the bright one

This male pillar is crucial to a Wehali house. Clan relics such as swords, pouches and betel-nut baskets are hung on it. In every harvest ritual, a whole maize plant is tied to it. Offerings for the ancestors are laid on the floor underneath this pillar. The male guardian of the house also offers his prayer facing this pillar. Compared to the focal position of the male pillar, the female pillar in the Wehali house is hidden behind the hearth and the two to three layers of storage racks above the hearth. It is located in the buttock (*kidun*) part of the house and therefore it gains the nickname *kakuluk uma kidun*.[18] Although situated in a 'hidden' place, it does not necessarily lack ritual importance. If the male post is the place where offerings of betel-nut are laid, the preparation of these offerings is done by a *ferik* (old woman) in front of the female pillar and the three cooking stones (*lali'an*). The betel-nut offerings prepared by the 'old woman' are described in ritual language as:

fuik tolu bua tolu	the three betel leaves the three areca nuts
hatasan hemu tasan	the cooked food the cooked drink

In this 'cooked' condition, not only the betel-nut offerings but also the woman who prepared them are categorically hot, sacred and therefore potentially can be harmful to human beings. To denote the 'sacred' nature of this female pillar, it is also called *kakuluk ha'i*, which can be translated

---

17   The literal meanings of 'language' and 'mouth' can be rendered as 'order' and 'message'.
18   One of the differences between Kamanasa and Wehali-type houses is the location of the female pillar. In the Kamanasa house, the female pillar is located in front of the hearth and therefore it is also called the 'fire pillar' (see also Francillon 1967: 270–271).

literally as the 'fire post'. The association with 'heat' makes this pillar not a place to ask for blessings (raw and cool). When the offering has been prepared, the woman hands it over to a man who is waiting at the male pillar. Now, the offering changes its status from the source of 'danger' to the source of 'blessings':

fuik hitu bua hitu	the seven betel leaves the seven areca nuts
hamatak hemu matak	the raw food the raw drink

The fourth and final step is indicated by the erection of the twelve 'orphan posts' (*rin kiak*) that support the rafters at the periphery. My informants explained that posts erected in the three steps described represent members of the household and therefore they are the first to be erected. The orphan posts represent 'others', therefore they are last to be erected. Like the nine *ksa'es* posts, no ritual event is associated with these orphan posts.

With the completion of the orphan posts, the essential building elements that have ritual significance have been erected in the correct place. The posts that represent various segments of society have been erected in the right order. But the owners of the land (*rai na'in*) have not yet been informed that 'human beings' (represented by the posts) have already intruded into their realm. The ritual to inform the *rai na'in* is also called *hahaan rai* (to feed the earth). The old man (*katuas*) moves again into the middle of the rectangular house ground toward the sacred betel-nut that has been laid there when the space was marked out. Using the knife set apart for this purpose, the old man scratches the edge of the silver coin so that its dust falls on the small cotton ball prepared for it. Together with one betel leaf and one slice of dried areca nut, this cotton ball is then slipped into the trunk of the post. Then a small amount of pig's blood is dropped on this 'sacred betel-nut'. The same activity is repeated for every ritual post beginning with the front right corner post and moving anti-clockwise, ending up on the male pillar. As has been mentioned, this ritual is observed specifically for the six ritual posts, namely the four corner posts (*rin lidun hat*) and the two main pillars (*kakuluk*). The information given to me, as to Francillon is that the 'failure to carry out this ritual … would result in the earth taking the life of one of the house members' (Francillon 1967: 222).

There are still other rituals performed before and after the completion of the house as noted by Francillon, such as the 'ceremony of the walls' (1967: 236–243), 'feeding the house' (1967: 243–248) and 'the introduction of fire into the new house' (1967: 248–249). I was told that formerly in the hamlet of Manumutin before the tips of the roof of a new house are trimmed into a nice tidy look, a short ritual must be conducted. This custom is based on a myth possessed only by the Manumutin people. According to this myth, when the house of Maromak Oan was built, the clan of Lawalu (the male servants of Maromak Oan) had the task of trimming the tips of the roof. The Lawalu could not execute the job well and therefore proved their lack of knowledge. So, Maromak Oan called on the clan of Umanen (the female servants). Umanen took advantage of this to show off their 'divine knowledge'. Instead of trimming the tips off using scissors, the Umanen trimmed using fire for a faster and better result.

Inner House and Platform

The Wehali house is conceptualised as divided into two spaces. The first space is the 'inner house' (*uma laran*) and the other is the platform or verandah. The Tetun word for platform is *labis*, which literally means 'layer'. Although the inner house and the platform are under the same roof, the difference in the terms applied to these two areas of the house creates the impression that the former is the 'true' living space, while the latter is only another space attached to the living space. This impression is strengthened by the way walls are installed in both parts of the house. Walls encircling the inner house are 'properly' attached to the main building elements, while walls surrounding the platform are only 'temporarily' installed. The difference between 'permanently installed' and 'temporarily installed' is quite significant, so a technical explanation concerning this type of 'wall' is unavoidable here.

The walls are made of gebang palm leaves, which are plaited coarsely to form leaf mats. The size of each mat depends on the length of the leaves. There are two types of wall mat known in the region (Figure 7.4).

The first type is called *kleni mane* ('male mat'). This type of mat is plaited (by women or men) using whole leaves that are not split from their original stalk. So the original stalk becomes the base of the mat, while the tips form its periphery. The tips of the leaves are plaited to make up a fan-shaped mat. These shaped mats are arranged neatly to comprise a wall panel of 8–10 cm thick on average. Just like planting a tree, the trunk part of the mats are arranged at the bottom of the panel, while the tips are at the upper part. These wall panels, which consist of hundreds of *kleni mane*, are used to enclose the inner section of the house.

Kleni mane   Kleni feto

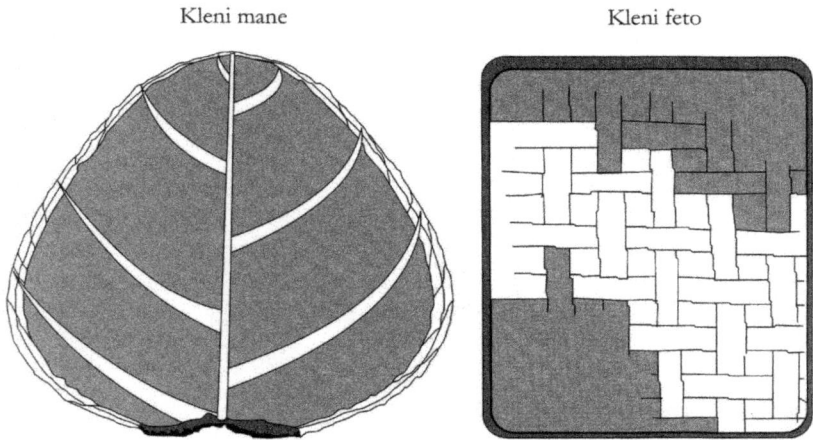

Figure 7.4: Male and female wall mats

The second type of wall mat is called *kleni feto* ('female mat').[19] This mat is plaited using palm leaves that have been split from their stalk. These leaves are interlaced into a rectangular shape like ordinary sleeping mats. Like the male mat, the female mat is also coarsely plaited by women. To encircle a platform one only needs an average of 18 to 20 mats. The way a *kleni feto* is installed to become the enclosure of the platform indicates that it is not a permanent wall. Two pieces of cord are tied at the two edges of each screen. To install the 'wall', these cords are hung on a stick of wood added to the main building elements. This construction suggests a temporary installation of 'walls' surrounding the platform. The temporary nature of this 'wall' is also indicated by the common usage of this type of mat in daily life. Apart from its function as 'moveable' walls, these (female) mats are also used for different purposes: during rainy days, they are used as umbrellas; and in various social gatherings, these mats are laid on the ground as sitting mats. It must be noted that in a social gathering members of the named house have a right to sit on the platforms, while the 'new man', the sons-in-law who reside in their wives'

---

19   The wall screen (*kleni*) is plaited in the same way as an ordinary sleeping mat (*biti*). The differences between these two items are due to their functions. As a sleeping mat, a *biti* is made longer than a *kleni*; the leaves used for the screen are divided into small strips; and before plaiting, those strips of leaf are refined, so as to produce a smooth surface. By contrast, a *kleni* is shorter than a *biti*; its size depends on the length of the palm leaf; and the leaves are plaited without prior refinements. Therefore, a *kleni* is rougher than a *biti*.

houses, sit on the mats spread on the ground. So the right to sit on the platform for an *adat* meeting or to sit on the mat signifies a man's status with respect to the named house concerned.

My informants particularly drew my attention (without elaborating further) to two implications raised by the distinction between the male and female wall mats: first, the male mats are used to encircle the inner house, the living space of women, and the female mats are used to encircle the platform, the sleeping space of men; second, the male mats are installed properly to form solid, 'permanent' walls, while the female mats are hung loosely to suggest 'temporary' walls.

The 'permanent' and 'temporary' construction of these two types of walls relates to a more complex ideology concerning the nature of masculinity and femininity. Accordingly, women are associated with 'immobility', since they are surrounded by permanent walls, in contrast to men who are mobile just like the 'temporary' construction of the walls of their platforms. Women are also associated with 'cooked' and 'heat', while men are 'raw' and 'cool'. The lack of ventilation within the inner house, the thick wall established around it and the 'unclimbed' door that remains closed make this section darker than it would otherwise be. Natural light does not get into the house. Thus, the only light is from the hearth burning inside the house. From this perspective, the house associates women with 'dark', 'fire' and 'heat'. Together with the ritual function of a woman to prepare sacred betel-nut, these associations articulate the sacred nature of women. As noted above, the forbidden betel-nut (*mama lulik*) prepared by women is in ritual language termed 'the cooked food, the cooked drink'.

By contrast, platforms as men's spaces are only surrounded by the 'temporary' walls that give an impression of coolness. 'The cooked food, the cooked drink' (*haa tasan, hemu tasan*) prepared by the woman inside the house becomes 'the raw food, the raw drink' (*haa matak, hemu matak*) in the hands of the men. According to this analysis, the female in Wehali is associated with fire, dark, heat, cooked, sacred and immobility. Not all of these categories are in contrast to those associated with men. But the notions of outside, bright, cool and blessing in terms of wealth are closely associated with the masculine.

The marked difference between the inner house and its outer area (verandah or platform) is also evident in the different terms of reference applied to members of the household. The inner house is a space restricted to women, children and parents. When a boy is considered eligible to carry betel-nut pouches, an indication of adulthood, he will join his father on the platform. Even a son-in-law has limited access to join his wife in the inner section of the house. By contrast, the platform is the realm of men. Male guests are entertained only in this section of the house. 'To enter the inner house' is another metaphor for having sexual intercourse. When a man marries a woman of this house, he resides in his wife's house as a 'new man'. An honorific term of reference for this new man is 'platform master' (*labis na'in*). By contrast, his wife (and their children) are referred to as the 'house master' (*uma na'in*). The difference in these terms of reference suggests that even a son-in-law is not part of the inner house. This space is reserved for the new man's wife, her mother and the younger children.

The space of the inner house as the realm of women and the platform as the realm of men is demarcated by a floor beam called *kotan*. When Wehali draw on this *kotan* for metaphor, they refer not only to a spatial boundary, but as I describe below, also to a social boundary within their society.

Social Boundary

In general, a *kotan* is a floor beam that runs in a lateral direction and functions as a borderline between two spaces. In the Wehali house, these beams are part of the building elements of the inner house.[20] There are two types of *kotan* within a house, and are often mentioned by the Wehali when notions of 'boundary' are discussed (Figure 7.5).

The outside cross-beam (*kotan lor*) is physically observable because it is located above the floor level. Its physical appearance evokes the impression that the *kotan lor* is the threshold of the front male door (Morris 1984: 117). However, more than just a threshold, it serves as a borderline between the inner house and the space of the platform. From various discussions concerning the cultural function of this beam, I became aware that for the south Tetun the *kotan lor* separates the outsiders from the insiders: as a demarcation line between the realm of women inside the house and the realm of men outside the house, it serves to separate the *uma na'in* (literally, 'house masters') from the *labis na'in* (literally, 'platform masters'). When

---

20   In the Kamanasa type, *kotan* also occurs in the platform section, where it runs in a north–south direction (cf. Francillon 1967: 254–257).

a young man comes to court a young woman in the house, neither the man nor the woman are permitted to cross over this beam. So the woman stays inside the house while the man sits on the platform. 'Crossing the beam' (*hakur kotan*) is thus a phrase to denote misconduct. The other cross-beam, called *kotan uma laran*, is not physically observable since it is located under and functions as support for the house floor. However, as this beam joins the 'unclimbed' door to the female door, one could locate it simply by looking at the position of these doors. This *kotan* marks the separation between the adult women's section (consisting of quarter 1—delivery room; quarter 2—hearth; quarter 3—for the storing of water jars) and the space available for other members of the household (quarter 4—parents and children; quarter 5—young women). In the next chapter, I discuss the ritual significance of this beam as a demarcation line that separates a mother during the rite of seclusion after childbirth from the rest of the household.

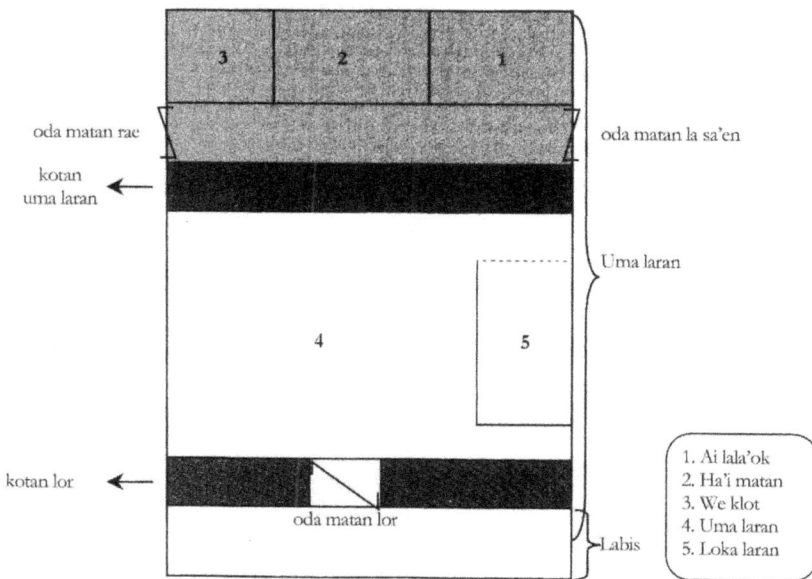

Figure 7.5: Cross-beams of a house

In keeping with the notion of *kotan* as a boundary that demarcates both spaces and people, Wehali origin myths draw on idiom to mark other social boundaries as well. So, just as a *kotan* separates outsiders from insiders and men from women in a Wehali 'house', there is an imaginary boundary demarcating insider clans from outsider clans and clans that are ritually regarded as male from those that are regarded as female.

Engaging this house metaphor, Wehali conceive of the present ordering of their society as rendered in and derived from the origin myth (Reference Text 2). There, it is narrated that when Ho'ar Makbalin Balin Liurai was of marriageable age, 'a man from the sun above', Na'i Loro Leten also known as Na'i Luru Mea, 'spat or flung down betel spittle' towards her. This phrase is a literal translation from the text of the myth *tuda kmusan*, referring to sexual intercourse between nobles. As a result, Ho'ar became pregnant and gave birth to Bano Ha'in Liurai. The relations between Ho'ar and Na'i Luru Mea are depicted in a romantic poem as follows:

anin nakis onan	the gentle breeze is blowing (crying)
nakis onan	is blowing (crying)
anin nadais onan	the wind is sobbing
nadais onan	is sobbing
nadais namodok fui no bua sia	sobbing to ripen the betel leaves and areca nuts
nakis namodok fui no bua sia.	crying to ripen betel leaves and areca nuts.
ama na'i maromak na'i maromak	the glowing father, the glowing one
matuun kmaun baa takan Wesei	sends down dew to the betel leaves of Wesei
matuun kmaun baa bua Wesei	sends down dew to the areca nuts of Wesei
bua Wesei ami tahan bea ida	the areca nuts of Wesei, we are in the same garden
takan Wesei ami tuun leo ida	the leaves of Wesei, we are under the same shade
sa'e be ku'u hodi basu liu onan	climb on to pinch, take (us) away
sa'e hikar baa fatin inan maromak	return to the place of the bright mother
sa'e hik ar baa fatin aman maromak	return to the place of the bright father

After quoting this poem, the *adat* historian added that 'with this birth, Wehali then had a Maromak Oan and a Liurai'. This birth, therefore, marks the opening of the era of Wehali's earlier inhabitants and their system of government. Among the inhabitants of that earlier era were two female ancestors, Balok Liurai and Se'uk Liurai, from whom the present inhabitants of inner Wehali who occupy the 'trunk of the hill' and 'the feet of the sea' are said to originate. It was Se'uk Liurai who gave birth to Dini Kotan and Luruk Kotan. Concerning the birth of Dini Kotan and Luruk Kotan, the myth recounts as follows:

Se'uk Liurai nahoris baa Dini Kotan Luruk Kotan[21]	Se'uk Liurai gave birth to Dini Kotan and Luruk Kotan
Dini Kotan Dini Liurai	Dini Kotan (entitled) Dini Liurai
Luruk Kotan Luruk Liurai	Luruk Kotan (entitled) Luruk Liurai
hodi kotan leten katak raiklaran	(they come) to demarcate the world above, to tell the world below

Dini and Luruk are common men's and women's names respectively, while *kotan* refers to the floor-beam that delineates spaces in a house. So according to folk exegesis, with the birth of Dini and Luruk, a *kotan* has been laid to demarcate women the 'insiders' from men the 'outsiders'. The descendants of Dini Kotan, the male ancestor, are the present 'periphery people' (*ema molin*), while the descendants of Luruk Koran, the female ancestor, are the present 'centre people' (*ema laran*). Thus, the division of Wehali society into male clans and female clans, centre and periphery began with the birth of Dini Koran and Luruk Koran, who laid a 'cross-beam' between these societal segments.

The notion of *kotan* that marks the physical boundary within the house between the realm of men and the realm of women is employed by the Wehali to create a social boundary and distinction within their society. So, in Wehali, people speak about inner or centre clans, which are ritually considered female, versus outer or periphery clans, which are ritually considered male. Here the insiders have precedence over the outsiders, the centre over the periphery. The claim made by the Wehali that their society is the centre, the female, and therefore has precedence over other societies, is justified in the same origin myth that recounted the laying of the 'cross-beam' between eras. This origin myth, which I sketch in Figure 7.6, uses the dual categories of male/female, first to dry/last to dry and first-born/last-born to proclaim Wehali's superiority over other societies.

---

21 In another version of the myth, the name Kotan is replaced with Katan. In Tetun the word *katan* means 'to sew' or 'to close'. Despite the change of terms used in the two versions of the myth, the notions of 'border' and 'enclosure' are also reflected in this name.

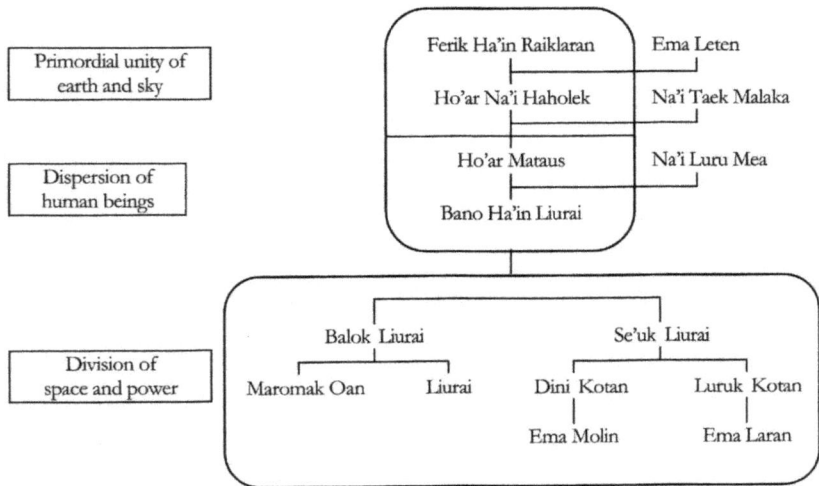

Figure 7.6: Social division

The claim made by the Wehali that their society is a female society is based on the origin myth I sketch above. The first four female ancestors lived in what is now Wehali. Three of them married 'outside' men. These men each resided in their wife's houses. The origin myth always places emphasis on the phenomenon of 'outsider' men coming to marry the insider women. These women, who lived in present-day Wehali, were the prime cause of the first dry land emerging and the present order of the earth. The claim that the first dry land to emerge was in Wehali derives from this part of the myth. Therefore, the asymmetrical relation between Wehali and other territories is based on the notion of *maran uluk* (literally, 'first to dry') and *maran ikus* (literally, 'last to dry'). The territory described as the 'first to dry' was occupied by female ancestors, so this territory constituted a female territory or a female society.

A dyadic structure of government is narrated in the myth in conjunction with the expanding of the dry land when the earth was fully populated. This era is marked by the birth of Balok Liurai and Se'uk Liurai. It was the descendants of Balok Liurai who were entitled to the offices of Maromak Oan (the ritual ruler) and Liurai (the executive ruler). The descendants of Se'uk Liurai then become the guardians of these two rulers who are portrayed as 'those who eat reclining, drink reclining'. The 'guardian people' are further divided into the 'centre people' and the 'periphery people'. The line of demarcation between centre and periphery is marked by the conceptual cross-beam (*kotan*). Those who belong to the centre are categorically female societies and those who are on the periphery are categorically male. Just like the division of male and female in a house, these societies also inhabit different localities. The descendants of Dini Kotan (the periphery people) live at the 'feet of the sea', the present hamlets of Kletek and Fahiluka, while the descendants of Luruk Kotan (the centre people) live at the 'trunk of the mountain', the present hamlets of Kateri and Umakatahan.

Such oppositional categories provide a basis for understanding the hierarchical nature of Wehali society. In daily discourse, Wehali claim superiority over other societies based on two things. First, Wehali is the origin place of the dry land (*maran hun*). Second, in this *maran hun* lived the female ancestors of all human kind. Thus, these two categories (gender and temporality) are associated with Wehali.

Although as a whole Wehali is considered as female, within inner Wehali herself, one finds a division into male and female societies. The pattern of asymmetrical relations between the female Wehali and the male Wehali is also organised as an order of precedence. The male gives precedence to the female because the latter gives birth to the former. The first-born (female) takes precedence over the last-born (male). These categories define an order of precedence, as Fox (1989a: 52) has suggested, through their recursive application (Figure 7.7).

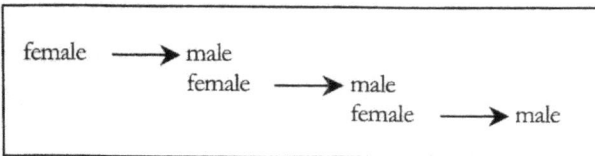

```
female ——→ male
         female ——→ male
                  female ——→ male
```

Figure 7.7: Order of precedence

In Wehali representations, this process itself recurs, both temporally and spatially as I have tried to demonstrate here, at all levels of social and ritual organisation.

Concluding Remarks

This chapter has analysed how a Wehali house serves as a representation of the cosmos and human society. This representation is articulated through a set of opposed categories. The categories used most frequently to express the cosmological ideas encoded in a house are those of sky/earth, upper/lower and mountain/sea. The inner house, which is built higher than the platform, thus becomes symbolic of the sky above. By contrast, the platform, which is constructed lower than the inner house, is associated with the flat lowland of the seaside. This lowland is further associated with the gender category of male because in the origin myth the male ancestors came from that direction. The primordial marriage between the mistress of the inner house and the master of the platform produced the inhabitants of the earth.

These cosmic categories of vertical relations are projected into the horizontal categories of centre/periphery, inside/outside and male/female. So, when Wehali speak about social division, they contrast the centre with the periphery, the inside with the outside and the male with the female in societies.

The two idioms Wehali use to describe their houses suggest that these physical habitations are alive. Like a tree, a Wehali house is growing from the trunk to the tips; like a human being, the Wehali ho use is facing the southern sea of Timor while its back is against the trunk of the mountains in the northern part of Timor.

More than simply a place to dwell, the Wehali house provides a model for their political organisation. The mother who 'sits' in the inner house and the father who is on the platform become perfect symbols of power and authority. She who dwells at the centre is the one who eats reclining, drinks reclining. The highest authority is entrusted into her hands. She is the source of life and fertility, while the peripheral man becomes the protector of the central authority. To him is entrusted the physical well-being, in terms of wealth and security, for the whole house of Wehali.

Last but not least, the Wehali house is an ancestral house. Like most Austronesian houses, it is a place to commemorate the ancestral paths of a particular origin group. It is a 'memory palace' (Fox 1993c: 141).

8

Life-giving Rituals

Introduction

Tetun believe that life can be maintained or even promoted if certain prohibitions are carefully observed. So heavy is the emphasis on 'prohibitions' that a casual observer may come to the conclusion that the Tetun 'religion' or world-view focuses on prohibition. To underline the importance of observing prohibitions as a means to achieving a successful life, this chapter includes an analysis of the Tetun concept of *lulik*, which can be translated as 'prohibition' and 'sacred' with reference to 'avoidance ritual'. The bulk of the chapter, however, explores a variety of dual categories used in south Tetun society as expressed in ritual, particularly two complex series of rituals: first, rituals for childbirth; and second, rituals that follow agricultural activities. Regarding the first series, I focus on rituals observed for pre-childbirth, childbirth and post-childbirth. Regarding the second series, the emphasis is on rituals held during pre-planting and planting, harvest and post-harvest seasons.

Both series of rituals or even each ritual observed in these two cycles, rely on somewhat different symbolic 'operators' (Fox 1989a: 45). Collectively, however, they express the same notion concerning the flow of life from women to men and from inside to outside. The quality of life-giving inherent in these separate rituals is manifested in the Tetun word *hahoris* (*halo* = to make, *moris* = life). Following the Tetun description, the function of a midwife to 'give life' (*hahoris*) to a pregnant woman and the function of 'an old man' (*katuas*) is to 'give life' (*hahoris*) to a seed. *Hahoris* then becomes a key term in understanding both childbirth and agricultural rituals. Thus, ritual in Tetun society is, to use Traube's expression (1986: 12), considered as a technique of life-giving or promotion of life.

The Tetun recognise only two kinds of rituals which they symbolically name using terms related to temperature; *halirin* (to make cool) that can be associated with cool (*malirin*) and *hamanas* (to make hot) that can be associated with heat (*manas*). These two categories of ritual employ certain symbolic oppositions: for example, cool/heat, raw/cooked, tasteless/salty and life/death.

Rituals that are associated with 'heat' are observed in order to redress a broken rule. For example, when a couple finds the solution to a serious dispute that might have led to their divorce, or a person has failed to observe a prohibition agreed upon previously, such as the restriction on harvesting coconuts during a certain period of time, they are obliged to 're-heat the *adat* rule' (*hamanas ukun badu*). In other cases, rituals that are associated with 'heat' aim to change a person metaphysically. A person who has been endowed with 'heat' is potentially a source of danger to people's lives and at the same time is immune from every possible threat. Rituals associated with heat are therefore needed when someone engages in warfare. The ritual to heat up a person is called *hamanas kakaluk hatuda* (to make heated the war pouch) or *hasa'e kakaluk hatuda* (to ascend the war pouch). When the war is over pouches have to be cooled off in another ritual called *halirin kakaluk hatuda* or 'to descend the war pouch' (*kasu kakaluk hatuda*). In principle, this rite deals with the preserving of the lives of those who partake in the ritual and not with the death of others, although it does potentially threaten the lives of others. On the other hand, rituals that are associated with 'cool' aim to give life, well-being and fertility, both to those who take part in them and to the community at large. Conceptually then, rituals that are associated with both 'heat' and 'cool' deal with the importance of life-maintaining and lifegiving symbols.

In this respect, I need to clarify a few technical terms that are used throughout the chapter, particularly the terms for 'ritual' and 'harvest'. In everyday speech the Tetun use only one word, *ukur*, to refer to the notions of both 'rites' and 'ceremony'.[1] Literally, the noun *ukur* refers to cords or threads that link the edges of a rectangular loom. In ritual

---

1   Firth distinguishes a rite from a ceremony as follows: 'A ceremony may be described as enforced by conventional sanctions, whereas a rite is enforced by mystical sanctions' (1967: 73).

language this word is paired with *lahan*, which also means 'threads' as in *kabas lahan* meaning 'a length of cotton thread'. But the word *lahan* also has another meaning, 'a block of land used for cultivation'. With reference to this latter meaning, the phrase *kabas no lahan* means 'rite' or 'ceremony'. No longer associated merely with 'cotton' and 'thread', instead it relates to the classical sexual division of labour: women are the weavers and men are the farmers. Similarly the work of weaving is represented in the word *ukur*, whereas the work of farming is represented in the word *lahan*. Thus, when a Tetun speaks of a rite or ceremony, the emphasis is given to activities that involve both women and men. In a ritual, it is the task of a woman to prepare an offering of betel-nut (*halo mama*) and the task of a man to invoke the ancestors through it (*sera mama*). When it comes to rituals, women are the workers, men are the talkers.

Tetun does not have a generic term for 'harvest'.[2] Concerning the harvest of maize, the Tetun employ two descriptive phrases: 1. *silu batar* (literally, to break off maize cobs) and 2. *baa batar nurak* (literally, to eat baby maize). The phrase *silu batar* is only used to 'harvest' maize cobs when they are ripe. People will not use this term to imply the harvesting of young edible maize. They refer to the latter simply as *haa batar nurak*. The different terms used to denote the two stages of harvest have different connotations in ritual. When people harvest young maize, a small part of the harvest is given to the man's natal house. When people harvest ripe maize, seven cobs are delivered to Maromak Oan as a gift of homage. Different names are also given to the two rituals that accompany these two stages of maize harvest. The ritual in the first stage is called *hamiis*, which for convenience sake can be glossed as ritual to make maize edible. The ritual observed at the second stage of harvest is called *batar mana'i*, literally translated as 'maize of homage'. Due to the different connotations of these two phrases, I refer to the first stage of harvest as 'first harvest' and the second stage of harvest simply as 'harvest'.

---

2   Tetun has different words for 'harvesting' different plants, for example:

silu batar	to break off maize cobs
korut batar ai naruk	to strip sorghum
ku'u hare	to harvest (literally, pinch) rice paddy
taa hudi	to cut banana
fokit li'is	to pull garlic
sahit tabako	to pick tobacco leaves
sau nuu	to pick up coconut

Myth, Ritual and Polity

In this section, I consider the reasons for observing particular rites as they relate to origin myths.[3] To examine the relationship between myth, ritual and social life in this respect I focus on two sets of myths according to their indigenous classification. First, myths that deal with the origin of the earth and human beings, which are called 'language of the earth' (*rai lian*). Second, 'true tales' (*lia tebes*) which concern the origin of food. This latter type of myth was called 'the path of Liurai' by the narrator. Myths concerning the origin of food, according to this classification, are not part of *rai lian*, even though they are still considered to be sacred charters and are therefore treated as 'old and respected language' (*lia tuan*) or 'the source of all languages' (*lia na'in*) as some prefer to call it. In accordance with their nature and function as origin myths, these two complex sets of myths depict two types of rites. Rites narrated in 'language of the earth' deal with people in supplication toward 'the man above' (*ema leten*), who was later known as Maromak (the bright one) for granting them dry land on which to live. On the other hand, *lia tuan* or *lia na'in* deal with rituals that follow the trajectory of human life and the agricultural cycle.

1. 'Language of the Earth'

The myth cited in Reference Text 1 reveals that in the beginning people did not yet know how to prepare a sacrificial offering. The 'mytheme' concerning the first-ever ritual starts with a supplication from Ferik Ha'i Raiklaran (Ho'ar's mother) to Maromak, who lived in the sky above. In her appeal she asks Maromak to widen the origin land, which at that time was only as big as a chicken's eye and a slice of areca nut. In accordance with the Tetun custom in which every plea toward a noble must be accompanied with a 'gift' as a sign for submission, in the plea to widen the living space Ferik Ha'in Raiklaran mentions the importance of bringing an offering as a gift. However, since at that time the earth was still unformed and therefore had not yet produced anything, people on earth could not provide 'gifts' to Maromak. Instead Ferik Ha'in Raiklaran asked

---

3   I emphasise the word 'particular' for two reasons. First, on pragmatic grounds, not all rituals observed by the Tetun can be traced to myths. Second, more theoretically, it aims to avoid the presumption that myths are developed to justify rites and therefore that every rite must be explained in myths. It is true that in some cases certain rites are justified in myths, but it does not prove the primacy of myths over rites or vice versa. Kluckholn in his analysis (Lessa and Vogt 1979: 66–78) argues that both are intricately interrelated because they reveal the social life of a particular people.

Maromak to send down birds so that she could roast them as a sacrificial meal (*lamak hatetu//lamak harani*) for him. So the initial ritual as narrated in the myth is related to the plea of the first woman on earth to expand the inhabited place. As narrated in the myth, Ferik Ha'in Raiklaran asked the man above to provide a place with edges. She pleads to Maromak:

lolo liman la to'o	that cannot be reached by stretching out hands
bi'i ai la dai	that cannot be reached by standing on tiptoes
husu natuun mantarun[4] mai	to send down his sign of power
lamak hatetu, lamak harani[5]	the sacrificial meal, the offering meal
atu hodi halo rai husar, rai binan	to make the navel land, the umbilical cord land
luan no kblean	wide and broad
atu hodi haluan, atu hodi sesu.	to widen and expand.
Maromak na'ak: sa'e mai. ko'i atu fo tone, atu hodi haluan rai ne'e.	The bright one said: come up here. On your return I will give a sharp sword, a sharp machete to widen the land.

As common in Tetun ritual speech, the communication between the woman and the man constitutes 'a ritual dialogue' (Fox 1988: 21, 22). In this formalised verbal communication the man invited the woman to approach him. In the text the man is called Maromak (the bright one). On her return, she was accompanied by two male retainers called Mau Leki and Mau Mauk. The retainers carried things conferred by the man above, namely 'a valuable blow pipe' (*hahuuk kmurak ida*) and 'a wild pigeon bird' (*manu do'u*, in Indonesian *burung dara*). The latter is to be considered as nourishment for royalty and is therefore described in the verse above as *lamak hatetu lamak harani*. This bird made a nest on the only banyan tree that grew there and was left to eat fruits from the tree. Not long afterwards the birds began to multiply.

---

4   The compound word *mantarun* derives from *manu* (rooster) and *tarun* (to bet). So, *mantarun* literally means money received from cockfight gambling. In Tetun it means 'king's property'. The ruler of the petty domain, Le'un Klot, Na'i Klau, jokingly said that this word proves that the Tetun nobles are gamblers.

5   Literally the Tetun word *lamak* refers to 'plates made of banana leaves'. But *lamak* is also a polite word to denote food as nourishment for nobles. The dyadic pair *hatetu harani* is translated as 'gifts' and 'offerings'. Literally the word *hatetu* means 'to lay s.t. on the ground' while *harani* means 'to lay s.t. above', 'to perch'.

In order to prepare for gifts of offering, Mau Leki and Mau Mauk were ordered to hunt a bird with the blow pipe. This first act of hunting is also sealed in the myth in the form of a short poem (*knanuk*), as follows:

Mau Leki Mau Mauk la'o ruu manu	Mau Leki Mau Mauk went to blow down the bird
ruu manu la sala, do'u laluuk ida	they did not miss the target, it was a wild pigeon *laluuk*
do'u laluuk ne'e tunu ba saa	but they did not know where it could be roasted
do'u laluuk ne'e taka ba saa.	but they did not know where it could be placed.

The heroic hunting performed by Mau Leki and Mau Mauk is still repeatedly chanted and sung by women during many ceremonial events. But despite their success as hunters, they failed to perform the obligatory rite. Another version of the myth narrates that Mau Leki and Mau Mauk brought the dead bird as an offering to Maromak without even roasting it. Consequently the offering rotted. The bright one was so displeased that he ordered them to take the uncooked meat back to the earth and exchange it for cooked meat. Both versions of the myth states that Mau Leki and Mau Mauk failed to perform their duty in preparing a correct offering because at that time the land was still watery. There was as yet no dry place to lay down the bird, and, on top of that, there was no fire to roast the bird. When they raised the matter with Ferik Ha'in Raiklaran, she ordered them to fetch fire from the man above. Upon their arrival the man above said he no longer had any fire since, when Ferik Ha'in Raik laran descended to the earth, she took the fire with her. With this answer, Mau Leki and Mau Mauk returned to the earth and somehow managed to roast the bird.

The sacrificial meat which consists of roasted bird is called in the myth *lamak hatetu, lamak harani*. The dyadic pair *hatetu*//*harani* in ritual language is also paired with *hana'in* (literally, to acknowledge someone as a ruler, homage) and *hahulu* (to acknowledge someone as a leader). In other contexts, as when gifts of homage consisting of seven cobs of maize were taken to the hamlet of Laran to be presented to Maromak Oan, the *adat* historian from the hamlet of Kateri explained this tribute of maize as a sign of submission. He humbly revealed the people's submission in the following way:

hodi tama mai hatetu no harani	we come to offer gifts and presents
hodi tama mai hana'i no hahuiu	we come to praise the ruler and to acknowledge his leadership

In the context of the first harvest rite just mentioned, *lamak hatetu, lamak harani* became a symbol of submission by the people towards Maromak Oan, the guarantor of people's well-being and fertility. The sign of submission is revealed in the dyadic pair: *hana'i//hahulu*. The man above was offered food as a sign of submission in return for blessing.

Ritual offerings are also used by the people seeking an agreement from ancestors and/or the man above on their actions. This is explicitly expressed in the myth of origin narrated in the Wewiku region. According to this myth (see Reference Text 4), when the three female ancestors landed on the beach of Fatumea, they planted a banyan tree which produced three different species of branches. These three branches represent three domains. The branch of *ai hali* (banyan tree) represents the domain of Wehali, the branch of *ai biku* (*biku* tree) represents the domain of Wewiku, while the branch of *ai katimun* (*katimun* tree) represents the domain of Haitimuk. To establish the founding of these domains, the three female ancestors who planted this tree offered *lamak hatetu, lamak harani* to the man above. The purpose of the offering is described as follows:

hodi haiamak hodi haioon	to ask and to request
hodi hatebes hodi hametis	to establish and to make firm

In summarising the aims of the ritual form manifested in the myths above, I have attempted to highlight the purpose of giving as a mode of exchange. This theme is also one of the significant concepts elaborated by Traube in her discussion of rituals among the Mambai. When she analyses their cultural conception of life, she points out that for the Mambai, life is a gift that requires a countergift (1986: 11). The principle of 'exchange' is obvious in her statement. Life is not a 'free-floating vitality' as she phrases it, but is a limited good that needs a countergift in exchange. As for the Tetun, Maromak, who grants life, demands a countergift of *lamak hatetu, lamak harani* from his people. One message communicated in this type of myth is that life granted by the authority must be countered with submission from the subjects. Such a notion of life as a gift in exchange is further elaborated in the other types of myth to be discussed here entitled 'the path of Liurai'.

2. 'Path of Liurai'

In contrast to the myths discussed so far, in which the principal figure is the Maromak, this second set of myths (see Reference Text 7) deals with the Liurai, the executive rulers of the realm of Wehali-Wewiku. Here, one of the Liurai is praised not only as a food-giver, but also as Wehali's protector. As a food-giver, the myth depicts how various edible crops and fish that people consume derive from parts of the Liurai's body. Even 'gunpowder' (*kilat rahun*) which people used to defend themselves was derived from a particular part of the Liurai's body.

Another feature in this myth that needs to be highlighted is the emphasis on place names. Almost every crop, fish and even the gunpowder that came out from particular parts of the body are associated with certain regions. So, the myth contains descriptions of: 1. parts of the body; 2. edible crops and other items that stem from specific parts of the body; and 3. descriptions based on the names of the places associated with these edible and other items.

The Wehali *adat* historian, Piet Tahu Nahak, began his version of the myth concerning 'the path of Liurai' with a brief introduction which states that when Maromak sent people down to earth, he also sent along a rice called *hare ekero* and foxtail millet (*tora*). 'When the earth came into being, these two kinds of food already existed', stated Piet Tahuk Nahak. Due to this 'history', the foods *hare ekero* and *tora* are considered nobles' delicacies. As for the commoners, it was the responsibility of the Liurai to provide foodstuffs for them both to feed themselves and to offer to Maromak Oan. In the myth, six Liurai ruled the realm of Wesei Wehali: Tabein Liurai, Liurai Brehi, Liurai Seran Asa, Liurai Klan, Liurai Dasa and Liurai Lelek. Then, in order to provide food, one of the Liurai had to be sacrificed so that food could grow out of the parts of his body. It was decided that the second Liurai (Liurai Brehi) would be sacrificed.

According to the myth, the head of the Liurai gave rise to red and green coconuts. The red coconut (*nu mea*) was then planted in the area towards the sunset, in Fatumea Talama, a region that is located at the western end of the domain of Wewiku. In ritual language the name Fatumea is always paired with either the name Talama or Tunama. According to native exegesis, Talama is a disguised form of *tunama*, a compound word of *tunu* (to roast) and *ama* (father). Based on this name, the *adat* historian from Kateri claimed that the myth concerning the sacrificing of the ruler is a true story (*lia tebes*). The name proves that it was in Fatumea that the man's head was 'roasted' (*tunu*).

The green coconut (*nu modo*) was planted in Fatumea Takolo, a region which is located in the land toward the rising sun. At present, this region is part of East Timor province. From the left hand came the mung bean, which was planted at Akani. To make the mung beans flourish, they were taken back to 'the four-corner land' and were planted at the 'junction of the Maubesi River'. Piet Tahu Nahak identified the area as located in the southern region. The flourishing mung bean is praised in the myth as a source of nourishment and wealth for the people:

| *Fore kmodo Wehali najua kmurak* | The mung beans of Wehali develop strong nodules |
| *nahabut besi, najua kmurak.* | develop strong nodules, develop valuable beans. |

From the right hand, came the *luan* banana and from the teeth, maize (*batar malae*). Banana and maize in this myth are not associated with particular regions. They are people's food growing in every garden. His stomach (Latin: *ventriculus*) and intestine (Latin: *intestinum tenu*) were 'bundled in Wehali' (*butuk baa rai Wehali*). From the stomach came pumpkin and from his intestine, pumpkin vines. His blood was poured into the south sea and became a mullet fish. Later a man called Na'in Bakalo Na'in caught the fish. From the head of the fish came sorghum (*batar tasi*, literally 'maize of the sea'). The feet were taken to Sulit Anemeta, a region located to the north. It was in this hamlet that these two feet were burned into 'gunpowder' (*kilat rahun*). Sulit Anemeta is ritually recognised as the gate and the fence of Wehali. The association between parts of the body, food and gunpowder and place names is summarised in Table 8.1.

Table 8.1: Vicarious death of Liurai Brehi

Part of the body	Crops and others	Place name
head	green coconut	Fatumea Talama
	red coconut	Fatumea Takolo
teeth	maize	not specified
right hand	banana	not specified
stomach	pumpkin	Wehali
intestine	pumpkin vine	Wehali
blood	mullet fish	south sea
legs	gunpowder	Sulit Anemeta

Regarding the fate of the other five Liurai, it was narrated that Liurai Lelek, the youngest, died in Lo'o Maten. From his bones came snakes. Therefore, according to the explanation given in the myth, the Sukabi Lulik and Busa Belo people will not plant their seeds until a snake perches in one of their sacrificial baskets (*ksahat lulik*), a place to store seeds. The same is true of the harvest of young maize. People will wait until a snake perches in the *ksahat lulik* before harvesting can be conducted. Tabein Liurai waged war against the Likusaen (the present Liquiça regency in East Timor province) and died there. His head was buried in the land of Nanaet (the present Batugade of East Timor region) 'to demarcate mountain, to demarcate sea' (*nanaet tasi kre'is, nanaet foho kre'is*). Liurai Dasa went to the 'trunk of the hill' in Mande'u and died there. His head was taken back to Wehali and was buried next to a well (*we knuk*) in the hamlet of Batane. Liurai Klan died in Namfalus, Suai, in a place called Debu Klan. Liurai Seran Asa died in We Seran Asa in the village of Kamanasa.

According to the narrator of the myth, formerly, when the annual tribute was still delivered to Maromak Oan, the people of those regions mentioned in the myth were entitled to pay their tributes in the form of crops specified for their regions. Others disagreed with this view. They suggested that during the delivery of the tributes, people from far-away domains brought gold and silver, regions to the south brought coconut and salt, while the rest delivered maize to Maromak Oan.

Numerous studies have been written on vicarious death, analysing myths concerning head-hunting or the murder or killing of someone. Needham, drawing on data from societies in Southeast Asia, emphasises 'the association between the taking of heads and the acquisition of all forms of fertility and well-being' (1976: 74). Downs, using written records mainly from Indonesian societies, particularly the Bare'e-speaking Toraja of Central Sulawesi and the Ngaju Dayak of Borneo as well as written documents from the islands of Flores, Solar, Adonara, Lembata, Sabu and Timor concurs that there is a connection between head-hunting and fertility 'because it repr esents a repetition of the cosmic cycle of life and death' (1983: 123).

In Timor island, old stories of head-hunting are still an effective tool for parents to ban children from going out at night. My encounters with people from Dawan in north Tetun as well as the Dirma of south Tetun suggest that narratives of head-hunting as told to Middlekoop (1963) are still current. In the two Tetun areas mentioned, people preserve *ksadan* as a place to 'perform' the trophy head. One logical reason given by the people as to why they consider it important to maintain this kind of sacred site is that the head-hunting ritual is only a small part of a complex set of agricultural rituals celebrated at such places. Thus, *ksadan* is not solely a place to perform the trophy heads, rather it is a place where rituals connected to planting and harvesting are concentrated. Indeed McWilliam (1994), in his recent paper on *dawan* childbirth, head-hunting and circumcision also emphasises that the 'affirmation of life' and the welfare of the community in terms of achieving 'coolness' (*mainikin*) are the main concerns of such rituals.

Unlike the Dawan and the north Tetun, the south Tetun (with the exception of the Dirma and the Mande'u) who occupy the plains of Wehali-Wewiku do not have a tradition of head-hunting and therefore the classical interpretation of the severed head as containing soul substance is irrelevant to them. Besides, in the myth summarised above, the foodstuff and gunpowder came from various parts of the ruler's body and not only from his head. Actually, this south Tetun myth is not peculiar to that area. In the context of eastern Indonesia, the myth that edible plants stem from various parts of a human body is also shared by peoples of other areas, including Seram (Downs 1983: 131–132). In the Timor region, however, this story is overridden by the more 'spectacular' story of head-hunting. Yet, both the myth concerning head-hunting and the myth concerning the vicarious death of a person deal with the same concern, as phrased by McWilliam, the 'affirmation of life'. The connection between killing (death) and fertility (life) is evident in both myths.

What I do consider peculiar to the Wehali, though, is the association between particular crops and particular regions. Their persistence in relating specific plants to specific regions and their insistence that the fruits of those same plants were brought as tribute to the Maromak Oan prove that this myth is a political charter. So, in the context of the Wehali, it is not enough to analyse this myth solely in terms of which part of the body the crops symbolise, but also how this myth is used to chart political relationships. In accordance with the political ideology of the south Tetun, a supreme ruler is the one who 'eats reclining, drinks reclining'. For the Wehali, this figure is represented by Maromak Oan. His superiority is marked by his passivity. In contrast, other people's subordination is marked by their obligation 'to feed the one who is reclining' as phrased by the Tetun. So, subordination means work and activity. The myth concerning the path of Liurai 'reflects'[6] this political ideology. Liurai, the ruler who is responsible for feeding the Maromak Oan, sacrificed himself so that there would always be food for the supreme. These 'foods' are cultivated by his subjects, who live in regions to the east, west, north and south. They are the children of Maromak Oan, who were appointed to live in those regions and work for him there.

In the Wehali diarchic political system, Maromak Oan is the supreme ritual ruler of a land called 'the four-corner land'. As a ritual ruler he is not involved in daily political affairs, but the fertility and well-being of the land and its people are laid in his hands. In the myth, the status of this ritual ruler is elevated from political affairs to religious spheres. He is not simply the ruler of 'the four-corner land', but also the ruler of the earth (*raiklaran*). A good agricultural season, for example, marked by an appropriate amount of rainfall at the right time and a successful harvest, is related to a function of Maromak Oan. By bringing the gift of homage to Maromak Oan, the ruler, people pay homage to Maromak Oan, the guarantor of life and fertility. In the same manner, the refusal to acknowledge the authority of Maromak Oan, the ruler, means the refusal to acknowledge the authority of Maromak Oan, the source of life and fertility.

Maromak Oan's counterpart is the Liurai. They are responsible for executing Maromak Oan's orders. So, the actual and practical government is in their hands. As an executive of Maromak Oan, they are responsible for ensuring that people bring tributes as gifts of homage to Maromak Oan. Due to this function, the second myth deals with the sacrificing of Liurai Brehi and not Maromak Oan. As described in myths and symbolically acted out in ritual, people owe their lives to Maromak Oan, but food, security and protection to the Liurai. The annual rite of 'delivering maize of homage' (*hatama batar mana'i*) to some extent re-enacts the conviction revealed in the two myths above that Maromak Oan is the source of life and the Liurai are the source of security and protection.

---

6   Following Schulte Nordholt's argument concerning the relationship between myth and social realities (1971: 255), I also suggest that the myths summarised above 'reflect' political ideology as conceived by the south Tetun. This argument runs in contrast to van Wouden's suggestion that the Tetun myths 'embody' political ideology (1968: 41).

Ritual of Avoidance

The Tetun, like many other traditional societies do not concern themselves with abstract ideas about the structure of the cosmos nor the extent to which it may be marked by any separation into realms of sacred and profane. What matters for them is how to deal with these two aspects of their own experience. In other words, the Tetun are more concerned with procedures which must be followed in order to attain a successful life. These procedures come in the form of 'prohibitions'. This gives the impression that the Tetun belief system constitutes systems of rules and procedures or in Hoskin's phrase 'systems of prohibitions' (1987: 137). Such a system is clearly manifested in the concept of *lulik*.

Lulik is a Tetun word for: 1. 'holy' and 'sacred'; and 2. 'taboo', 'prohibition' and 'forbidden'. In some other Timorese societies, such as the Dawan, these two core meanings are represented by two words *le'u* and *nuni* respectively. Schulte Nordholt regards the Tetun word *lulik* as etymologically equivalent to the Dawan *nuni* (1971: 147). In addition to the word *lulik*, the Tetun also have the word *badu*,[7] which I translate as 'ban'. Although the latter sense of *lulik* (taboo and forbidden) is closely related to the meaning of the word *badu*, these two terms are used in different contexts and for different purposes.

In marriage arrangements, a woman is considered to be betrothed when the man's house presents betel-nut (*fuik badu labis*) to 'ban' the platform from other men, as people phrased it. At a particular time of the year, the custodian of gardens or, following the Tetun description, 'the inspector of gardens' (*lalawar*)[8] in a ceremony called *tara horak* announces an annual 'ban' (*badu*) on harvesting coconuts for a certain period of time. In both cases, those who break the agreed *badu* will be penalised by exacting a previously agreed form of penalty. For example, those who transgress the agricultural banning will be penalised by having to pay a fine of pigs or chickens. The difference between *lulik* and *badu* lies in the consequences of failing to follow their directives. Breaking a rule of prohibition agreed together (*ukun badu*) will result in penalties levied on the individuals concerned. But breaking a *lulik*, which is customarily recognised as a 'rule of the earth' (*ukun rai*), will harm not only the individual concerned but

---

7   Apparently the Tetun of East Timor pronounce it as *bandu*. Morris regards *bandu* as a Portuguese loan word, *bando*, meaning 'prohibit', 'forbid' (1984: 10).
8   The North Tetun call this official *makle'at*.

also the community at large as well as the earth. Even though the Tetun are close kin to the Mambai, who have the same word for 'to ban', the two societies apply it in different ways. The Mambai do not separate *ukun rai* from *ukun badu*. Instead they speak only of one 'path' or, in Traube's translation, 'walk of rule and ban—*ukun nor badun ni lolain*' (Traube 1986: 54–56).

My introduction to the concept of *lulik* came when I started learning to use the 'right' words and phrases for speaking to a noble or a respected elder. My language 'tutors' keep reminding me that it is *lulik* to say this word or to say that word. Instruction about observing *lulik* 'language' is evident if we notice interaction within the village. Often parents or older people remind the youngsters to say acceptable words when talking to older people. In an effort to understand the Tetun concept of *lulik*, I wrote in my fieldnotes that *lulik* has something to do with 'people'.

Besides 'people', *lulik* is also associated with 'places'. There is a consensus or rule that an *adat* meeting or discussion can only be held in a man's house (*uma katuas*) and not in a woman's house (*uma ferik*). People explain that it is *lulik* to conduct a meeting in a woman's house. When one approaches the hamlet of Laran, the seat of Maromak Oan, certain *lulik* must be observed. It is *lulik* to make noises within the hamlet area; shoulder cloths must be tied around the hips; and when something is dropped, it cannot be picked up. These avoidances are also called *lulik*. So, it is not the place that must be avoided; rather certain rules (*lulik*) must be observed when one is in a sacred (*lulik*) place.

In relation to people, the Tetun emphasise the observance of *lulik* not only in their behaviour towards the nobles, older and respected people, but most of all to ancestors, the 'dark people' (*ema kukun*). In accordance with the Tetun concept of their social universe, the earth is populated with both living human beings (*ema roman*—literally, 'bright people', the clear ones, or those who are visible) and ancestors (*ema kukun*—literally, 'dark people', or those who are invisible). Social relations among the living are, to some extent, defined in terms of the status of their ancestors. The recruitment of lineages (*uma*) reflects a strong interest in the maternal group. For example, in a hamlet (*leo*) originally consisting of houses of *inan bin alin, maun bin alin* (literally, M, eZ, yZ, eB, yB) groups, the sisters' houses make up a unit of female houses and the brothers' houses are the male houses. The power to govern the hamlet lies in the hands of the old women (*ferik*) and old men (*katuas*) of named houses. They constitute an informal council of *ferik katuas leo*. The *ferik* and *katuas* of the hamlet claim that the power they have to govern the hamlet derives from their ancestors. They are the human actors who rule the hamlet on behalf of the ancestors, the unseen actors. To symbolise their representativeness, these *ferik* and *katuas* are in charge of guarding the sacred betel-nut baskets and pouches, which belong to the ancestors and other regalia of the house. So, just like their ancestors, who are categorically *lulik*, the rulers are also considered as *lulik*. The rulers and their descendants then form what Keesing called 'an ancestral kin group' (Keesing and Fifi I 1969: 157; cf. Keesing 1981: 248; 1992: 25, 26).

At the named house level, the *ferik* and *katuas* of the house are the powerful figures that represent the male and female ancestors of the house. At the hamlet level, the powerful figures are the *ferik katuas leo*. At the domain level, the powerful figures are represented by Maromak Oan and the Liurai. Sacrifices to the entire community are only valid if they are made through these leading figures. In ritual language, these rulers are called *manas lulik wa'ik, klak lulik wa'ik* (the great sacred heat, the great sacred burning charcoal). As for the ordinary people, success in gardening and, formerly, in warfare, and success in the accumulation of wealth and well-being in general are determined by their relation with the rulers and thereby the ancestors. When people follow proper agricultural rituals and observe *lulik* relating to these rites, the ancestors will grant them enough rain, healthy plants, protection from diseases and prey, as paths to success.

Lulik also has something to do with 'space' and 'place'. Just as members of a clan, an ancestral origin group, share an array of common ancestors, they also share common sacred places. Take the hamlet of Laran as an example. Spaces and places that are considered to be sacred in this hamlet are the sacred banyan trees (*ksadan lulik*), the spring of Maromak (*we matan maromak*), the 'royal dark garden' (*to'os etu kukun*), sacrificial pillars in the middle of each garden (*troman*), the 'dark burial grounds' (*rate kukun* and *fatu taman rik*), 'the cannon of Liurai' (*kilat inan liurai*), the named houses (*uma mahoo naran*), the front male pillar (*kakuluk lor*) of each named house and the sacred paraphernalia that hang down on those pillars. Hicks argues that these places are considered as *lulik* because they function as transitional points between the sacred underworld and secular upperworld. They are the 'thresholds between the two halves of the cosmos' (1987a: 37, 38; 1990: 89–95; cf. Capell 1943: 211). As noted before, the division between the sacred underworld and the secular or profane upperworld that prevails among the east Tetun is unheard of in south Tetun. With the lack of vernacular to translate the meaning of 'secular' or 'profane' in south Tetun, the notion of 'transitional points' becomes irrelevant to understand their world-view. What matters for the south Tetun is that their obligation to look after these *lulik* persons and places guarantee the 'raw and cool' (*matak no malirin*) in their community.

Rituals Concerning Mother and Baby

Asking a Wehali about birth rites, one will get information not only concerning the baby, but also concerning the mother and the place where the birth will occur. This is consistent with my daily observations that a child is not the main focus of a family.

When parents are receiving guests, children are forbidden to hang around the platform. They will be ordered to sit quietly inside the house or play somewhere else. I often heard the adults warn the children to be quiet because it is *lulik* (forbidden) for the children to make noise while the mature people are talking. But saying this does not necessarily mean that the Wehali do not love their children. Children are also the object of parents' admiration. Girls are called the 'flowers' (*funan*) of the house and boys are its 'young sliced areca nuts' (*klaut*). From daily conversations with many parents in the villages, I have the impression that mothers are more eager to talk about their own children than are the fathers. In contrast, fathers prefer to talk more about their sisters' children than their own.

1. Rite of the Cleaning up the Path

The polite terms used to describe pregnancies are either *netan* (literally, begot) or *ko'us* (literally, to carry in the arms). These two words refer to both the existence of the mother and the forthcoming child. To promote the welfare of the expectant mother and the forthcoming baby, a shaman (*matdok*)[9] is invited to perform the rite called *kasu ai kanaer*. In general, the verb *kasu* means 'to dismiss' or 'to acquit' (Morris 1984: 103). *Ai knaer* is a rope or string that has been joined at its two ends to form a circle. It is used by men to climb coconut trees or areca nut trees. Thus, the phrase

9 The phrase matdok consists of two words: *mata* = eye; *dok* = far, distant. So, a shaman is 'one who can see 'far' into the future and 'far' into current inauspicious happenings' (Hicks 1984: 98). As a term of address, a shaman is called *bei dok*.

kasu ai knaer literally means 'to untie the string'. The rite of *kasu ai knaer* is held for particular purposes—namely, to arrange the movements of the foetus, to secure a healthier pregnancy and to ensure a successful delivery.

According to belief, most unsuccessful pregnancies derive from a failure in social relations. A miscarriage, for example, is associated with the unsympathetic behaviour of the husband and wife towards their ancestors and other people. In the case where a husband and wife know that there are people who dislike them for certain reasons, it is their job to seek pardon and plead for 'cleaning the path' (*hasori dalan*) of the coming baby. However, there are other possible factors that can hinder a successful pregnancy (and future delivery)—namely, the displeasure of ancestors and unheard curses cast by other people. To combat these 'enemies', a person with special knowledge of the 'unseen forces' needs to be invited, that is the shaman.

To invite a shaman, the family is expected to prepare certain items needed 'to clean the path of the baby'. These consist of either a pig or a chicken, a small amount of dry-field rice, seven betel leaves, a knife, a white bowl and a sorghum blossom or a small branch of leaves used for sprinkling liquid. An expert with knowledge of medicine, the shaman is expected to free the expectant mother from curses and to shield her from other curses that might befall her. Using the knife prepared by the family, the shaman cuts one of the chicken's right toes. Drops of blood from the cut toe are mixed with water contained in the bowl. Then, the blossom of the sorghum (*knar batar tasi*) is immersed in that liquid. Having prepared the 'cool blood', the shaman then swings the betel leaves seven times around the mother's head in an anticlockwise direction to indicate that he is unbinding something. Using the same betel leaves, the shaman goes on rubbing the mother's body, starting from the head and going down to the stomach. With these acts, the shaman uses his magic power to unbind the umbilical cord that is supposed to be twisted around the foetus as a result of curses that have befallen her. Having finished 'the unbinding' acts, the shaman discards the betel leaves in the direction of the sunset.[10] To cool the mother's body, the shaman picks up the blossom that has been immersed in the liquid and rubs the mother's body from the head to the

---

10   When I was in the field, a cholera epidemic claimed many villagers' lives. To cleanse the villages from this deadly disease, people performed a cleansing rite. In this rite each household took its disused household utensils (such as broken pottery, plaited screens and all sorts of plaited baskets) to the western part of the village.

stomach. This blossom is also discarded to the west. Normally, no formula is cited following the rubbing of the woman's body. However, with the 'new awareness' that '*adat* and religion are one', the following formula is often said nowadays as a prayer:[11]

Ah ... matabian sia, tuan no nurak, na'in no ala	Oh ancestors, old and young, nobles and commoners
Ami tama mai husu mai hakmasin	We humbly come in front of you
Matak no mali·nn bodik funan no klaut	Asking for raw and cool for the flower and the nut
Sara no lituk, banin no satan bodik funan no klaut ne'e	Close and protect, border and shut the flower and the nut
Hosi anin no loro manas no krakat	From wind and sun, heat and anger
Hosi lia at lia moras	From curse (lit. bad words) and condemnation (sick words)
Bei sia iha kukun kalan, feto no mane, tua no nurak, na'in no ala	Grandparents in the dark and night, women and men, old and young, nobles and commoners
hodi husu kmaan no muti mos baa funan no klaut ne'e.	(We) plead for forgiveness (lit. light) and pardon (white) for this flower and nut.

In this prayer, phrases related to forgiveness and pardon common in Christian discourse are translated into traditional terms. This combination produces an unusual form of prayer characterised by an idiosyncratic paired phrasing of *kmaan* (light) and *muti mos* (clean white).

The payment for the shaman depends on his reputation in curing all sorts of diseases. A well-known shaman such as Frans Tae Mauloko of the village of Kletek, a young man of 22 years, deserves compensation up to a small pig for this sort of work. For other relatively unknown shaman, a chicken or even a plate of food is enough. If the capability of a shaman is questioned,[12] the family is free to call in other shamans to 'clean up the baby's path'.[13] Of course, the more rites that are performed the better the result will be.

---

11 This 'prayer' was recited for me by a Protestant minister, the Reverend Gabriel Bria, who is himself a member of the Wewiku people, from the hamlet of Uma To'os Fatuk.
12 People question the shaman's capability if the sickness persists, or when a member of the patient's family has a bad dream.
13 My key informant on '*adat* language', Piet Tahu Nahak, has a son who is considered by his parents and the villagers at large as a *bulak* (lunatic). Several shamans have been invited to cure him. So far, there has been no indication that his sickness is improving. For the parents, it is a matter of choosing the right shaman to clean up the boy's path.

Despite these efforts to guarantee the success of a pregnancy, the expectant mother herself must refrain from certain 'behaviours' that can be interpreted as resulting in the entangling of the umbilical cord around the baby's neck. For example, she is prohibited from sitting at the threshold of the door. 'Sitting in the middle of the door' as they phrase it means blocking the flow of life from the inside of the house to the outside. The effect will be that the umbilical cord will become entangled around the baby's neck, which can cause death. To guard herself, everywhere she goes she has to take along the knife used by the shaman to cut a chicken's toe to indicate her readiness to clean up the baby's path. During her pregnancy, she is not permitted to take a bath at dawn because that is the time when evil spirits come out to harm pregnant women. As far as food taboos are concerned, the expectant mother has to refrain from eating hot meals. She is also forbidden from eating goat meat because, according to the Tetun classification, goats belong to the hot-blooded animal group. As for the husband, when his wife is in the advanced stage of pregnancy he cannot wear a belt or bracelets. These things are claimed to be the cause of a difficult birth.

2. Making the Baby Come Alive (Birth Rite)

When the time for delivery is near, a midwife (called *makaer kmi*) is invited to the house. The literal translation of *makaer kmi* is the 'holder of candle-nut'. Following the Tetun description, her main task is 'to cause the baby to arrive' (*nato'o oan*), 'to take the baby out' (*nasai oan*) or 'to make the baby come alive' (*nahoris oan*). The office of midwife is hereditary and is therefore associated with a particular lineage (*uma makaer kmi*). Using candle-nut powder mixed with coconut oil as the primary medicine, she rubs the expectant mother's stomach to ensure that the head of the baby is facing downward. The following were listed as items needed for delivering a baby.[14] Their importance is due to their practical purpose as well as their ritual significance:

1. Firewood. For a childbirth, the husband has to prepare bundles of firewood. One log of wood is tied to the female pillar of the house. This log is called *ai kabuka* (literally, the searching wood). This is because during parturition people who are waiting outside use this particular piece of wood as a medium to 'search for information' on the gender of the new-born baby.

---

14   This type of list was also reproduced by a Catholic priest, the Reverend Piet Manehat SVD, who happens to be a Tetun, when he wrote an article in the *Agenda Budqya Pulau Timor* (1) (1990: 85).

2. A bunch of *luan* banana. This kind of banana is commonly used as baby food, both by the Tetun and the Dawan peoples. When these people(s) make a trip away from home, they bring along the *luan* banana as their prime food provision.

3. A pottery bowl, which is a container used for boiling water, called *omas*.

4. A big pot used for water storage called *knaras*.

5. A small pot to store the umbilical cord (*alin fatik*).

6. A strong piece of string used in parturition.

7. A knife made from a specific bamboo, called *fafulu*, or a stalk of sorghum. People claim that this type of knife can be sharper than an ordinary-bladed knife. In many births, according to my informants, many infections derive from using an unclean-bladed knife.

8. A piece of black cotton thread, spun by the mother only for this purpose (*tais lima rasan*).

9. A black handmade sarong used only for parturition (*tais hahoris*). This 'birth sarong' is also transmitted from mother to daughter. When this sarong is no longer used because it has worn out, it becomes a sacred item and is stored together with other regalia of the house.

When the time for delivery arrives, the expectant mother lies on a mat spread on the floor in a particular space within the house, which is used only for a mother to give birth. This place is called *ai lala'ok*. It is located between the east door and the hearth. During parturition, the woman holds a string hung especially for this purpose. Men are not allowed to stay in the house. The parturition is only assisted by a midwife and the woman's mother and other female relatives. Once the first crying of the baby is heard by men who are waiting outside, a young man rushes to the female pillar where the piece of firewood (*ai kabuka*) has been tied to its trunk. The midwife takes the knife and pretends to cut the umbilical cord. At the same time, the young man takes his sword and pretends that he is going to cut the cord binding the wood to the female pillar. The midwife starts counting from one to seven loudly, so her voice can be heard outside. Every time the midwife counts a number, the young man also counts the same number. When the midwife and the young man reach seven, they both cut the cords. The midwife cuts the umbilical cord that joins the mother and the baby, while the young man cuts the string that joins the wood to the female pillar. If the baby is a boy, the midwife *klalak* (shouting, imitating a man calling for a friend or the shouting when men go hunting). Upon hearing the *klalak*, the young man who was asked to chop the cord in front of the female pillar mimics the shouting. If the baby is a girl, the midwife *hahaek* (gives out laughter, a typical woman's laugh).[15] The young man would then mimic her.

Local custom dictates that the umbilical cord should be cut with a sliver of bamboo or a sliver of sorghum stalk. According to my informants, a straight sliver of bamboo or sorghum stalk gives the child a strong body, a soft heart and a just, straightforward mind. When choosing a midwife and a young man to cut the umbilical cord of the baby and the string that binds the wood on the female pillar respectively, parents always consider choosing those who are physically strong but possess a soft heart and a just mind. The umbilical cord is cut a few inches above the baby's navel. Then it is tied using the black cotton thread spun by the mother particularly for this purpose. Every day the remaining cord attached to the baby's stomach is rubbed with warm coconut oil until it falls off. This usually takes four to five days. When the remaining cord has dropped off, it is hidden under the upper part of the mother's sarong (*kabonan*) until an appropriate time to take it outside the house. It is worthwhile noticing that the Tetun distinguish the terms for umbilical cord (*ka'an* or *alin*) from the remaining cord attached to the baby's navel (*husar*), but they do not use different terms for the 'placenta' and 'the adjacent cord' as we do. Thus, for the Tetun the term *ka'an* means both the 'placenta' and the 'umbilical cord'. People refer to this *ka'an*[16] as *alin*, which literally means 'younger brother/sister'. The pot to store the *alin* is called *alin fatik* (the younger brother/sister place). Before the afterbirth is placed in it, the pot is broken into two pieces. Only one half is used as a storing place. The other half is left behind to symbolise 'the elder brother/sister's place'.

Before the child's remaining umbilical cord (*husar*) drops off, the woman goes back to the place where she gave birth (*ai lala'o*) 'to heat and cleanse her body with her back to the fire'. The Tetun term for heating the body after giving birth is *hatuka ha'i*. So, while the baby's navel is heated with coconut oil, the mother's back is 'roasted' over the fire. The mother cannot stop cleansing her body until the baby's *husar* has dropped off. The importance of *hatuka ha'i* for the mother is clearly pointed out by

15 Tetun differentiates a woman's laugh (*hahaek*) from a man's laugh (*hanasa*).
16 Morris makes an interesting comment on the meaning of *ka'an* or *ka'a* as follows: '*ka'an, ka'an*, sister-in-law, a name which indicates that the sisters-in-law are regarded as sisters, cf. *rian*; *ka'an mane* or *ka'an feto*—male or female placenta, also known as *mane malun* or *feto malun*' (1984: 91).

the people as a way to cleanse the dead blood left in her body and for other health reasons, such as restoring the mother's strength lost in labour, 're-shaping' the mother's body and preparing enough breast-milk for the baby. Although the symbolic importance of *hatuka ha'i* is not always clear, my *adat* informants attempted to explain it in relation to the origin myth. According to the myth, after Ho'ar Na'i Haholek was born, her mother took her:

baa hatuka ha'i iha lolo leten baa	(they) go to heat her body over the fire in the world above
wai matan natene, wai oan natene	(that is) to be nurtured and becomes knowledgeable

In this myth, it is narrated that both mother and baby went to the world above to warm the mother's back over the fire. Both of them were secluded for a period of time 'to be nurtured and receive knowledge about life'. To elaborate on the symbolic purpose of this ritual heating, I was told that, after the birth, both the mother and the baby are ritually 'hot' and 'wild'. The ritual heating is then a liminal phase between ritual heated/wild and cool/tame. Being 'heated' and 'wild' persons, they represent a danger to life and therefore must be isolated. During the period of seclusion, the heat of the fire will turn them ritually into 'cool' and 'tame', that is 'to be nurtured and to become knowledgeable' as stated in the myth. Thus, both the mother and the baby are described as going through a domestication process during which they change from wild and ignorant persons to tame and knowledgeable persons.

Similar to the notion of domestication mentioned in the myth, the mother enters a period of seclusion after giving birth. She goes back to the place where she gave birth to heat her back the fire. The place to heat her back in a house is called *ai lala'ok*, which literally means 'behaviour' or 'custom'. Here in this place, the 'wild' mother is ritually 'tamed' to be a 'civilised' person who will not harm the community at large. Thus, in addition to the practical reasons for cleansing one's body, heating oneself is also a category of rite that marks the passage of a woman from a wild to a tame person. As for the baby, the period of seclusion is also a liminal phase between the physical birth of the child inside the house and the social birth of the child outside the house, as I discuss in the following section.

This liminal phase is indicated by 'rules' that must be observed by both the mother and the child. These rules place more emphasis on what a woman (and her child) cannot do than on what she can do, on what their obligations are rather than what their rights are. The commonest rule discussed by people is that the mother cannot leave the house at any time unless it is necessary. If for certain reasons she has to go outside, she must make sure that no one will recognise her by disguising herself. In this case, she has to wear a pyramid-shaped plaited basket (*hanematan*) to cover her head and face. The only time she feels free to go outside is at night. Even then she has to walk in silence so that she will not attract people's attention. If she happens to come across other people, she is not allowed to greet or even to respond to the greetings of those people. The only access to the outside is through the female door.

Her space within the house is also limited to the three blocks located at the back of the house, namely the place to give birth (*ai lala'ok*), the hearth (*ha'i matan*) and the place to store water (*we klot*). There is a floor beam within the inner house that divides these three places from the parents' and young women's sleeping quarters. This beam (*kotan uma laran*) marks the demarcation line between the other members of the household and the young mother. Members of the household can cross the beam, for example, from the main sleeping area to the hearth and vice versa. But the young mother is not permitted to cross the beam at any time. In practice, this means she cannot even go into her room to get her own clothes. Her needs are supplied by the rest of the household. Regarding the child, only one rule applies to him/her. The child can be carried by members of the household inside the house, but not outside. There is a time for the child to be introduced to the outside world. Prior to this time he/she must not be taken outside. People say that the 'bad wind' and the heat of the sun will harm the baby. How long this restriction is observed varies between the first child and the following children. For a first-born child, the mother and the baby must stay in the house for at least two weeks, but subsequent children are not expected to stay secluded any longer than a week.

3. The Rite of Taking Out the Hot Ashes

If the heating ritual may be described as a rite of seclusion, the rite of taking out hot ashes may be analysed as a rite of incorporation, in which the mother and the baby are incorporated into society. This rite is also called *hasai naran* (taking out name). This ritual marks the end of a series of rituals concerning childbirth.

The process of the ritual is as follows. A young man who is related to the mother as a marriageable cousin (*talain*) is designated to pick a coconut. The coconut is preferably selected from one of the trees planted by her mother's brothers (*tua na'i*). There are also 'rules' that must be observed by the one who is designated to pick the coconut. The coconut cannot be dropped from the tree. He has to carry it with his hands down to the ground. When he removes the husk of the coconut, he must make sure that the whole husk remains joined together and is not broken into pieces. The coconut is then divided into two halves. The half towards the eyes of the coconut is chopped smaller than the other. When he removes the flesh of the coconut, he must also make sure that the flesh is not broken into pieces but rather joins together to comprise a 'cord' of coconut flesh. The young mother then burns the husk (together with the rind of *luan* banana) in order to get ashes, which she keeps in one half of the coconut shell.

The flesh of the coconut, which she keeps in a pyramid-shaped plaited basket (*hanematan*), is used to rinse the young mother's hair. The ashes are used to shave the child's hair. The actual shaving of the child's hair is the task of the woman's mother's brother (*tua na'i*). Sometimes this task is executed by the head of a particular lineage within the clan who is known as *la'e tua* (literally, 'the respected husband'). The prepared ashes are then mixed with water, and used as a shaving rinse. When the *tua na'i* shaves the child's hair, he does it extra carefully so that the hair will not drop to the ground. The hair of the baby is kept in the smaller half of the coconut shell toward its eyes. The storing of hair in this half of the coconut shell is a symbol of life since a new plant grows from this part of a coconut.

After shaving the child's head, the *tua na'i* takes advantage of his position as a respected elder of the husband-taking group to impose his superordinate power by taking the dirty water and unexpectedly watering the son-in-law's feet. The Tetun call this action *habasak we* (throwing of water). This unexpected throwing of water creates the impression that the thrower is playing a practical joke. Everybody laughs at the son-in-law who is being teased by his WMB. In relation to the pouring of water during an agricultural ritual observed by the Dawan, Schulte Nordholt states that 'the fact that the water is dirty and that an element of teasing is involved is a result of the superordinate position of the bride-giver group in respect of the bride-receiving group' (1971: 62). While the same notion may be observed during Tetun childbirth rituals, the splashing of water is also a re-enactment of the birth of the child into the community.

The remaining mud in the water is used 'to rub' (*kose*) the forehead, neck, shoulders, elbows, wrists and knees of the baby. According to the Tetun, these parts are the weak spots in the human body. By rubbing them, the child becomes invulnerable to any outside 'attacks'. The remaining water is taken outside to splash the waiting audience and the mud is used to 'give invulnerability' to those people. My informants enthusiastically told me the joyful experiences they had when they were attending this rite. Laughing, teasing and putting down others by splashing them with dirty water are attractive elements remembered by those who participated in this rite. Although the flinging of dirty water at the men who are waiting outside the house is considered only as a practical joke, this noisy event has similar symbolic significance to the solemn rite of 'sprinkling the seeds'. Society needs to be cooled off to keep the new-born baby alive. On the same principle, the earth needs to be cooled off so that the seeds can grow and promise a good harvest.

In the meantime, the 'dark food' (*lamak kukun*) is prepared. 'Dark food' is an eating ceremony, where those who participate in the ritual eat a sacrificial meal. By doing this they inform the 'ancestors' (*kukun*, literally, 'dark') that their grandchild is going to be taken outside the house (*hasai naran*).[17] The 'dark food' consists of seven piles of grilled fish (*na'an knase*) and sorghum. This food is then distributed to those who took part in the birth of the baby: the midwife gets three plates of meat and three plates of rice; the young man who chopped the cord off the firewood gets one plate of meat and one plate of rice. Some meat and rice is put in coconut shells and divided amongst the children to eat. The mother's brother (*tua na'i*) who helped with shaving the child's hair is entitled to be served separately. Beside this 'dark food', his status as the most respected elder of the house (*tua na'i ama etuk*) obliges others to serve him with the head of a pig that has been slaughtered especially for this purpose. Usually the pig's head is then shared with the head of the clan (*fukun katuas*) and other senior members of the hamlet. Accomplishing the 'dark food' eating ceremony indicates that the ancestors have been informed and, therefore, the hot ashes from the hearth can be cleansed.

---

17 The phrase *hasai naran* that literally means 'to take the name out' is understood to mean 'make oneself famous'. In the context of the birth rite, I propose to translate *hasai naran* as 'reborn in the community'.

When the ashes are about to be carried out of the house, the midwife opens the door, which is conceptually regarded as facing the sunrise (*oda matan la sa'en*). The young mother comes out from the female door, which is conceptually regarded as facing the sunset (*oda matan rae*). Her child and the pot with the umbilical cord (*ka'an* or *alin*) are cradled in her sarong. She is accompanied by the midwife who brings along the sarong worn by the woman during her delivery. When they reach the ground, the young mother lets drop the remaining umbilical cord that she has hidden in the upper part of her sarong, called *kbonan*. The woman's party then go to a type of shrub called *ai kalaan*.[18] There is no particular *kalaan* shrub chosen for the whole clan as a 'placental shrub', such as is evident in some other societies (cf. Graham 1991: 62, 63). Each house or even each member of the household may designate their own shrubs for the temporary installation of the umbilical cord. This kind of shrub is chosen because the name *kalaan* is associated with another Tetun word -*lalaan*-, which means 'warmly wrapped up' or 'warmly protected'. For example, when a sister walks between her two brothers, she is said to be 'warmly protected' (*lalaan*) by the two men. So, when the mother carefully lays down the 'younger brother/sister' (the pot with umbilical cord), she whispers to the shrub (*kalaan*) to warmly protect (*lalaan*) the baby:

Lalaan oan nu'u inan naneras	Shelter the baby warmly, like a mother wrapping her baby

With the placement of the umbilical cord and the afterbirth, the young mother has completed her work. She has given birth to the child in the house and also borne the child into the community. Now it is the task of the young man who picked the coconut to take the coconut shell containing the baby hair to a banyan tree, which has been chosen by the clan of the mother as the sacred place of the clan. This place is called *ksadan*.[19] He lays down the coconut shell at the foot of the banyan tree. After placing the hair, he goes to the *kalaan* shrub where the cord has been laid down. He removes the cord from the pot and brings it to a coconut tree. He chops the tree and permanently installs the umbilical cord into the cut. Having done so, he then climbs the coconut tree. When he reaches the peak of the tree he cuts a bunch of coconuts and a branch of palms. He has to make sure that each is chopped with only one strike. People believe that failure

---

18   This kind of shrub is known as *pohon buah tinta* in Indonesian because the liquid of its berries is like the colour of ink.

19   The *ksadan* of the Kamanasa are located in the centre of the hamlets. In contrast, the Wehali locate their *ksadan* either at the eastern or southern part of the hamlet.

to observe this 'chopping rule' will cause death to the new-born baby. When the man chops the coconuts and the palms, the new mother should sit under the tree without any protection. However, this latter custom (sitting under the tree) is rarely practised now. The reason for avoiding this rite, I assume, relates to 'accidents' that might have happened in the past. However, many old women explained that in their time, 'when *adat* was still fully observed', accidents never occurred.

In conclusion, the process of childbirth elaborated above reveals at least two symbolic meanings. First, it denotes that a child is not only born from the physical womb of a woman, but also from the symbolic womb of society. Second, with the birth of the baby, the mother's and the father's lineages are united.

The physical birth of a child from the womb of a woman is marked by the cutting of the baby's umbilical cord. The symbolic birth of the child from the womb of society is symbolised by the cutting of the cord that ties the firewood to the trunk of the female pillar. The falling of the remaining part of the umbilical cord from the baby's body is re-enacted by the mother when she, for the first time after the birth, 'officially' descends from the house with the baby. She drops the umbilical cord to the ground in front of the members of her husband's house.

The splashing with water further emphasises that the symbolic birth has taken place in the community. Concerning this, David Hicks rightly suggests that the splashing of water symbolises the political union between the father's group and the mother's group (1984: 48). The two houses, of which the husband-taker is superior to the husband-giver, are then united with the birth of the child.

Agricultural Rites

The two principal times of the year for agricultural rituals are at planting and at first harvest time. When the annual planting season arrives,[20] but there is still no rain, the ancestors are informed by people visiting their places of origin. Every hamlet has its own 'old hamlet'. For the Kamanasa

---

20   In Chapter 2, I described the way the Tetun read 'the signals of nature' by observing the emergence of a particular star at a given time of night, the sound of certain birds and the blossoming tamarind trees.

people, 'the fortress of Fatisin' (*kota* Fatisin) is the original hamlet. For the Kareana people, their place of origin is the 'old hamlet of Anemeta' (*leo tuan Anemeta*). In this 'old hamlet', there are five named houses. The plea for rain is conducted in *uma Fore Na'in* (the Mung-bean house), the plea to stop a whirlwind is made in *uma Rai* (the Earth house), while the plea for good sunlight is conducted in *uma Loro Tuan* (the Old Sun house). Other hamlets recognise sacred forests (*alas lulik*) as their places of origin. But for the people of Wehali as a whole, their place of origin is located in Marlilu Haholek, the mythical place where the first dry land emerged and the first human beings lived. These places of origin are where people assemble to make a plea for rain.[21] The same is true of harvest time. When the harvest is due but rain keeps falling, the ancestors have to be informed by visiting the sacred places. In the following sections, I focus on the three principal agricultural rituals celebrated by the Wehali: the ritual designed to 'give life' to the seeds, which is called *hisik fini*; the ritual designed to 'make the fruits edible', called *hamiis*; and the delivery of tributes to the Maromak Oan, which is known as 'the delivery of seven cobs of maize' (*hatama batar fulin hitu*) or 'the bringing in of maize of homage' (*hatama batar mana'i*).

1. To Sprinkle the Seeds (*hisik fini*)

The aim of this ritual as formulated by the people themselves is to 'make the seeds live'. When the soil is considered moist enough after a heavy rain, preparations for the planting season begin. Every single mature man that has a garden is obliged to bring their seeds to be 'cooled' (*halirin*) in the *uma Fukun*, the house of the head of the clan. It should be noted that not all seeds or crops cultivated by the people are included in this ritual. Wet rice, for example, is not 'ritual rice'. Only the rice cultivated on dry land (*hare leten*—literally, the above rice) is ritual rice. In addition, no yam is part of the ritual. Seeds and fruits that are considered as ritually important are foxtail millet (*tora*), sesame (*lena*), sorghum (*batar tasi*), maize (*batar malae*), dry land rice (*hare leten*) and a few varieties of melon that grow wild in the jungle and are known as *babuar* (cognate with *kabuar* meaning 'round', 'circular'). Maize, a relatively newly introduced crop, is considered as 'native' to the area. I was told that only native plants can be 'blessed' (Indonesian, *diberkati*) in this ritual.

---

21 When I was in the field I had the opportunity to participate in the Kamanasa ritual for invoking rain.

The day before, a young man is ordered to climb a coconut tree. He has to pick a young, unformed coconut (*nuu kalabuk*) and bring it down himself from the top of the tree. According to my informants, a coconut that has produced flesh inside it is considered 'cooked'. A cooked coconut cannot do the job of cooling the seeds. Only an unformed young nut (*nuu kalabuk*) is suitable. The top part of the nut is chopped carefully so that it does not separate from the rest of the nut. A few drops of the blood of a pig, which has been slaughtered as sacrificial meat, are then put inside the nut to mix with the coconut juice. This nut is then hung on the rack above the hearth. The same young man is also asked to pick a small branch of leaves then known as *ai tahan malirin* (the cool leaves). This branch of leaves is later used to sprinkle the liquid from the nut onto the seeds and people who gather around the ritual place.

When all the seeds needing to be 'blessed' have been piled together in front of the front male pillar of the *fukun* house, the female guardian of the house (*ferik*) begins to prepare for the betel-nut offering (*halo mama*). Betel-nuts are used as a medium to communicate with the ancestors. The communicator is always a man, in this case the head of the hamlet. With the help of his female partner, he distributes the betel-nut into the betel-nut boxes and pouches hung on the male pillar of the house. One slice of areca nut covered with a betel leaf is carefully placed inside each of these paraphernalia. With the offering of betel-nut, the ancestors are informed of the purposes of the rite. In regard to the rite of cooling the seeds, the *fukun* will make a plea in front of the male pillar, asking for the seeds to flourish, for good rain, and for protection from pigs and other predators that might destroy the plants. On the plains of south Tetun, where gardens are not fenced, people firmly believe that if they do not participate in the rite of *hisik fini* their plants will be destroyed by pigs and other prey.

In the hamlet of Labarai, the Bunak-speaking people, who have occupied the village of Kamanasa for the last 90 years, incorporate dancing that runs the whole night into the rite of *hisik fini*. Both women and men hold hands around a sacrificial pillar (*ai toos*), located in front of the *fukun* house, while dancing and singing. Early in the morning, when birds are still in their nests and pigs yet sleep, men bring their seeds quietly into their gardens. Total silence is needed so the sleep of these predators is not disturbed. Consequently, the seeds can be safely planted. However, before planting begins, the owner of the garden has to cool the soil. Coconut juice from a young unformed nut is sprinkled in a small area in the middle of the garden called *troman*.[22] A *troman* is made up of a post called *ai toos* (literally, the strong wood) on which to hang the coconut, and a few flat stones as places to offer sacrificial meat. In response to my query, Piet Tahu Nahak recited for me the following invocation that he used to say in front of the male post.

Aa bei sia ama sia	Oh ancestors, fathers
bei tuan bei nurak	old ancestors, young ancestors
bei atan bei na'in	commoner ancestors, noble ancestors
ita hato'o lai, basu lai, ita hato'o liu lai	please forward (this plea) on, please pass it, pass it on please
amikan hakmasin, amikan hakro'an	our misery (literally, saltiness), our agony
ba ama naran la kaka, ama naran la temi	to the father that can't be summoned by name, the father that can't be called by name
iha metin baa, iha as baa	(that lives) in the low tide, in (the place) above
iha lolo liman la to'o, iha bi'i ai la dai	that cannot be reached by stretching out hands, by standing on tiptoes
natodan du'uk, nabesi du'uk	the one that only sits, only firmly sits
iha fitun fohon, iha fulan fohon	on the top of a star, on the top of the moon
natuun matak mai, natuun malirin mai	send down the raw, send down the cool
udan wen di'ak, loro wen di'ak	a good rain, a good sunlight
ba te hutun raik laran, hutun rai tenan	for the people of the world, the people of the old world
ba hodi ko'o tua, ba hodi hafaho rai	to tap the palms, to weed gardens
be to'os be no isin, tua be no wen	so gardens produce harvest, palms give juice

---

22 The north Tetun spell *troman* as *toro uman* (Seran 1992: 11). Unfortunately, Seran does not explain further the meaning of that phrase. I am not aware if the Tetun have the word *toro* in their vocabularies. For sure, the word *uman* is a possessive form of *uma* (house). By pronouncing 'the centre of the garden' as *toro uman*, Seran indicates that the garden is associated with 'house' (*uma*). The south Tetun, however, do not associate the centre of the garden with the notion of *uma*. For the south Tetun, *troman* is a compound word. The letter *t-* is derived from either *tur* (to sit) or *ta* (to cut). My informants are not certain about this. But they are certain that the word *roman* means 'bright'. So, according to folk interpretation, a *troman* is the first spot in the garden that was 'cleared off' (*ta*) from shrubs when the garden was founded. Within this clear spot, 'the bright people' (*ema roman*) sit (*tur*) while offering their sacrifices to the ancestors, 'the dark people' (*ema kukun*).

Only when the seeds and the earth have been ritually cooled can the planting begin. Depending on the size of each garden, the planting is conducted by men and women, young and old. There is no further differentiation of who does what. With the completion of this rite, the seeds have been ritually born or become alive (*moris*). No other rituals are needed to guarantee the continuation of the plants' growth unless there is a disease or natural disaster that threatens the life of the plants. The south Tetun have only one word for all sorts of plant diseases and two kinds of 'ordinary' disaster—namely, a prolonged dry season or the overflowing of water due to excessive days of rainfall. The word for all these is *klakar*.[23] If either of these two types of disaster occur, a ritual called *soe at* (literally, throwing out the bad) is performed at the western part of the gardens.

2. The First Harvest Rite (*hamiis*)

This ritual is mainly observed in relation to the first harvest of maize. When the maize is considered ready to be consumed, a rite for the first harvest needs to be prepared. My informants also said that this ritual is observed so that children who love to eat young maize can start eating it without waiting any longer for the maize to ripen.

Literally, the compound word *hamiis* derives from the word *halo* (to make) and *miis*. The latter word has two meanings. Fresh water is called *we miis*. The term *miis* in this context is paired with *masin* (salty). In myths, when a storyteller narrates the origin of the earth, we often hear the comment 'at that time we did not know whether the sea was *masin* or *miis*'. In the Tetun mind, the opposite of *miis* is *masin*. Therefore, the word *miis* (in *hamiis*) can be translated as 'unsalted', 'tasteless' or 'fresh'. The second meaning of *hamiis* is 'to cool'. When a person's talisman is still 'active', it is said that the talisman is 'hot'. A hot talisman can endanger others. To domesticate or to tame this hot wild talisman, its owner has to cool it. Taking all the notions conveyed by the word *miis* just mentioned and the purpose of conducting this ritual, I suggest translating the term *hamiis* as 'to make fresh' or 'to cool'.

Thus, although the maize is considered ready to eat, it is still in the stage of 'heat' and 'salty'. Under these conditions, the maize is a potential danger to those who consume it. According to the people, eating it before

23   *Oan klakar* is a phrase used for children of an invalid marriage.

performing *hamiis* will give the individual concerned a serious illness and his/her garden will not produce enough food for several years. To this point, the maize is considered to contain heat because it is occupied by the spirit of ancestors (*kmalar*), which makes the maize and other plants flourish. To make this maize edible, the heat must be taken out of it by informing the ancestors of the people's intention to consume the fruits.

Hamiis is a rite that attracts a large audience. Compared with the *hisik fini* rite, the *hamiis* involves not only people of the hamlet but also those who come from related hamlets. This rite is not centralised in the house of the head of the clan. Each named house conducts its own first harvest ritual. When a named house is conducting its rite, the word for an invitation or a 'reminder' (*hamenon*), as they call it, is delivered to the mother's brother who is in charge as the 'old man' (*katuas*) of the named house and to every son of the named house who has married out and resides in his wife's house. These sons are referred to as *mane maksai uma* (literally, men that go out from the house). The message is communicated by the sons-in-law, who are the married-in men and therefore are called *mane maktama uma* (literally, men that enter the house). Upon receiving the notice, those who are going to participate in the ritual go to their gardens. They pull out seven or eight 'whole' maize plants—that is to say, plants consisting of roots, cobs and blossoms. One plant is erected inside the garden and tied to the post in the *troman* area. A few small pieces of cooked chicken or pig (depending on the size of the garden) are laid on the stones surrounding the post. To offer betel-nuts, four tiny sticks are erected beside the pillar with the tips pointing upward. The top end of the sticks are split into four strips. On top of these four strips, betel-nuts are offered. One stalk of maize is tied to the front post of the garden hut (*laen*). Four maize plants are erected at the four corners of the garden to feed the 'owners of the land' (*rai na'in*), who usually get access to the garden through its four corners. I was told that if the owners of the land are not fed, the garden will not produce enough for the people. 'We take one bunch, the owners of the land will take four or five bunches', claimed the people. Having completed the garden ceremony, each man takes a bunch of maize cobs home, together with one or two whole maize plants. One plant is then erected in the place his wife or his mother-in-law uses to weave cloths. If the house raises cattle, one plant is erected on the gate of the stable.

One bunch of maize cobs is the man's offering to his natal house. During the time of celebration, I encountered people carrying bunches of maize cobs to their natal house. Usually the man goes alone to his natal house, without his wife and children, who celebrate the first harvest ritual in their own house. For those who live in far-away hamlets, they are expected to arrive one or two days before the actual time of celebration. Those who live nearby arrive on the day of the celebration. Since the *hamiis* rite involves the eating of young maize, it is conducted in the middle of the day.

The time of the first harvest ritual is also a great time for 'family reunion'. During this time, I noticed, some people who had achieved success in cities took the opportunity to come back to display their wealth. For ordinary farmers, the *adat* obligation of a bunch of maize cobs is sufficient tribute in homage to their natal houses. For the 'city dwellers', their contributions may consist of pigs, bundles of betel-nuts, coffee and sugar, cakes and other luxuries for the villagers. The attend ance of successful sons raises the prestige of a named house in the village.

Like other rites, the *hamiis* rite also commences with 'the preparing of betel-nut' for the ancestors. In order to elaborate in detail on the process of *hamiis*, I will focus on a named house in the hamlet of Le'un Klot. Before commencing the rite, betel-nut was prepared in the house of Makde'an Rai. Bei Katuas Laran brought in one whole maize plant. This whole plant was then erected in front of the male pillar. Meanwhile Ferik Rai distributed seven betel leaves and seven slices of areca nuts into the betel containers and the pouches. Having done so, Bei Maksia Rai recited the following 'prayer':

Ah bei sia iha kukun kalan	Oh ancestors in the dark, in the night
bei feto bei mane.	female ancestors and male ancestors.
ama Tiku bei Tiku[24]	father Tiku and ancestor Tiku
Emi kre'is ama Maromak	You are the ones that live closer to Father, the Maromak
iha leten baa	(who lives) above
iha as baa	(who lives) in the height

24 *Ama Tiku bei Tiku* is the founder of Le'un Klot. According to the history of the hamlet, this ancestor in the company of four others came to Le'un Klot from Ua Hun, following the track of a dog. In ritual language the dog is called *asu mata balada oin balada, asu besin, asu kai sa*. This journey was narrated as crossing a sea. At one stage of the journey they came to a place called Kalisuk. In this place they discovered that water dripped from the legs of the dog. They became excited, because it was an indication that they had arrived in a place suitable for habitation. Since this place is quite narrow, they call it Le'un Klot.

Titu tuun baa ami	Observe us from the above
hutun no renu	(your) folk and people
iha hoku fatik[25]	(who live) in the muddy place
iha abut kakias	(who live) in the orphan roots
Iha Le'un Klot	in Le'un Klot
iha uma Makde'an.	in the house of Makde'an.
Ohin loron ne'e ami at hakserak tinan foun	Today we offer the new year
loron ami to'o mak ohin loron	our day is due today
dadi ohin loron ne'e ami ho'i hakne'an ne'e	so, today we want to kneel down
ama Tiku bei Tiku	father Tiku, ancestor Tiku
klaut no funan	the sliced nuts (boys) and flowers (girls)
atu rodi netik lilin oan ida	are going to disturb you by lighting candles
atu rodi netik batar oan ida	disturb you by bringing maize
atu rai baa bei sia	(they) want to offer them to you
iha tafatik	in palaces
iha uma kukun	in dark houses
iha uma kalan	in night houses
iha let	in narrow (places)
iha luan.	in broad (places).
Dadi ha'ukan hakmasin bei sia iha leten iha as	So, my plea, oh ancestors who live in the height above
ta'an tilu hanono	open your ears and listen
tan ohin loron ne'e	because today
klaut no funan	the sliced nuts and flowers
atu rai netik manu oan ida baa emik tanasak, emi kakaluk	will disturb you by offering a chicken in your baskets and your pouches
no tenik batar oan ida fulin ida ka rua	and also one or two cobs of maize

---

25 *Hoku fatik* is a muddy place where buffaloes lie down in the heat of the day.

atu rain baa emi rate sia iha uma kukun uma kalan.	(they) will lay down those things on your graves, in the dark houses, the night houses.
Dadi lia hau mak ne'e dei	That is all I want to say

The invocation signifies that the first harvest of maize has officially commenced. The maize brought as tributes of homage was taken out to the graves. As soon as the maize was laid on the graves, children rushed forward to collect it and take it home. According to the explanations I received, other's children gathered maize offered by their father's sister's houses, while sister's children collected from their mother's brother's houses. At the same time, some women lit candles on the graves.

In the meantime, the offering of meat is prepared in *uma* Kakaluk. Although a pig is slaughtered, in ritual language it is referred to as *manu lamak oan ida* (a small nourishment of chicken). When the pork is ready to be taken inside the house, the east door (*oda matan la sa'en*), which always remains closed, is now opened. In contrast to ordinary practice, when food is taken inside the house through the female door (*oda matan rae*), in this ritual pork and maize are taken into the house through the male door (*oda matan lor*). The pork is then boiled, without adding any salt for flavour. Cobs of maize are also boiled, without salt, in separate cooking pots. The emphasis on 'without salt' is necessary to understand the whole concept of *hamiis*. When maize is ripe, it is considered 'cooked' (*tasak*). Cooked and salty (*masin*) items together with heat (*manas*) are categorically 'dangerous' and therefore harmful for human beings. So, in rites where the focus is on asking for 'raw' (*matak*) and 'cool' (*malirin*), food has to be offered 'plainly', 'without taste' and 'unsalted'. These terms are simply translated by one Tetun word, *miis*. While the food is being cooked, the male and female guardians of the house bring out some foxtail millet (*tora*). They come out from the house through the normally closed east door (*oda matan la sa'en*), which is opened especially for these occasions, to pound millet. They call this activity *fai tora lulik* (pounding the sacred millet). It is important that while they are pounding, the pounders do not hit each other or it would be a bad omen for the entire house.

When the food was cooked, the head of the boiled pig and a few cobs of maize were brought to the male pillar. After a short plea asking for 'raw' and 'cool' for their future work in the gardens, the male guardian peeled a few cobs of maize and threw them backwards over his shoulder. Similarly with the pieces of pork, he pinched small pieces of pork and threw them backwards over his shoulder. The throwing behind him symbolises that the ancestors, who are the 'dark people' (*ema kukun*) have been fed by the living. Only then can the pork and maize be consumed. The eating of this food is called *lamak kukun* (nourishment for the dark). The male guardian of the named house, who is also a *tuak* (the most 'respected' figure in the house, a term of address for mother's brother) is entitled to have the pig's head. The rest of the food was shared equally by members of this named house.

On every occasion involving the ritual 'eating for the dark' (*lamak kukun*), the pig liver divination is considered an important part. 'Reading the liver' (*leno aten*) as they phrased it, involves the interpretation of the size, colour and other uncommon features observed on the pig's liver (see Figure 8.1). Thus, *hamiis* rite performed by the Le'un Klot people was also accompanied by a 'reading of the liver'.

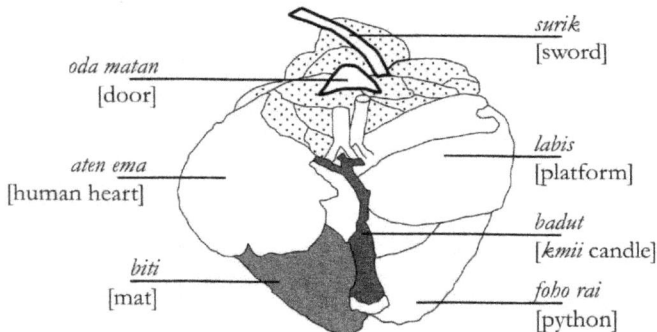

Figure 8.1: Pig liver divination

Names given to specific parts of the liver are metaphorically related to house symbolism. To begin with, I will briefly recall the placement in a house of certain items whose names also designate the specific parts of the liver. The male pillar is one of the most sacred pillars within a named house. It is situated at the front part of the inner side of the house next to the male door (*oda matan lor*). As a matter of fact, this pillar is part of the door's frame. Among paraphernalia hung on this pillar are swords with a long curved shield called *surik samara*. These swords (and for a particular named house, a staff granted by the Dutch during the sandalwood trading of the colonial era) are important regalia for a named house or even a domain. Thus, *surik samara* and *oda matan lor* represent sacred paraphernalia located at the inner part of the house. In accordance with the south Tetun house design, the verandah or platform (*labis*) is not considered as part of the inner house. Rather, it is attached (*labis*) to the inner house, therefore it belongs to the outer part of the house.

The inside/outside symbolism communicated in a house design becomes a kind of standard classification for the pig liver divination. Although the anatomy of a pig liver is not divided into inside and outside, names given to the specific parts of the liver manifest this dual classification. Using the sketch of a pig liver provided by Popesko (as given in Kuipers 1990: 103; see Figure 8.1), the outside parts are represented by different names given to specific parts of the liver. These names represent components commonly associated with outside such as 'platform' (*labis*), 'human heart' (*aten ema*), 'mat' (*bitu*), 'python' (*foho rai*) and 'candle made from candle-nut' (*badut*). There are also other parts of the pig's organs that need to be examined in a liver divination. These parts are not included in Popesko's sketch. But for the Tetun, they are important parts within a liver divination, and comprise the liver's milt (*surik* = sword) and the pork fat that links the liver and the milt called *oda matan* (door). The pork fat looks like a screen. A healthy pig, according to people's exegesis, always has a small hole in the 'screen', which is associated with 'door'. Both the 'sword' and 'door' in a liver divination represent the two sacred paraphernalia one commonly finds in a house. Unmistakably, names given to the specific parts of the liver symbolise the dual categories of inside/outside discussed in the context of house symbolism. It should be added that this analogy does not harm the indigenous concept of 'reading the liver' (*leno aten*) since the Tetun themselves gave names to those parts of the liver according to the inside/outside arrangement within a house.

In a divination, the 'sword' and 'door' are the first parts of the organ to be examined. Normally, a sword has only one sharp edge. If both edges are sharp, it is a bad omen for the house. The same is true of the 'door'. It must remain open, which is indicated by the existence of a hole in the 'screen', to allow fortune in terms of wealth to flow into the house. A closed door indicates the refusal of good fortune. The 'outside' parts of the liver are examined starting from the 'platform' and running anti-clockwise to the 'human heart'. The surfaces of 'platform' and 'python' must appear smooth without any blemishes or holes, otherwise misfortune might befall the house. As for the bile sac or '*kmii* candle', a good omen is indicated by the colour and volume of liquid contained in the sac. A good life for the house is indicated by light greenish liquid that fills three-quarters of the sac. Using a kerosene lamp as an example, my 'tutors' explained that dirty kerosene fully filling the lamp will cause the house to catch fire. In contrast to the 'platform' and 'python', the 'mat' and 'human heart' should have blemishes. The 'mat' should have a rough surface while the 'human heart' should have curves. If in 'reading the liver', these two parts look smooth (in contrast to their normal condition), the house will soon suffer great misfortune. In a divination, it is important that a diviner knows what is regarded as the 'natural condition' of these specific parts of the liver.

The mention of 'sword' as sacred regalia because it was owned by the founding fathers of the named house, and the mention of human heart, platform and other equipment that can be associated with outside, permit us to develop more categories within a symbolic classification as shown in Table 8.2.

Table 8.2: Liver omen categories

Inside	Outside
oda matan, surik	*labis, aten ema, biti, fobo rai, badut*
sacred paraphernalia	daily equipment
ancestral space	human space
women	men

My last comment aims to address the goal of the ritual as manifested in invocations during the offering of betel-nuts. As clearly spelled out by Bei Maksia Rai in the invocation cited above, the purpose of conducting this first harvest ritual is to offer meat and maize to the ancestors as well as lighting candles on their graves. The offering of meat and maize to the ancestors is a common practice throughout the entire region. But lighting candles on graves is a new practice adopted from outside.

If we look more carefully at the form and content of the above invocation, we will notice some peculiarities. The first concerns the addressee. Bei Rai summonses the ancestors who are living 'in the dark//in the night' (*iha kukun//kalan*). In traditional ritual discourse, the paired phrasing dark//night as the place where ancestors dwell is a common reference that can be found in any invocation or other ritual recitations of histories and genealogies. Some people would add more predicates to emphasise the origin place of the first human being, Fatumea//Marlilu Haholek. Others would mention the sacred house, the house of origin of a particular clan, such as 'the black house, the sacred house' (*uma metan//uma lulik*).

These expressions are standard conventions in ritual discourse in the area. What is uncommon, however, is the expression *emi kre'is ama Maromak*, which I translate as 'you are the ones that live closer to Father, the Maromak'. The Tetun do not differentiate Maromak from ancestors. For them, their ancestors are the Maromak. Therefore one could invoke the ancestors by summoning *ama maromak*, but at the same time this phrase must pair with the phrase *ina maromak*, as in the following:

Ah bei sia, tua no nurak	Oh ancestors, young and old
ah Fatumea ee Marlilu Haholek	oh Fatumea, Marlilu Haholek
uma metan sia ee uma lulik sia	oh the black houses, the sacred houses
bei sia iha kukun kalan	ancestors who are in dark and night
ah ina maromak ama maromak	oh mother maromak, father maromak

The peculiarity one discovers in the prayer summons by Bei Rai, as cited before, reveals a new element introduced by Christianity. The expression 'you are the ones who live closer to the *ama Maromak*' is a Christian theological conception concerning the existence of a mediator between humans and God. In the invocation cited above, Bei Rai, who is considered as an expert in *adat* matters, left this sentence without matching it with another parallel sentence. The same is true of the *phrase ama Maromak*. In the Christian Bible, 'God the Father' is translated as *ama Maromak*. This loaded phrase cannot simply be paired with *ina Maromak* (God the Mother), the paired phrasing found in many traditional ritual discourses. If he had matched the phrase *ama Maromak* with *ina Maromak* he would have met the *adat*'s convention but not the Christian conception. Bei Rai's solution is to leave the loaded sentence and phrases as they are, which results in the creation of an unusual form of 'prayer'.

The second peculiarity relates to the purpose of celebrating the first harvest rite. Bei Rai explicitly mentioned in his invocation that children of his village are gathering to offer meat and maize and to light candles. Even though these are common practices in a *hamiis* rite, it is not the main purpose of the rite. Some people said that the goal of conducting the first harvest rite is to inform the spirits of the ancestors (*kmalar*) to stay in the garden so that in the future the garden will keep producing a good harvest. The reason given by these people is as follows: 'We believe that the presence of ancestors' spirits (*kmalar*) caused the maize to flourish. If the maize is harvested without prior "information" to the ancestors, their *kmalar* will leave the garden and so in the future the garden will not produce any more.'

Although this answer is consistent with the practice of hiding a few seeds of sorghum under the sarong during harvest to prevent the escape of the *kmalar* contained within the seeds, this aim is not literally spelled out in the invocations. In the few invocations that I recorded, the aim of the first harvest ritual is clearly spelled out: 'We come to ask for raw and cool'. This goal is expressed as follows:

natun matak mai, natun malirin mai	grant us your raw, grant us your cool
udan wen di'ak, loro wen di'ak	a good rain and a good sun light
ba hutun raiklaran, renu rai tenan	for your people in this inhabited earth, for your folk in this eternal world
rori ko'a tua, rori rafaho rai	for them to tap palms, for them to clear gardens
bodik to'os bee no isin, tua bee no wen	so that gardens can produce, palms give juice

3. Maize of Homage (*batar mana'i*)

There are two consecutive activities related to this ritual. The first is the harvesting of sorghum planted in 'the royal dark garden' (*to'os etu kukun*) located in the eastern part of the hamlet of Laran, and the second is the bringing of the 'seven cobs of maize' (*batar fulin hitu*) as a gift of homage to the Maromak Oan, who resides in the hamlet of Laran. In the sequence of these two activities, we are dealing with an irreversible order of harvesting activities: first, the harvest of the 'ancestors' garden' and, second, the harvest of 'living humans' gardens. The former is marked by 'silence', while the latter is marked by 'festivity'. The former involves only *adat* officials who are responsible for planting and harvesting the sorghum. The latter involves a large number of people who bring their gifts of homage. These differences in the two sequential rituals affect the amount of information one can obtain. Despite the number of people who participate in them, given the nature of these rituals, people are more eager to speak about the latter than the former. The difference in the symbols used in these two rituals also encourages me to discuss them separately in chronological order.

Informants mentioned that in former times people could not harvest their maize if sorghum planted in the *to'os etu kukun* had not been harvested. It was the function of the 'garden inspector' (*lalawar*) to ensure that this rule was followed by everybody. Heavy fines of silver coins, pigs, jars of palm gin and bunches of betel-nut were levied on those who broke it. At present, although the injunction is no longer observed, the rites connected with harvesting the sorghum and the giving of the seven cobs of maize are still solemnly practised.

When the sorghum is considered ripe enough to be harvested, *lalawar*, the garden inspector arranges for the preparation of harvesting the sorghum, which is called *koto batar etu kukun*. When I was in the field, the *lalawar*, a man whose natal house is in the hamlet of Batane but who resides in his wife's house in the hamlet of Lo'o Sina, was not asked to perform his duty.[26] At that time, the *lalawar* was replaced by Bei Ai Tou, a lineage head who lived in *le'un Loro Monu*, within the hamlet of Laran. He erected a small hut (*laen*) roofed with coconut leaves. In front of the hut, he spread a mat called *biti ulun* (literally 'the head mat'). This mat was taken from the most sacred house in the whole realm of Wesei Wehali called Ai Lotuk. He also prepared other items needed for the rites, such as a small bamboo jar used as a drink container (*au kenu*); the shell of a kind of fruit used to gather the sorghum seeds (*kso'e*); a betel-nut container (*kabir inan*); a small pointed stick erected in front of the mat called *kaledik* to represent the male pillar of a house; a bottle of palm-gin tied with a slice of palm-leaf; two big hexagonal baskets (*baliki*) and two sorghum blossoms (*batar knaar*). These items are needed during the rite called *hahaan rai* ('to feed the earth').

The person who was responsible for the 'feeding of the earth' was Bei Nufa,[27] the guardian of the house of Ai Lotuk. He lives in Le'un Klot, within the hamlet of Laran. He was also in charge of harvesting the sorghum. When Bei Ai Tou had erected the temporary hut, Bei Nufa went to harvest the sorghum. The sorghum was then spread on the mat. The bottle of palm-gin was tied to the stick. The hexagonal baskets, the betel-nut container and the fruit shell used for gathering the seeds of the sorghum were placed upside-down. I was told that by placing them upside-down, the spirits of the ancestors (*kmalar*) who were occupying the ritual paraphernalia would not escape. The bamboo container was

---

26 A few months afterwards, when I visited the hamlet of Lo'o Sina, I asked him about his absence in this important rite. He avoided mentioning the dispute that had been taking place in the hamlet of Laran concerning the appointment of the Maromak Oan, in which he was among those who opposed the nominee advanced by the Laran people.

27 Normally Bei Lulik, as the sacred holder of Maromak Oan's sacred regalia, is in charge of feeding the earth. But due to the current dispute, Bei Lulik was not present. He also informed me that he did not know the exact time for conducting the harvest of the sacred sorghum.

then filled with palm-gin together with a few drops of the blood of a pig slaughtered especially as a sacrifice. The sacrificial pork was put into two pyramidal baskets called *hane matan*. The meat was taken from particular parts of the pig known as *fahi lolon* (literally, the body of the pig). The parts consisted of the head, including the tongue (*nanaan*), the lungs (*afaak*) and the kidneys (*fuan*). These things were put into one of the pyramidal baskets. The other pyramidal basket was filled with liver (*aten*), liver milt (*surik*), the right leg (*kelen kwana*), right haunch (*kidan*) and ribs (*sorin balu*). The former basket was taken inside the garden to 'feed the centre of the garden' (*hahaan troman*). The latter basket was taken to 'feed the mat' (*hahaan biti ulun*). I was told that the feeding of the centre of the garden symbolises the people's thanksgiving to the ancestors, who brought sorghum as food for the people. The feeding of the mat symbolises their thanksgiving toward Maromak Oan, the guarantor of their livelihood.

Having finished the feeding of the earth, Bei Nufa carefully gathered the sorghum seeds and transferred them to the hexagonal baskets using the fruit shell (*kso'e*) as a scoop. Every time he scooped he took a few seeds and hid them under his sarong. After scooping up the sorghum, the scoop (*kso'e*) was laid upside down on top of the seeds before putting the lid on the basket. The sorghum was then taken by Bei Nufa's sister (Maria Abuk Baria), the female guardian of the Ai Lotuk house. She walked in silence, carrying the sorghum on her head, to the ancestral house. The remaining food was then consumed by the participants in the harvesting of the sorghum, mainly women from *le'un* Klot. The eating of this sacrificial meal is called *lamak kukun*, 'eating for the dark'. This marked the end of the rite.

In former times, when the sorghum had been installed in the ancestral house (Ai Lotuk), 'royal gongs' (*tala etu*) were beaten to inform people that they could start harvesting their gardens. A few days afterwards, Maromak Oan called for a meeting with his assembly—'the four old women and the four old men' (*ferik hat, katuas hat*). They came from the hamlets of Kateri, Umakatahan, Kletek and Fahiluka. The aim of this assembly was to negotiate the 'time' for delivering their gifts of homage to the Maromak Oan. The exact 'date' for the delivery is in the hands of Maromak Oan. Maromak Oan's decision is conveyed by messengers (Bei Ai Touk and Bei Nufa). These men passed around a rope with knots called *kbabukar*, which signified how many days were left until the gifts would be delivered to the hamlet of Laran. Usually, the number of knots in a rope ranges from three to seven, since, according to my sources, odd numbers are associated with sacred elements and ancestors, while even numbers belong to human beings. Every day a knot was untied. The remaining knots delineated the number of days left. The passing on of the rope follows an order of precedence. From the hamlet of Laran, the centre of Wesei Wehali, the rope was sent to the four surrounding hamlets. The rope was first passed to the hamlets of Kateri and Umakatahan. As discussed in earlier chapters, following the house metaphor these two hamlets are delineated as the two corner posts located at the back of a house. These posts are therefore considered as female posts. As they are in the category of 'female' posts, they are considered as the trunk of the house. In ritual language these two hamlets are described as 'the trunk of the hip//the trunk of the ladder' (*knuba hun//tetek hun*). *Fukun* of these two hamlets are ritually known as 'the old women of the trunk of the mountain, the old men of the trunk of the mountain' (*ferik foho hun, katuas foho hun*). It was the task of the *fukun* of those two hamlets to pass the rope on to the next two hamlets, namely Kletek and Fahiluka. In the house analogy, these two hamlets are delineated as the front corner posts. Being categorised as 'front', these posts are considered to be male posts. These two hamlets are ritually known as 'hamlets of the edge of the sea' (*leo tasi tehen*). *Fukun* of these two hamlets are referred to as 'the old women of the leg of the sea//the old men of the leg of the sea' (*ferik ain tasi//katuas ain tasi*). Thus, the passing of the rope symbolises starting from the insiders to the outsiders, from centre to periphery, from mountain to sea, from trunk to edge, and from female to male. The actual passing of the rope is illustrated in Figure 8.2.

Bei Ai Tou who lives in the *le'un Loro Monu* ('plains areas towards the sunset') was charged with communicating the message to the clan heads who live in the hamlet of Kateri, the 'trunk' hamlet. From there, the message was passed on to the peripheral hamlets (*leo molin*), as far as Bi'uduk Fehan, Bi'uduk Foho and Kakaniuk. Bei Nufa was charged with communicating the message to the *fukun* of Umakatahan. It was the task of the *fukun* of those two hamlets, who are known as 'the old women of the trunk of the mountain and the old men of the trunk of the mountain' (*ferik foho hun, katuas foho hun*) to pass on the message of the *kbukar* rope to the *fukun* who live in the hamlets of Kletek and Fahiluka and other peripheral hamlets such as Manumutin, Tabene, Bakateu and Dirma. The *fukun* of the hamlets of Kletek and Fahiluka are known as 'the old women of the edge of the sea, the old men of the edge of the sea' (*ferik tasi tehen, katuas tasi tehen*).

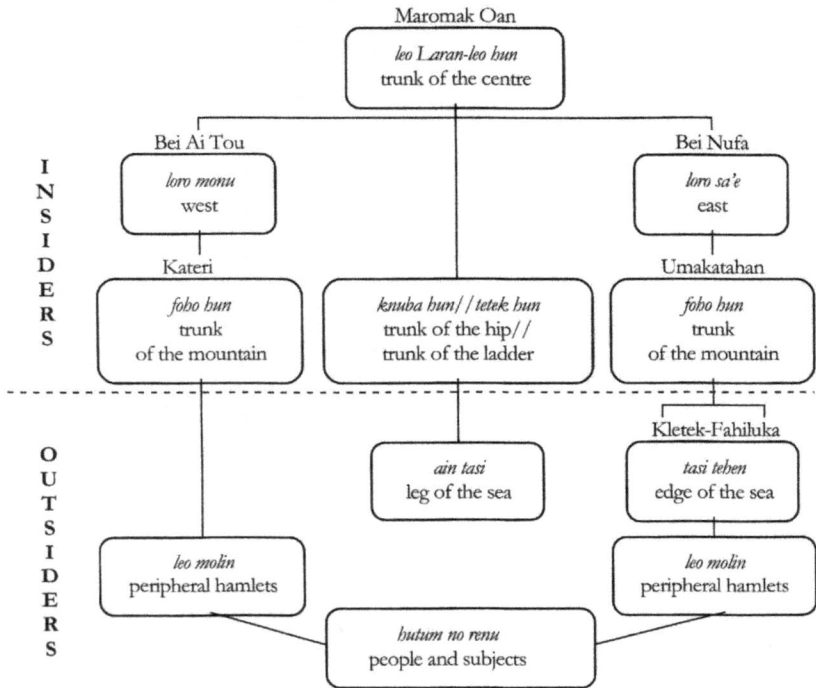

Figure 8.2: Order of precedence in the passing of rope of announcement

On the chosen day, 'old women and old men' from these four hamlets assembled in the hamlet of Laran. When I was in the field the ritual was conducted on 17 July 1993, almost four months after the assembly of 'the four old women and the four old men'.[28]

Compared with the harvesting of the sorghum, the delivery of gifts of homage was a joyous occasion. Women beat drums (*bibliku*) while dancing with snake-like movements (*likurai*). Men lead the women, dancing, while unsheathing their swords. Cockfighting, a traditional game enjoyed by the people during this type of ritual, has long been banned by the government. With the confiscation of traditional guns (*kilat*), men can

---

28 The meeting of the assembly of 'the four old women and the four old men' (*fukun ferik hat katuas hat*) was held on 22 March 1993. This means that the delivery of the gift of homage occurred almost four months after the meeting. This postponement, according to official information, was related to the cholera epidemic that claimed many lives. Government officers and police, at that time, did not want to issue *Izin mengadakan keramaian* (permission for conducting festivity) until the epidemic was regarded as over. However, there was another rumour that the government was reluctant to give permission because, according to them, the gift of homage is a practice of feudalism. Celebrating it meant reviving the old feudalism.

no longer show off to the women their skill in firing the guns. Despite these 'handicaps', the celebration was conducted as joyfully as ever. The taking of gifts of homage was accompanied not by the firing of guns, but by shouting men (*kalalak*), just like in former times when trophy heads were taken into the hamlets.

The seven cobs of maize brought by people from various clan heads within the four-corner land were assembled in front of the three bigger named houses (*uma mahoo naran bot*). Since the hamlet of Laran is the seat of Maromak Oan, two named houses are referred to as 'palaces' (*tafatik*, literally 'place to sit'), while the third one is simply called *uma mahoo naran*. Those clan heads (*fukun*) knew exactly in which *tafatik* and *uma* they had to assemble. In response to my query, Na'i Niis who sits in the *tafatik* Leko (the house of Maromak Oan), Na'i Mea who sits in the *tafatik* Mako'a Rai, and Na'i Nona who sits in the *uma* Marii Lia (the house that is considered as the 'gate' to Ai Lotuk), together offered me a list of named houses and hamlets that are considered as 'their subjects' (see Table 8.3).

Table 8.3: Distribution of *fukun* named houses

Tafatik Leko	Tafatik Mako'a Rai	Uma Marii Lia
Uma Bei Rai–Kateri	Ume Tema–Kateri	Uma Komu Han–Tabene
Uma La'e Tua Klolok–Bi'uduk Fehan	Uma Fukun Makwar–Bolan	Uma Manekin–Bolan
Uma La'e Tua–Bi'uduk	Uma Na'i Kasak–Bolan	
Umasukaer Hanematan Babenik–Banibin	Uma Makbukar–Brama	
Uma Atok Ama Klau Nahak–Umasukaer	Uma Kaliduk–Tabene	
Uma Atok Ama Klau Laran–Umasukaer	Uma Katuas–Kletek	
Uma La'e tua Lia Rian–Manumutin	Uma Lo'o–Kletek	
Uma Bei Muti Bei Katuas–Umanen		
Uma Katuas–Batane		
Uma Lalawar–Umakatahan		
Uma Lor–Umakatahan		
Uma La'e Tua Hali Abut–Umakatahan		
Uma Bunuk Lo'o Latar–Umakatahan		
Uma Makta'en–Bakateu		

Tafatik Leko	Tafatik Mako'a Rai	Uma Marii Lia
Uma Mamulak–Fahiluka		
Uma Badare–Fahiluka		
Uma Paki Besi Liurai–Fahiluka		
Uma Si'a Kaliduk–Kakaniuk		
Uma Tien Tua Mau Ra'e–Mande'u		
Uma Bau Mauk–Mande'u		

I was also told that when gifts of homage are taken to the centre (*leo* Laran), those who deliver the gifts are usually entitled to pick people's coconuts or catch other people's pigs along the way to the hamlet of Laran. They will then bring to Maromak Oan the 'maize of homage' as well as the produce that they have gathered along the way. The custom of collecting others' property is called *baboen*.[29] The custom of *baboen* is also observed by the people of We Oe in a similar rite of delivering gift of homages. But their ritual is called *hanematan loro* (gifts for 'ruler', *loro*, which are offered in *hanematan* baskets). In the case of Wehali, in the meeting of the assembly of 'the four old women and the four old men' held on 22 March 1993, it had been decided that the custom of *baboen* would not be practised. One of the reasons given for the cancelling of *baboen* was that many people no longer understood its value. The elders were concerned about the social tension that might occur due to the misunderstanding of the custom.

When the people had assembled in front of the noble houses and torches made of palm fronds (*ai klunus*) had been lit, a few bunches of maize were exchanged among the noble houses. People call this event *hadomi malu/ / hatias malu* (show love to each other//show affection to each other). Before the crowd proceeded to Ai Lotuk, the *adat* historian of Kateri, Benedictus Bere Seran, delivered a short speech that I recorded as follows:

Fukun sia	All the *fukun*
Ita hoi hukun no hanatar ne'e, emi ha'ak mana'ik	The execution of rule and the hunting of food, which people call homage
ha'ak fore lai dikin batar lai dikin	is the offering of tips of mung bean vines, tips of maize leaves

---

29 The people translate *baboen* into Indonesian as *lelang* (auction), but the way they explain the meaning of *lelang* suggests that it must be translated as 'to rob', a translation that they would certainly not recommend.

iha dato has ain dato has ulun	from the four leg rulers, the four head rulers
iha ferik hat katuas hat	the four old women, the four old men
hodi tama mai hana'i	We deliver (them) to pay homage
hodi tama mai hatetu no harani	We come to present and to offer
hodi mai hana'i no hahulu	we come to pay homage and honour
iha kwaur ha'in aa as ha'in aa	to the exclusive one, to the supreme one
iha lolo liman la to'o, bi'i ai la dai	to the one that cannot be reached by stretching out hands, by standing on tiptoe
bat hodi husu uda wen naketak loron wen naketak	we come to plead for the boundary made for rain days separated from sun days
bat hodi simu matak simu malirin.	we come to acquire raw, to acquire cool.

With this short speech the crowd proceeded to the Ai Lotuk. The party from the palace of Mako'a Rai called on the party who were waiting at the palace of Leko. Together they called on the house of Marii Lia. Although these houses are only located metres away from each other, the 'call up event' (*haksee*) is considered an important ritual. The crowd then went on shouting like people coming back from the battle field, while carrying the maize on their shoulders. The crowd consisted only of men because the delivery of the seven cobs of maize is a men's event. This is the opposite to the delivery of the sorghum to the Ai Lotuk, which is considered to be a women's event.

On arrival at the Ai Lotuk, people formed a square shape in front of the female door (*odamatan rae*) of the Ai Lotuk house, while maize was placed in the middle of the square. Maromak Oan[30] took off his shoulder cloth and spread it in front of him. Betel leaves and areca nuts harvested from the sacred forest situated right in front of Ai Lotuk were carefully ordered on top of the cloth. A slice of areca nut, the symbol for man, was placed on one betel leaf, the symbol for woman. The number of betel-nuts represented the number of elders assembled. Young men collected betel-nut containers from all the elders. The betel-nuts were then placed in those containers. This event is called *simu kmusan, simu matak no malirin* (acquiring betel-chew, acquiring raw and cool). This is the end of the ritual because the exchange of wealth and life have taken place. The subjects

---

30 On this occasion, Na'i Muti, the nominee of the Laran people, acted as Maromak Oan.

receive a guarantee of life (in the form of betel-chewing) and the hope of future well-being (raw and cool) in exchange for wealth in the form of products of their gardens. With the receiving of *kmusan* (betel-chew), the union of male (areca nut) and female (betel leaf) has occurred, fertility has been guaranteed. Thus, the flow of life from centre to periphery and the flow of wealth from the periphery to the centre revealed in many ritual speeches discussed in earlier chapters are re-enacted in these rituals.

Concluding Remarks

It is evident from the above accounts that rituals relating to the process of childbirth and the agricultural cycle, two events observed separately by the Wehali, are constructed on the same cultural categories and therefore reveal the same symbolic meaning. The Tetun employ the same term for both rituals: *hahoris batar* (to make the maize alive) for the agricultural ritual and *hahoris oan* (to make the child alive) for childbirth. The key word in these two events is hahoris which derives from mons meaning 'alive'.

Life, fertility, raw, tame and cool are necessary conditions one needs to achieve in order to make both people and plants 'alive'. This is the reason why on every occasion during the two cycles of rituals, we hear people plead in a stereotypical formula:

natuun matak mai	send down the raw
natuun mafirin mai	send down the cool

However, it is not valid to conclude that the opposite categories (death, cooked, salty, wild and heat) are conditions that need to be avoided. Actually, both categories are mutually interrelated. In order to achieve 'cool' one needs to pass through the 'heating' process. In the same manner, at a particular time in one's life-history one needs to be heated from a 'cool' condition. The process of achieving the condition of either 'cool' or 'heat' involves the offering of betel-nut and animal blood. The red betel chew and the blood therefore act as a passage from cool to heat and vice versa. They are considered as substances that 'weaken the boundaries separating categories', as described by Hicks (1990:92). Concerning animal blood, the Tetun believe that a goat's blood is necessary to achieve the 'heat' condition. In contrast, the blood of chickens and pigs is an agent for achieving 'cool'.

The three rituals described above in the process of childbirth and the agricultural cycle reflect the three stages in the life cycle introduced by van Gennep (1960). The first stage, concerning rituals of separation, is represented by the rite of 'cleaning up the path' (*hasori dalan*) and the rite of 'sprinkling the seeds' (*hisik fini*). In 'cleaning up the path' the expectant mother is 'separated' from every possibility that might threaten the life of the woman and her offspring. In this ritual of separation she is forbidden to eat foods that are traditionally considered as stimulating heat or to behave in a manner that is considered as inviting danger to her pregnancy. In the agriculture ritual, the separation between the dual categories of cool and heat is identified by a clear-cut division between the cool seeds and the hot earth. In order to make the seeds alive the earth must be cooled early in the morning before getting hot. The earth is also cooled with juice from an unformed coconut. The unformed coconut is contrasted with the ripe coconut. The former is considered as having the 'cool' and 'raw' substances needed for a life-giving ritual.

The next stage, the liminal stage, is represented by the rite of seclusion (*hatuka ha'i*) and the first harvest rite (*hamiis*). In this stage both the young woman and the crops (particularly maize) are still in a transitional stage. The young woman has not yet become a mother and the edible maize is not yet suitable to be harvested. In this stage, the oppositional dual categories are re-ordered: the 'wild' woman is 'tamed' and the 'heat' maize is 'cooled'.

The last stage is that of re-incorporation. It is represented by the rite of 'to take out name' (*hasai naran*) and the 'delivery of the maize of homage' (*hatama batar mana'i*). After a period of seclusion the mother is considered 'cool' and 'tame' and able to be re-incorporated safely into the community. In this final stage of the life cycle, the mother is identified as having given birth to her child. The final stage of the agricultural cycle is marked by the delivery of the maize of homage to the Maromak Oan. Within the agricultural context this final ritual emphasises the notion of re-affirming the source of life. With the delivery of the maize of homage, the Tetun re-affirms Maromak Oan as the giver of life.

9

Conclusion

In the course of this study I have been dealing with the use of dual categories by the south Tetun to order their social relations. Many of these Tetun local categories are related to the cultural expressions of other Austronesian-speaking peoples, which thereby constitute a common reservoir of 'metaphors for living' (Fox 1980: 333). As I have attempted to show, the south Tetun continue to draw on these categories that are expressed vividly in myths and other forms of ritual language.

In this final chapter, I expand my focus to include the Atoni or the Dawan, as the Tetun term this neighbouring ethnic group. There are two reasons for including these Dawan-speaking people. The first reason is based on historical considerations. Although Schulte Nordholdt (1971: 157) fails to use the support of oral tradition narrated by the Dawan specialists as a basis for comparing these two societies and therefore he has to rely on historical documents, nevertheless he also came to the conclusion that there was a historical tie between the south Tetun and Insana, Biboki and, to a certain degree, with Molo (1971: 231, 276). While acknowledging the lack of any comprehensive research on oral traditions narrated in these two regions, the recorded myths available and informants' recapitulation of past history led Cunningham (1962: 54) to conclude that, although Insana is culturally Dawan, past political allegiance was to the Liurai of south Belu rather than to Sonba'i. Ataupah (1990: 146–152) in his dissertation points to the south Tetun connection with Insana and Molo based on oral traditions narrated in those regions. A rather ambitious work is Parera's (1971) unpublished typescript (1994 published edition) that attempts to connect the south Tetun, and more particularly the Wehali, with all the Dawan-speaking peoples.

The second reason for making this comparison with the Dawan has to do with considerations in the literature on these societies. Within the last 30 years, an accumulation of ethnographic accounts based on substantial fieldwork has enriched our knowledge of the Dawan area. Among those who contributed to this build-up of ethnographies are Cunningham, Schulte Nordholt, McWilliam and Ataupah.

I delimit this comparative exercise by focusing on three features of Wehali society, which are described in local categories: 1. Wehali—the 'female', 2. Wehali—the insider, 3. Wehali—the 'trunk', the 'centre' and the 'first to dry'. As a background to this analysis, I begin with a short description on how the south Tetun perceive the Dawan as revealed in oral tradition and other symbolic representations.

Dawan as Seen from South Tetun

Myths that I recorded in south Tetun provided mixed information on how much the south Tetun 'know' about the Dawan. In the following description of the Dawan, I do not mention all the ethnic groups that compose this 'dry land people' simply because I want to highlight how south Tetun myths reveal the relation between these two neighbouring peoples. From the first time I learned of the origin myths narrated both in Wehali and Wewiku, I noticed the south Tetun regular emphasis on location and generational categories that distinguish themselves and the Dawan as an entity: the Dawan are the people of the setting sun; the south Tetun are the people of the navel land. Liurai Sonba'i was a son of Wehali sent by his 'mother and father' to protect them in this 'trunk land'. Comparing the Liurai Wehali with the Liurai Sonba'i, the former is regarded as eldest brother. Reference Text 2, for example, has to be understood in terms of these kinds of dichotomies. It was narrated that when Ho'ar Na'i Haholek and Na'i Taek Malaka had sons, two were sent to the land of the rising sun, the next two were sent to the land of the setting sun and the last two sons remained in Wehali. The name 'Mataus' (literally, 'to protect') was given to these six sons, alluding to their cultural function as 'protectors' of their natal land.

Beside this general knowledge of the Dawan, there are also myths that connect the south Tetun to particular groups of the Dawan-speaking peoples. The myth cited in Reference Text 3 explicitly names five groups of Dawan: Biboki, Insana, Amanuban, Amanatun and Amarasi. According to this myth, when the land had already dried, a group of ten men (entitled Loro) came:

hat iha Wehali	four of them remained in Wehali
nen la'o	six went on
loro mane kwa'ik aa baa iha Likusaen Bauboe	the elder *loro* went to Likusaen Bauboe
ida baa iha Biboki	one went to Biboki
ida baa iha Insana	one went to Insana
ida baa iha Amanuban	one went to Amanuban
ida baa iha Amanatun	one went to Amanatun
ida baa iha Amarasi	one went to Amarasi

The mention of Amarasi in this myth is crucial since other myths narrated in Wewiku do not include this group. According to the Wewiku version, the four brothers who went to the land of the setting sun were Natu Taek, Nuba Taek, Sana Taek and Boki Taek. These four brothers later became ancestors of the respective domains of Amanatun, Amanuban, Insana and Biboki. Wewiku elders informed me that in former times when the *adat* of 'sending the food of Liurai' (*hatama liurai lamak*)—that is, when the annual delivery of the tribute of homage was still observed—these four domains were among those who were entitled to bring their products of the land. From the Wewiku perspective, Amanatun, Amanuban, Insana and Biboki are the 'stables of Liurai, the paths of Liurai' (*knokar Liurai, inuk Liurai*); they are the Liurai's 'cultivation' area and therefore people of these domains are entitled to pay their tribute to the Liurai, the 'one who eats reclining, drinks reclining'. The absence of Amarasi both in Wewiku's version of the myth and in the agricultural rituals of homage celebrated both by the Wehali and Wewiku show that Amarasi is not considered Liurai's 'cultivation space'. The only explanation given to me concerning the relation between Amarasi and Wehali was in regard to the sacred regalia belonging to the house of Liurai (see Chapter 5, note 27). Included in the regalia registered as belonging to Liurai Luis Sanaka Tei Seran is a saddle made of Amarasi woven cloth. Luis Sanaka added, 'it is a proof that Sonba'i originated from the house of Liurai'.

The mention of the domains of Amanatun and Amanuban as founded respectively by Natu Taek and Nuba Taek is also problematic. Living with the people in We Oe and Akani who share a border with Amanatun,

I constantly heard stories concerning the dispute between the Wehali-Wewiku and Amanatun, which ended in tribal warfare. People in the hamlet of Uma To'os Fatuk even have an 'amulet' house (*uma kakaluk*) called Seran Fuik Luan Fuik where their warriors sought invulnerability when these two societies were in tribal war. Despite the intermarriage between the nobles of the domain of Amanuban with nobles from Uma Lor in the domain of Wewiku, the 'language of the earth' and other types of origin myths that I recorded both in Wehali and Wewiku do not reveal much about the relations between these two regions.

Another group of Dawan who need to be addressed are those of Molo. The 'languages of the earth' do not explicitly mention the name Molo, although Liurai Sonba'i is considered as the younger brother of the Liurai Wehali. Myths recorded both in south Tetun and in the Dawan-speaking area reveal that when the first Sonba'i (named Na'i Laban in the Dawan myths) discovered empty space in which to dwell upstream of the river of Benenai, he sent this 'good news' to his elder brother who lived in Wehali at the mouth of the river of Benenai. It is the Benenai River that links these two brothers. To send the message to his elder brother, Sonba'i filled a bamboo container (Dawan: *tukek*) with fresh water and floated it down the river of Benenai. Having received this 'good news' from his younger brother, the Liurai Wehali brought this bamboo container and planted it on the eastern part of the hamlet of Laran. This bamboo grew densely there. I was told that the location where this first shrub of bamboo grew was in the eastern part of the hamlet of Laran. This area had been sold by Laran nobles to the Catholic mission. My Tetun friends regretfully mentioned that the place where the first bamboo was planted had been converted into a dam.

Beside myths that I use as a means to depict relations between the south Tetun and various groups of Dawan, there are also names given to ancestral houses that indicate relations. With the focus on the ideology of Wehali as the origin place from which other societies including the Dawan originate, one would expect that there are named houses in Wehali that refer to this mythical origin of the Dawan. In this regard there are two hamlets that are worth noting, namely the hamlets of Batane and Laran. In Wehali symbolic organisation of space, the hamlet of Batane (glossed as 'campsite') is a resting place. I was told that in former times when people of domains under the hegemony of Wehali still brought their tribute to the Maromak Oan, who resides in the hamlet of Laran, they used the hamlet of Batane as a 'campsite'. Every ruler of a domain would stay overnight in a named house to which their ancestors originally belonged. There are three important named houses that are inhabited by three female siblings: *uma* Makaer Lulik (elder sister), *uma* Bei Luruk (middle sister), and *uma* Tudik (younger sister). The first house symbolises the house that gave birth to the Maromak Oan; the second symbolises the house that gave birth to the Liurai; the last house gave birth to the Liurai Sonba'i, the *liurai* of the domains of the setting sun and the Liurai Likusaen, the *liurai* of the domains of the rising sun. Piet Tahu Nahak, the Wehali *adat* historian whose trunk house is the *uma* Makaer Lulik, explained that the name *uma Tudik* (Knife house) given to this house refers to the task given to Sonba'i (and the Liurai of Likusaen) as Maromak Oan's workers who were in charge of 'providing food as offering, food as gifts' (*koto lamak hatetu, lamak harani*) for the Maromak Oan.

As regards Sonba'i subjects, they came to deliver the tribute of homage following another procedure. I was told that they came to Laran via the domain of Haitimuk as their first campsite. From there the procession went to the hamlet of Laran. In this hamlet they gathered in a named house called *uma* Insana (or *uma* Sonba'i as referred to by others), which is located in the *le'un Loro Monu* (the *le'un* of the setting sun).

Based on the evidence in myths, ritual and named houses one is able to draw a sketch of how the south Tetun perceive people of the neighbouring Dawan regions. More often the Dawan are identified in general terms as the Sonba'i. In other instances they are referred to by their own identity. From among the ten groups that make up the Dawan, the south Tetun associate themselves more with Insana, Biboki, Molo and also Amanuban. Despite the different perceptions of the various groups of Dawan, the south Tetun have a common cultural conception that the Dawan territories are the Liurai's cultivation areas.

Major Features of Wehali

1. Wehali — the 'Female'

In a recent study comparing the Buru people with the Timorese Mambai, Grimes (1993: 286) notes that 'much of the Mambai world is pre-gendered'. Throughout the study, I have shown that the notion of gender is but one set of categories that is used in structuring the Tetun societies. It is true that in these societies gender is used to identify certain things such as parts of the house, sets of goods presented at marriage as bridewealth; two lines of ritual language or two dyadic words can also be grouped into gender categories. What is significant in these societies, however, is the dynamic nature of these gender categories. To limit the discussion in this comparative context, I focus on gender symbolism in political structure.

Most eastern Indonesian societies discuss their political organisation based on the symbolic division of powers between male and female. Fox has defined this type of diarchic system as 'a rigorous division between spiritual authority and temporal power predicated on a conceptual opposition between female and male' (1982: 25). This system of diarchy particularly resounds among Timorese societies.

Ethnographic accounts of the Dawan suggest that: (1) Dawan political organisation is encoded in a system of dual classification; (2) this system is based on the complementary opposition of gender categories; (3) the political structure is organised on quadripartition. To say this does not necessarily provide a ready-made model to study the political structure of the Dawan. In fact, it is fair to say that this is not so. If one takes two groups of the Dawan (Insana and Amanuban), for example, one will realise that these two Dawan groups order their political structure according to different kinds of precedence.

The quadripartition of Insana political organisation is based on the female principle. The central authority is in the hands of the Atupas, the one who reclines. He is conceptually female, holding ritual authority: 'He had no secular duties and was required to remain in the court area (ba'af)' (Cunningham 1964: 65). This female ruler is surrounded by the palace chiefs, conceptually male, who act as his 'mouth' in executing his orders. Official positions in the polity are ascribed to the four great fathers (amaf naek) who represent the four houses (Cunningham 1964: 68; Schulte Nordholt 1971: 188).

The study conducted by McWilliam in southern Amanuban (among the Nabuasa origin group) shows the same principle of quadripartition as found in Insana and the rest of Dawan societies, but its political structure is based on a male principle. Comparing the Nabuasa group and the Insana studied by Cunningham and Schulte Nordholt, McWilliam (2002: 116) draws the conclusion that:

... it is the male aspect which is given precedence and central priority in the structure. The meo naek Nabuasa, stands on the periphery of Amanuban as one of the 'four males, the four bulls'. The essential 'masculinity' of the meo naek Nabuasa, results in the political centre of the domain, becoming conceptually male.

Based on McWilliams' diagram (2002: 115), one could depict a political structure of the Nabuasa group where as a 'great cat' (*meo naek*) he was encircled by the four groups of 'small cats' (*meo ana*): Benu, Neonane, Sopaba and Toislaka. These 'four fathers' (*atoin amaf*) as the Dawan term these 'small cats' acted as 'soldiers for Nabuasa and fought under his name with the ritual protection Nabuasa offered ...' (2002: 102). Beside the 'warfare' idioms used to delineate the cultural function of these 'four fathers', they are also depicted as gardeners who are entitled to 'feed' the Nabuasa at the centre. Thus in agricultural idioms, the 'four fathers' are gardeners who 'serve' the central Nabuasa. These two idioms, as pointed out by McWilliams (2002: 103), have placed the 'four fathers' in a state that appears to be ambiguous. As warriors they are the male superior. As 'servants' they are the female inferior.

Discussing the notion of gender in the political structure of the south Tetun, the 'land of women' (*rai feto*) whose societies are described as 'matriarchic' by Francillon (1967), one would expect to begin with the female principle. The Wehali claim to be 'the land of the woman' is based on origin myths. Reference Texts 2, 5 and 6 recapitulate how 'the First Woman on Earth' (*Ferik Ha'in Raiklaran*) gave birth to the genetrix of Wehali. The name of this genetrix, as recorded in Reference Texts 2 and 6, is Ho'ar Na'i Haholek. The emphasis on female origin is significant in developing the notion of precedence. Although later Ho'ar married an 'outside' man and produced offspring, who are said to rule most domains on the island of Timor, it was Ho'ar who gave life and therefore Wehali must take precedence over other domains.

The emphasis on female origin is also replicated in their political organisation. As a centre domain, the Maromak Oan is the supreme ruler. Although the Maromak Oan is a man, he is conceptually female. The female category applied to this figure is indicated, among others, by his ritual designation as 'the one who eats reclining, drinks reclining'. Thus, the female, immobile and passive are categories relevant to this designation.

As the supreme ruler, he is not actually entitled to exercise power. This power is in the hands of the Liurai, his male subordinates. There are three Liurai who act as his executive rulers: Liurai Likusaen who represents domains toward the sunrise, Liurai Wehali who represents domains at the centre of the island (known as Wesei Wehali), and Liurai Sonba'i who represents domains toward the sunset. These Liurai are conceptually male rulers who act as gates and doors to inner Wehali, the domain of the Maromak Oan.

Within the territory of Wesei Wehali, the Liurai who is otherwise conceptually male, is also referred to as 'the one who eats reclining, drinks reclining'. With this female categorisation, he is not then entitled to rule. The power to rule is delegated to his male subordinates with the title *loro* (sun). There are four *loro* representing four domains: Wewiku, Haitimuk, Lakekun and Dirma. These four domains are depicted as surrounding and protecting the fifth domain, known as 'the four-corner land'. This is the centre domain where the Maramak Oan resides. This domain is glossed as 'inner Wehali', and therefore those four domains are regarded as 'outer Wehali'.

To encapsulate the political structure of the realm of Wesei Wehali, which in Tetun cosmology includes both the Liurai Likusaen (representing domains of the rising sun) and Liurai Sonba'i (representing domains of the setting sun), the territory of 'the four-corner land' as the navel land is bordered by sets of 'pillars'. The outer pillars are the Liurai Likusaen, Liurai Wehali and Liurai Sonba'i, each represents the east, central and west gates respectively. The second set of pillars are represented by Loro Wewiku, Loro Wehali, Loro Lakekun and Loro Dirma. These four Loro symbolically represent the four corner posts of a garden. In 'garden' symbolism, inner Wehali is delineated as situated in a fenced garden. The access to Wehali is through a 'ladder' mounted on the fence. This 'ladder' is represented by the hamlet of Sulit Anemeta. The third set of pillars, which in this work I translate as 'posts', are represented by the male *fukun* of Kateri, Umakatahan, Kletek and Fahiluka. These four *fukun* symbolise the four corner posts of a house.

In 'the four-corner land', the Maromak Oan is assisted by his two nobles. One is called Na'i Umanen and the other is called Na'i Lawalu. The gender classifications of female and male respectively are also applied to these nobles. Na'i Umanen is chosen from male members in a house in the hamlet of Umanen and Na'i Lawalu is similarly chosen from a house in the hamlet of Bi'uduk Fehan. The Na'i Umanen is female; the Na'i Lawalu is male.

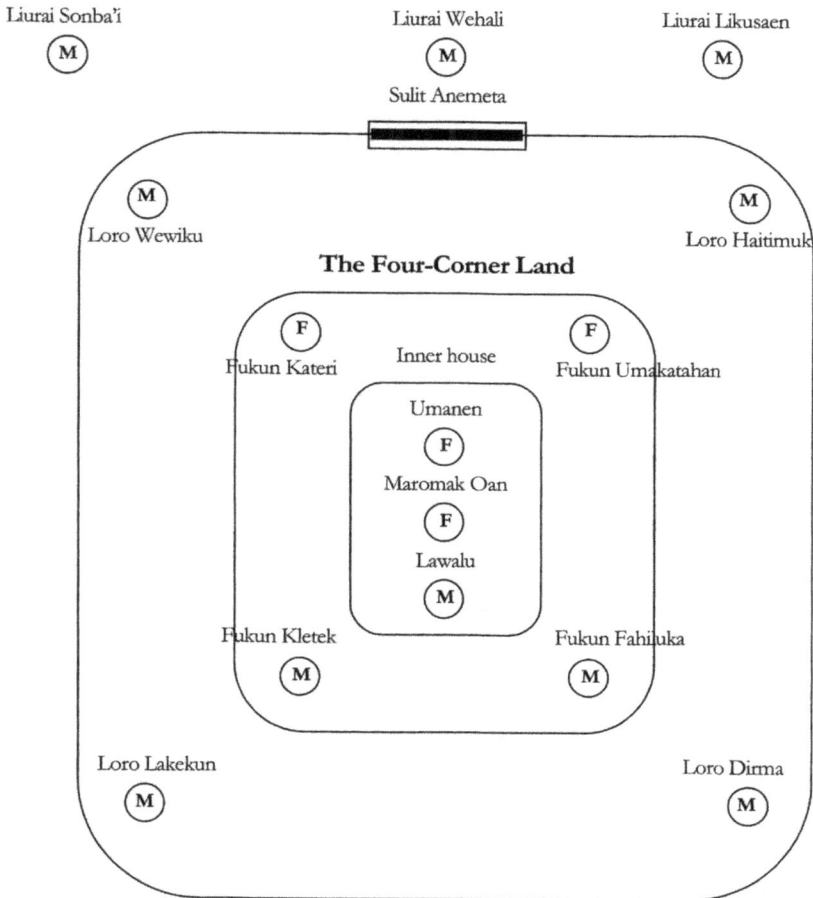

Figure 9.1: Conceptual structure of the Wesei Wehali polity

The Maromak Oan, Umanen and Lawalu are surrounded by the assembly of 'the Four Old Women, the Four Old Men' (*Ferik Hat, Katuas Hat*) who are chosen from the four hamlets that make up the territory of 'the four-corner land'. They are titled 'female *fukun*' (*fukun ferik*) and 'male *fukun*' (*fukun katuas*).

At this origin group level, these *fukun* are referred to as 'those who eat reclining, drink reclining'. They are surrounded by their male subordinates—that is, the custodians or guardians of named houses. The latter are called 'old women' and 'old men'. This division of the male and female principle is replicated down to the level of the named houses, where the 'old women' and 'old men' are those who 'eat reclining,

273

drink reclining'. In turn, members of these named houses serve as sons for these 'old women' and 'old men' who are categorically considered as 'those who eat reclining, drink reclining'. Thus the division between spiritual authority and temporal power is replicated down to this named house level.

What is significant in this political organisation is not the structuring of gender itself, which is evident elsewhere in eastern Indonesia (Needham 1973; Fox 1980), nor the set of categories based on a system of precedence that is also observed among the Dawan, but rather it is the use of female categories to undermine the strength of the rulers of other predominantly patrilineal neighbouring domains.

Wehali has every right to be protected by these patrilineal domains because it has given away its men in marriage to its peripheral domains and retains only the vulnerable women; it has delegated the power to rule, but still maintains the privilege of conveying its life-giving force; it has 'emptied' itself in order to make others 'well-off'. In the analogy of a 'sword', the Wehali claim that they have given away the 'blade' and retain only its 'sheath' (*mola isin mela knuan*). This notion of 'giving' and 'retaining' developed by the Wehali generates a matrilineal society amongst the predominantly patrilineal societies of Timor.

2. Wehali — the 'Insider'

Inside/outside, inner/outer or interior/exterior as social categories are closely related to the symbolic organisation of habitation space. Using the dichotomy of 'inside' and 'outside' in house design as metaphors, people develop asymmetrical relations among houses, hamlets and domains. Both the south Tetun and the Dawan employ these house metaphors to depict the inferior and superior relations in their own societies. The unmistakable importance of these house metaphors among the Dawan is reflected in the degree of concentration on the house provided by ethnographers who have worked in the region: Cunningham (1962: 54–84, 269–442), Schulte Nordholt (1971: 186–261, 428–432) and McWilliam (2002: 223–248).

In comparing the political organisation of Sonba'i and the Liurai of Wesei-Wehali, for example, Cunningham (1962: 55–56) quoted his Insana informants who grouped each realm into the so-called 'inner rulers' and 'outer rulers', as follows:

Liurai		Sonba'i	
Inner	**Outer**	**Inner**	**Outer**
Wewiku	Amanatun	Kono	Beun Uf
Haitimuk	Amanuban	Oematan	Kune Uf
Dirma	Insana	Babu	Afoan Uf
Lakekun	Biboki	Bifel	Lasi Uf

The superior/inferior relations revealed in the categories of inner (*nanan*)/outer (*mone*) were in fact recognised by Cunningham when he explained Amfo'an's way of grouping the outer Sonba'i domains into Ambenu, Amfo'an, Amarasi and Amanuban. Rulers of these four domains are not the 'outer' Sonba'i but rather 'outside' Sonba'i, meaning that 'they were never tribute-paying subjects of Sonba'i' (1962: 57). The 'outer' and 'outside' translation of the Dawan word mone is irrelevant in this comparative exercise. What is of interest, however, is the association between the categories of 'inner' or 'inside' with superiority and 'outer' or 'outside' with inferiority.

The term *nanan* is related to the space inside a fence that marks a boundary of a hamlet, which means both 'inside' and 'centre'; it also refers to the interior of the house. The dyadic opposition to *nanan* is *mone*, which refers to both the open space outside the fence of a hamlet as well as the exterior of a house. The interior of a hamlet and more particularly that of a house is conceived of as female space in contrast to *mone*, which happens literally to mean 'male'. It is the gender associations attached to the concept of *nanan* and *mone* that are able to transform the 'inside' into that which is superior and the 'outside' into that which is inferior. By associating *nanan* with 'female', 'it refers to the immobile, ritual centre by which orders are issued ...' (Schulte Nordholt 1971: 221). McWilliam also arrives at the same conclusion that the 'inner female area is relatively superior ...' (1989: 168).

Linguistically, Tetun has separate words for 'inside' (*laran*), 'centre', 'interior' (*klaran*) and 'source', 'trunk' 'origin' (*hun*). Conceptually, these terms share a similar focus of 'centre' and 'inside' and therefore sometimes they are used in a subtly related way. The dyadic opposition of *laran* both in the sense of 'inside' and 'centre' is *molin*, which in this study I gloss as 'outside' and 'periphery'. However, the dyadic opposition of *hun* is never *molin* but *tehen* (edge). Using the house symbolism of 'inner house' (*uma laran*) and 'platform' (*labis*), and the general habitation symbolism of *laran* (inside, centre) and *molin* (outside, periphery), both the *uma laran* and *laran* are conceived of as female. In contrast the *labis* and *molin*, which are the areas 'outside' the inner house and immediately surrounding the hamlets are conceived of as male. Like the neighbouring Dawan, the gender categories attached to notions of inside/outside, centre/periphery and trunk/edge contribute to the development of an ideology of superior/inferior.

This ideology of superior/inferior as developed by the Wehali and the south Tetun in general is expressed in two different contexts: marriage and affinal relations, and ritual. In marriage ceremonies, the right of sitting on the two 'storeyed' platforms indicates social status. The higher platform (*labis leten*) is occupied by the bride's mother's brother and all respected members of his named house. This is the superordinate position in contrast to members of the husband-giving house, who sit on the subordinate 'lower platform' (*labis kraik*). In ritual speech during the marriage ceremony, members of the husband-taking house are referred to as the 'female house' (*uma feto*), in contrast to the husband-giving house, the 'male-house' (*uma mane*). Members of the *uma feto* in the context of this marriage ceremony constitute the inner group who are treated by the outer male group as living in 'darkness', 'heat', 'danger' and 'sacred' circumstances, conditions related to superiority.

The superiority of the husband-taking (*uma feto*) is also expressed in a ritual context. As categorically male and outsider, the husband-giving house is relatively inferior because it provides the 'workers' who come to feed the 'recliners'. The analogy of the husband-taking house as 'those who eat reclining, drink reclining' and the husband-giving house as 'workers' who feed the recliners is a theme that has been discussed in various contexts of the study. Thus, at this point, the south Tetun differ from the Dawan as depicted by Schulte Nordholt, who sees the superiority in economic terms: the bride-givers 'are economically superior because they "feed" the ruler by bringing them the harvest of gifts ...' (1971: 221). In south Tetun, it is the recliners who are superior because they are conceptually female.

3. Wehali — the 'Trunk', the 'Centre' and the 'First to Dry'

Reading diagrams provided by Cunningham as a summary to what he calls 'the picture of the Traditional Princedom' of Insana (1962: 152–157) and the comparative diagrams given by Schulte Nordholt, both about Insana (1971: 229, 1980: 240) and other petty domains in the Dawan-speaking area (1971: 246, 247), one notices the concentric circles of the Dawan political system where the superior is located at the 'centre of the centre' while the less superior are located at the 'periphery of the centre', which, in turn, is enclosed by an outer circle termed as the 'masculine exterior' (Schulte Nordholt 1971: 229). Circle after circle enclose a central authority which, in the case of Insana, is in the hands of Atupas and Us Bala. This encirclement provides the basis for the Dawan to talk about their political system using the concept of *usan* (navel) and *eno-lalan* (gate-path). Using the four cardinal points as a model, every movement from periphery to the centre (navel) must proceed through appropriate 'gates' and 'paths'. Both Cunningham and Schulte Nordholt describe in detail the names and functions of *eno ma lalan* associated with the cardinal points, which are considered as encircling the navel of the realm. Whether Schulte Nordholt's diagram can be taken as a typical model of the Dawan political system has been seriously questioned by McWilliam (1989: 13), but this argument is not the concern of the present work. What is of interest in this regard is how the Dawan develop the concept of 'navel' (*usan*) versus 'gate' (*eno*) and how the concepts of *eno* and *lalan* are used to express the social relationship.

Without pretension to be able to summarise in a few paragraphs the elaborate study produced by McWilliam (1989) who titled his thesis 'Narrating the Gate and the Path', a few quotations directly from his work will, hopefully, represent what the Dawan mean by these metaphors:

> The path is at once the historic journey of the ancestors and the personal journey of one's life … The notion of the path expresses the relationship between affines through marriage exchange, mortuary rituals and continuity of alliance. The number of affinal paths (*lanan*) of a name group is the measure of its social network (1989: 220–221).

> Gates represent boundaries in a variety of contexts. Gates (*eno*) to political domains, community settlements and house yards are all thresholds that distinguish levels of social enclosure. Gates are markers of events and points of transition. They serve to limit and define the direction and extent of the connecting paths (1989: 221).

The conceptual categories of 'gate' and 'path' are also used by the south Tetun to express social and political relations. The social relations are revealed in terms of 'paths' while the political relations are expressed in terms of 'doors' (gates) and borders. However, unlike the Dawan, the Tetun do not pair 'gate' with 'path'. These two terms are separated in their usages as well as their functions. Concerning 'gate', the south Tetun employ different terms, which can be translated literally as 'door' and conceptually as 'border' or 'boundary'. They use three different words to translate the notions of 'gate' as used by the Dawan. Access to a fenced garden or hamlet is through a ladder mounted on the fence. This ladder is called *tetek*. This is the first notion of 'gate'. In ritual language the word *tetek* is paired with *riin* (post) in the sense of the corner posts of a fenced garden or hamlet and the four corner posts of a house. So a second notion, that of *riin* (post), is also conceptually linked in political terms to 'gate'. The third meaning is 'door' of a house (*oda matan*). In ritual language, ladder, post and door are depicted as the 'place to knock, place to tap' (*deku na'in baa nia, dare na'in baa nia*). In the territory of 'the four-corner land', for example, the Liurai is symbolised as the 'male door', the two *fukun* of the hamlets of Kateri and Umakatahan are depicted as the 'female posts', the two *fukun* of the hamlets of Kletek and Fahiluka are the 'male posts' while the *fukun* of the Sulit Anemeta is the 'ladder'. These people function as 'gate-keepers' and 'border-guards' of the navel land. Using house symbolism, the order of precedence between them is expressed in terms of the degree of closeness to the 'inner house', the place where the Maromak Oan resides. Thus in political discourse people speak about the hierarchy of 'door', 'post' and 'ladder'. Liurai in this house symbolism is depicted as 'the male door' (*oda matan lor*). Being relatively closer to the Maromak Oan he is depicted in ritual language as wearing the Maromak's mark and becoming the Maromak's fence and door. The Liurai is:

babetan Maromak	the Maromak's ankle ornaments
knokar Maromak	the Maromak's fence
deku na'i baa nia	the place to knock
dare na'in baa nia	the place to tap

People claim that the decision as to whether an origin group is a door, post or ladder within a higher order origin group has been established in myths that present historical narratives of that particular group. These narratives of the journey of the ancestors become the sacred history of the group concerned. It is their 'old track, old path' (*inuk tuan, dalan tuan*).

The Wehali claim to be the centre of all societies that originated from the 'old path, old track'. In primordial time when the earth was covered with water, the first dry land emerged on a spot of a hill that at present is known as Marlilu Haholek. This dry land was formed from 'the navel, the umbilical cord' (*husar, binan*) of a woman named Ho'ar Nai Haholek. From this historical narrative, the Wehali gained a status as 'the navel land, the umbilical cord land' (*rai husar, rai binan*), the trunk land (*rai hun*) in the sense of the 'centre' of the universe.

When this first dry land was formed, it was quite small and so in ritual language it is depicted as 'the land as a chicken's eye, land as a sliced areca nut' (*rai manu matan, rai bua klaras*). The gradual expansion of the dry land from 'the trunk land' to its present reality provides Wehali with a form of discourse to speak about an order of precedence based on the categories 'the first to dry' (*maran uluk*), 'the last to dry' (*maran ikus*). Wehali as the region where the first dry land began is called the centre land. As the dry land expanded so did its people. The expansion of dry land to comprise the territory of 'the four-corner land' and the people who occupy it is given in Figure 7.6. In that figure, those who occupied the subsequent dry land are depicted in terms of 'borders' and 'gates' to the navel land. So the Liurai is the 'door', Dini Kotan and Luruk Kotan, the ancestresses of 'the four corner clans', became peripheral because they occupied the relatively 'last to dry' regions. As the land is continually expanding, the last to dry land became the trunk of the latest to dry land and so forth. Thus, we encounter layers of 'first to dry' (*maran uluk*) and 'last to dry' (*maran ikus*) regions encircling the trunk-centre-female land of Wehali. The first ancestors who occupied these successive expanding dry lands are depicted as 'border-guards' and 'gate-keepers'.

The categories of first to dry/last to dry also gave rise to the development of the division of the inhabited cosmos into 'dwelling space' and 'cultivation space'. In the myth cited as Reference Text 5, for example, areas that are regarded as 'dwelling space' are the Bakiruk, the first to dry territory. As the dry land expanded, one ancestress named Harek was sent:

baa darek	to dry up (herself)
fo ba furi no kada	she was sent to scatter (the seeds) and to plant (seedlings)
ba loro karas no kbelan	to the areas toward the chest and ribs
nodi nameti rai lidun hat	to make firm the four-corner land

In house design, the front part of the house is called the 'chest' while the right and left sides are the 'ribs'. Using this house symbolism, the 'chest' part of the territory of 'the four-corner land' is represented by the hamlets of Kletek and Fahiluka. While the 'ribs' point to areas toward the sunrise and the sunset. These are the cultivation space, 'to scatter (the seeds) and to plant (seedlings)'.

To summarise, the south Tetun do not simply use the metaphors of path, border and gate to reveal the political order of their society or the historic journey of ancestors, although these are also significant concepts for them. But more than that, they reveal the path of life that flows from the centre to periphery, from the first to dry land to the last to dry land and from dwelling space to cultivation space. Based on this paradigm, the annual agricultural ritual called 'delivering the maize of homage' (*hatama batar mana'i*) or 'delivering the seven cobs of maize' (*hatama batar fulin hitu*) is delineated by the Wehali as the path of wealth that flows from the cultivation space to the dwelling space. Thus the flow of life is reciprocated by a flow of wealth.

In this present work, I have attempted to describe the social cosmology and political ideology of Wehali based on local categories as expressed in myths and other forms of cultural representations. These primary categories serve as 'operators' in Wehali symbolic classification and therefore become a cultural marker that distinguishes Wehali from other societies. However, as the reference texts provided in the Appendix show, there are still more complex categories that need to be explored in future research.

Language Texts

Reference Text 1

Narrator: Piet Tahu Nahak
Type: 'Homage Language' (*Lia Rik*)

Halo tuir kbabukar	In accordance with the 'rope of order'
halo tuir mamenon	in accordance with the invitation
mamenon Liurai	the invitation from the Liurai
kbabukar Liurai	the 'rope of order' issued by the Liurai
ba uma Wesei na'in	from the household of Wesei
Wehali na'in	the household of Wehali
malaka na'in	the source of flame
mamanas nain	the source of heat
mane Umanen	the son of the Umanen
mane Lawalu	the son of Lawalu
ro makaer lulik sia	together with custodians of the forbidden (regalia)
makaer manas sia	guardians of the heat (paraphernalia)
ro sasian sia	together with all who assist them
ro tatanen sia	together with all who support them
at rakerek rola tian	as have been informed
badaen rola tian	as have been brought to attention
ba inan Maria	concerning the mother of Mary
susu Maria	suckling Mary
no oan manek kmesak na'i Yesus Kristus	and the only son Jesus Christ

nak at halo kdahur tan	that (we) are going to make festivity
halo klibur tan	making a great gathering
at fafudi hola	to come humbly into his (bishop) presence
at talara hola	to receive him with open arms
at sei ba hakau lai	to lift him gently on (our) arms
sei hamaan lai	to lighten his steps
makaer lulik bot	holder of the great taboo
makaer manas bot	holder of the mighty heat
rak noi natodan du'uk oan	who is enthroned
noi nabesi du'uk oan	who sits
iha uma metan maromak	in the bright black house
riin mean maromak	in the bright red post
iha namon matan	in the main harbour
we matan Atambua	the main spring of Atambua
iha Lidak, ama Lawalu ne'e	in the domain of Lidak, the father of Lawalu
Tukuneno ne'e, manu aman ne'e	in Tukuneno, the rooster
Banmetan ne'e, Bankase ne'e	the Banmetan, the Bankase
foin rak fafudi hola ti'an	having been entertained
tatane hola ti'an	accepted him with open arms
foin sasi'an sia	then all the helpers
tatanen sia	all the supporters
rakau ro mai	lift him in their arms
raman ro mai	lighten his steps
tuir inuk tuan	tracing the old track
tuir dalan tuan	tracing the old path
inuk Liurai	the track of the Liurai
dalan Liurai	the path of the Liurai
ha'ak, mai la basu ha'i	he did come and not just simply passed through
mai la liu ha'i	he came and not passing by
Bautok ne'e, Taekto ne'e	to Bautok, Taekto
lali'an tohe	driving the fire from the hearth
karaen tohe	chasing the fire away

fatuk baki Dafala	the stony fort of Dafala
uma metan Dafala	the black house of Dafala
iha dero kmasin ne'e, Lelowai ne'e	at the salty orange, the Lelowai
iha klobor matetek	at the ladder of the granary
hisa riin matetek	the supporting step of the post
ra'ak klobor Halikelen	the granary of Halikelen
laen Halikelen	the hut of Halikelen
foin basu mai	then he proceeds towards here
foin liu mai	then he comes here
mai buka nola	comes to search
mai naktan nola	comes to find
na'ak ee Kasulisu ne'e, Halilulik ne'e	Kasulisu, Halilulik
Debuktetuk ne'e, Welaka ne'e	Debuktetuk, Welaka
rin besi ne'e, nanaet ne'e	this strong post, the separator
Tetikama ne'e, Labur ne'e	the Tetikama, the Labur
Bakus ne'e, Tulama ne'e	the Bakus, the Tulama
ra'ak iha Wehali solat	in Wehali, the place to live
iha Likusaen solat	in Likusaen, the place to live
foin titu nola	he visits
foin raree rola	he greets
dato alin ida, dato maun ida	the younger *dato*, the elder *dato*
loro alin ida, loro maun ida	the younger *loro*, the elder *loro*
ra'ak iha Mande'u, rai manas ne'e	(who live) in Mande'u, the heat land
Tintua ne'e, Maurae ne'e	in Tintua, Maurae
sera we ne'e	the place to offer water, the place to offer oil
sera mina ne'e	the place to offer oil
Etuwain ne'e, Rafou ne'e	Etuwain, Rafou
iha klobor manu maus	at the granary of the tame rooster
iha laen manu maus	at the hut of the tame rooster
iha tali metan ki'ik	at the small black rope
tali metan kwa'ik	big black rope
iha Seon ne'e	in Seon
mota sorun ne'e	the junction of the river

fatuk metan ne'e	the black stone
bua ahan ne'e	the *ahan* fruit (of the forest)
asu kmeda ne'e	the civetcat dog
fahi kmeda ne'e	the civetcat pig
foin ra'ak ee soe lerek mata ba nia	(in those places), he simply casts down his eyes
soe lerek oin ba nia	casts down his face there
hakau liu dei	he is lifted to pass through
haman liu dei	he is enlightened to pass through
tuir inuk tuan	tracing the old track
tuir dalan tuan	tracing the old path
inuk Liurai	the track of the Liurai
dalan Liurai	the path of the Liurai
mai la basu ha'i	come, don't just pass by
mai la liu ha'i	come, don't just go on
ra'ak sikun manaran	the named (important) corner
tias manaran ida	the exclusive place
ra'ak iha Bo'as ne'e, nanasa ne'e	in Bo'as, the place to laugh
si'a Tae ne'e	the supporting house of Tae
La'e Tua Taen	the La'e Tua Taen house
iha Maibiku ne'e, nanono ne'e	in Maibiku, the place to listen
Maibiku hat	the four Maubiku
rafa'e hat	the split four
hat balu ba	four on this side
hat balu mai	four on the other side
oan natar hat	the four children of the paddock
oan lalu'an hat	the four children of the stables
wee, ra'ak soe lerek mata ba nia	casts down his eyes there
soe lerek oin ba nia	casts down his face there
rakau liu dei	they lift him and pass by
ramaan liu dei	they lighten his steps
ba la basu ha'i	to the place that cannot be bypassed
ba la liu ha'i	to the place that cannot be passed through

ra'ak klobor bot ida	a big granary
laen bot ida	a big hut
ra'ak klobor Liurai	the granary of Liurai
laen Liurai	the hut of Liurai
iha Sulit Anemeta	in Sulit Anemeta
kfan lulik ne'e	the sacred *kfan* tree
taloban ne'e	the small hut on stilts
sera ki'ik ne'e	the place to lay small offering
soe ne'e	the place to discard things
foin tama basu	then he goes onward
foin tama liu	then he passes by
tuir inuk tuan	tracing the old track
tuir dalan tuan	tracing the old path
inuk Liurai	the track of the Liurai
dalan Liurai	the path of the Liurai
ra'ak foi matak bot	the big half-ripe fruit
babasa bot ne'e	the big *babasa* fruit
mae nain ne'e	the lord of the yam
maroman ne'e	the one who is bright
Unani ne'e	the Unani
Tubaki ne'e	the Tubaki
foin rakau tama mai	then they lift him to enter here
foin tama mai	then they lighten his steps toward here
mai ba hoku fatik	comes to this place to wallow
iha natar fatik	in the paddock
iha hatodan fatik	in the sitting place
iha habesi fatik	in the enthronement place
iha knua Wehali	in the shield of Wehali
iha knua Wesei	in the shield of Wesei
betun inan Wehali	mother *betun* (the bamboo trunk of Wehali)
au inan Wehali	mother bamboo of Wehali
ferik rua	two respected women (*ferik*)
katuas rua	two respected men (*katuas*)

na'i Akatahan	the lord of Akatahan
na'i Batane	the lord of Batane
ferik hali abut	*ferik* of the root of the banyan tree
katuas hali abut	*katuas* of the root of the banyan tree
feto ra tuan sia	the respected female retainers
klosan tuan sia	the respected male retainers
ro Wesei na'in	together with the household of Wesei
Wehali na'in	the household of Wehali
malaka na'in	the source of flame
amanas na'in	the source of heat
na'i mane Umanen	the lords of the Umanen house
mane Lawalu	the lords of the Lawalu house
ro sahutun sia	together with all the people
sarenu sia	all the subjects
iha maksatan hat	in the four enclosures
iha makdidin hat	in the four edges
iha loro Diruma	in the territories of the *loro* of Dirma
loro Lakekun	the *loro* of Lakekun
loro Wewiku	the *loro* of Wewiku
loro Haitimuk	the *loro* of Haitimuk
rodi kdahur rai tolus	to make festivities in the three lands
klibur rai tolus	get together in the three lands
bibliku lian di'ak	the beautiful sound of drums
tala lian di'ak	the beautiful sound of gongs
rakau tama ba	lift him on the arms to enter
raman tama ba	lighten the steps to enter
uma metan maromak	the bright black house
rin mean maromak	the bright red post
temi mama	pronounce the betel chewing
namoo mama	rinse out the betel chewing
nodi nakmasin	ask humbly
nodi hakro'an	make a request

ba ama naran la kaka	to the father whose name cannot be pronounced
ama naran la temi	to the father whose name cannot be called
iha leten ba	in the height
iha as ba	in the above
iha lolo liman la to'o	to the (place) that cannot be reached by stretching out hands
kni'it ai la dai	cannot be reached by standing on tiptoes
ra'ak iha kfitun fohon	the top of stars
iha fulan fohon	the top of moon
at natun matak mai	to send down the raw
natun malirin mai	to send down the cool
udan wen di'ak	good rains
loro wen di'ak	good sunlight
batu nahutun sia	for those who are (his) people
narenu sia	for those who are (his) subjects
hutun raiklaran	all people of the earth
renu raiklaran	all subjects of the earth
rori ko'a tua	to tap the palms
rafaho rai	to weed the gardens
to'os isin naksoran	harvest of the gardens will multiply
tua wen nak soran.	palm juice overflow.

Reference Text 2

Narrator: Piet Tahu Nahak
Type: 'Language of the Earth' (*Rai Lian*)

Rai foin nahuu dadi.	The earth starts to emerge.
Uluk fohon rai klaran ne'e sei makukun totoon	A long time ago the earth was still very dark
rai klaran ne'e, kroman sei la natetu	The light of the earth was not yet perfect
kalan bee sei la natetu	nor was the night complete
foin ema ne'e sia na'ak	after that, people say that
loron ikus to'o ti'an	the time had arrived
naruka bei ok feto ida	(he) asked your grandmother
naran Ferik Ha'i Raiklaran	known as the 'Only Woman on Earth'
natiu basu	(she) carried the message in her hand
natiu lia	carried the message on top of her head
ba tasi fohon	came to the top of the sea
meti fohon	the top of the tidal flats
nariik ba tasi fohon	she stood right on top of the sea
meti fohon	on top of the tidal flats
atu lolo liman la to'o	tried to stretch out her hands, but she couldn't reach
fila nikar ba rai aa	she returned to the land (above)
manfatin natiha na'ak:	the order slipped down, saying:
'Simu mola manfatik boot ne'e	'Receive this great order
simu mola naleka liman rua ne'e.'	receive with your two hands stretched out.'
Manfatik aa simu mola ha'i	She could not receive it
monu liu ba tasi wen	the order dropped further into the sea
manfatik ohin monu ba tasi wen fohon ne'e dadi ba na'an knase ida	the order that had just fallen into the sea turned into a *knase* fish
mosu sa'e mai	(the fish) ascended to appear
bei ok nariik tetek oan ba na'an knase fohon aa	so that grandmother stood on the small fin on the *knase*'s back
nariik ti'an ba	once she stood (on the fish's back)

foin bei ok, ema leten aa na'ak:	the man above said:
'Ta'an tenik manfatik.'	'Accept (this order) again very carefully.'
Manfatik natiha tenik	The order descended again
simu nola ti'an	after accepting it
ko'us nola ti'an	after carrying it on her arm
hakee, netan ti'an	she became pregnant
loron to'o	days passed
kalan to'o ti'an	nights passed
foin netan ti'an ba Maromak Oan ne'e.	then she gave birth to the child: this 'Small Bright One' (*Maromak Oan*).
Kalan to'o	Nights passed
loron to'o	days passed
nahoris ti'an foin nia britahan nasa'e ba ema leten aa nakloke	after giving birth she revealed her plea to the person above
naruka feto raa no mane klosan batu mai riti rola ko'us rola Maromak Oan ne'e	asking for female and male retainers to come and rock this Maromak Oan
foin Maromak natun feto ida mane ida	after that the Bright One (Maromak) lowered down a woman and a man
natun mai na'in feto no mane naruka ra'ak	after the woman and the man descended they cut
kotu ti'an Maromak Oan husar aa	the umbilical cord of the Maromak Oan
hodi Maromak Oan ba hatuka ha'i iha lolo leten ba	(then they) brought Maromak Oan (and the woman) to heat body over the fire in the world above
wai matan natene, wai oan natene	(that is), to be nurtured and become knowledgeable
hela ka'an iha rai ne'e, ha'ak:	the umbilical cord was left behind in this land:
'Rai manu matan	'The land as a chicken's eye
rai bua klaras.'	the land as a slice of areca nut.'
Hanaran rai ne'e Rai Marlilu Haholek	This land was called Marlilu Haholek (the first to dry land)
ka'an ne'e tubu ti'an ba hali aa	the umbilical cord grew into a dense banyan tree
foin ha'ak:	and so the saying goes:

'Maromak nahonu hali leon di'ak	'The Bright One has provided a good dense banyan tree
soe nahon la sar karas haat ne'e	its shade provides shelter to the chest of the house
soe nahon la sar kbelan haat ne'e	its shade provides shelter to the ribs of the house
nalo kbelan haat ne'e nahon tutuir	the four side branches grew into each other
nalo karas haat ne'e nahon tutuir	the four front branches grew into each other
Sei Bere Lelo Babesi hali leon di'ak	Sei Bere Lelo Babesi was a good leafy banyan tree
sorin balu leo feto	one half of the shade is called the female hamlet (clan)
balu leo mane	the other half is the male hamlet (clan)
leo feto leo mane balu lasisin'.	the female hamlet (clan) and the male hamlet (clan) were both in the shade.'
Nuu nia, ka'an tubu ti'an dadi ba hali	So the umbilical cord had grown into a banyan tree
rai manu matan bua klaras mos moris ti'an	the land as a chicken's eye, the land as a slice of areca nut already existed
sia hariik ba nia	they (the land and the tree) were there
hali leon di'ak	the good leafy banyan tree
hodi hola ktetuk, hodi hola nesan	(the leaves of the tree) were spread evenly
foin mane no feto ne'e sa'e hikar ba leten ba	then the two retainers went back to the world above
iha ema bot lolo liman la to'o	went to the great man that could not be reached by stretching out the hand
bi'i ai la dai	and by standing on tiptoes
husu natun mantarun mai	asked to send down his sign of power (lit. money bet in cockfighting)
lamak hatetu, lamak harani	the sacrificial meal, the offering meal
atu halo rai husar rai binan	to make the navel land, the umbilical cord land
luan no kbelan	wide and broad
atu hodi haluan atu hodi sesu.	to widen and expand.
Maromak na'ak:	The Bright One said:

290

'Sa'e mai ko'i atu fo tone, atu hodi haluan rai ne'e. Nia ne'e surik kro'at, taha kro'at nia ne'e.'

'Come up here. On your return I will give a sharp sword, a sharp machete to widen the land.'

Feto no mane ne'e sa'e ba ratun rola hahuuk kmurak ida

The woman and the man brought back a valuable blow pipe

no lamak hatetu, lamak harani, ha'ak manu do'u ida

together with food for sacrificing and an offering, which was a *do'u* bird

nia hanahon oan ba hali aa

the bird made a nest in that banyan tree

naa hali fuan nia

ate the fruits of the banyan tree

naran ha'ak dou' Laluuk

the bird was called Do'u Laluuk

foin Leki no Mauk rola manu do'u ne'e. Knanuk na'ak:

then Leki and Mauk (the two retainers) took the bird. It was said:

'Mau Leki Mau Mauk la'o ruu manu

'Mau Leki Mau Mauk went to blow down the bird

ruu manu la sala, do'u laluuk ida

they did not miss the target, it was a wild pigeon Laluuk

do'u laluuk ne'e tunu ba sa

but they did not know where it could be roasted

do'u laluuk ne'e taka ba sa'.

but they did not know where it could be placed'.

Foin atu tunu do'u ne'e

Then (they) were about to roast the bird (as an offering)

ne'e be hodi haluan rai manu matan

to ask for expanding the land as a chicken's eye

rai bua klaras.

the land as a slice of areca nut.

Ma'is ha'i la no

But there was no fire

tan nia ferik ne'e naruka mane ne'e na'ak

therefore the woman asked the man, saying:

'sa'e ba musu ema bot, fo ha'i mai atu tunu lamak hatetu, lamak harani, hodi koto, ne'e be hodi haluan rai manu matan, rai bua klaras'.

'go up there and ask the great man to send fire for us to roast the bird as a sacrificial meal, offering meal, as preparation for expanding the land as a chicken's eye, the land as a slice of areca nut'.

Nia sa'e ba nia na'ak:

The man went up, but the man above said:

'Lale. Ha'i aa nia tun ba nodi kedan. Ha'i nia ha'u kela ha'i iha ne'e.'

'No. When the woman descended (to the earth), she brought the fire along. I do not retain the fire here.'

Foin naruka hosak feto.

So she asked the woman retainer to go up again.

Maromak na'ak: 'ha'i aa nia nodi kedan. Nia nodi ha'i ti'an. Ha'u atufo sa ida tenik'. Feto na'ak: 'Lale. Mamfatik hatebes ha, britahan ne'e, ne'e be hahata tun hikar ba atu hodi katak mamfatika aa'.

The Bright One said: 'she has taken the fire with her. What else can I offer you'. The woman (retainer) said: 'I only ask your confirmation, so that when your servant goes back, she will inform that noble woman'.

Feto ne'e tun nikar mai.

The woman (retainer) went back to the earth.

To'o mai ni nasara na'ak:

On her arrival she informed the noble woman, saying:

'Ina. Maromak na'ak mamfatik tun mai, hakroros mai, hodi kedan'.

'Mother, according to the Bright One, when you descended, when you departed, you took the fire along'.

Nia nasa'e nawan, na'ak:

She (the noble woman) held her breath, saying:

Haruka Leki ba nu Mauk, haruka Mauk ba nu Leki'.

'Asking Leki is as bad as asking Mauk, asking Mauk is as bad as asking Leki'.

Foin ema rua ne'e hanaran ha'ak Mau Leki Mau Mauk,

That is why these two persons are called Mau Leki, Mau Mauk,

knanuk na'ak:

as said in the poem:

'Tua tahan ba dedon keta masee

'Do not greet (someone) when the palm leaves are rustling

tua tahan nakbohar keta masee

do not greet (someone) when the palm leaves make a noise

keta masee na'i baba tuak Lekik

do not greet Lekik, the respected mother's brother

na'i loro tua Lekik, tuak maktun hori leten sia mai

the respected prince who comes down from above

na'i baba tua Lekik, baba maktun hori as sia mai

the binder, the mother's brother that comes down from the heights

tun to'o raiklaran fila naree

descends to the earth, returning to inspect

tun to'o rai tenan falu naree

descends to the wide earth to watch

falu naree ha'i lakan oan ida

returns to inspect a little flame

fila naree ha'i len oan ida

returns to watch a little glowing

ha'i laka len ne'e Marlilu Haholek leten sia ba	the flame and glowing is in Marlilu Haholek, the place above
ha'i laka len ne'e Marlilu Haholek as sia ba'.	the flame and glowing is in Marlilu Haholek, in the heights'.
Sona Fahi natete kiki rai tarutu nosi Maromak iha wa'i matan natene, wa'i oin natene	Sona Fahi flew down from the Bright One to the place to be nurtured and achieve knowledge
ti'an ma foin nalo suman no matan ne'e	then he made these springs and wells. One is called the male spring
suman feto ida suman mane ida	one is called the female spring
foin nia ha'ak wa'i mata.	this is the source of upbringing.
Foin nia nusu ba ama Maromak, na'ak:	Then he asked the Bright One, saying:
'Manftin laliki tatuna dadi Wehali	'By your waving command, Wehali exists
sama raiklaran, sama no sa	trample the earth, with what did you trample
naluli raiklaran, tun no sa	to sanctify the earth, how did you descend
naluli raiklaran, tun rai tenan	sanctifying the earth, descend to the wide world
tun to'o raiklaran falu ba maliku takan Wesei	descend to earth to nurture the betel leaves of Wesei
tun to'o rai tenan fila ba maliku bua Wesei	descend to the wide world to nurture the areca nut of Wesei
takan Wesei manu semo la tadu	the leaves of Wesei, birds can not break through
bua Wesei mosa loron no kalan'.	areca nut trees of Wesei grow night and day'.
Foin nawa'i takan Wesei bua Wesei iha rai manu matan bua klaras	Then he nurtured the betel leaves of Wesei, the areca nut of Wesei in the land as a chicken's eye, a slice of areca nut
foin ha'ak ee wa'i feto wa'i mane	it is the place to nurture both women and men
takan Wesei bua Wesei	the betel leaves of Wesei
hun baras ba lolon	covered the whole vines
hakon sarat ba rai	the areca nuts of Wesei hung all over to the ground

foin ha'ak ee manu semo la tadu ne'e	it was said that birds could not force their way through
husu ema loro leten mai bet sau	asked people from the sun above to harvest
ema loro leten aa nuu wain ee kfitun na'in ne'e	the people above were the lords of the stars
mai uluk mai sau takan Wesei	firstly, they came to pick the leaves of Wesei
fitun na'in aa natiha mai ne'e nola takan Wesei bua Wesei ne'e nodi ba maa iha loro leten ba	the lords of the stars came down to fetch the betel leaves of Wesei, the areca nuts of Wesei, then took them up
ba mama morin	when they chewed, it was sweet smelling
tan nia feto hitus natene rola ra'ak: 'Ita ho'i mama buat morin ne'e ita hola iha sa?'	because of that aromatic flavour, the seven noble women above asked: 'Where did you get that which you are chewing?'
'Na'i keta lai te buat ne'e iha raiklaran ba. Mais buat ne'e badu. Na'i mane ida makdakar buat ne'e'.	'Wait a minute' (came the reply), 'these things are from the earth down there. However, they are forbidden. A noble man guards these things'.
'So'in'.	'That is fine' (the noble women replied).
Ratene rola ti'an, feto hitus sia tun mai.	Knowing this, the noble women descended to the earth.
Mai rakbasak takan kau bua kau	They came to chew the young betel leaves and the soft areca nuts
mai rakbasak kalan ida, kalan rua sei	they did this for two nights
kalan ida, sia rakbasak to'o rai atu naroma ma na'in mane mai suba nola liras aa	one night they chewed the betel nuts until almost dawn. Then came the noble man and hid a pair of wings
suba nola ti'an liras aa, sasawan aa na'in feto atu leten nikar be liras aa iha ha'i ti'an	because he had hidden the wings, in the morning when the noble women were about to fly back up, the wings were missing
tan nia na'in nen fila nikar, ida hela	because of this six returned, leaving one
hela ti'an ma na'in mane nafe nola	then the noble man took her as his wife
nafe nola ti'an, netan ba feto ida naran Ho'ar Na'i Haholek	she became pregnant and gave birth to a girl named Ho'ar Na'i Haholek

Ho'ar na'i Haholek sura ha'ak wa'i matan ona, wa'i oin ona	When she had come of age
to'o nia mane ida mos mai labu ona. Mane mai maklabu ne'e naran Taek Di'ak, Taek Ha'in Malaka.	a man came to court her. His name was Taek Di'ak, Taek Ha'in Malaka.
Feto ne'e lorloron tuur iha Marlilu Haholek. Uma niak aa uma Rai-Lale'an	This woman lived in Marlilu Haholek. Her house was called the house of Earth-Sky
lale'an ne'e nia knanuk na'ak ee:	the 'sky' is described in verse as follows:
'Hali ne'e nahako kraraik oan	'The banyan tree produces a lot of branches
hali ne'e natahan kraraik oan basuk	the banyan tree produces a lot of leaves
morin ne'e kato'o rai Malaka	its aroma reaches the land of Malaka
di'ak ne'e kato'o rai Malaka	its goodness reaches the land of Malaka
bosok nola dei na'i Taek Malaka	it tricks Taek Malaka
beur nola dei na'i Taek Malaka	it deceives Taek Malaka
mai tiha iha Marlilu hun aa	to come and cast his fishing net under the trunk of Marlilu
mai ee hali ne'e hun aa'.	comes to the trunk of the banyan tree'.
Mai tiha ne'e, nia nodi niak klosan na'in rua. Ida naran Bria Nahak, ida Bria Berek.	When he came to fish, he brought along his two male retainers. One was called Bria Nahak, and the other Bria Berek
nia naruka nia klosan rua aa, na'ak ee:	He (Taek Malaka) ordered his two retainers, saying:
'Emi tama kokos ba rai manu matan, rai bua klaras, hodi haree kokon iha uma Rai-Lale'an. Ne'ebe ferik rai leten sa'e leten aa, nahusar talin rai iha nia. Ita sa'e bete ita ruas hodi haree'.	'Go to the land as a chicken's eye, the land as a slice of areca nut and have a look into the house of Earth-Sky. Try to find out if the woman from the world above left behind the umbilical cord when she ascended back to the world above'.
'So'in.'	'All right'.
Ne'e, Ho'ar na'in Haholek nia feto ra tuan nia Se'u Harek, Ho'ar Harek.	Ho'ar Na'i Haholek had two female retainers called Se'u Harek and Ho'ar Harek.
To'o nia mai sia tama iha Rai-Lale'an	So the two male retainers entered the house of Earth-Sky
sia tama to'o Rai-Lale'an bete fafudi	they came to the house of Earth-Sky to converse

feto ra rua ne'e rasee ra'ak:	the two women (retainers) greeted them saying:
'Ee mane Baria Nahak Baria Nahak	'Oh brother Baria Nahak, Baria Nahak
mane Baria Berek Baria Berek	Oh brother Baria Berek, Baria Berek
sama ami seisawan	visiting us this early morning
kma'un sei la monu	when the dew has not yet fallen
modi lia sa?	what news do you bring?
mai ami seisawan	coming to us this early morning
kma'un sei la mosar	when the dew has not yet dived
modi lia sa?'	what news do you bring'?
Na'ak ee:	They (the two male retainers) said:
'Fetosawa sia	'Sisters
ami atu katak ba, emi be mate dei	if we tell you, you will die
ami katak ha'i bee emi mate dei	if we do not tell you, you will die too
ami tutur bei ok na'i Taek Malaka nia manfatin bot aa na'ak ee ami mai iha umaRai Lale'an ne'e, bete ami haree Bei Ferik Ha'in Raiklaran ba sa'e leten sa'e as, nia nela nahusar kotu husar rohan ba raiklaran ne'e ka lale'.	we carry orders on our heads from your honourable Taek Malaka. He ordered us to come to this house of Earth-Sky and find out whether the honourable Ferik Ha'in Raiklaran left behind an umbilical cord, when she ascended back to the heights above'.
Na'ak ee:	(The two female retainers) said:
'Nela ee na'i. Mais ami katak be, ami mate dei Ami katak ha'i be, ami mate dei'.	'She actually left it here. However, if we tell you, we will be dead. If we do not tell you, we will be dead too'.
To'o nia ma sia katak ra'ak ferik ha'i maklen sa'e leten sa'e as nela husar kotu, nahusar rohan. 'Nia ne'e ami ho'i dakar ne'e'.	Then they said that the respected woman, the glowing one, when she ascended to the heights above, she left behind an umbilical cord. 'We are in charge of looking after it'.
Hotu Bria Nahak Bria Berek rodi rikar lia ba na'i Taek Malaka ne'e.	Then Bria Nahak and Bria Berek brought the news back to Taek Malaka.
Rodi rikar lia mai, tama liu mai rika fafudi atu hamimak.	After receiving the news, he (Taek Malaka) returned to court her (Ho'ar Na'i Haholek).

Mai hamimak ne'e, feto no mane lia aa makonak ba malu. Feto no mane rola malu ona.

During the courting, the two spoke the same language and so the man married the woman.

Na'i Taek Malaka nola ti'an Ho'ar Na' Haholek, foin tee ba mane nai'n nen, fetoq na'in ida.

Na'i Taek Malaka married Ho'ar Nai Haholek and had six boys and one girl.

Mane ulun Na'i Saku Mataus, Na'i Bara Mataus, Na'i Ura Mataus, Na'i Meti Mataus, Na'i Leki Mataus, Na'i Neno Mataus.

The first born was Na'i Saku Mataus (Mataus – lit. the protector), and Na'i Bara Mataus, Ura Mataus, Meti Mataus, Leki Mataus, Neno Mataus.

Ikun aa feto naran Ho'ar Mataus Ho'ar Makbalin Balin Liurai.

The last born was a girl named Ho'ar Mataus, entitled Ho'ar Makbalin Balin Liurai (lit. Ho'ar, the one who was in charge of appointing Liurai).

Foin ne'e na'i Ho'ar Makbalin Bali liurai ohin ne'e, na'i Lurumea na'in nosi loro leten na mama ti'an, nodi kmusan mean tuda

Then the noble of Lurumea from the sun above fed (threw) red betel chewing to Ho'ar Makbalin Balin Liurai

netan ti'an ba Bano Ha'in Liurai.

then she became pregnant Balok Liurai.

To'o nia knanuk na'ak ee:

As said in the poem (concerning this marriage):

'Anin nakis onan

'The gentle breeze is blowing (crying)

nakiis onan

is blowing

anin nadais onan

the wind is sobbing

nadais onan

is sobbing

nadais namodok

gently blow to ripen

fuik no bua sia

betel leaves and areca nuts

nakis namodok

gently blow to ripen

fuik no bua sia

betel leaves and areca nuts

ama Na'i Maromak, na'i Maromak

The bright father, Na'i Maromak

matun kma'un ba takan Wesei

sends down dew to the betel leaves of Wesei

matun kma'un ba bua Wesei

sends down dew to the areca nuts of Wesei

bua Wesei, ami tahan bea ida

the areca nuts of Wesei, we are of one leaf

takan Wesei ami tun leo ida

the leaves of Wesei, we descended from one hamlet (clan)

sa'e be ku'u hodi basu liu onan

come up here, pick us up, take us away

sa'e hikar ba fatin inan Maromak	bring us back to the place of the glowing mother
sa'e hikar ba fatin aman Maromak'.	bring us back to the place of the glowing father'.
Nia foin ee Balok Liurai Se'uk Liurai moris ti'an	Then the Balok Liurai, Se'uk Liurai were born
Balok Liurai tee ba, emi ha'ak ee	Balok Liurai gave birth to the so called:
Hobuk funan mala.	Hobuk the strange flower
Banasa isin ida funan malae	Banasa the strange flower
Se'uk Liurai nahoris ba Dini Kotan Luruk Kotan	Se'uk Liurai gave birth to Dini Kotan, Luruk Kotan
Dini kotan Dini Liurai	Dini Kotan (entitled) Dini Liurai
Luruk Kotan Luruk Liurai	Luruk Kotan (entitled) Luruk Liurai
hodi kotan leten	(they come) to demarcate the world above
katak raiklaran.	to tell the earth.
Luruk Kotan nahoris ba ferik tasi tehen rua	Luruk Kotan gave birth to respected women (*ferik*) at the edge of the sea
Balok Liurai Se'uk Liurai ne'e ha'ak ee ferik foho hun	Balok Liurai, Se'uk Liurai were the *ferik* of the trunk of the hill
ferik foho hun emi ha'ak:	the *ferik* of the trunk of the hill were:
Na'i Akatahan na'i Batane	the noble of Akatahan, the noble of Batane
ferik Hali Abut	the *ferik* of Hali Abut (lit. roots of the banyan tree)
katuas Hali Abut	the respected men (*katuas*) of Hali Abut
Ferik Rai	Ferik Rai (the respected woman of the earth)
Katuas Rai.	Katuas Rai (the respected man of the earth).
Foin to'o oras mai iha rai Sabete Saladi na'ak to'o ohin loron na'ak Wesei na'in moris ba ne'e, Wehali na'in moris ba ne'e.	Until now people say that in the land of Sabete Saladi (lit. sitting cross legged) rulers of Wesei have been born here, rulers of Wehali have been born here.
Ha nuu ee lia husar, lia binan	Accommodating the language of the navel, the language of the umbilical cord
ema ha'ak:	it is said:
'Rai Wesei Wehali	'The land of Wesei Wehali
betun inan Wehali	the bamboo trunk of Wehali

au inan Wehali	the mother's bamboo of Wehali
iha ferik ruas, katuas ruas	in the territories of the two *ferik*, the two *katuas*
na'i Akatahan ee, na'i Batane	the noble of Akatahan, noble of Batane
na'i Hali Abut ee, Katuas Hali Abut'.	the noble of Hali Abut, *katuas* of Hali Abut'.
Ita ha'ak:	We say:
'Rai husar ni ne'e, rai binan ni ne'e	'This is the navel land, this is the umbilical cord land
lo'o lor Ida	(it has only) one group of garden houses on the seaside
lo'o rae ida'.	one group of garden houses on the hillside'.
Ho'ar Bokis Saniri funan malae	Ho'ar Bokis Saniri, the strange flower
nafunan ba loro Dirma, Loro Lakekun.	flowered the *loro* of Dirma, the *loro* of Lakekun.
Bano Asa Sabu'a klaut malae	Bano Asa Sabu'a, pieces of the strange fruit
nafunan ba ferik tasi tehen, katuas tasi tehen.	flowered *ferik* at the edge of the sea, *katuas* of the edge of sea.
No ti'an ferik tasi tehen, katuas tasi tehen,	The (offices) of *ferik* of the edge of sea, the *katuas* of the edge of sea have been founded
bete emi ha'ak:	people say:
'Klara meti lia	'The voice of crabs in tidal flats
tiri tasi lia'.	the voice of small fish in the sea'.

Reference Text 3

Narrator: Bau Fahik Larosi
Type: 'Language of the Earth' (*Rai Lian*)

Ema mak tun raiklaran ne'e Leki no Mauk no Liurai Asa Ai Sorun.	Those who descended to the earth were Leki and Mauk, and Liurai Asa Ai Sorun.
Sia tun mai sia rodi hali Karlele.	When they descended, they brought along a banyan tree called *hali Karlele* (lit. the floating banyan tree).
Hodi hali Karlele, rai maran ti'an mais ra mamar basuk, sei we.	when they brought this tree, the earth was still soft, still water.
Asa Ai Sorun naruka Leki no Mauk ba bolu malaka na'in, Bria Bauk	Asa Ai Sorun asked Leki and Mauk to fetch Bria Bauk, the source of flame
Bria Bauk mai nodi hali Tutulis	Bria Bauk brought along a banyan tree called *hali Tutulis* (lit. the erecting banyan tree)
nia nodi hali Tutulis, nia nalo	with this banyan tree, he made:
ulun noku, ai noku	firmed the head, firmed the food
belan toba, karas toba	let sleep the ribs, let sleep the chest
nia naruka ba nikar nola nia alin sia na'in tolu.	he asked again (the two retainers) to fetch his three brothers.
No nia dadi mane hat.	With himself, there were already four people on earth.
Mane hat tun ta mai.	(So) there were already four people.
Sia naruka Mau Leki Mau Mauk ba nola Bebelera	They asked Mau Leki and Mau Mauk to fetch Bebelera
rai mos maran ti'an.	the land had already dried.
Hotu Bebelera la'o ba to'o Balibo	Then Bebelera went as far as Balibo
Bebelera mate iha nia.	Bebelera died there.
Bebelera mate iha nia moris nikar ba to'o Larantuka.	When he resurrected, he travelled to Larantuka.
To'o Larantuka tubu ba fatuk no hun	On his arrival, he grew on stone and tree
rai mos moris ti'an	the land was already alive

nia mate iha nia, iha Larantuka.

he died there, in Larantuka.

Tubu moris nikar, ba iha India.

When he grew alive, he went as far as India.

Bebelera la'o ti'an hotu mane sanulu mai

When Bebelera departed, a group of ten men (entitled *loro*) came

hat iha Wehali nen la'o.

four of them remained in Wehali, six went on.

Loro mane kwa'ik aa ba iha Likusaen Bauboe, ida ba iha Biboki, ida ba iha Insana, ida ba iha Amanuban, ida ba iha Amanatun, ida ba iha Amarasi

The elder *loro* went to Likusaen Bauboe, one went to Biboki, one went to Insana, one went to Amanuban, one went to Amanatun, one went to Amarasi

hat hela ba Haitimuk, Wewiku, Dirma, Lakekun.

four men were left in Haitimuk, Wewiku, Dirma and Lakekun.

Mane hat ne'e sai husi Wehali, dadi sia loro Wehali.

These four men departed from Wehali. So they are the *loro* of Wehali.

Hotu mane sanulu tun tenik mai, usi man sanulu, mane sanulu Bereliku.

Then another group of ten people descended again entitled *usi*. They were the ten men of Bereliku.

Mane sanulu ne'e mai tuka ti'an

these ten men were the last group of people descended to earth

tan rai no kbatak no kiadik ti'an

because the land had already its border and its edge

rai maran no kmetis ti'an.

the land was already dry and firm.

Mane sanulu ne'e sai hosi Wehali

These ten men left Wehali

sia la'o ba Ambon Keser, Lautem, Mantutu, Tutuala, Fohoren, Kaladi, Maukari Tulakain, Laka'an, Mande'u. Ida tun tasi iha Suai.

and went to Ambon *Keser*, Lautem, Mantutu, Tutuala, Fohoren, Kaladi, Maukari Tulakain, Laka'an and Mande'u. One went down to the sea at Suai.

Reference Text 4

Narrator: Sam Kehik Seran (Wewiku Version)
Type: 'Language of the Earth' (*Rai Lian*)

Rai ne'e nahuu	When the earth started to originate
rai ne'e dadi	the earth came into being
na'ak ee:	as it is happened:
'Wee iha leok lema rai	'Oh, in the hovering world above
kbetek lema rai	in the smooth world below
sia na'in rua rola ibu du'uk	the two of them consented
rola lia du'uk	the two of them agreed
foin kraik simu iha leten	then below received above
leten mos simu iha kraik	above received below
leten simu ti'an kraik	above having received
kraik simu ti'an leten	below having received above
foin atu fila ba malu	they turned to each other
ramaas ba malu	whispered to each other
los ha'in a tebes	true to each other
ha'in a iha la kaka naran	faithful in the face of the one whose name cannot be pronounced
la temi naran	whose name cannot be called
malore uit	become a little clear
mahosu uit	appear a little
foin atu natudu	then about to show
foin atu namosu	then about to cause to appear
foin leok lema rai iha leten ne'e ha'ak iha leten	then that which was hovering above was called 'the land above'
kbetek lema rai iha rai ne'e ha'ak iha kraik	that which was smooth on earth was called 'the land below'
sia ruas katak ti'an malu	the two of them having spoken together
ramaas ti'an malu	having whispered to each other
sia ibu kmesak	they were of one mouth
sia lia kmesak	of one language

foin sia ha'ak, hasee du'uk	then the two of them invoked
dobar oan ida	a little thickened liquid
wen oan ida	a little liquid,
nu'u dobar oan ida	like a little thickened liquid
wen oan ida	a little liquid
foin ra'ak:	then it was said:
kmemetin ha'in a	the firming
kmamaten ha'in a	the tightening
kmetis rola ti'an foin ramaten	having made firm, then it was tightened
foin mate ba nia	then it was tight there
kmetis ba nia	firm there
tan sia ha'ak:	because they said:
leok lema rai nakees nola ti'an	that which hovers above has spoken
kbetek lema rai nakees nola ti'an	that which is smooth on earth has spoken
foin no kmetis no ktobar	then there was firmness, there was thickening
foin sia haree ba	then they looked
ktobar ti'an kmetis ti'an	it was thickened liquid already, it was firmness already
tan kmetis ti'an foin tadu	because only after it was firm, did it appear
tadu ti'an foin haree rai Wesei, rai Wehali	only after it appeared did one see the land of Wesei, the land of Wehali
foin babaur, fatik kaka fatin:	then the place was called, the place was pronounced:
'mosu Maralilu, haree Fatumea'	'Maralilu appears, Fatumea is seen'
Mosu Maralilu, Haree Fatumea du'uk be sia rua mosu a isin	Although the names were 'Marlilu appears', 'Fatumea is seen', both places appeared at once
be inan a mosu tebes	even though, it was the mother who fully appeared
naran no kakaba Fatumea Talama.	it was called and pronounced Fatumea Talama.
Mosu ti'an foin sia mosu ba mai kaka rola ema tolu:	Having appeared then they called three people (sisters):

Ema ida naran Bi Lasai, ida naran Bi Kou, ida naran Bi Mali	One was called Bi Lasai, one was called Bi Kou and one was called Bi Mali
ema na'in tolu ne'e, raneo ralo raneo, ranoin ralo ranoin	the three persons deeply contemplated and meditated
atu hodi ba hanaran ba sa:	how to name these places:
'hanaran ba rai Wesei	'named them the land of Wesei
hanaran ba rai Wewiku'	named them the land of Wewiku'
Wewiku sia ha'ak, oik, na'ak: kwa'ik	they called Wewiku *oik* meaning 'elder'
Wehali sia ha'ak, hak, na'ak: ikun.	they called Wehali *hak* meaning 'younger'
Haitimuk sia ha'ak, la, na'ak: klaran	they called Haitimuk *la* meaning 'middle'
tan na'in tolu ne'e raneo rola la son resik	these three persons contemplated together without any success
la mamar resik	the earth was still soft
foin no tadu	after a while, it emerged
tadu ti'an ema raree ba Fatumea	when it fully emerged, people saw Fatumea
to'o ne'e foin hamate, foin hamemi:	only then (these places) were confirmed and pronounced:
'rai Wewiku ida, rai Wehali ida, rai Haitimuk ida	'the land of Wewiku, the land of Wehali, the land of Haitimuk'.
hahina ba rai Wewiku'.	the two of them honoured Wewiku as their mother.
Tan sa inan rai Wewiku?	Why was Wewiku the mother?
tan feto tolu ne'e iha rai Wewiku	because these three women were in Wewiku
naran sei nafati dei	the name is still there
naran aa tubu iha Fatumea inuk	the name grew in the track of Fatumea
ai hun aa sei nafati dei	the tree (as proof) is still there
ai ida Biku, ai ida Katimun, ai ida Hali	one (branch) of the tree is the Biku branch, other branches are Katimun and Hali
hun a ai Biku, iha rai Wehali, iha rai Wewiku	the trunk is the Biku tree, (grows) in the land of Wehali, the land of Wewiku
ne'e, hodi rai Wewiku foin hodi hanaran:	it was from the domain of Wewiku, then it was called:
'ama Wesei	'father of Wesei

inan Wesei	mother of Wesei
ina Wesei naran la kaka	mother of Wesei, the unpronounceable name
ama Wesei naran la temi	father of Wesei, the unspeakable name
hodi halamak	to offer sacrifice
hodi haloon	to invoke
hodi hatebes	to be true
hodi hametis.	to be firm.
atu hodi sa hanaran	how (Maromak Oan) would be named
atu hodi sa hamemi?	how (he) would be pronounced?
hodi kaka duni ba	just calling
hodi temi duni ba	just pronouncing
hana'i ho oan	just pay the respect
haboot ho oan	just praise
ba naran la kaka	to the name that can not be pronounced
naran la temi'.	the name that can not be called'.
Foin ami temi no kaka ha'ak:	Then we pronounce and call:
'iha dadoko fatin ka	'(to the one) in the cradle
tatuna fatik ka	in the place where he was swinging
hodi ha'ak hahaan du'uk ba	to feed him
haroo du'uk ba	to rock him
do'u oan sia	the little pigeon
kawak oan sia'.	the little crow'.
(Do'u oan no kawak oan ne'e tuir ami ema fehan ne'e ha'ak Maromak Oan.)	(For the plains people, Maromak Oan is just like a baby pigeon, a baby crow.)
Ulun ba Maromak Oan	the head was Maromak Oan
Maromak Oan tadu	Maromak Oan had appeared
at se nahaan?	(but) who is going to feed (him)?
at se naroo?	who is going to rock (him)?
at se naluku?	who is going to veil (him)?
at se balu?	who is going to cover (him)?
Mesti no ema makbalin	There must be someone to take care of him

no ema maklituk iha uma laran	there must be someone
atu haree, atu titu ba Maromak Oan	to look after and to take care the Maromak Oan
hanesan ema maho beran bot	there must be someone who has great authority
maho ukun bot.	who has power.
Tan nia, foti rola ema na'in rua ne'e ha'ak	For that reason two people where appointed
leo walu nen, leo hitu nen, leo nen nen	the clan of eight-six, the clan of seven-six
Umanen Lawalu makbalin no makdakar ba Na'i Maromak Oan	Umanen and Lawalu take care and guard the lord Maromak Oan
sia mak hakwana	they are the ones that decide to the right
no hakaruk	and to the left
iha hadak no labis	on the bamboo floor and platform

Reference Text 5

Narrator: Mako'an Benedictus Bere Seran
Type: 'Language of the Earth' (*Rai Lian*)

Dadi oras ne'e ha'u mai mulai atu kakees hosi rai Bakiruk.	So, now I am going to talk about the territory of Bakiruk.
Rai Bakiruk, ema mak dakar rai naran Ferik	The person who guarded the Bakiruk region
Ha'in Raiklaran iha Marlilu Haholek, Marlilu Hahoiek Sona Fahi Atebes	was called Ferik Ha'in Rai Klaran in Marlilu Haholek. (She lived in) Marlilu Haholek Sona Fahi Atabes
nia mesan dei iha Marlilu Hahoiek	she was all alone in Marlilu Haholek
nia mesan dei naneo na'ak la di'ak.	being totally alone, she felt sad, felt it was not good.
Ida moris tan teni naran Ho'ar Na'in Haholek	Someone else was born (came into life) called Ho'ar Na'in Haholek
Ho'ar Na'i Haholek iha Marlilu ki'ik	Ho'ar Na'in Haholek lived in the small Marlilu
nosi Marlilu Ki'ik foin naholek	she started to squirm in the small Marlilu
naholek ba, nahoiek ba nia, foin tasi wen no	only when she squirmed there did the sea
rai maran fa'e malu	water and the dry land separate
tasi wen no rai maran fa'e malu ba nia ti'an	after the sea and the dry land separated there
rai maran titin nola teni uit	the dry land expanded a bit
mais sei dauk nakroma	but it had not yet become light
loro sei dauk la iha	the sun did not exist
fulan sei dauk la iha	the moon did not yet exist
rai sei makukun	the earth was still dark
nia tee rai kroman rai titin nola tenik uit mai iha rai naran Natar Klese Uma Rua	then the bright earth expanded a little again to a place called Natar Klese Uma Rua
titin nola teni ba Natar Kiese Uma Rua, ita ema no kabau moris hamutu iba Natar Klese, Uma Rua	it expanded again to Natar Klese Uma Rua; we people and buffalo were born together there

dadi ita ema, uluk ita kabau	formerly we people were buffalo
kabau wa'in ne ita ema mak ne nia	these buffalo were us
kabau dadi ba ema	buffalo turned into people
ita ema haa hae la hatane, foin kabau dadi ba ema, ema dadi nikar ba kabau	because we people did not know how to eat grass, we turned into people, and people turned back into buffalo
tan kabau naa hae natene, ita haa hae la hatene	because buffalo know how to eat grass but we do not know how to eat grass
nia te ema ne, naran sei la no	these people had no name yet
la'o dadaun rai iori teni uit mai iha rai naran Ba'a Fetok	gradually the earth expanded again to a place called Ba'a Fetok
lori mai iba Ba'a Fetok, feto ida no mane	in Ba'a Fetok, there was a woman and a man (there)
mane naran Bei Kelu Toba	the man was called Bei Kelu Toba
feto aa Lesek toba	the woman was called Lesek Toba
nia ti'an sia rua mesan dei	the two of them were alone
naanmane taa ai aa, katak fetsawa na'ak, 'ses!	the brother was cutting wood, and said to the sister, 'Go away!
ai kroek kti tan o, lulik	it is taboo for the wood chips to hit you'
fetsawa la fiar	the sister did not believe
dadi ai kroek aa kti tan ni fetsawa, ni permisi ita hotu hotu fetsawa netan	so the wood chip hit his sister, his sister became pregnant
ai kroek kona nia1 Jetsawa netan ti'an	when the wood chips touched her, she was pregnant
netan ti'an, te uluk pertama mane ida, Mane Seran	after being pregnant, she gave birth firstly to a first son named Seran
nia tee sia rua rola malu na man onan	then they (mother and son) married each other there
sira feto-naan rola rikar malu, te teni mane na'in rua	they, sister and brother married each other again, and gave birth to two more sons
te teni mane na'in rua, naran Seran hotu	she gave birth to two more sons. The sons were all called Seran
ida mane ulun naran Na'i Seran Tabada Boki Bakiruk	the oldest son was called Seran Tabada Boki Bakiruk
mane nomor dua naran Seran Bei Rai	the second son was called Seran Bei Rai

mane nomor tiga naran Seran Di'ak Sedi'a	the third son was called Seran Di'ak Sedi'a
nee Seran Tabada Boki Bakiruk, rai maran luan no kbelar ti'an	(when Seran Tabada Boki Bakiruk was born) the dry land was already wide and broad
nia ba nalolon rai	he went to measure the land.
Ba to'o Larantuka Baboi	He went as far as Larantuka Baboi
fila nikar mai Seran Bei Rai sa'e ba Liurai	when he returned, Seran Bei Rai 'ascended' to Liurai
Liurai nariik ti'an	the office of Liurai already existed
Seran Di'ak Sedi'a dadi ba Wehali Maromak Oan	Seran Di'ak Sedi'a become Maromak Oan in Wehali
foin na'i Seran Tabada Boki Bakiruk ha'ak loro Inan Bakiruk ba nia	then Seran Tabada Boki Bakiruk became/ was called the mother *loro* of Bakiruk
nia ti'an, te no teni feto nen	after that she also gave birth to six daughters
feto ida naran Ae Ro, feto ida naran Ae Bauk, Ida ne Tora Bauk	one daughter was called Ae Ro, one daughter was called Ae Bauk, this one was called Tora Bauk
Ae Ro fo ba Wehali	Ae Ro was sent to Wehali
Ae Bauk Jo ba Haitimuk	Ae Bauk was sent to Haitimuk
Tora Bauk Jo ba Wewiku	Tora Bauk was sent to Wewiku
hela Harek, Bui no Se'uk	there remained Harek, Bui and Se'uk
Harek, ba darek	Harek went to dry up (herself)
fo ba furi no kada	she was sent to scatter (the seeds) and to plant (seedlings)
ba loro karas no kbelan	to the areas toward the chest and ribs
nodi nameti rai lidun hat	to make firm the four corner land
Bui no Se'uk nafati ba rai Bakiruk to'o ohin loron.	Bui and Se'uk remained in Bakiruk until now.
Lia to'o ne'e dei.	That is all.

Reference Text 6

Narrator: P. Seran Luan
Type: 'Language of the Earth' (*Rai Lain*)

'To'os ai fatik	'The (first) garden place
tua ai fatik	the (first) palm place
Marlilu Haholek leten sia ba	Marlilu Haholek above
Sona Fahi Latebes as sia ba'.	Sona Fahi Latebes up high'.
Uluk fohon raiklaran ne'e sei makukun	In the beginning the earth was still dark
tan lale'an ne'e no raiklaran ne'e sei taka malu	as the sky and the earth still touched each other
to'o mai lale'an ne'e no raiklaran ne'e nakloke	then the sky and the earth separated
lale'an ne'e nakloke nela raiklaran ne'e no kroman	when the sky and the earth separated, the earth was left with light
no ti'an kroman foin klosan rua tun nosi leten naran Mau Leki Mau Mauk	after there was light two retainers descended from above, named Mau Leki and Mau Mauk
Maromak ha'in naruka tun mai matan raiklaran ne'e	The Bright One ordered (them) to come down to the source of the earth
tun mai matan raiklaran ne'e, emi ha'ak:	(they) came down to the source of the earth, just as the saying:
'Tobu tuir laliran kaban	'Step on the spider saliva thread
sama tuir labadain kaban	trample on the spider web
sama nikar ain atu kotu la kotu.	trample again without breaking it
tobu nikar ain atu kotu la kotu'.	step again without breaking it'.
Mai naree raiklaran ne'e mesa we	They came and saw that the earth was (still) all water
no ha'i sa ida	there was not a thing
sia sa'e rikar ba rasara ba Maromak ha'in a, na'ak:	they ascended back to inform The Bright One, saying:
'Ema bot, raiklaran ne'e ami tun ba haree ti'an be mesa we tanan	'Your Greatness, we have gone down and seen the earth already, but it is all just water
no ha'i sa ida'	there is not a thing'

Na'ak 'so'in	(The Bright One) said 'All right
metak metak oan lai kaneo	wait a little, while I contemplate
matek matek oan lai kanoin	wait a little, while I think
lai kaneo kola leten oan ida	let me contemplate how to make a small surface
lai kanoin kola maran oan ida'.	let me think about how to make a small dry (land)'.
Rola kalan hitu Leki no Mauk tun nikar mai	On the seventh night Leki and Mauk came back down
no ai hali ida Karlele iha tasi wen fohon a	there was a banyan tree called Karlele, 'floating' on the surface of the sea
sedaun no leten sedauk no maran	there was no dry land yet
sa'e rikar ba ema bot a, ha'ak e:	they ascended back to the honourable man, saying
'Ema bot, raiklaran ne'e no ha'i leten no maran be no ai hun ida iha tasi wen laran'.	'Your Greatness, this earth has no dry land yet, but there is a tree trunk in the sea'.
Na'ak 'so'in,	He said, 'All right,
loron hitu tun nikar ba, te nariik onan ka sei'.	on the seventh day you descend again, and see whether it is already upright or not yet'.
Loron hitu ne'e to'o sia tun rikar mai, ohin ai Barlele ai hun ne'e nariik ti'an	When the seventh day arrived they came back down, and the 'Barlele' tree trunk was already upright
sia rua sa'e ba katak	the two of them ascended and told him
'Maromak ami tun ti'an te ba, ai a nariik ti'an'	'Maromak, we have already gone down, and the tree is upright already'.
Ai a bot ti'an, ma manu raiklaran ne'e nakonu	The tree is already large, it is full of birds
Leki no Mauk tun mai	Leki and Mauk came down
mai be atu ru'u man do'u ba nia	they came down in order to 'blow' shoot with a blowpipe a wild pigeon there
to'o mai, ru'u rola ti'an atu tunu ba sa?	having arrived, and having shot one, how were they to roast it?
te raiklaran ne'e sei we	because the earth was still water
ai hun ne'e sei we	the base of the tree was still water

311

rodi hikar sa'e ba, buat ne'e dois

they brought it back up, and this thing smelled

dois ti'an, sei kdok Maromak nusu na'ak

because it already stank, when they were still far off Maromak asked

'Se mak hodi buat at ne'e?'

'Who is it that brought this bad thing?'

To'o nia ida tama nasaran na'ak:

(Confronted with that question), one went in to inform him, saying:

'Ami at hatasak lamak hodi hatetu bee buat ee at ti'an tan no ha'i leten no ha'i maran

'We want to cook the sacrificial meat to offer, but this thing is bad already because there is no dry land

ami at hatasak lamak a ba sa?'

how are we to cook this sacrificial meat?'

'So'in,

'All right,

kalan hitu fali ba hikar

on the seventh night, go back

nia no leten no maran ti'an'.

it will have become dry land'.

Kalan hitu sia tun rikar mai, no leten no maran ti'an

On the seventh night they went back down, and it was already dry land

hali hun aa ta'u mesak

the base of the banyan tree was very muddy

ru'u rola do'u muk rodi sa'e e, tunu ba hali abut

they shot the squawking wild pigeon which they were to carry up, and roasted it at the banyan roots

rodi sa'e hikar ba, tasak, morin

they carried it back up, and it was cooked and sweet smelling

no leten no maran ti'an bee, sei ta'u bee, tasi wen aa basak mesak.

there was dry land already, but it was still muddy, and the sea was rough.

Sa'e rikar ba sia ra'ak 'no ha'i ema hein ami iha raiklaran ba ho dale'.

Ascending again, they said, 'there is no one waiting on earth to talk with us'.

Nia ti'an nia na'ak, 'so'in,

Then he said, 'All right,

kalan hitu ti'an ba hikar

on the seventh night you go back

sa ida iha nia'.

there will be something there'.

Tun rikar mai, nu'u buat oan ida, nu'u bata musan ida kaa buat sa ida, sihak iha hali nian abut aa

Having come back down, there was a small thing, like a corn seed or something, entangled in the roots of the banyan

rodi rikar rasa'e ba ema bot aa:

they brought it back up to the Greatness one:

'Buat e nu'u rak ee nu'u sa ida bee sihak iha hali abut aa'.

'This thing is like blood or something, but it was entangled in the roots of banyan roots'.

'So'in,

'All right,

kalan hitu ne'e tun nikar ba'.

just go back on the seventh night'.

Kalan hitu ti'an tun nikar ba, Ferik Ha'in Raiklaran ne'e moris ba nia.

On the seventh night when they went down again, Ferik Ha'in Raiklaran (lit. the only woman on earth) was born there.

Moris te ba nia, atu kotu oan aa husar, atu kotu ba saa

When she was born people did not have the right tools to cut her umbilical cord

husar aa naa nikar ba hali abut aa

the umbilical cord entangled inside the roots of the banyan tree

mola besi bee at mai kotu (?)

Fetched an iron blade to chop (?)

sa'e rikar ba rusu

they ascended back to ask

'Kotu hodi fafulu'.

'Cut with a sliver of bamboo' (came the reply)

Kotu hodi fafulu a tan ba nia.

(The tradition) of cutting (the umbilical cord) using (sliver of) bamboo is related to this story.

Oan ne'e at se mak nahaan, se mak naroo, ita la haree tan ne'e Maromak nia beran

Who fed this child and who gave her drink, we do not know because that was Maromak's power

oan ne'e foi-wa'ik ti'an, nia nakdobos nela hali hun ne'e tan maran naksesik nalo ui-uit ti'an

when this child was grown up, she crept away from the base of the banyan, because the dry land had already gradually expanded

knanuk na'ak hoku fatik e hanatar fatik ba iha nia

the poem says there was the place to lie down, to rest

nia ti'an, nia nakdobos

then she went further

nakdobos mai rai iha uma kain kmesak

she came and was put in a household by herself

nia mesan dei

she was just alone

susun a kmesak ida

she had one breast

mais ema ne'e oin a rua, feto ida mane ida

but this person had two faces, one female and one male

nia lori mai, mai to'o uma rua a, nia nahoris ba nia

she came, came to the second house, and she gave birth there

foin taka natoos tasi matan a, tase wen a, nodi we mis nariis oan ne'e	then she tightly covered the source of the sea, and she bathed the child with fresh water
nia be adat moris ba nia	then *adat* began there
nia ti'an sia rola rikar malu te nola ba Ho'ar Na'i Haholek, te nola tenik ba Ho'ar Samara Morin	then they married and gave birth to Ho'ar Na'i Haholek, and gave birth again to Ho'ar Samara Morin
Samara Morin la'o lema rai	Samara Morin walked to explore the earth
fila nikar mai haree ha'i lakan no len iha rai Marlilu Haholek	when he came back he saw a flame and glowing fire (a woman) in Marlilu Haholek
hola nikar Ho'ar Na'i Haholek.	he married Ho'ar Na'i Haholek.
Te nola sia na'in hitu: Na'i Ura Mataus, Saku Mataus, Neti Mataus, Bara Mataus, Neno Mataus, Leki Mataus, Ho'ar Nahak Makbalin	she gave birth to seven children: Ura Mataus, Saku Mataus, Neri Mataus, Bara Mataus, Neno Mataus, Leki Mataus and Ho'ar Nahak Makbalin

Reference Text 7

Narrator: Piet Tahu Nahak
Type: 'True Language' (*Lia Tebes*)

Liurai ne'e sia na'in nen	There were six Liurai
Liurai ida, mane ulun aa naran Tabein Liurai	the first was called Tabein Liurai
mane dala rua naran Liurai Berehi	the second was called Liurai Berehi
mane dala tolu niakan naran Liurai Dasa	the third was called Liurai Dasa
mane dala haat niakan naran Liurai Seran Asa	the fourth was called Liurai Seran Asa
mane dala lima niakan naran Liurai Kalaan	the fifth was called Liurai Kalaan
mane dala nen niakan naran Liurai Lelek.	the sixth was called Liurai Lelek.
Ba oras nia rai Wehali ne'e hahaan no ha'i	At that time, there was no food in Wehali
tan nia sia rodi malu rakees ramutu lia raak:	therefore they (the six Liurai) discussed amongst each other, saying:
'Ita ne'e haa be la no, hemu be la no	'We have absolutely no food, no drink
at halo saa be at haa kmaus Wehali, hemu kmaus Wehali'.	how are we going to domesticate Wehali with food, to tame Wehali with drink'.
Nia foin Liurai ida dala rua naran Liurai Barehi ne'e naak,	Then the second Liurai, called Barehi, said:
'So'in	'Do not worry,
kalau nu nia emi hakara at halo haan ne'e, emi	if you want to provide food for the people, just
ho'o ha'u ba bat ee halo ba haan'.	kill me and turn parts of my body into food.
Nia foin naak sia tuir tenik malu naak, 'so'in'.	Then the remaining five Liurai accommodated his desire.
Ho'o ti'an nia ulun aa halo ba nu	after they killed him, his head was turned into coconuts
nu modo leik aa fo haan rai Fatumea Takolo iha loro sa'en	the green coconut was sent to feed the land of Fatumea Takolo, to the land of the rising of the sun

nuu mean aa fo haan rai Fatumea Talama iha loro monu

the red coconut was sent to feed the land of Fatumea Talama, to the land of the setting of the sun

nia ti'an be oras to'os molik ti'an udan ne'e tau rai, ema loro sa'en buka nuu mea sa'e nodi nisik todan foin furi.

(that is why) after the gardens were cleared, rain fell; the people from (the land towards) the sunset fetched a red coconut in order to sprinkle (the earth with coconut milk) before planting.

Kalau ema rai Wehali hola nuu modo ha'in (nuu kalabuk) be hodi hisik to'os laran foin furi

But the Wehali people took only the young green coconut to sprinkle the garden before planting

nia ti'a fokit ni'an aa halo ba batar malae, na'ak:

his teeth turned into maize, as the saying goes:

'Batar leki makerek

'The beautiful and colorful maize

batar nakfoli

is giving fruit

nakfoli nakabit

it bears seed

sorin no na'in

all over the cob'.

Nia foin foti ba to'os laran aa halo ba batar malae.

The teeth, then, were planted in the garden and became maize.

Nia ti'an foin hola liman ku;ana ne'e halo ba hudi luan, naak:

Then his right hand turned into *luan* bananas, as the saying goes:

'Taman hudi luan(n) lotuk

'Plant thin *luan* bananas

nalai kladik

plant in rows to make borders

feto sawa taa balu

sisters are on one side

naan taa balu'.

brothers are in the other side'.

Ne'e be to'o maifeto nia natene na'ak niakan fetosawa, mane mos nia natene na'ak namane malun. Ne'e be keta hala'e(n) hikar malu, keta hefee(n) hikar malu.

The planting of bananas around borders of a garden warned brother and sister not to marry each other.

Liman karuk ee halo ba fore, hodi ba furi iha rai Akani, naak:

The left hand turned into beans, to be planted at Akani, as is said:

'Fore nurak Akani

'Young beans of Akani

nurak Akani

young ones of Akani

la mea Akani

not red Akani

mea Akani'.

red Akani'.

To'o nia ma ema nosi Akanz Bei Liki Loku, nako'us nodi nikar mai, nariik ba rai Tatun, Bei Liki ne'e, foin bolu ema rai Wehali ne'e naak:	A person from Akani, called Bei Liki Loku, brought young beans to the land of Tatun, and called the people of Wehali, saying:
'Fore kmodok Wehali ne'e la ber ha'i, la duun ha'i'.	'These green beans of Wehali, (Wehali people) don't want (to plant)'.
Be mai oras hikar be ema hodi ba furi seluk ba at hodi be huli hikar fini lok Wehali	So the Akani people brought the seed back to replant it; in order to feed Wehali
ne'e huli hikar mai furi ba hamolik hola (iha) rai mota hasan	then they took (the beans) back and planted them in the riverbed – at the junction of streams of water
fore knau Sanbei makasuk	the unexpected mung beans planted by Sanbei
foin fore nia haknau ba nia	then the beans grew unexpectedly there
haknau ba nia foin knanuk na'ak ee:	when the beans germinated there, the saying goes
'Fore kmodok Wehali	green beans of Wehali
nahabut besi	develop strong nodules
nafua kmurak	develop valuable beans
nahabut besi nu nia	develop strong nodules
nafua kmurak ba nia	develop valuable beans
iha rai mota hasan	in the junction of the river
rai fore knau Sanbei Lakasuk	the land of unexpected beans planted by Sanbei Lakasuk
iha baki Liurai	at the stronghold of the Liurai
besi uurai	at the fort of the Liurai
iha natar besi	at the productive paddock
lalu'an besi	the productive animal pen
kakehen hat	at the four flat plain areas
lalidun hat	at the four corners
loku hasan mak erek hat	at the place where men wear male bracelets
riti hasan makerek hat	at the place where women wear female bracelets

317

foin ha'ak, lifun isin manun isin'.	then it is said, all living things are fruitful'.
Nataman be haak:	Having planted (the mung beans), people say:
'Fore kmodo Wehali	'The mung beans of Wehali
'Nahabut besi ti'an	develop strong nodules
nafua kmurak ti'an'.	develop valuable beans'.
Teik aa no kawa'i aa butuk ba rai Wehali ne'e	the guts and the intestine piled up in Wehali
fuan ne'e ninia, ne'e kmodo fuan ne'e	the intestine became pumpkin fruit
teik aa ninian kmodo kain ne'e sia.	the guts became vines.
Raan aa hodi kakin ba tasi laran dadi ba na'an knase	The blood poured into the sea and became a *knase* fish
na'in Bakalo na'in fola nola	*na'in* Bakalo caught the fish
dadi ti'an ba batar tasi musan	it turned into a seed of *batar tasi*
tan tasi no ema raiklaran nalo funu	because the sea fought with the people of the earth
ho'o hola na'an tasi nia ulun	someone caught the fish and cut off its head (lit. killed the fish's head)
Bakalo na'in meti lor na'in ne'e baka ibun ulun fatuk ne'e foin hataan hola na'an batar tasi ne'e musan ida	called Bakalo, Lord of the tidal flats, he chopped through the mouth to the skull and caught the small bone, the sorghum seed
nodi ba furi iha to'os etu kukun aa	he took it and planted it in the royal dark garden
ha'ak Maromak Oan niakan	the garden owned by Maromak Oan
foin haree dadaun to'o loron hat dadi ba batar tasi ni ne'e.	after four days it became *batar tasi*
Ain aa ai Kanikur hodi ba hamotu iha rai Sulit Anemetan Talobo	the legs (looking like) Kanikur tree trunks were burned in Sulit Anemeta Talobo
foin hodi halo ba kilat rahun	then they turned into gunpowder
hamotuk ti'an halo ra'ut hola ahu kesan aa	once the legs were burned to ashes
halo ba kilat rahun aa foin hodi halo funu	someone scooped ash in their hands to make gunpowder for warfare

hodi husi iha knuu halo ba rahun no fuan bat ee hodi hasoru funu no ledo.

in order to wage war they made gunpowder and bullets, to wage war.

Kilat rahun rai iha Uma Makbukar, Uma Akar Tahan

The gunpowder was placed in the house of Makbukar, the house of Akar Tahan

'makbukar na'in Liuraz banin Liurai '.

'the right hand of Liurai, the border of Liurai'.

Hudi luan aa

Concerning *luan* bananas

liman kwana niak halo hudi luan aa

it was the right hand that became *luan* bananas

tan bat nu e oras oa(n) ida ukur no manaran ee hakoir to'o mai at hodi ukur halo los ba nuu ohin ee ne ha'ak naa los hudi luan ne'e dei.

therefore according to *adat* one must eat only *luan* bananas for the occasions of childbirth, first haircut, and naming of a child.

Reference Text 8

Narrator: Johannes Seran Kehik
Type: 'Story to be Remembered' (*Ai Knanoik*)

Ferik ida te nola oa mane na'in ne'en no oa feto ida

A woman gave birth to six sons and one daughter

oa feto mak ikun.

the girl was the youngest.

Feto ne'e sia ki'ik, nia sei la natene sa ida, mane na'in ne'en ne'e ba buka sotir ba buka uan iha ema rain.

When the girl was still small, and still knew nothing, the six men went to seek their fortune, to seek their luck in other people's land.

Mane ne'en ne'e nola to'os ko'a tua hodi hahaan ina Wesei Ama Wesei.

The six men worked the gardens and produced juice to feed the mother of Wesei, the father of Wesei.

Sia sei nahaan ina Wesei Ama Wesei, sia ha'ak sei la di'ak, sei la kbit sia atu ba futu, manu, ba lak a manu.

While they were still feeding the mother of Wesei and the father of Wesei, they said it was still not good, still not strong, they would go cockfighting.

Sia na'in ne'en tene nola malu ha'ak nola malu, ba futu manu, ba laka manu, iha rai loro lakan, iha rai loro len, iha rai ulun.

The six of them arranged together to go cockfighting in the land of the sun's glow, the land of the sun's flame, in the head land.

Ba futu manu no Liurai Lakuleik. Taru osan tam morteen, to'o mos, sia na'in neen taru isi lolon.

They went cockfighting with Liurai Lakuleik. They gambled precious metal and beads until they were all gone. Then the six of them gambled themselves.

Tan nia, mane kwa'ik taru uluk mane ki'ik na'in lima. Mane ki'ik na'in lima ne'e Liurai Lakuleik taru nola ti'an.

So the oldest first gambled the youngest five men. Liurai Lakuleik gambled and took the youngest five.

Mane Kawa'ik mos taru no isi lolon, nia mos Lakuleik taru nola no.

the oldest also gambled himself, Lakuleik gambled and took him too.

Tan nia, sia fila mai la bele. Na'in Lakuleik na'in nalo sia ba niakan atan. Kesi sia iha kidun uma kotuk.

Because of this they couldn't come back. The noble of Lakuleik made them his slaves. He tied them up at the back of the house.

Dadi dadaun feto bot lai, nia matenek.	When the girl grew up, she knew what was gomg on.
Nia sa'e ba kadadak leten ne'e, ma naree. niakan nan siakan buti: Nia naree buti ne'e sia, mak hanesan kahuuk no kaleik, tan uluk hana kaleik	She climbed onto the top of a shelf and saw her brothers' bracelets. These bracelets were formed just like a blowgun and a *kaleik* vine because in the past people used to shoot *kaleik*.
Tan nia, nia nusu niakan inan. Nia inan sei neli na'ak buat ne'e sia, ami moris ami haree kedan. Nu nia mos feto ne'e nusu tenik:	Because of this, she asked her mother. Her mother concealed the truth, saying when we were born, we already saw these things. But she kept asking:
'Ina, keta ha'u moris mai ko namane e lale'.	'Mother, when I was born did I have brothers, or not?'
Ina na'ak: 'Lale, o moris mai a mesa dei, la mo namane'.	Her mother said: 'No, when you were born there was only you, you had no brothers'.
To'o loron ida, nia naruka keu hirik	Then one day, she ordered her father to cut strips of palm leaves for twine
keu nola hirik ne'e, sia tutan foin nia soru	having cut the strips of leaves, they joined them together, then she wove
ba oras nia sei soru, manu Taun mai katak.	while she was still weaving, Bird Taun came and talked.
Oa feto ne'e naran Ho'ar Nahak Samane Oan	The girl's name was Ho'a Nahak Samane Oan
naran ne'e ikus. Naran uluk Sakadu, naran kadua Ati Batik. Naran ikus Ho'ar Nahak Samane Oan, tan dadi ba mane onan atu ba futu manu ba laka manu.	this was her last name. The first name was Sakadu; the second name Ati Batik. The last name was Ho'a Nahak Samane Oan because she was going to become a man, to go cockfighting.
Ba oras nia sei soru, manu Tauk oan mai ni lia, na'ak:	While she was still weaving, young Bird Tauk came with a message, saying:
'Ati Batik, feto ati Batik	'Ati Batik woman Ati Batik
Ati Batik maktuur tasi tehen sia ruma	Ati Batik who sits at the edge of the sea
Ati Batik maktuur meti tehen sia ruma	Ati Batik who sits at the edge of the tidal flats
o atu sei soru manook lai	you would keep weaving, be quiet first
o atu sei ta manook lai	you would keep striking, be quiet now

manook ho atis lian sia lai	silence your loom
manook ho knuban lian sia lai	silence your loom
manook be ha'u katak fo tone	be silent so that I will tell you
manook be ha'u de'an fo tone'.	be silent so that I will speak to you'.
Tan nia, Atik Batik na'ak:	Because of this, Atik Batik said:
'Hei! Manu ne'e manu sa? O naran manu sa?'	'What bird is this? and what is your name?'
Manu Tauk na'ak: 'Ha'u ne'e Manu Tauk	Bird Tauk said: 'My name is Bird Tauk
manu Tauk dadoko rai Wehali'.	Manu Tauk rocks the land of Wehali
dadoko nakiak rai Wehali'.	Cradles and raises the land of Wehali'.
Ati Batik katak ba manu Tauk na'ak:	Ati Batik spoke to Bird Tauk saying
'So'in, O katak lia sa?'	'All right. What is your message?'
Manu Tauk na'ak: 'o moris mai mo ama, mo no namane	Bird Tauk said: 'when you were born you had a father and also had brothers
okan nan sia, mane ne'en	your brothers were six men
sia ba futu manu la fila mai	they went cockfighting and didn't come back
oh, ba futu manu sia loro len ba, ba laka manu sia loro lakan ba'.	Oh, they went cockfighting in the sun's glow in the sun's flame'
Ati Batik soe niakan atis, nia ba nusu niakan inan:	Ati Batik threw away her weaving stick and went to ask her mother:
'Ina, loron a ha'u kusu o, o meli	'Mother, that day when I went to ask you, you concealed the truth
manu Tauk mai katak na'ak ha'u moris mai, ha'u ko ama etuk, ko namane'.	Manu Tauk came and told me that when I was born I had a mother's brother and had brothers'.
Ina na'ak: 'Tebes na'i	Her mother said: 'yes dear
o moris mai mo ama etuk, mo namane	when you were born you had a mother's brother and had brothers
mais okan namane na'in ne'en ba futu manu	but your six brothers went cockfighting
mais Lakuleik na'in taru nola hotu sia	but the noble of Lakuleik gambled and took all of them

tan nia, sia la bele fila mai, foin o la mo namane'.

because of that, they could not come back. After that you had no brothers'.

Ati Batik na'ak: 'Ha'u musti ba buka sia, ba kola kikar sia'.

Ati Batik said: 'I must go and look for them, go and fetch them back again'.

Inan nusu: 'ba mola mak nu sa?'

Her mother asked: 'How will you fetch them?'

Ati Batik nusu: 'Ina, ita ho hutun no renu ka lale?'

Ati Batik asked: 'Mother, do we have subjects and commoners or not?'

'Ita ho hutun ho renu', ina na'ak.

Mother said 'we have subjects and commoners'.

Tan nia feto ne'e na'ak ina, di'ak liu katak hutun no renu sia mai ta rola ro ida bodik ha'u.

Because of this the girl said: 'Mother, it would be better if we asked our subjects to come and cut a canoe for me.

Ha'u atu tuir ha'ukan namane sia, ne'e be ha'u taru kola hikar'.

'I will follow my brothers, so that I will gamble them back'.

Bolu hutun rai tolu, renu rai tolu mai ta ro.

they called the subjects from three lands, commoners from three lands to come and then cut a canoe.

Ta ti'a ro ne'e nale naktomak, bolu renu feto renu mane mai halo bakae

Having cut the canoe and finished it, they called the female commoners and male commoners to come and prepare travelling food

halo ti'an bakae hasa'e ba ro

having prepared the food for the journey, they put it up in the boat

hasa'e ai maran, hasa'e we

they put in dry wood, put in water

hasa'e saasa ne'e nakonu ro ti'an, nola niakan manu nasa'e ba to'o kakuluk leten

having put things in until the boat was full, she took her cock and put it into the top of the boat

manu rani ti'an manu kokoreek

once the cock had perched, it crowed

kokoreko!

kokoreko!

Ho'ar Nahak Samane Oan lele ai onan

Ho'a Nahak Samane Oan floated the boat

Ho'ar Nahak Samane lori loit onan

Ho'a Nahak Samane brought money

lori loit ba laka manu sia ona

brought money to go cockfighting

lori loit ba futu manu sia ona

brought money to go cockfighting

Ho'ar Nahak Samane la'o ba onan

Ho'a Nahak Samane went

323

WEHALI

nia ba no Leki no Mauk bodik atu naruka	she went with Leki and Mauk to whom she could give orders
nia la'o to'o sikun ida nia nusi kilat	on her arrival on a corner, and she shot a firearm
ema sai mai nusu nia, oh ro ne'e ro Ekekero e ro Kailaku?	people came out and asked her if the name of the boat was Ekekero or Kailaku
Ho'ar Nahak Samane na'ak: 'ha'u ne'e la Ekekero Kailaku'	Ho'ar Nahak Samane said: 'I am not Ekekero Kailaku
ha'u la'o atu futu manu laka manu'.	I am travelling for cockfighting'.
'Oh, atu futu manu sia la'o liu ba	'Oh, to fight cocks, go further
atu laka manu sia basu liu ba	to fight cocks, pass on further
rai ne'e la futu manu sia fatin	this area is not a cockfighting place
rai ne'e la laka manu sia fatin'.	this area is not a cockfighting place'.
Nu'u nia ema katak ba Ho'ar Nahak Samane.	Thus said the people to Ho'ar Nahak Samane
Nia la'o dadaun to'o rai Lakuleik na'in, nia nusi tenik kilat.	She kept going to the land of Lakuleik, and again shot a firearm.
Na'i Lakuleik na'in sai mai nasoru na'ak oh ro ne'e ro Ekekero e ro Kailaku?	Lakukeik came out to meet her, asking whether her boat was an Ekekero or Kailaku
Ho'ar Nahak Samane na'ak: 'Ha'u ne'e la Ekekro Kailaku	Ho'ar Nahak Samane said: 'I am not Ekekero Kailaku
la'o futu manu la'o laka manu'.	I am travelling for cockfighting, travelling for cockfighting'.
Lakuleik na'in na'ak:	the Lakuleik said:
'Atu futu manu sia, bara lai ona	'To fight cocks, stop now
atu laka manu sia bara lai ona	to fight cocks, stop now
rai ne'e rai futu sia fatin	this area is the place for fighting cocks
rai ne'e rai laka sia fatin'.	this area is the place for fighting cocks'.
Ho'ar Nahak Samane natene ti'an iha neon laran oh, ha'ukan namane sia iha ne'e.	Ho'ar Nahak Samane already knew in her heart oh, my brothers are here.
Lakuleik na'in nusu: 'O mai ne'e o mane ka o feto?'	The noble of Lakuleik asked: 'You who came here, are you a man or a woman?'
Ho'ar Nahak Samane na'ak: 'Ha'u mane. Ha'u feto ha'u mai ha'i'.	Ho'ar Nahak Samane said: 'I am a man. If I were a woman I would not come'.

324

Nia sa'e nosi tase wen, nia nalo batane ida iha hali bot ida leon	She ascended from the sea water, and made a temporary shelter in the shade of a banyan tree
hotu nia katak ba Lakuleik na'in, na'ak 'Ha'u kanawa kosar lai, awan foin ita hasoru malu, atu futu manu laka manu'.	then she said to the noble of Lakuleik: 'I will rest now. Tomorrow we'll meet each other, to fight cocks'.
Seisawan foin sia futu manu laka manu	In the morning they did cockfighting
sia taru osan muti, osan mean to'o marten	they gambled silver and gold, and then beads
futu manu, Ho'ar Nahak Samane manaan terus Lakukeik na'in.	cockfighting, Ho'ar Nahak Samane consistently defeated the noble of Lakuleik.
Dadaun Ho'ar Nahak Samane na'ak: 'Kalu okan osan mos ti'an, ita rua taru ata dei	Eventually Ho'ar Nahak Samane said: 'If your money is all gone, we two will gamble slaves
tan ha'u hodi kedan ata rua.	because I have brought two slaves.
O mo ata ka lale?'	Do you have slaves or not?'
Lakuleik na'in na'ak: 'Ha'ukan ata na'in ne'en sia iha ohak laran ne'e'.	The noble of Lakuleik replied 'my six slaves are below'.
nia natudu ba mane na'in ne'en mak nia kesi iha ohak laran.	he pointed to six men whom he had tied up below.
Hotu sia futu manu	Then they fought cocks
sia taru uluk ata rua no ata rua	first they gambled two slaves against two slaves
ata hat ne'e tur mutuk	these four slaves sat together
sia na'in rua futu manu	the two of them fought cocks
Ho'ar Nahak manaan	Ho'ar Nahak won
Ho'ar Nahak Samane nusu tenik masai tenik na'in rua!	Ho'a Nahak Samane again requested to bring out another two
ata rua mai tenik tur tan ba Ho'ar Nahak niakan ala rua	again two slaves came and sat by Ho'ar Nahak's two slaves
sia rua mulai futu tenik manu	the two of them started again to fight cocks
Ho'ar Nahak manan tenik	Ho'a Nahak won again

325

dadaun to'o niakan namane ne'en nis nola hotu	and so on until she had taken all her brothers
nia nodi niakan namane ne'en ne'e ba nariis tan sia mesa kdor	she brought these six brothers of hers to bathe because they were very dirty
sia hariis ti'an, Leki no Mauk te'in etu fo ba sia ha	when they had bathed, Leki and Mauk cooked rice and gave it to them to eat
hotu Lakuleik na'in naruka Leki no Mauk ba katak Ho'ar Nahak Samane ne'e be sia sei atu sukat malu	then the noble of Lakuleik ordered Leki and Mauk to go and tell Ho'ar Nahak Samane that they would still test each other
sukat malu uluk fohon sia sukat mi	they first tested each other in a test of urinating
se niakan sai sasoi kdok liu se	whose would land further than whose?
tan Ho'ar Nahak ne'e jeto, join nia mos nakerat	only because this Ho'ar Nahak was a woman, she was smart
tan nia na'ak: 'Ha'u sei ba batane	she said: 'I'll go to my hut
ha'u sei ba hemu we	I'll go and drink water
tan ha'u du'uk mi la sai'.	because of itself urine will not come out'.
Nia to'o batane ba, nia nola au fafulu naruk ida	When she got to the huts, she took a long piece of bamboo
nia nodi lama ba hariis fatin	she took it with her entering bathing place
mia mos mi	and she urinated
mi sai, nia ta'an au fafulu ba niakan oin, mi sai tuir au fafu nia sai kdok basuk, liu na'in Lakuleik niakan.	when the urine came out, she put the bamboo in front of her. The urine came out along the bamboo, and went very far, further than the noble Lakuleik's.
Lakuleik na'in nusu tenik atu sukat malu hodi hariis mutu iha hariis fatin laran	The noble of Lakuleik asked again to test each other by taking a bath together inside the bathing place
Ho'ar Nahak Samane nata'uk tan feto	Ho'ar Nahak Samane was afraid as she was a woman.
keta Lakuleik na'in natene na'ak nia feto, hariis. mutu oin susun sai ona	She didn't want the noble of Lakuleik to know she was a woman. If they bathed together, her breasts would show.
Nia fila ba batene, nia mos tanis tan nata'uk no moe.	She returned to her hut. And she cried because she was afraid and ashamed.

Nia sei tanis ba laho mai na'ak: 'Tan sa o tanis?'

While she was still crying, a rat came and said: 'Why are you crying?'

Ho'ar Nahak na'ak: 'Ha'u tanis tan ha'u mai futu manu ha'u hodi ti'an

Ho'a Nahak said: 'I am crying because I came to fight cocks and I've already won

ami sukat malu hodi hariis (mii), ha'u hodi ti'an

we tested each other in urinating, and I won

mais oras ne'e, ami sukat tenik malu hodi atu hariis mutu

but now we are again testing each other by bathing together

ami hariis mutu, Lakuleik na'in natene ha'u feto onan'

if we bathe together, the noble of Lakuleik will know that I am a woman'.

Laho na'ak: 'O keta tanis. Fo mak o maruka okan maun sia hasa'e hotu saasa nia ba ro laran

The rat said: 'Don't cry. Order your older brothers to put all the belongings up into the boat

hotu, o maruka Leki no Mauk ba sar no butuk hali tahan ne'e sia halo butuk rua

then, order Leki and Mauk to sweep and pile up these banyan leaves into two piles

ne'e be sunu hali tahan nia ne hak okan batane ha'i na

so that when these banyan leaves are ignited it means you say fire is devouring your campsite

o mos malai mela Lakuleik na'in ba sa'e ro

then you run leaving the noble of the Lakuleik and go up into the boat

Lakuleik na'in niakan ro sia, ha'u mak ba'at halo bon'.

as for the noble of Lakuleik's boats, I will line holes through them'.

Ho'ar Nahak Samane nalo tuir laho lian

Ho'a Nahak Samane acted according to the rat's advice

hotu nia ba sukat malu no Lakuleik na'in nariis uluk nodi nein

then she went to test with the noble of Lakuleik. He was bathing first, waiting

Ho'ar Nahak sei kolu faru tan niakan faru kran hitu

Ho'a Nahak was still taking off clothes as she had seven layers of clothes

Lakuleik na'ak: 'Mai ona, ha'u hariis uluk ti'an'.

Lakuleik said: 'Come now, I am already bathing ahead of you'.

Ho'ar Nahaksei kolu faru.

Ho'a Nahak was still taking off clothes.

Lakuleik na'in naree ti'an Ho'ar Nahak karas kbo'uk.

The noble of Lakuleik had already seen that Ho'ar Nahak's chest was rounded.

Lakuleik nanasa nodi bolu

Lakuleik laughed and called out

Ho'ar Nahak Samane na'ak: 'Keta lai, ha'u sei kolu faru ne'e'.

Ho'a Nahak Samane said: 'Wait. I'm still taking off these clothes'.

Kolu ti'an ida nia sei leno, nodi fudi na'ak faru no utu	Having taken off one layer she still inspected them, on purpose, saying the clothes had lice
Ho'ar Nahak nalo nu'u nia nodi nein ha'i na hali tahan	Ho'a Nahak acted like this while waiting for fire to consume the banyan leaves
oras ha'i na ti'a hali tahan, nia katak ba Lakuleik na'ak: 'O mein ha'u lai tan ha'u susar ti'an. Ha'i na ti'an ha'ukan batane'.	when the fire was already devouring the banyan leaves, she told Lakuleik: 'You just wait for me because I am in difficulty. Fire is devouring my camp site'.
Nia nalai nela Lakuleik terus ba sa'e ro no la'o.	She ran leaving Lakuleik and immediately went up into the boat and left.
Sa'e to'o ro laran, nia ta'e bibiliku na'ak:	Having gotten up into the boat, she hit the drum saying:
'Bibiliku benai, bibiliku benai, hodi feto ida talik mane oan ida la natene'.	'Drum of the river of Benai, drum of Benai. A woman tricked a man and he did not know it'.
Na'in Lakuleik rona bibiliku lian foin nia sarebak no natene,	When the noble of Lakuleik heard the sound of the drum he was surprised and understood,
'Ah! Liurai ne'e feto. Nia nalai ti'an'.	'Ah! This Liurai is a woman. She has run away'.
Laho ba'at Lakuleik niakan ro sia nalo bon hotu.	The rat filed Lakuleik's boats putting holes in all of them.
Lakuleik na'in rona bibiliku lian, nia nalai tuir mai, mais nia la toma ti'an	The noble of Lakuleik heard the sound of the drum. He ran following her, but did not catch up
nia sa'e ba ro ida ro bon	he got up into one boat, and the boat had holes in it
sa'e teni ba ro ida ro bon	he went up again onto another boat, and the boat had holes in it
Ho'ar Nahak Samane la'o ha nodi ta'e bibiliku: 'Bibiliku benai, bibiliku benai, hodi feto oan ida talik mane oan ida la natene'.	Ho'ar Nahak Samane went hitting the drum: 'Drum of Benai, drum of Benai, a woman tricked a man and he did not know it'.
Lakuleik na'in na'ak: 'Ho, so'in'.	the noble of the Lakuleik said: 'Oh, never mind'.
Fulan mosu	The new moon appears

Ho'ar Nahak Samane Oan to'o mai nikar no niakan namane ne'en

Ho'ar Nahak Samane Oan returned with her six brothers

tan nia, nia nasa'e nikar niakan namane ne'en sia nalo ba ulun, ne'e be rai ne'e no nikar ulun, lale rai ne'e no ha'i ukun badu.

then she raised up her six brothers again to make them heads, so that each land would again have a head, otherwise the land would not have rule

Ho'ar Nahak Samane katak kananuk atu nodi nasa'e nikar niakan namane ne'en ne'e ba ulun, atu hodi ka'er ukun ba rai ne'e na'ak:

Ho'ar Nahak Samane said a poem to raise her brothers to headship again in order to grasp the rule of this land. She said:

'Eh, manu aman malae nadu be nadu nadu nak nia heti ren sia monu

'The foreign roosters have come (appeared) come and say that their head-cloths have already fallen

nadu na'ak nia so'e ren sia monu

appear and say that their head accessories have already fallen

so'e ren sia monu kain Maubesi

their head accessories fall on the stalk of Maubesi

heti ren sia monu tenan Maubesi

their head-cloths fall on the wide land of Maubesi

foin atu ba foti le'u lai ulu

then the head-cloths are rescued and have re-encircled on their heads

foin at ba foti kaku rei ulu

then the head accessories were rescued and have been re-installed

mane alin mane maun, na'ak atu natetu nikar ba fatin

the younger brothers and the elder brothers resumed their positions

mane alin mane maun na'ak atu nasa'e nikar ba fatin

the younger brother and elder brother's were restored back to their places

sa'e nikar ba fatik dato na'in dato uma ne'en lawalu

restored to the position of *dato* of Umanen, Lawalu

tetu nikar ba fatin loro na'in loro uma ne'en lawalu'.

Re-enthroned in their positions as *loro* of Umanen, Lawalu'

Tan lia ne'e, rai ne'e foin halo no ukur.

Only after that did this land have rule and measure.

Hotu, Ho'a Nahak Samane Oan mai ba nia inan: 'Ina, ita katak hutun no renu musti ta ai ida. Taa ai oi ida hanesan nu'u ha'u, tan Liurai Lakuleik atu tuir ha'u mai nola. Ta ai oi ida nu'u ne'e-be Liurai Lakuleik maiJo ba nodi'.

then Ho'ar Nahak Samane Oan came to her mother: 'Mother, ask the subjects and commoners to cut a tree. Carve the wood in my image, because Liurai Lakuleik will follow me to come and fetch me. Cut a statue so that when Liurai Lakuleik comes you can give it to him to take'.

Sia hahuu ta ai oi ona

They started to cut a tree/wood

ta iha fatin ida naran Ai Makerek

they cut it in a place called Ai Makerek (lit. patterned wood)

naran Ai Makerek ne'e, tan ko'a ai oi iha nia

this name 'patterned wood' was because people cut a statue there

ko'a ai oi ne'e halo naktomak hanesan niakan isi lolon

they cut this statue exactly like her body

sai ba Malefatin, ne'e be ema Malefatin halo buin ida, halo nu'u niakan oin

they went to Makfatin, so that the people of Makfatin would make the head of the statue like her face

hola mai, tau ba niakan kakorok, hotu hola tenik tuanasu wen tau ba buin laran

they brought it back, put it on her neck, then again fetched sugar palm juice and put it inside the head-statue

hotu, sia hola kabau ikun tau ba buin hotu le'u babani hikar hanesan Ina Ho'a Nahak Samane oan niakan.

then they fetched a buffalo tail and put it on the head-statue; then they twisted it like Mother Ho'ar Nahak Samane's.

Dadi, Julan mosu kilat no lia

So when the moon appeared, there was the sound of a firearm

sia sai ba hasoru, ra'ak Liurai Lakuleik mai ti'an

they went out to greet, saying, Liurai Lakuleik has arrived.

Liurai Lakuleik sa'e mai nodi kedan osan no isin, atu nodi nafoli nola na'in feto ne'e

Liurai Lakuleik came bringing money to pay (bridewealth) toward this noblewoman

sia hasai biti ba odamatan ne'e, foin Liurai. Lakuleik mai tate osan ba

they brought out a mat, spread it out at the door. Then Liurai Lakuleik came and scattered the money on it.

Sia ho'o na'an, atu ha mutu ho Liurai Lakuleik

They killed a beast to eat together with Liurai Lakuleik

Liurai Lakuleik tur nosi labis, Ho'ar Nahak Samane Oan tur nosi loka laran, mais ai oi tur ba odamatan for.

Liurai Lakuleik sat on the platform. Ho'ar Nahak Samane Oan sat inside the single girl's room, but the statue sat at the front door.

Liurai Lakuleik nakees no Ho'ar Nahak Samane Oan ai oi nia naho'uk dei

When Liurai Lakuleik talked with Ho'ar Nahak Samane the statue, she just agreed

Liurai Lakuleik na'ak: 'Ita la'o hikar mai loro laka loro fen, o maho'uk ka lale? Tan o, foin ha'u atu tolo o'.

Liurai Lakuleik said: 'If we go back to the domain of the flaming sun, the glowing sun, do you agree to or not? Because I would like to marry you'.

Ho'ar Nahak Samane Oan naho'uk.

Ho'ar Nahak Samane Oan nodded.

Sia haa hotu ti'an, ho ina ama ka'er lima ti'an hasa'e ti'an ba tasi wen. To'o tasi wen klaran, Lakuleik no nakees nia nataa ha'i.

When they had finished eating, they shook hands with mother and father, raised themselves and their belongings, went to sea. When they were in the middle of the sea, Lakuleik talked (to her) but she did not answer.

Tan nia nataa ha'i, foin Liurai Lakuleik ta'e kokon ba ulun

Because she did not answer, Liurai Lakuleik slapped her on the head

tan ta'e ba ulun, ulun be'o, tuanasu wen kakin.

Because he hit the head, the head shattered, and the sugar palm juice spilled.

Liurai Lakuleik na'ak:

Liurai Lakuleik said:

'Hei! Liurai ne'e, tan sa ita ta'e lerek dei nia bele be'o?'

'Hey! how come this Liurai's head can shatter when we just hit it?'

Hotu nia nola ran belo

Then he took the spilled 'blood' and licked it

hotu nia na'ak:

then he said:

'Hei! Liurai ne'e ran kmidar

'Hey! This Liurai's blood is sweet

tan nia, ha'u, oras ne'e, ha'u la bele kola tenik Liurai ne'e ha'u kola tenik, ha'u mate'.

because of that, now I can not marry this Liurai again. If I marry, I'll die'.

Tan nia, ami (Umanen) no (Lakulo) Lakuleik ne'e, luli malu.

Because of this story, the people of Umanen are prohibited to marry the (Lakulo) Lakuleik.

'Ami hola ha'i malu

'We don't marry each other

331

tan ibu sala	because our mouths wronged each other
tan Ho'a Nahak Samane Oan butar ti'an nia nodi ai oi butar'.	because Ho'ar Nahak Samane Oan deceived him, deceived using a statue'.
Lakuleik na'in ftla ti'an, Ho'ar Nahak Samane.	When the noble of Lakuleik had returned,
Oan sa'e ba niakan tur fatin la hos iha rai ne'e	Ho'ar Nahak Samane Oan ascended to her dwelling place not in this land.
Nia tur iha rai ida naran Tanebesi, Besi na'in	She lived in a place called Tanebesi, master of iron
Nia potor ema hutun rai ktomok halo kdahur iha rai Basadebu	She got the populace to have a celebration at Basadebu
ta'e tala, he'uk, tulu, futu manu	they played gongs, did women's dances (using drums), and fought cocks
futu manu nia, ema rai rai rona hotu	people everywhere heard about the cockfighting
tan Liurai Lakuleik mos mai no.	so, Liurai Lakuleik came too.
Mai nikar futu manu nia iha rai Basadebu ne'e	He came back to engage in cockfighting in this land of Basadebu
tan rai Basadebu ne'e; ita kbasa-basak nia ha'ak kbasa debu e kadadak, tula besi e tula lia ba	we named Basadebu, because in this land we slap a muddy pool as a sign of solemn promise
lia futu kmetis e, lia rai kmetis	words of promise, words of oath
jadi, hotu hotu futu lia kesi lia, iha rai Basdebu Kadadak.	So everybody make a promise, make a vow in the land of Basedebu Kadadak
Dadi Lakuleik na'in mai, nodi manu niakan naran Falahok Laro Lakan	So, the noble of Lakuleik came, bringing his cock called Falahok Loro Lakan
Ho'ar Nahak Samane Oan niakan naran Knase Wesei Wahali	Ho'ar Nahak Samane Oan's was called *knase* fish of Wesei Wehali
sia na'in rua hasoru nikar malu, iha kdahur no klibar iha rai Basadebu	the two of them met each other again at the festivity at Basadebu
sia futu hikar manu iha nia	they engage in cockfighting again
Lakuleik na'in nodi osan mean osan mutin	the noble of Lakuleik brought gold and silver
Ho'ar Nahak Samane ne'e taru nola nalo mos	Ho'ar Nahak Samane gambled and took all of it

nia menan	she won
dadaun Lakuleik osan mos.	eventually Lakuleik's money was gone.
Ho'ar Nahak Samane katak ba Lakuleik na'ak: 'Belu, ita na'in rua taru rai bele ka lale?'	Ho'ar Nahak Samane said to Lakuleik: 'Friend, can we wage our land, or not?'
Lakuleik na'ak: 'Bele'.	Lakuleik said: 'All right'.
Sia taru rai	They went out and gambled their land
Ho'ar Nahak Samane Oan taru niakan rai, Lakuleik taru niakan rai.	Ho'ar Nahak Samane Oan gambled her land; Lakuleik gambled his land.
Lakuleik na'in niakan rai iha rai ulun, Ho'ar Nahak Samane Oan niakan rai iha rai husar rai binan.	Lakuleik's land was the head land; Ho'ar Nahak Samane Oan's land was the navel land, the umbilical cord land.
Hotu, sia na'in rua binoor	Then the two of them competed
Ho'ar Nahak Samane Oan nodi niakan tara knuan ba sana iha Fatumea	Ho'ar Nahak Samane Oan took the shield of the blade (used in cockfighting) to Fatumea
nia sana ba ai ida naran Ai Sorun Tolu: hun hali, sorin ba abiku, sorin katimun	she hung it on a tree called Tree of Three Forks: the trunk was a banyan (*hali*), one side *abiku*, the other side was *katimun*
nodi tara knuan ba sana iha nia, nia nabusik manu iha rai Besinai	she brought the blade to hang and released her cock at Besinai
nia nameti ti'an tara iha nia, nodi tara knuan ba sana, mai nikar foin nodi manu ba nasori Lakuleik na'in atu futu.	having secured the shield there, she brought the blade back to face the noble of Lakuleik in cockfighting.
Na'ak: 'Belu, ita hakotu, kalu ha'u manan o, rai okan ha'u kola ba ha'u;	(She) said: 'Friend, let us conclude our bet. If I beat you, your land will be mine
o manaan ha'u, rai ha'ukan o mola ba o'.	if you defeat me, my land will be yours'.
Lakuleik na'ak, 'Bele'.	Lakuleik said, 'All right'.
Sia rua futu	The two of them fought cocks
Ho'ar Nahak Samane Oan manan	Ho'ar Nahak Samane Oan won

manu Knase Wesei Wehali manaan manu. Falahok Laro Lakan

cock called *knase* fish of Wesei Wehali defeated Falahok Loro Lakan.

Sia na'in rua ka'er liman.

The two of them shook hands.

Lakuleik na'in mos hotu. Nia na'ak: 'Belu, oras ne'e, ha'u mos hotu ti'an

The noble of Lakuleik was finished. He said, 'Friend, now I am finished

rai faro lakan mos okan ti'an

the land of the sun's flame is yours

rai husar binan mos rai okan

the navel umbilical cord land is also yours

ha'u ba hikar rai loro lakan mos rai okan

if I go back to the land of the sun's flame, it is yours also

ha'u tur iha rai ne'e mos rai okan

if I stay in this land, it is your land too

di'ak liu, ha'u tur kafatin ba ne'e'.

what if I stay here'.

Ho'ar Nahak Samane Oan na'ak: 'Belu, tebes

Ho'ar Nahak Samane Oan said, 'Friend, it is true

di'ak liu o tur ba ne'e

it would be better if you stay here

o ba rai loro lakan, nia rai ha'uk

if you go to the land of the sun's flame, it is my land

iha ne'e mos rau ha'uk

here too is my land

di'ak liu o tur ba ne'e'.

it is better if you stay here'.

Dadi, Liurai Lakuleik ne'e, hatama ba iha

So, this Liurai of Lakuleik was inserted into

Wehali na'in, fo ba dakar bua kau Wehali, takan kau Wehali

Wehali and was in charge of looking after the soft areca nut of Wehali, the young betel leaves of Wehali.

Dadi nia no Leki no Mauk sia, dakar bua kau Wehali, takan kau Wehali.

So he accompanied Leki and Mauk in looking after the soft areca nut of Wehali, the young betel leaves of Wehali.

Bibliography

Agerbeek, J.R.

1916   Memorie van overgave van onderafdeeling Beloe. Atamboea,
        29 November 1916 (unpublished).

Almagor, U.

1989   Dual organization reconsidered. In David Maybury-Lewis and
        Uri Almagor (eds), *The attraction of opposites: thought and society
        in the dualistic mode*, pp. 19–32. Ann Arbor: The University of
        Michigan Press.

Anonymous

1932   *Militaire Memorie van Timor*, Juni 1932 (unpublished).

1958   Minute of an *adat* court case, 9–13 May 1958 (unpublished).

        Monografi Kabupaten Belu.

Anrooij, Francien van

1979   *Between people and statistics: essays on modern Indonesian history
        presented to P. Crentzberg*. The Hague: M. Nijhoff.

Ataupah, H.

1990   Ekologi dan Jati Diri Sosial Suku Bangsa Meto di Timor Barat.
        Dissertation UI, Jakarta.

Barnes, R.H.

1974   *Kedang: a study of the collective thought of an eastern Indonesian people*.
        Oxford: Clarendon Press.

1977   Mata in Indonesia. *Oceania* XLVII(4):300–317.

1987   Avarice and inquiry of the Solor fort. *Bijdragen tot de Taal-, Land-en
        Volkenkunde* 143:208–236.

Bere Tallo, A.A

1957   Pandangan Umum Wilayah Belu. Typescript.

Bijlmer, H.J.T.

1929 *Outlines of the anthropology of the Timor-Archipelago.* Weltevreden:
G. Kolff & Co.

Bobbio, N.

1979 Gramsci and the conception of civil society. In C. Mouffe (ed.),
Gramsci and Marxist theory. London: Routledge & Kegan Paul.

Bocock, R.

1986 *Hegemony.* England: Ellis Horwood.

Bohannan, P.

1965 Introduction. In Lewis H. Morgan (ed.), *Houses and house-life of the
American aborigines,* pp. v–xxi. Chicago: University of Chicago Press.

Bork-Feltkamp, A.J. von

1951 *A contribution to the anthropology of Timor and Roti after data
collected by Dr W.L.*

Meyer. Amsterdam: Uitgave Koninklijk Instituut voor de Tropen.

Bourdier, Jean-Paul and Nezar Alsayyad (eds)

1989 *Dwellings, settlements, and tradition: cross-cultural perspectives.*
Lanham: University Press of America.

Boxer, C.R.

1947 *The Topasses of Timor.* Amsterdam: Indisch Instituut. Series:
Koninklijke Vereeniging Indisch Instituut. Mededeeling no. 73.

1948 *Fidalgos in the Far East 1550–1770.* The Hague: Martinus Nijhoff.

1949 Notes and comments. *The Far Eastern Quarterly* 9:63–65.

Brandewie, E. and S. Asten

1976 Northern Belunese (Tetum) marriage and kinship: a study of
symbols. *Philippine Quarterly of Culture and Society* 4:19–30.

Bria, J.S.

1985 *Pantun Bahasa Tetun Timor.* Kupang: Yayasan Oemata Moris.

Bruijnis, J.K.

1919 Zuid Beloe. *Tijdschrift van het Koninklijk Nederlandsch
Aardrijkskundig Genootschap (TKNAG)* 36(2):178–198.

Capell, A.

1943–45 Peoples and languages of Timor. *Oceania* xiv(1):191–219; 311–337;
xv:19–48.

Castro, A. de

1867   *As Possessoes Portuguezas na Oceania*. Lisboa: Imprensa Nacional.

Catedra, M.

1991   Through the door: a view of space from an anthropological perspective. In

D.M. Mark and A.U. Frank (eds), *Cognitive and linguistic aspects of geographic space*, pp. 53–56. Dordrecht: Kluwer Academic Publishers.

Childs, S.M.

1976   The study of myth as a political document. *Asian Folklore Studies* xxxv(2):29–42.

Clamagirand, B.

1980   The social organization of the Ema of Timor. In J.J. Fox (ed.), *The flow of life: essays on eastern Indonesia*. Cambridge: Harvard University Press.

Clarence-Smith, W.G.

1992   Planters and small holders in Portuguese Timor in the nineteenth and twentieth centuries. *Indonesia Circle* 57:15–30.

Clement, P.

1982   The spatial organization of the Lao house. In K.G. Izikowitz and P. Sorensen (eds), *The house in east and southeast Asia: anthropological and architectural aspects*. Scandinavian Institute of Asian Studies Monograph, No. 30. London and Malmo: Curzon Press.

Cortesao, A.

1967   *The Suma oriental of Tomé Pires and the book of Francisco Rodrigues*. 2 vols. Nendeln: Krans Reprint.

Cunningham, C.E.

1959   An ethnographic survey of the island of Timor in eastern Indonesia. B. Litt. thesis. Exeter College, Oxford.

1962   People of the dry land: a study of the social organisation of an Indonesian people. PhD thesis. The University of Oxford.

1964   Order in the Atoni house. *Bijdragen tot de Taal-, Land-en Volkenkunde* 120:34–69. Reprinted in Rodney Needham (ed.), *Right and left: essays on dual symbolic classification*, pp. 204–238. Chicago: The University of Chicago Press (1973).

1971   Types of social structure in eastern Indonesia. F.A.E. van Wouden. *American Anthropologist* 73:843–845.

Das Dores, R.

1907   Diccionario Teto-Portugues, Lisboa.

Diffie, B.W. and G.D. Winius (eds)

1977   *Foundations of the Portuguese empire, 1415–1580*. Volume I. Minneapolis: University of Minnesota Press.

Douglas, M.

1973   Symbolic orders in the use of domestic space. Reprint 179:1–9.

Downs, R.E.

1983   Head-hunting in Indonesia. In P.E. de Josselin de Jong (ed.), *Structural anthropology in the Netherlands: a reader*, pp. 117–149. Dordrecht: Foris Publication.

Duarte, Jurge

1964   Barlaque, *Secara* 2:92–119.

Durkheim, E. and M. Mauss

1963   *Primitive classification*. Translated from the French by Rodney Needham (ed.). London: Cohen & West.

Ellen, R.F.

1978   *Nuaulu settlement and ecology: an approach to the environment of an eastern Indonesian community*. Verhandelingen van het Koninklijk Instituut voor Taal-, Land-en Volkenkunde 83. The Hague: M. Nijhoff.

1986   Microcosm, macrocosm and the Nuaulu house: concerning the Reductionist fallacy as applied to metaphorical levels. *Bjidragen tot de Taal-, Land-en Volkenkunde* 142(1):2–30.

Ellen, R.F. and D. Reason (eds)

1979   *Classifications in their social context*. London: Academic Press.

Errington, S.

1987   Incestuous twins and the house societies of insular Southeast Asia. *Cultural Anthropology* 2(4):403–444.

Evans-Pritchard, E.E.

1973   Foreword. In Rodney Needham (ed.), *Right and left: essays on dual symbolic classification*, pp. ix–x. Chicago: University of Chicago Press.

Felgas, H.A.E.

1956   *Timor Portugues*. Lisboa: Agencia Geral Do Ultramar.

Fernandes, P.

1937   Abilio Jose – Missao em Timor (1561–1931). Macau.

Ferreira, C.

1987   *Palauan cosmology: dominance in a traditional Micronesian society.*
        Goteburg: Acta Universitatis Gotheburgensis.

Firth, R.

1967   *Tikopia ritual and belief.* Boston: Beacon Press.

Forbes, H.O.

1883   On some of the tribes of the island of Timor. *Journal of the Royal
        Anthropological Institute* 13:402–430.

Forth, G.

1981   *Rindi: an ethnographic study of a traditional domain in eastern Sumba.*
        Verhandeilingen van het Koninklijk Instituut voor Taal-, Land-en
        Volkenkunde 93. The Hague: M. Nijhoff.

1991   *Space and place in Eastern Indonesia.* Centre of South-East Asian
        Studies Occasional Paper No. 16. Kent: University of Kent at
        Canterbury, Centre of South-East Asian Studies.

Fox, J.J.

1973   On bad death and the left hand: a study of Rotinese symbolic
        inversions. In Rodney Needham (ed.), *Right and left: essays on dual
        symbolic classification*, pp. 342–368. Chicago: University of Chicago
        Press.

1977   *Harvest of the palm: ecological change in Eastern Indonesia.*
        Cambridge: Harvard University Press.

1982   The great Lord rests at the centre: the paradox of powerlessness in
        European–Timor relations. *Canberra Anthropology* 5:22–32.

1988a   Introduction. In J.J. Fox (ed.), *To speak in pairs*, pp. 1–28.
        Cambridge: Cambridge University Press.

1988b   Origin, descent and precedence in the study of Austronesian
        societies. Public Lecture in connection with De Wisselleerstoel
        Indonesische Studien, given on 17 March 1988. Rijksuniversiteit te
        Leiden, The Netherlands.

1988c   Foreword. In E.D. Lewis (ed.), *People of the source: the social and
        ceremonial order of Tana Wai Brama on Flores.* Dordrecht: Foris
        Publications.

1989a   Category and complement: binary ideologies and the organization
        of dualism in Eastern Indonesia. In David Maybury-Lewis and Uri
        Almagor (eds), *The attraction of opposites: thought and society in the
        dualistic mode*, pp. 33–56. Ann Arbor: University of Michigan Press.

1989b   F.A.E. van Wouden (1908–1987), A tribute. *Bijdragen tot de Taal-, Land-en Volkenkunde* 145:425–429.

1990   Arguments in a theory of precedence: sisters since the trunk of heaven, brothers since the rim of the earth: progenitor lines of origin in some societies of Eastern Indonesia. Paper prepared for the Conference on Hierarchy, Ancestry and Alliance, 25–30 January. Canberra: The Australian National University, Research School of Pacific Studies.

1994   Installing the 'outsider' inside: an exploration of an Austronesian cultural theme and its social significance. Paper prepared for the First International Symposium on Austronesian Studies, Universitas Udayana, Bali, 14–16 August.

1995   Sunan Kalijaga and the rise of Mataram: a reading of the Babad Tanah Jawi as a genealogical narrative (typescript).

Fox, J.J. (ed.)

1980   *The flow of life: essays on Eastern Indonesia.* Cambridge: Harvard University Press.

1988   *To speak in pairs: essays on the ritual languages of Eastern Indonesia.* Cambridge: Cambridge University Press.

1993a   *Inside Austronesian houses: perspectives on domestic designs for living.* Canberra: The Australian National University, Research School of Pacific Studies.

1993b   Comparative perspectives on Austronesian houses: an introductory essay. In J.J. Fox (ed.), *Inside Austronesian houses: perspectives on domestic designs far living,* pp. 1–29. Canberra: The Australian National University, Research School of Pacific Studies.

1993c   Memories of ridge-poles and cross-beams: the categorical foundations of a Rotinese cultural design. In J.J. Fox (ed.), *Inside Austronesian houses: perspectives on domestic designs far living,* pp. 140–174. Canberra: The Australian National University, Research School of Pacific Studies.

Fox, J.J. and S.A. Wurm

1981   Lesser Sunda Islands and Timor. In S.A. Wurm and S. Hattori (eds), *Language atlas: Pacific area.* No. 40. Canberra: The Australian Academy of the Humanities.

Francillon, G.

1967   Some matriarchic aspects of the social structure of the southern Tetun of middle Timor. PhD thesis. The Australian National University.

1974   Sociological interpretation of differences in musical styles of the southern Tetun (Timor). In M. Taib Osman (ed.), *Traditional drama and music*, pp. 345–349. Kuala Lumpur: Dewan Bahasa dan Pustaka, Kementrian Pelajaran Malaysia.

1980   Incursions upon Wehali: a modern history of an ancient empire. In J.J. Fox (ed.), *The flow of life: essays on Eastern Indonesia*, pp. 248–265. Cambridge: Harvard University Press.

1989   Un Profitable exchange de freres chez les Tetun du Sud, Timor Central. *L'homme* 29:26–43.

Friedman, J. and M.J. Rowlands (eds)

1977   The evolution of social systems. Proceedings of a meeting of the Research Seminar in Archaeology and related subjects held at the Institute of Archaeology, London University. London: Duckworth.

Gennep, A. van

1960   *The rite of passage*. London: Routledge & Kegan Paul.

Gewertz, D. (ed.)

1988   Myths of matriarchy reconsidered. *Oceania Monograph* 33. Sydney: University of Sydney.

Graham, P.

1985   Issues in social structure in Eastern Indonesia. MA thesis. University of Oxford.

1991   To follow the blood: the path of life in a domain of eastern Flores, Indonesia. PhD thesis. The Australian National University.

1994   Alliance against hierachry: affinal distinctions and sovereign rights in Eastern Flores, Indonesia. In Margaret Jolly and Mark S. Mosko (eds), *Transformation of hierarchy: structure, history and horizon in the Austronesian world*, pp. 339–362. Chur/Reading: Harwood Academic [History and Anthropology].

Gramsci, A.

1971   *Selection from the prison notebooks*. Ed. and tr. by Q. Hoare and G. Nowell Smith. London: Lawrence and Wishart.

Granet, M.

1973   Right and left in Central China. In Rodney Needham (ed.), *Right and left: essays on dual symbolic classification*, pp. 43–58. Chicago: University of Chicago Press.

Grijsen, H.J.

1904   *Mededeelingen Omtrent Beloe of Midden-Timor*. 's-Gravenhage: M. Nijhoff.

Grimes, B.D.

1993   The pursuit of prosperity and blessing: social life and symbolic action on Buru Island, Eastern Indonesia. PhD thesis. The Australian National University.

Grimes, C.E. and K. Maryott

1991   Named speech registers in Austronesian languages. In Tom Dutton and Darrell Tryon (eds), *Language contact and change in the Austronesian world*. Berlin: Mouton de Gruyter.

Groeneveldt, W.P.

1960   *Historical notes in Indonesia and Malaya — compiled from Chinese sources*. Djakarta: C.V. Bhratara.

Haan, H.C. de

1947   Memorie van overgave betreffende de onderafdeling Beloe. Atamboea, 22 October 1947 (unpublished).

Hertz, R.

1973   The pre-eminence of the right hand: a study in religious polarity. In Rodney Needham (ed.), *Right and left: essays on dual symbolic classification*, pp. 3–31. Chicago: The University of Chicago Press.

Hicks, D.

1971   Eastern Timorese society. PhD thesis. University of London.

1972   Timor-Roti. In G.N. Appell (and others), *Ethnic groups of insular South-east Asia*, 1:97–98. New Haven: Human Relations Area Files Press.

1973   Tetum narratives: an indigenous taxonomy. *Ethnos* 38:93–100.

1978   Mata in Tetum. *Oceania* 48:299–300.

1981   A two-section system with matrilineal descent among the Tetum of eastern Indonesia. *Sociologus* 37(2):175–180.

1984   A maternal religion: the role of women in Tetum myth and ritual. Monograph Series on Southeast Asia. Special Report No. 22. Dekalb: Northern Illinois University, Center for Southeast Asian Studies.

1987a   Space, mobility, time, and symbol in Tetum religion. In R.S. Kipp and S. Rodgers (eds), *Indonesian religions in transition*, pp. 35–47. Tuscon: University of Arizona Press.

1987b   Tetum descent. *Anthropos* 82:47–61.

1988   Literary masks and metaphysical truths: intimations from Timor. *American Anthropologist* 90(4):807–817.

1990   *Kinship and religion in eastern Indonesia.* Goteborg: University
            of Goteborg.

Hoare, R. and G.N. Smith (eds)

1971   *Selections from the prison notebooks of Antonio Gramsci.* London:
            Lawrence & Wishart.

Hook, R.H. (ed.)

1979   *Fantasy and symbol: studies in anthropological interpretation.* London:
            Academic Press.

Hoskins, J.A.

1987   Entering the bitter house: spirit worship and conversion in West
            Sumba. In R.S. Kipp and S. Rodgers (eds), *Indonesian religions in
            transition,* pp. 136–160. Tuscon: University of Arizona Press.

1988a   Etiquette in Kodi spirit communication: the lips told to pronounce,
            the mouths told to speak. In J.J. Fox (ed.), *To speak in pairs,* pp. 29–63.
            Cambridge: Cambridge University Press.

1988b   Matriarchy and diarchy: Indonesian variations on the domestication
            of the savage woman. In D. Gewertz (ed.), *Myths of matriarchy
            reconsidered,* pp. 34–56. Oceania Monograph 33. Sydney: University
            of Sydney.

Josselin de Jong, J.P.B. de

1983   The Malay archipelago as a field of ethnological study. In P.E. de
            Josselin de Jong (ed.), *Structural anthropology in the Netherlands:
            a reader.* Dordrecht: Foris Publications.

Josselin de Jong, P.E. de (ed.)

1982   W.H. Rassers and his critics: an introduction to the second edition
            of his collected essays. In WH. Rassers (ed.), *Panji, the culture hero:
            a structural study of religion in Java.* The Hague: M. Nijhoff.

1983   *Structural anthropology in the Netherlands.* Dordrecht: Foris
            Publications.

Kana, N.L.

1978   Dunia Orang Sawu: Satu Lukisan Analitis tentang Azas-azas
            Penataan dalam Kebudayaan Orang Mahara di Sawu, Nusa Tenggara
            Timur. Doctoral dissertation, Universitas Indonesia.

1980   The order and significance of the Savunese house. In J.J. Fox (ed.),
            The flow of life: essays on Eastern Indonesia, pp. 221–230. Cambridge:
            Harvard University Press.

Keesing, R.M.

1981   *Cultural anthropology and contemporary perspective*. New York: Holt, Rinehart & Winston.

1992   *Custom and confrontation; the Kwaio struggle far cultural autonomy*. Chicago: University of Chicago Press.

Keesing, R.M. and J. Fifi I

1969   Kwaio word tabooing in its cultural context. *The Journal of the Polynesian Society* 78(2):154–177.

Ketaren, P. et al.

1991   Identifikasi wilayah miskin clan upaya penanggulangannya di propinsi Nusa Tenggara Timur. Kupang: Pusat Penelitian Social Ekonomi Pertanian, Departemen Pertanian. (unpublished).

King, M.J.E.

1965   Fishing rites at Be-Malai, Portuguese Timor. *Records of The South Australian Museum* 15:109–117.

Kipp, R.S. and S. Rodgers (eds)

1987   *Indonesian religions in transition*. Tucson: University of Arizona Press.

Klerck, E.S. de

1938   *History of the Netherlands East Indies*, vol. II. Rotterdam: W.L. & J. Brusse.

Klinken, C.L. van

1994   Consonant clusters in Tetun. Paper presented at the 7th International Conference on Austronesia Linguistics, Leiden.

1999   *A grammar of the Fehan dialect of Tetun, an Austronesian language of West Timor*. Canberra: Pacific Linguistics.

Kluckhohn, C.

1979   Myths and rituals: a general theory. In W.A. Lessa and E.Z. Vogt (eds), *Reader in comparative religion: an anthropological approach*, fourth edition.

Koentjaraningrat, R.M.

1958   Beberapa Metode Antropologi dalam Penjelidikan 2 Masjarakat clan Kebudajaan di Indonesia: Sebuah Ichtisar. Dissertation, Djakarta: P.T. Penerbitan Universitas.

Kuipers, J.C.

1990   *Power in performance: the creation of textual authority in Wryewa ritual speech*. Philadelphia: University of Pennsylvania Press.

Lammers, H.J.

1948   *De Physische Anthropologie van de Bevolking van Oost-Dawan (Noord-Midden-Timor)*. Nijmegen.

Laan, P.

1969   Missiewerk op Timor. Translated into Indonesian as Karya Missi di Timor (1860–1914) by H. Embuiru. Typescript (1993).

Lapian, A.B. and P. Abdurachman

1980   Sejaran Timor Timur. *Berita Antropologi* XI 36:9–36.

Leitao, H.

1948   *Os Portugueses em Solor e Timor de 1515 A 1702*. Lisboa: Tip. da Liga dos Combatentesde Grante Guerra.

Lessa, WA. and E.Z. Vogt (eds)

1979   *Reader in comparative religion: an anthropological approach*, fourth edition. New York: Harper & Row Publishers.

Leur, J.C. van

1955   *Indonesian trade and sociery: essays in Asian social and economic history*. Translated by J.J. Holmes and A. van Made. The Hague: W. van Boeve.

Lévi-Strauss, C.

1963   *Structural anthropology*. Translated by C. Jacobson and B.G. Schoepf. Middlesex: Penguin Books.

Lewis, E.D.

1982   Tana Wai Brama: a study of the social organization of an eastern Florense domain. PhD thesis. The Australian National University.

1988   *People of the source: the social and ceremonial order of Tana Wai Brama on Flores*. Dordrecht: Foris Publications.

1989   Idioms of kinship in the cosmological thought of the Ata Tana' Ai. *Mankind* (19):170–180.

Locher, G.W.

1968   Preface. In F.A.E. van Wouden (ed.), *Types of social structure in eastern Indonesia*, pp. v–vi. The Hague: M. Nijhoff.

Manehat, P.

1990   Bahan Bahan yang Disiapkan oleh Suami Istri sebelum Bersalin. In P. Manehat and G. Neonbasu (eds), *Agenda Budqya Pulau Timor* (1). Kupang: cv Budaya.

Manehat, P. and G. Neonbasu (eds)

1990   *Agenda Budqya Pulau Timor* (1). Kupang: cv Budaya.

Mark, D.M. and A.U. Frank (eds)

1991   *Cognitive and linguistic aspects of geographic space*. Dordrecht: Kluwer Academic Publishers.

Masinambouw, E.K.M.

1980   Bahasa bahasa di Timor Timur. *Berita Antropologi* Thn XI, 36:68–81.

Mathijsen, A.

1906   *Tettum-HollandscheWoordenlijst*. Batavia: Albrecht & Co.

1967   Testamento Tuan: nian dale hodi lia Tetun. Ende: Percetakan Arnoldus.

Mauss, M.

1970   *The gift: forms and functions of exchange in archaic societies*. Translated by I. Cunnison. London: Cohen & West.

Maybury-Lewis, D.

1989   The guest for harmony. In David Maybury-Lewis and Uri Almagor (eds), *The attraction of opposites: thought and society in the dualistic mode*, pp. 1–17. Ann Arbor: University of Michigan Press.

Maybury-Lewis, D. and U. Almagor (eds)

1989   *The attraction of opposites: thought and society in the dualistic mode*. Ann Arbor: University of Michigan Press.

McWilliam, A.R.

1989   Narrating the gate and the path: place and precedence in South West Timor. PhD thesis. The Australian National University.

1994   Case studies in complementary opposition as process: childbirth, headhunting and circumcision in West Timor. *Oceania* 65:59–74.

2002   *Paths of Origin, Gates of Life: A study of place and precedence in southwest Timor*. Leiden: KITLV Press.

Meilink-Roelofsz, M.A.P.

1962   *Asian trade and European influence in the Indonesianarchipelago between 1500 and about 1630*. 's-Gravenhage: M. Nijhoff.

Metzner, J.K.

1977   *Man and enviromnent in eastern Timor: a geological analysis of the Baucau-Viqueque area as a possible basis for regional planning*. Development Studies Centre Monograph No. 8. Canberra: The Australian National University.

Middlekoop, P.

1960   Curse-retribution-enmity. Dissertation Utrecht. Amsterdam.

1963   *Head-hunting in Timor and its historical implications.* Oceania
        Linguistic Monographs No. 8. Sydney: University of Sydney.

Molnar, A.K.

1994   The grandchildren of the Ga'e ancestors: the Hoga Sara of Ngada in
        West-central Flores. PhD thesis. The Australian National University.

Morais, A.F. de

1944   *Solor e Timor.* Lisboa: Divisao de Publicacoes e Biblioteca, Agencia
        Geral das Colonias.

Morgan, L.H.

1965   *Houses and house-life of the American aborigines.* Chicago: University
        of Chicago Press.

Morris, C.

1984   *Tetun-English dictionary.* Pacific Linguistics Series C No. 83. Canberra:
        The Australian National University, Research School of Pacific Studies.

Mouffe, C. (ed.)

1979   *Gramsci and Marxist theory.* London: Routledge & Kegan Paul.

Mubyarto

1990   *Masyarakat Desa Timor Timur: Laporan Penelitian Socio-
        anthropologis.* Jogyakarta: Pusat Penelitian Pembangunan
        Kependudukan dan Kawasan.

1991   *East Timor, the impact of integration: an Indonesian socio-anthropological
        study.* Northcote, Victoria: Indonesia Resources and Information
        Program.

Muskens, M.P.M.

1973   *Sejarah Gereja Katolik Indonesia*, vol. I. Jakarta: Bagian
        Dokumentasi-Penerangan, Kantor Wali Gereja Indonesia.

Needham, R.

1973   Introduction. In Rodney Needham (ed.), *Right and left: essays on
        dual symbolic classification*, pp. xi–xxxix. Chicago: The University of
        Chicago Press.

1976   Skulls and causality. *Man* II:71–88.

1979   *Symbolic classification.* Santa Monica, California: Goodyear
        Publication.

Needham, R. (ed.)

1973   *Right and left: essays on dual symbolic classification.* Chicago: University of Chicago Press.

Newitt, M. (ed.)

1986   *The first Portuguese colonial empire.* Exeter: University of Exeter.

Nowell, C.E. (ed.)

1962   *Magellan's voyage around the world: three contemporary accounts.* Evanston: Northwestern University Press.

Oliveira, Luna de

1949   *Timor na Historia de Portugal.* Lisboa: Agencia Geral Das Colonias.

Ormeling, F.J.

1957   *The Timor problem: a geographcial interpretation of an underdeveloped island.* Groningen; Djakarta: J.B. Wolters.

Overakker, N.Th.

1926   Nota van toelichting betreffende her landschap Beloe (unpublished).

1927   Memorie van overgave van de onderafdeeling Beloe. Atamboea, 28 December 1927 (unpublished).

Parera, A.D.M.

1970   Maromak Oan dan Keradjaan Pulau Timor (Maromak Oan and domains in Timor). Kupang, April 1970 (unpublished). A speech delivered in front of the assembly of People's Representative Council (DPR).

1971   Sedjarah Politik Pemerintahan Asli (Sedjarah Radja Radja) di Timor (Political history of indigenous government in Timor). Kupang (unpublished).

Phillips, N. and K. Anwar (eds)

1981   *Papers in Indonesian languages and literatures.* London: University of London, School of Oriental and African Studies.

Rassers, W.H.

1982   *Panji, the culture hero: a structural study of religion in Java.* The Hague: M. Nijhoff.

Reid, A.

1981   A great seventeenth century Indonesian family: Matoaya and Pattingalloang of Makassar. *Masyarakat Indonesia* viii(l):1–28.

Rogge

1865   Memorie van overgave van de onderafdeeling Beloe. Atapoepoe, 13 Juli 1865 (unpublished).

Rooney, D.F.

1993   *Betel chewing traditions in South-East Asia.* Oxford: Oxford University Press.

Sá, A.B. de

1961   *Textos em Teto da Literatura Oral Timorense*, vol. 1. Lisbon: Junta de Investigacoes do Ultramar.

Sather, C.

1993   Posts, hearths and thresholds: the Iban longhouse as a ritual structure. In J.J. Fox (ed.), *Inside Austronesian houses: perspectives on domestic designs for living*, pp. 64–115. Canberra: The Australian National University, Research School of Pacific Studies.

Schulte Nordholt, H.G.

1971   *The political system of the Atoni of Timor.* Verhandelingen van het Koninklijk Instituut voor Taal-, Land-en Volkenkunde 60. The Hague: M. Nijhoff.

1980   The symbolic classification of the Atoni of Timor. In J.J. Fox (ed.), *The flow of life: essays on Eastern Indonesia*, pp. 231–247. Cambridge: Harvard University Press.

Sejarah Gereja Katolik Indonesia. Jilid I.

1974   Ende. Flores: Percetakan Arnoldus.

Seran, H.J.

1992   Hakserak: the rites of sacrificial offerings among the Belunese on Timor island, province of East Nusa Tenggara, Indonesia. Paper delivered in Conference of Sacrifice in Eastern Indonesia, University of Oslo, 19–23 June 1992.

Silva, Manuel da

1900   *Nocoes da Grammatica Galoli.* Macao.

Silva, S.M.

1889   *Diccionario de Portuguez – Tetum.* Macao.

Sowash, W.B.

1947   Colonial rivalries in Timor. *The Far Eastern Quarterly* 7:227–235.

Staatsblad van Nederlandsch-Indie

1859   No. 101. 's-Gravenhage: Staatsdrukkerij-en Uitgeverijbedrijf, pp. 1–3.

1909   No. 214. 's-Gravenhage: Staatsdrukkerij-en Uitgeverijbedrijf, pp. 1–10.

Stanley, H.E. and A. Pigafetta

1963   *The first voyage round the world by Magellan*. Translated from the accounts of Pigafetta, and other contemporary writers; accompanied by original documents with notes and introduction by Lord Stanley of Alderley. New York: Burt Franklin.

Stapel, F.W. (ed.)

1955   *Corpus Diplomaticum Neerlando-Indicum*, pt 6 (*1753–1799*). 's-Gravenhage: M. Nijhoff.

Suparlan, P.

1980   Orang Timor Timur. *Berita Antropologi* XI, 36:37–54.

Swetnam, J.J.

1988   Women and markets: a problem in the assessment of sexual inequity. *Ethnology* xxvii:327–338.

Tambiah, S.J.

1969   Animals are good to think and good to prohibit. *Ethnology* 8(4):423–459.

Teixeira, M.

1961   *The Portuguese mission in Malacca and Singapore 1511–1958*. Vol. I–II. Lisboa: Agencia Geral Do Ultramar.

Thomaz, L.F.F.R.

1981   The formation of Tetun-Praca, vehicular language of East Timor. In N. Phillips and K. Anwar (eds), *Papers on Indonesian languages and literatures*. London: University of London, School of Oriental and African Studies.

Traube, E.G.

1980   Mambai rituals of black and white. In J.J. Fox (ed.), *The flow of life: essays on Eastern Indonesia*, pp. 290–314. Cambridge: Harvard University Press.

1986   *Cosmology and social life: ritual exchange among the Mambai of East Timor*. Chicago: University of Chicago Press.

1989   Obligation to the source: complementarity and hierarchy in an Eastern Indonesian society. In David Maybury-Lewis and Uri Almagor (eds), *The attraction of opposites: thought and society in the dualistic mode*, pp. 321–344. Ann Arbor: University of Michigan Press.

Troeboes

1987   *Struktur bahasa Tetun*. Jakarta: Depdikbud.

Villiers, J.

1986   The Estado da India in Southeast Asia. In M. Newitt (ed.), *The first Portuguese colonial empire*. Exeter Studies in History No. 11. University of Exeter.

Vischer, M.

1992   Children of the black patola stone: origin structures in a domain on Palu'e Island (Eastern Indonesia). PhD thesis. The Australian National University.

Visser, B.J.J.

1934   *Onder de Compagnie: Geschiedenis der Katholieke Missie van Nederlands Indie 1606–1800*. Batavia: Uitgave G. Kolff.

Vroklage, B.

1948   Bride price or dowry. *Anthropos* 47:133–146.

1953   *Ethnographie der Belu in Zentral-Timor*. Volume 1. Leiden: E.J. Brill.

Wade-Marshall, D. and P. Loveday (eds)

1988   *Contemporary issues in development*. Darwin: The Australian National University, North Australian Research Unit.

Waterson, R.

1991   *The living house: an anthropology of architecture in South-East Asia*. Singapore: Oxford University Press.

Wortelboer, W. von

1955   Zur Sprache und Kultur der Belu (Timor). *Anthropos* 50:155–200.

Wouden, F.A.E. van

1968   *Types of social structure in Eastern Indonesia*. Translated by R. Needham. The Hague: M. Nijhoff.

Wurm, S.A. (ed.)

1976   *Austronesian languages: Neu; Guinea area languages and language study*. Vol. 2, Pacific Linguistics Series C No. 39. Canberra : The Australian National University, Research School of Pacific Studies.

Wurm, S.A. and J. Wilson

1975   *English finderlist of reconstructions in Austronesian languages*. Pacific Linguistics. Series C No. 33. Canberra: The Australian National University, Research School of Pacific Studies.

A Note on Language

The Catholic missionary Father von Wilco Wortelboer, SVD, includes a brief but useful sketch (1955: 176–177) of Tetun. Morris (1984) describes aspects of Tetun in the introduction to his dictionary. As far as I know, there is only one published monograph on Tetun language (Troeboes et al. 1987). As mentioned by the authors (1987: 11), the analysis presented in their work was based mainly on data collected in north Tetun, a dialect known locally as *Tetun foho* (hill Tetun). Dr Catharina van Klinken, in the context of her doctoral program at The Australian National University, has conducted linguistic research on south Tetun, known locally as *Tetun fehan* (plains Tetun). It is hoped that these studies will encourage further descriptive and comparative study in this region. Here, I highlight some aspects of Tetun relevant to following the vernacular data incorporated in this present work. A few dialectal differences are summarised below as background for understanding some of the different cultural interpretations noted in the ethnographic literature.

Troeboes et al. claim that Tetun has five vowels and 19 consonant phonemes (1987: 14). The vowels are / *a, e, i, o, u*/. They note the vowel sequences / *io*/, / *ie*/ and / *ou*/ appear to be unheard of in Tetun. In my transcription, I treat long vowels as significant features of the Tetun language, written as a double vowel. In this system the syllable takes the word stress. For example: *hare* 'rice' but *haree* 'see'; *kbon* 'smoke' but *hakboo* 'evaporate'.

The 19 consonant phonemes referred to by Troeboes et al. (1987: 22–28) include six consonant clusters: / *kb, kd, kl, km, kn, kr*/. Van Klinken (1994) has argued that these should be considered sequences of two consonants rather than complex phonemes, so these six are not considered here as part of the Tetun phonemic inventory. The remaining consonants (after van Klinken 1994) are as follows: / *t k b d f s h l r m n w*/. In this study the glottal is represented orthographically by an apostrophe as in *na'an* ('meat').

Tetun words consist of one to four syllables. One- and four-syllable words are relatively rare. Most lexical roots are two syllables.

Beside rhythmic and intonational differences between 'hill' and 'plains' Tetun (commonly noted by native speakers), both von Wilco Wortelboer and Troeboes noted some additional dialectal differences, adapted and summarised below.

From my personal familiarity with both the north and south dialects, I have no difficulty understanding von Wilco Wortelboer's notes (1955: 176–177) as summarised in points 1 to 3 in the table. Using Testamento Tuan, the Old Testament in Tetun language, as translated by Father A. Mathijsen (1967) and reference texts in this study as a basis for comparison, one would note the same differences. However, Troeboes et al. (1987: 10–11) note four additional differences (4 to 7), which may reflect the bias of being familiar with only one dialect and thus not encountering additional forms in another. Therefore, additional dialect research, including statistical work, is clearly needed, but such research is beyond the scope of the present study.

alin	term of address for yB, yZ; umbilical cord
alin fatik	small pot to store the umbilical cord
alin-maun	patrilineal descent groups (yB, eB); (a man, his brothers, father, father's brothers, grandfather and great-grandfather, with their children and his unmarried sisters belong to this group)
ama	'father'; addressing ego's father and ego's FB; FB; one's father or father's brother (kin term); polite address used to greet all male seniors, just like the usage of the term *bapak* in Indonesian
ama etuk	term for FZH
ama na'i	polite address used to greet all male seniors (like the usage of the term *bapak* in Indonesian)
ama uiu	father who is the eldest in his family
amaf naek	great fathers
amak	top end of pillar
aman besik	true father (FB)
aman maun alin	persons whose fathers are brothers
aman ten	biological father (children refer to their)

astanara	the high anvil
asu ikun	dog-tail millet
asu ikun knasak rua	two dog-tailed millet
asu ikun knasak tolu	three dog-tailed millet
aten	liver
aten ema	human heart
atmas Ema	Ema people
atoin amaf	'great fathers'
au kenu	drink container
ba'af	court area
baban	to attach
baboen	auction (Indonesian *lelang*); collecting others' property
babuar	cognate with *kabuar* meaning 'round', 'circular' (varieties of melon that grow wild in the jungle)
badaen	knowledgeable person (male category)
badi lulik mutin	knife with silver holder
badu	ban
badut	candle made from candle-nut
baen	old age
baliki	hexagonal baskets
balu feto foun	half new woman
balu mane foun	half new man
bandu	prohibit, forbid (Tetun of East Timor), (Portuguese loan word, *bando*)
banin	affines of the first ascending generation; ditches; paired with the word *satan* meaning 'to close' or 'enclosure'
batane	campsite
batar ai naruk	long stalk maize (sorghum)
batar au kale'an	third crop of maize
batar fulin hitu	seven cobs of maize
batar knaar	sorghum blossoms
batar knau	second crop of maize
batar malae	foreign maize

batar mana'i	maize of homage
batar na'an tasi	maize that derives from a fish (in ritual language)
batar tasi	maize of the sea (sorghum)
batar ut	maize powder
bei	someone at the second genealogical level
bei ala	an accountable grandparent
bei dok	a shaman (term of address)
bei feto	female PP; MM and FM
bei kla'ok	PPPP
bei klutis	iguana grandparents
bei mane	male PP; FF and MF
bei sia	they, the PP (ancestors are addressed by general term)
bei ubu	PPP
bei ut	PPPPP; one who is already worn out
beik	foolish
bein	ancestors
bein dalan	ancestor's path
bein hot	respected sun (ethnic groups: Lamaknen)
bein oan	child
bibliku	drums
bin	term of address for eZ
bin alin ten	sisters who were born from the same womb (express their consanguinity as *feto malun*)
biti	sleeping mat
biti ulun	the head mat
blai	kitchen
bouw	blocks (of land) (Dutch)
bua klaras	dried, sliced nuts
buka sotir no ua	to search for luck and money
bulak	lunatic
butuk baa rai Wehali	bundled in Wehali
cafres	heathen (Portuguese term)
Casa da Misericordia	House of Mercy (church)

chita	calico (Portuguese loan word, Indonesian term *kain cita*)
daerah hak bapak dibatasi oleh laut perempuan sedangkan daerah hak ibu dibatasi oleh laut lelaki	'the patriarchal region is demarcated by the female sea, while the matriarchal region is demarcated by the male sea' (Indonesian)
dato	minor male rulers
datos Belos	noble
de'an	to swear; be angry
de'an lia	citing of a story, poetry or a myth
desa	villages
desa gaya baru	new style villages
diberkati	be 'blessed' (Indonesian)
dikin	tips; pointed end of the crown of the tree
dikur ro'a ida	a full arm span of buffalo horn
dusun	an administrative designation for hamlet (Indonesian)
ema fehan	plains people
ema foho	mountain people
ema ita	insider (our people)
ema kukun	the dark people
ema laran	centre people
ema leten	the man above
ema matak	outsider (raw people)
ema molin	periphery people
ema roman	the bright people
ema taruik	hills people
eno	gates (Dawan)
eno-lalan	gate-path (Dawan)
etu	food
fafudi	chatting
fafulu	knife made from a specific bamboo
fahi lolon	the body of the pig

fai tora lulik	pounding the sacred millet
falus	widower
fatu isin	flesh of the stone
fehuk	root crops that are inter-planted in conjunction with other staples
fehuk malae	sweet potatoes
feitor	factor (every *feitoria* is headed by)
feitoria	factory (Portuguese)
feitorias	trading posts (Portuguese)
fen	wife
ferik	an old woman; a respected mother
Ferik Ha'in Raiklaran	the First Woman on Earth; the Only Woman on Earth
ferik makaer lulik	the old woman who guards the forbidden objects
ferik-katuas	guardians of the house
feto foun	new woman
feto hitus	the seven princesses
feto ra	female servant; young women
feto talain	female cross-cousin
feton oan	brother's sister's children; ZC
fetosawa	patrilineal descent groups (the wife-taking house); sister
fetosawa-uma mane	type of marriage
fia kalo raek	small type of yam
fila	to go home (asking permission)
fo ba; fo baa	to give away
foho	mountain
foho rai	python
fokit li'is	to pull garlic
fore	cultivated beans
fore rai	peanut
fore tali	kidney bean
fore Wehali	mung beans
fortalezas	fortified strongholds (Portuguese)
fuan	fruit; kidneys

fuik	betel leaves
fuik badu labis	the verandah prohibition betel leaves; presentation of betel-nut (to 'ban' the platform from other men)
fuik bua oda matan	the front door betel-nut
fuik horak	prohibition betel leaves
fuik sasoka rua	bundles of betel leaves
fukun	clan head; heads of hamlets
fukun bot	the chief *fukun*
fukun ferik	female *fukun*
fukun ferik hat katuas hat	assembly of the four old women and the four old men
fukun katuas	male *fukun*; head of the clan
funan	'flowers' (girls) of the house; 'flowers' (literal meaning); 'daughters' (metaphorical meaning)
ha'i matan	the hearth
ha'i mate	the fire will die (Wehali discourse, without female children the kinship group will perish)
haa batar nurak	to eat baby maize
habasak we	throwing of water
hafu'ut	(noun) derives from the root verb *fu'ut* meaning 'to twist' (verb); man's shoulder cloth (noun) (Indonesian, *selendang*)
hafu'ut kabala	division of property; to divide the man's belongings into two halves (one half for the wife's kin and the other half for the husband's kin)
hahaan biti ulun	feed the mat
hahaan rai	to feed the earth
hahaan troman	feed the centre of the garden
hahaek	woman's laugh (laughter, a typical woman's laugh)
hahida bua baa oan feto no oan mane sia kabinan, sia kakaluk	to lay betel-nut in the female child's basket and in the male child's pouch
hahori	alive (derives from moris)
hahoris	give life (function of a midwife) to a pregnant woman; *halo* = to make, *moris* = life (Tetun word)

hahoris batar	to make the maize alive
hahoris oan	to make the child alive
hahulu	to acknowledge someone as a leader
hahuuk kmurak ida	a valuable blow pipe
hakane rai	to wound the earth (in the context of house construction)
hakneter haktaek oa feto	to respect and to praise the woman (bridewealth)
hakneter malu, hakmoe malu	mutually respect and honour each other
haknotak	to sleep; to stretch one's body
hakraik	lower oneself down from the raised verandah to the lower ground
hakse hawaka	greetings (to salute // to counsel)
haksee	call up event
haksera mama	betel-nut offerings to the ancestors
hakur biti kluni	to cross mat and pillow (incest, south Tetun)
hakur kotan	crossing the beam (phrase to denote misconduct)
halanu	intoxicate
halirin	cooled (seeds to be); to make cool
halirin rai	cooling down the earth
halo mama	betel-nut (woman to prepare) offering
hamaan	to walk as to enlighten one self
Haman mai ti'an?	Are you making light your steps here?
hamana	to make hot
hamanas (hikar) ukun badu	to re-heat the *adat* law
hamanas kakaluk hatuda	to make heated the war pouch
hamenon	reminder
hamiis	make the fruits edible; to make fresh or to cool
hana'in	to acknowledge someone as a ruler, homage
hananu	to sing (verb)
hanasa	man's laugh
hanawa	to rest

hane matan	pyramidal-shaped palm leaf basket
hanematan loro	gifts for 'ruler', which are offered in baskets
hanematan lulik	family's forbidden pyramid-shaped plaited basket
hanimak	'to play around' and 'to stop for a while' (period of courtship); young man who courts a young woman
hare ekero	type of rice
hare kake	cockatoo rice
hare leten	dry upland rice
hasa'e	ascended
hasa'e horak	lift the prohibition
hasa'e kakaluk hatuda	to ascend the war pouch
hasai naran	reborn in the community (birth rite)
hasan	junction (top end of the female pillar is cut in a V-shape)
hasee hawaka	to greet, to counsel (form of ritual speech)
hasori dalan	cleaning the path (of the coming baby)
hatalin	linking
hatama baa Wehali	taken into Wehali
hatama batar fulin hitu	delivering the seven cobs of maize (Wehali, annual agricultural ritual)
hatama batar mana'i	delivering the maize of homage; the bringing in of maize of homage (Wehali agricultural ritual)
hatama batar ulun	delivering the head maize
hatama liurai lamak	sending the food of Liurai
hatodan	to sit as to make oneself heavy
hatuda Manufahi	battle of Manufahi
hatuka ha'i	heating the body after giving birth; new mother has to 'roast' her back over the fire (ritual in childbirth)
He'e. Fafudi hein tian?	Yes. Are you waiting while chatting?
heli	to conceal, to cover up
hisik fini	'give life' to the seeds; 'sprinkling the seeds' (agricultural rite)
Ho'ar Makbalin, Balin Liurai	Ho'ar the Liurai adviser

hoku fatik	muddy place where buffaloes lie down in the heat of the day
hola malu	*hola* = to take; *malu* = to reciprocate
hola tehen	to take the roof off the house
hudi baen	the oldest fruit in a banana bunch
hudi ulun	'banana head' (returning of the; repayment in the form of another woman returned to them; returned woman)
hun	'source', 'trunk', 'origin'; 'trunk of tree'; source, trunk, origin (botanical terms)
hun (Tetun)	origin, derivation (Indonesian, *asal usul*)
hun beli meti	to tie the trunks together
husar binan	umbilical cord
husar oan (binan)	types of marriage
hutun no renu	commoners
hutun rai hat	the four tribes
ikun	tail; last born; youngest
ikus	last
imperator	supreme ruler
ina	mother; addressing ego's mother and ego's MZ
ina fetok	girl's MBW; man's MBW; MBW, FZ (potentially one's parents-in-law); WM, HM
ina no ama	mother and father
ina no ama Wehali	the mother and father of Wehali (immediate protectors)
inak	hole that joined *amak* with the ridge pole
inan	mother
inan bi alin	'mother elder-younger sister' (bond); 'mothers are sisters'; mother, elder and younger sisters' group
inan ten	biological mother (children refer to their)
isin	content; inwards
iskoma	type of bean
izin mengadakan keramaian	permission for conducting festivity
ka'a	WZ (term of address for)

ka'an	'placenta' or the 'umbilical cord'
ka'an and/ or *alin*	younger brother/sister; umbilical cord
ka'an or *ka'a*	'*ka'an, ka'a n*, sister-in-law, a name that indicates that the sisters-in-law are regarded as sisters, cf. *rian*; *ka'an mane* or *ka'an feto* — male or female placenta, also known as *mane malun* or *feto malun*
kabala	wrapping cloth used by men (Indonesian: *sarong* or a loin cloth (Indonesian: *sabuk*)
kabas lahan	a length of cotton thread
kabir inan	betel-nut container
kabonan	mother's sarong
kabupaten	regency
kacang-kacangan	beans
kadain	a kind of net sack
kadain talin	'chain marriage' (continuation of marriage links)
kahak rae	female attic (above the hearth)
kakaluk	pouch
kakaluk lulik	sacred pouches
kakuluk	grand post (Tetun Indonesian-speakers tiang aguni)
kakuluk feto	female pillar
kakuluk ha'i	fire post
kakuluk lor	front half of the house, which is conceptually oriented toward the sea-side; front male pillar
kakuluk mane	male pillar
kakuluk mesak	the only pillar
kakuluk rae	pillar oriented toward the high place in the mountain
kalalak	shouting men
kaledik	small pointed stick erected in front of the mat
kanoea (*knua*) or *kotta* (*kota*)	village
karas	chest; front half of the house (chest)
kasu	to dismiss or to acquit

kasu ai knaer	to untie the string (rite held for particular purposes: namely, to arrange the movements of the foetus, to secure a healthier pregnancy and to ensure a successful delivery)
kasu horak	dismiss the prohibition (in marriage)
kasu kakaluk hatuda	to descend the war pouch
katan	to sew or to close
katuas	male guardian; old man (of the house)
katuas makaer lulik	'the old man who guards the forbidden objects'
kaiven	marriage (probably originated from the Proto-Polynesian *qa(a)wana* meaning 'marriage')
kawen tama	'entering marriage' (Wehali; translation from Indonesian *kawin masuk*)
kawin syah	legal marriage (Tetun Indonesian-speakers translation of)
kawin tak syah	illegal marriage (Tetun Indonesian-speakers translation of)
khabukar	passing of a rope of command (from the centre to the periphery); rope with knots
kbelak	golden chest plate (worn by men)
kbonan	upper part of her sarong
ke'e rai	to dig the ground (to cut the earth)
kecamatan	administrative districts
kelek ksoik ida	one chicken drumstick
kelen kwana	right leg
kena'ian	amalgam of four domains
Keser	king (colonial title)
ki'i	WeZ (term of address for)
kidun	back half of the house called (buttock); buttock
kilat	traditional guns
kilat inan liurai	the cannon of Liurai
kilat rahun	gunpowder
kla'ok	(root word) (= *klala'ok*) is *la'o* meaning 'to walk'; adjective, *klala'ok* means 'behaviour' or 'conduct'
kladik	'border' (limit or border of one's own garden)

klalak	shouting
klaran	interior, inner side, centre; middle
klaut	fruits (literal meaning); 'sons' (metaphorical meaning)
kleik	type of shrub
kleni	wall screen
kleni feto	female mats
kleni mane	male mat
klosan	male servant; young men
klot	narrow
kmaan	light
kmalar	spirits of the ancestors
kmii	candle-nut
kmurak	silver coin
kmusan	betel-quids
knaban	palm leaf basket
knanuk	oral poetry; short poem
knar batar tasi	blossom of the sorghum
knaras	big pot used for water storage
knase	fish (mullet)
knawar	work (north Tetun verb)
knete	a small ladder erected at the front gate of a garden used as access to the garden
knua as	high sheath
knua kraik	low sheath
knua or kota	a conglomeration of six to twenty households
knua(n)	rind or sheath
ko'us	to carry in the arms (polite terms used to describe pregnancies)
koba	square palm-leaf container (categoically female, because it is a woman's betel-nut container)
koha lulik	baskets
kona lia	person engaged in a court case (in colloquial Indonesian: *kena perkara*)
kopiah	*hat* (Indonesian)

korut batar ai naruk	to strip sorghum
kose	to rub
kola	fortress (Portuguese loan word); city (Tetun)
kota or *knua*	a conglomeration of 6 to 20 households
kotan	floor beam
kotan lor	cross-beam (outside)
koto batar etu kukun	harvesting the sorghum
krade malae oan	a small wild duck
ksa'e(s)	rafter supporter posts
ksadan	ritual centre; sacred jungle
ksahat lulik	sacrificial baskets
kso'(e)	fruit shell (scoop)
ktuik	type of shrub
ku'u hare	to harvest (pinch) rice paddy
kuda	to plant
kukun	ancestral spirits, dark
kwa'ik	eldest
la'e tua	'the respected husband' (head of a particul ar lineage within the clan)
la'en	husband; huts
la'o sala dalan	walking the wrong path; walks the wrong path (person who has committed incest)
labis	platform (house symbolism)
labis klaran	middle platform
labis kraik	lower level platform
labis leten	higher level platform
labis na'in	platform masters
laen	garden hut; huts
lahan	a block of land used for cultivation; threads
laho dalan	path of rats
lain	tips of a tree as a whole
lakateu sina oan	a small Chinese dove
Lakuleik beik	the foolish Lakuleik
Lalaan	warmly protected

lalawar	garden inspector (North Tetun call this official *makle'at*)
lale'an	sky
lali'an	cooking stones
lamak	plates made of banana leaves; also a polite word to denote food as nourishment for nobles
lamak kukun	dark food
lanan	inside, interior
Larantuqueiros	Black Portuguese (whom the Dutch called)
le'un	a small section of narrow inhabited plain; sub-clans of hamlet
Le'un Has	four clans
le'un Loro Monu	the sunset *le'un*
le'un moris fatik	the birth place *le'un*
lelang	to rob
lena	sesame
leno aten	reading the liver
leo	hamlet; clan; origin unit
leo ain tasi	hamlets at the foot of the sea
leo feto	female hamlets
leo foho hun	hamlets on the trunk of the hill
leo klaran	middle clan or hamlet
leo laran	inner hamlets (female)
leo Liurai	hamlet of the Liurai
leo mane	male hamlets
leo molin	outer hamlets (male)
leo tasi tehen	hamlets at the edge of the sea
leon	the shade of a tree
leon feto	female shade
leon mane	male shade
let	gap; time
lia	Language; also means word, phrase or news; can also denote some serious business
lia fuan	a definite conversation, a message or a mandate
lia hatuda	battle stories

lia hun	the trunk language
lia na'in	the source of all languages; elevated language/speech; the noble language
lia riik	'honour language'; greetings (the stand up language)
lia sasaluk	'disguised language'; language that wraps up or enfolds (translated into Indonesian as *bahasa bungkus*)
lia tasi	language of the sea
lia tebes	a true tale; true story
lia tuan	an old, highly valued story
likurai	dancing with snake-like movements
likusaen	python
Liurai	derives from *liu* = to surpass and *rai* = land; above the earth; executive ruler (in Wehali system of government)
Liurai feto	female Liurai; a man who is ritually regarded as female *Liurai*
Liurai loro sa'e	ruler of Wehali's domains toward the sunrise
Liurai mane	male *Liurai*
loka laran	temporary compartment within the house for adolescent girl as her sleeping space
loloran	rolling waves
lor	horizon; low-lying ground, the tidal regions, seaside; south
loro	sun; male ruler (second rank of nobility in the structure of the Liurai's government); rulers
loro laran	the inside rulers
loro molin	outside or peripheral rulers
loro sa'en	the rising sun
loro toba	the sunset
lulik	forbidden; sacred; holy, taboo, prohibited
Madre de Deus	Mother of God (church)
mainikin	coolness
makaer kmi	holder of candle-nut (midwife)
makdakar	guardians; to look after; protectors
makerek	knowledgeable person (female category)

mako'an	*adat* historian; the one who cuts (*ko'a*) the words
maktane	supporters
maktukun	an inedible fruit (invalid wife)
malae	malay (can be translated as foreign)
Malaka *foun*	new Malaka (the present district of Malaka)
Malaka *tuan*	old Malaka (on the Malay peninsula)
malirin	cool
mama lulik	forbidden betel-nut (offerings); obligatory gifts
manas	heat; hot (*menas* is probably a disguised form of *manas*)
manas hun	the source of heat
mane aa tur ti'an iha uma nabaa	the man is married to a woman in that house (the man sits in that house)
mane foun	new man (status raised in the final stage of the marriage process, bridegroom)
mane lais	rest of the in-married men, who are standing and sitting on the ground (addressed as, quick men, helpers)
mane liman	men's arms
mane lor	the man of the wave
mane maksai uma	men who leave the house (term to refer to wife's brothers)
mane maktama uma	man who enters the house (married-in men); son-in-law
mane sanulu	group of 10 men
mane talain	male cross-cousin
mantarun	money received from cockfight gambling; derives from *manu* (rooster) and *tarun* (to bet). In Tetun it means 'king's property'
manu do'u	a wild pigeon bird (Indonesian *burung dara*)
manu ida	one chicken
manu lamak oan ida	small nourishment of chicken (ritual language)
maran hun	dry land
maran ikus	last to dry
maran uluk	first to dry

marii lia	to erect words, the house that has the authority to decide *adat* matters
ma-roma-k	derives from *roman* or *kroman* meaning 'bright' while *oan* means 'small' and 'child'
maromak oan	'the small bright one, luminous one'
masin	cooked and salty
mata musan	'giving back a seed' (bilateral cross-cousin marriage); 'source seed'; 'the pupil of the eye' (translated into Indonesian as *biji mata,* which means the '(father's) beloved'); ideology and practice of returning a woman to her father's natal house upon the death of her father
mata(n)	eye, any eye-like feature, focus, centre, orifice, spring, origin and source
matak	raw (translation of Christian notion of 'blessing')
matak no let	types of marriage
matak no malirin	raw and cool
matan	notions of primacy
matdok	consists of two words: *mata* = eye; *dok* = far, distant; a shaman is 'one who can see "far" into the future and "far" into current inauspicious happenings'; shaman
matenek	cleverness, tricks, out-smarting
maun	elder brother; term of address for eB
maun alin ten	brothers who were born from the same womb (express their consanguinity as *mane malun*)
maun uma kain	person's MZeS and FBeS
mengakali	out-smart
meo	hero (term used for wife's elder brother)
meo ana	small cats
meo naek	great cat
miis	plain taste; unsalted, tasteless or fresh (in *hamiis*)
molin	outside, periphery (general habitation symbolism); cultivation space; peripheral ('outside' the residential space); space outside a house, village or domain
monas	strength and invulnerability

moris	alive
moris ikus	last born
moris uluk	first born
mota dikin	tips of a river
murak tomak ida	silver coin
muti mo	clean white
na'an knase	fish
na'i	affectionate term used by grandparents for grandchildren
Na'i Lulik	priest, master of the forbidden
naan	sisters refer to their brothers and parallel cousins of the opposite sex
nababan	married-in man and persons in his generation
nahoris oan	to make the baby come alive
nakdobos	crawling like a baby (house idiom, polite way of moving down the levels)
nanaan	brothers; tongue
naran babaur	nickname
naran mata bian	ancestral names
nasai oan	to take the baby out
natar	a rice paddy field (east Tetun)
nato'o oan	to cause the baby to arrive
natoni	type of greeting (Dawan)
ne'e be rai ne'e no nikar ulun	so the land could have rulers
nea ksuik ida	a long boar's tusk
netan	begot (polite terms used to describe pregnancies)
nia nasa'e nikar niakan naan mane nen sia nalo ba ulun	she promoted the 6 brothers to become heads of the regions
nikah adat	*adat* marriage
nu mea	red coconut
nu modo	green coconut
nu'u mane la no fen, feto la no la'en	like a man without wife or a woman without husband

nuu kalabuk	young, unformed coconut
oa la'en	child husband (bridegroom)
oan	sons
oan feto	female child
oan klakar	phrase used for children of an invalid marriage
oan la'en	daughter's husband
oan mane	male child
oda matan	door
oda matan la sa'en	the unclimbed door; door facing the sunrise
oda matan lor	the male door (house symbolism)
oda matan loro sa'en	door of the rising sun
oda matan rae	door facing the sunset
odan	branches of bamboo (can also be translated as ladder)
oe mean	golden staff
omas	container used for boiling water
onderafdeeling	sub-divisions (Dutch)
pendatang	newcomers (Indonesian)
Perarakan Bunda Maria	the procession of Mother Mary (Indonesian)
pohon buah tinta	kind of shrub is known in Indonesian because the liquid of its berries is like the colour of ink
rae	a living space in the mountains, high regions on the mountains; associated with mountain, high (place)
rahaman	recently married couple (husband addressed as)
rahinan	recently married couple (wife addressed as)
rahuk	body hair
rai	earth, island, land, region, domain and dirt
rai bot	the great land
rai feto	land of women
rai hun	trunk land (centre of the universe); the original land
rai husar binan	navel of the earth
rai ikun	tail land
rai klaran	the middle, inside world, earth
rai leten	the above world, heaven

rai lian	language of the earth
rai lidun hat	the four-corner land
rai loro monu	land of the falling sun
rai loro sa'e	'the sunrise land'
rai loro toba	land of the setting sun
rai lulik	sacred land or domain
rai maran	dry land
rai na'in	owners of the land
rai saun	secular land or domain
rai sei we	land still covered with water
rai Timor	the island of Timor
rai ulun	the head land
rai Wehali	the domain of Wehali
ramas abut	to water the root
rate kukun and *fatu taman rik*	dark burial grounds
reinos	domains (Portuguese)
ri(n) lidun hat	four corner posts
riin	post
rin kiak	orphan posts (that support the rafters at the periphery)
rin lidun hat	four corner posts
ro'a	outstretched arms
roman	living human beings, bright
rumah adat	*adat* house
rumah sehat	healthier house (Indonesian)
rumah tidak seha	unhealthy house (Indonesian)
sadan	receive advice
sahit tabako	to pick tobacco leaves
sasadin	trying out period (before marriage)
sasaluk	a shroud obscuring or disguising the conditions of something
sasere	rhythm
sasi'an	a counsellor (noun)

sasolok	gifts
sasolok hohela feto foun	gifts that accompany the new woman
sau nuu	to pick up coconut
saun	secular
sera mama	betel-nut offering
silu batar	to break off maize cobs
Sina mutin Malaka	the white Chinese of Malaka
sistem pemerintahan asli di Belu	a system of government native to Belu (Indonesian)
sorin balu	ribs
surik	liver milt; sword
surik lulik Liurai	swords
surik samara	swords with a long curved shield
swapraja	self-governing domains (Indonesian)
taa hudi	to cut banana
taek	a small step in front of a house that provides access to the verandah
tafatik	palace (derives from two words: *tur* = to sit; *fatik* = place); place to sit (translated into Indonesian as '*istana*')
taha tur	weeding equipment (gifts in terms of money)
tais at	old used sarongs (ugly sarongs)
tais hahoris	birth sarong (black handmade sarong used only for parturition)
tais lima rasan	woven cloth made of local cotton
tak punya adat	someone as without *adat* (serious insult or even a curse) (Indonesian)
tala etu	royal gongs
talain	FZS; marriageable cousin
talain besik	true cross-cousin; true cousins (MBC and FZC)
talain uma kain	classificatory cross-cousins; person's MMBSC and FFZSC
talin	rope, cord or string
taman	to plant (Wehali)

tan lia ne'e, rai ne'e foin halo no ukur	we now have government in our land
tan rai ne'e moris uluk iha ne'e	because the earth was first born here
tanasak	baskets for storing goods (associated with women)
tane	to face, to hold up from underneath, to support
tara horak	to hang up the prohibition; announces an annual 'ban' (*badu*) on harvesting coconuts for a certain period of time
tara kakaluk	to hang up the pouch
tasak	cooked; ripe
tasi	sea
tasi feto	female sea
tasi mane	male sea
tasi sere	the beating of surf on the beach
tatakan	lid
tatane	a woven serving tray (noun)
tate rai halo we	making the canal to drive water
tehen	edge
ten	intestine
tetek	ladder; step
to'os etu kukun	the royal dark garden
tora	fox-tail millet
toro uman	the centre of the garden (north Tetun spell *troman* as *toro uman*)
troman	first spot in the garden that was 'cleared off' (*ta*) from shrubs when the garden was founded; sacrificial pillars in the middle of each garden
tua	palm juice; WyZ (term of address for)
tua botir ida	bottle of palm gin
tua kusi ida	one jar of palm gin
tua na'i	the most respected person; father's sister's husband (also addressed as *tuak*); girl's mother's brother (MB); mother's brothers; term for MB; MB, FZH (potentially one's parents-in-law); woman's mother's brother

tua na'i ama etuk	most respected elder of the house
tua sangkir ida	a cup of palm gin (referring to several bottles of palm gin)
tua(n)	old and respected (Tetun)
tuak	(MB) of his sister's children; 'the respected one'; the most 'respected' figure in the house (term of address for mother's brother); variety of palm tree (*Borassus Sundaica*)
tuan	notions of primacy
tubu	grew
tuda kmusan	sexual intercourse between nobles
tudik	knife
tukek	bamboo container (Dawan)
tunama	compound word of *tunu* (to roast) and *ama* (father)
tunu	roasted
tur	to sit (idiom to denote 'marriage'); reside
tuur fati	a sitting place (palace)
tuur lia	actual court or *adat* meeting (colloquial Indonesian: *duduk perkara*)
ubi-ubian	tuber plants; classified as root crops (in Indonesian)
udan baur	drizzle that sets in together with the appearance of a rainbow
udan fahi	the pig's rain
udan kakait	drizzle
udan lor	rain that sets in from the seaside
udan menas	unexpected rain
udan namate ahu kresan	rain that kills the hot ashes
udan narodan ai tahan	rain to shed leaves
udan tinan	annual rain; west monsoon
udan we toluk	type of rain is said only to last for three days
uem	house (pronounced as *uim* by the Tetun) is a metathesis from *ume*
uhi	native tubers
ukun badu	a rule of prohibition

ukun rai	rule of the earth
ukur	cords or threads that link the edges of a rectangular loom (noun); notions of both rites and ceremony
ulu	first born (adjective)
uluk	before, former or simply first in time (adverb)
uma	residential house
uma Ai As	the high post house
uma Amanas	heat house
uma at ida	an ugly house
uma Ferik	the house of the respectable woman
uma feto	female house; the house where the husband resides
uma fukun	house of clan head
uma hanawa kosar	house to dry one's sweat
uma hun	the origin house; the trunk house
uma inan bin alin	mother elder sister younger sister houses
uma kain	stalk of the house (signifies that the people concerned were not born in the same house but are related collaterally); born from a different womb
uma kakaluk	amulet house (popularly known as 'the medicine house')
uma Katuas	the house of the respectable man
uma kre'is	closest house uma kukun dark house
uma laran	inner house
uma lidun hat	rectangular house; the four corner house
uma lulik	the forbidden house; sacred house
uma maho naran	named house
uma maho naran ha'i	unnamed house
uma maksian maktane	the up-holding, the supporting house
uma malae	foreign house
uma mane	male house; patrilineal descent groups (wife-giving house)
uma metan	sacred black house
uma moris fatik	the birth place house

uma na'in	house masters; owner of the house; the lord of the house (term that refers to a man's wife)
uma Rai Lale'an	the house of Earth-Sky
uma Ro Malae	the foreign ship house
uma sasi'an tatane	supporting house
uma tasi	the sea house
uma tur fatik	the sitting place house
uma tur hanawa kosar	the house to rest one's sweat
usan	navel
ut	powder, residue, waste
Vaiquenos	designates both the people and the language of the Dawan (term used widely in East Timor)
wakil camat	deputy head (Indonesian)
we klot	space inside a house to store water
we knuk	well
we matan Maromak	spring of Maromak
we miis	fresh water

Parallel and Metaphoric Phrases

adomi malu// hatias malu	show love to each other// show affection to each other
akar Insana rohan// maek Insana rohan	edge of the gebang palm of Insana, edge of the tuber of Insana
Ami mai fo hatene ba emi tan oa feto isin manas ulun moras	We come to let you know that your daughter-in-law suffers from fever and headache (to convey condolences to the husband's kin)
asu mata balada oin balada, asu besin, asu kai sa	following the track of a dog
banin Wehali// satan Wehali	the border of Wehali, the enclosure of Wehali
besi Wehali, baki Wehali	the stronghold of Wehali, the fortress of Wehali
dakar bua kau Wehali// takan kau Wehali	looking after the young areca nuts of Wehali, the young betel leaves of Wehali

deku na'in baa nia, dare na'in baa nia	place to knock, place to tap
ema matak no let	the raw and gap people, 'stranger'
ferik ain tasi// katuas ain tasi	'the old women of the leg of the sea// the old men of the leg of the sea'
ferik foho hun, katuas foho hun	'the old women of the trunk of the mountain, the old men of the trunk of the mountain'
ferik hat, katuas hat	the four old men, the four old women (origin group of the four-corner land council)
ferik tasi tehen, katuas tasi tehen	the old women of the edge of the sea, the old men of the edge of the sea
foho hun ain tasi	'the trunk of the mountain and the tips (instead of foot) of the sea
fuik hitu, bua hitu	the seven betel leaves, the seven areca nuts
fuik let// bua let	the empty (literally, 'gap') betel leaves, the empty areca nut
fuik maho naran// bua maho naran	named betel leaves, named areca nuts
fuik tebes, bua tebes	the true betel leaves, the true areca nut
fuik tolu, bua tolu	the three betel leaves, the three areca nuts
haa matak, hemu matak	the raw food, the raw drink
haa tasan, hemu tasan	the cooked food, the cooked drink
hakro'an hakmasin	'to plead and to make oneself salty'; action of praying
halon hakmasin bodik uma kain foun ha'i kain foun	to bow and to salinise for the new house and the new fire
haloon// hakmasin	to make straight// to salinise
hatetu harani	'gifts' and 'offerings'; literally *hatetu* means 'to lay s.t. on the ground' while *harani* means 'to lay s.t. above', 'to perch'
hatodan fatik// habesi fatik	the place to sit, the place to strengthen oneself
hoku fatik// natar fatik	the place to lie down, the place to dwell
iha kukun// kalan	in the dark// in the night (ancestors who are living)
inuk tuan, dalan tuan	the old path, the old track

kabas no lahan	rite or ceremony
klobor na'in// laen na'in	the lord of granaries, the lord of huts
knokar Liurai, inuk Liurai	stables of Liurai, the paths of Liurai
knua Wesei, knua Wehali	the sheath of Wesei, the sheath of Wehali
knuba hun// tetek hun	the trunk of the hip// the trunk of the ladder
koto lamak hatetu, lamak harani	providing food as offering, food as gifts
labis no na'in ti'an	the platform already has its occupant
lamak hatetu, lamak harani	sacrificial meat that consists of roasted bird
liman lais ain kmaan	fast arms, light feet (the helpers)
loro foho leten// loro tauk dikin	sun mountain peak// sun rock edge
mahaa rik// mahemu rik	eat while standing, drink while standing
mahaa toba// mahemu toba	the one who eats reclining, drinks reclining
mahaa tur// mahemu tur	eat while sitting, drink while sitting
makaer lulik bot// makaer manas bot	holder of the great taboo, holder of the mighty heat
makdakar knokar Liurai	guardian of Liurai's stable
makdakar knokar Wehali	the guardians of the stable of Wehali
malaka na'in// amanas na'in	the owner of fire, the owner of heat
manas ha'in// klak ha'in	the only heat, the only burning charcoal
manas hun// lulik hun	the origin of heat and origin of sacredness
manas lulik wa'ik, klak lulik wa'ik	the great sacred heat, the great sacred of burning charcoal
mota la bele suli sa'e	water never flows upstream
nalaka ha'i, hamanas we	to light the fire, boil the water in their house

namon matan// namon tuan	main harbour// old harbour
nanaet tasi kre'is, nanaet foho kre'is	to demarcate mountain, to demarcate sea
nanan (inner)/*mone* (outer)	superior/inferior relations
no'i nafofek onan// no'i naknanik onan	is rowing (toward here)// is swimming (toward here)
oa natar hat// oa lalu'an hat	the children of the four enclosures// the children of the four stables
rai husar// rai binan	the navel land// the umbilical cord land
rai lidun hat, rai sikun hat	the four-corner land, the four-elbow land
rai loro lakan// rai loro len	the land of the flaming sun, the land of the glowing sun
rai manu matan, rai bua klaras	the land as a chicken's eye, the land as a slice of areca nut
riin besi hat// riin kmurak hat	the strong posts, the valuable posts
riin makerek// riin mean	the engraved post, the golden post
sadan uma kain foun, ha'i kain foun	to make a place for the new stalk of the house, the new hearth of the house
sasi'an// tatane	facing (uphold// support, Tetun)
simu kmusan, simu matak no malirin	acquiring betel-chew, acquiring raw and cool
su kanu foun, baki foun	to dig a new ditch, a new canal
tama soi// sai seti	easy to put in, but hard to take out
tanasak talin// kadain talin	links that connect the plaited baskets (Wehali ritual language)
tetek hun// knuba hun	'trunk of the house step// trunk of the garden ladder'
to'os ai fatik// tua ai fatik	the first garden, the first palm tree
tuir dalan tuan// tuir inuk tuan	tracing the old path, the old track
uma metan// uma lulik	the black house// the sacred house

Glossary

abut	root
adat	customary law
adat lalek	having no *adat*
adat sabete saladi	the custom of sitting cross-legged
afaak	lungs
afdeeling	divisions
afuan	spear divination
ahan	beans that grow wild in jungles
ahan alas	forest bean
ai biku	biku tree
ai fehuk	cassava
ai hali	banyan tree
ai kabuka	the searching wood
ai katimun	katimun tree
ai kletek	bridge (mediator)
ai klunus	palm leaves used as torch
ai knanoik or *ai knoik*	'story to be remembered'; a folk tale
ai lala'ok	place to give birth
ai lotuk	slender tree
ai sorun tolu	three branches of tree
ai tahan malirin	'the cool leaves' (branch of leaves)
ai tasi	mangroves
ai toos	the strong wood
ain	foot
akal	cleverness (Indonesian)

akar bone	variety of palm tree (Indonesian: *enau*)
akar lisa	gebang palm (Corypha Utan; Indonesian: *gebang* or *gewani*)
akaria	sago palm
alas lulik	sacred forests
alin	term of address for yB, yZ; umbilical cord
alin fatik	small pot to store the umbilical cord
alin-maun	patrilineal descent groups (yB, eB); (a man, his brothers, father, father's brothers, grandfather and great-grandfather, with their children and his unmarried sisters belong to this group)
ama	'father'; addressing ego's father and ego's FB; FB; one's father or father's brother (kin term); polite address used to greet all male seniors, just like the usage of the term *bapak* in Indonesian
ama etuk	term for FZH
ama na'i	polite address used to greet all male seniors (like the usage of the term *bapak* in Indonesian)
ama ulu	father who is the eldest in his family
amef naek	great fathers
amak	top end of pillar
aman besik	true father (FB)
aman maun alin	persons whose fathers are brothers
aman ten	biological father (children refer to their)
astanara	the high anvil
asu ikun	dog-tail millet
asu ikun knasak rua	two dog-tailed millet
asu ikun knasak tolu	three dog-tailed millet
aten	liver
aten ema	human heart
atmas Ema	Ema people
atoin amaf	'great fathers'
au kenu	drink container
ba'ef	court area
baban	to attach

baboen	auction (Indonesian *lelani*) ; collecting others' property
babuar	cognate with *kabuar* meaning 'round', 'circular' (varieties of melon that grow wild in the jungle)
badaen	knowledgeable person (male category)
badi lulik mutin	knife with silver holder
badu	ban
badut	candle made from candle-nut
baen	old age
baliki	hexagonal baskets
balu feto foun	half new woman
balu mane foun	half new man
bandu	prohibit, forbid (fetun of East Timor), (Portuguese loan word, *bando*)
banin	affines of the first ascending generation; ditches; paired with the word *satan* meaning 'to close' or 'enclosure'
batane	camp site
batar ai naruk	long stalk maize (sorghum)
batar au kale'an	third crop of maize
batar fulin hitu	seven cobs of maize
batar knaar	sorghum blossoms
batar knau	second crop of maize
batar malae	foreign maize
batar mana'i	maize of homage
batar na'an tasi	maize that derives from a fish (in ritual language)
batar tasi	maize of the sea (sorghum)
batar ut	maize powder
bei	someone at the second genealogical level
bei ala	an accountable grandparent
bei dok	a shaman (term of address)
bei feto	female PP; MM and FM
bei kla'ok	PPPP
bei klutis	iguana grandparents
bei mane	male PP; FF and MF

bei sia	they, the PP (ancestors are addressed by general term)
bei ubu	PPP
bei ut	PPPPP; one who is already worn out
beik	foolish
bein	ancestors
bein dalan	ancestor's path
bein hot	respected sun (ethnic groups: Lamaknen)
bein oan	child
bibliku	drums
bin	term of address for eZ
bin alin ten	sisters who were born from the same womb (express their consanguinity as *feto malun*)
biti	sleeping mat
biti ulun	the head mat
blai	kitchen
bouw	blocks (of land) (Dutch)
bua klaras	dried, sliced nuts
buka sotir no ua	to search for luck and money
bulak	lunatic
butuk baa rai Wehali	bundled in Wehali
cafres	heathen (Portuguese term)
Casa da Misericordia	House of Mercy (church)
chita	calico (Portuguese loan word, Indonesian term *kain cita*)
daerah hak bapak dibatasi oleh laut perempuan sedangkan daerah hak ibu dibatasi oleh laut lelaki	'the patriarchal region is demarcated by the female sea, while the matriarchal region is demarcated by the male sea' (Indonesian)
dato	minor male rulers
datos Belos	noble
de'an	to swear; be angry
de'an lia	citing of a story, poetry or a myth
desa	villages

desa gaya baru	new style villages
diberkati	be 'blessed' (Indonesian)
dikin	tips; pointed end of the crown of the tree
dikur ro'a ida	a full arm span of buffalo horn
dusun	an administrative designation for hamlet (Indonesian)
ema fehan	plains people
ema foho	mountain people
ema ita	insider (our people)
ema kukun	the dark people
ema laran	centre people
ema leten	the man above
ema matak	outsider (raw people)
ema molin	periphery people
ema roman	the bright people
ema taruik	hills people
eno	gates (Dawan)
eno-lalan	gate-path (Dawan)
etu	food
fafudi	chatting
fafulu	knife made from a specific bamboo
fahi lolon	the body of the pig
fai fora lulik	pounding the sacred millet
falus	widower
fatu isin	flesh of the stone
fehuk	root crops that are inter-planted in conjunction with other staples
fehuk malae	sweet potatoes
feitor	factor (every *feitoria* is headed by)
feitoria	factory (Portuguese)
feitorias	trading posts (Portuguese)
fen	wife
ferik	an old woman; a respected mother
Ferik Ha'in Raiklaran	the First Woman on Earth; the Only Woman on Earth

ferik makaer lulik	the old woman who guards the forbidden objects
ferik-katuas	guardians of the house
feto foun	new woman
feto hitus	the seven princesses
feto ra	female servant; young women
feto talain	female cross-cousin
feton oan	brother's sister's children; ZC
fetosawa	patrilineal descent groups (the wife-taking house); sister
fetosawa-uma mane	type of marriage
fia kalo raek	small type of yam
fila	to go home (asking permission)
fo ba; fo baa	to give away
foho	mountain
foho rai	python
fokit li'is	to pull garlic
fore	cultivated beans
fore rai	peanut
fore tali	kidney bean
fore Wehali	mung beans
fortalezas	fortified strongholds (Portuguese)
fuan	fruit; kidneys
fuik	betel leaves
fuik badu labis	the verandah prohibition betel leaves; presentation of betel-nut (to 'ban' the platform from other men)
fuik bua oda matan	the front door betel-nut
fuik horak	prohibition betel leaves
fuik sasoka rua	bundles of betel leaves
fukun	clan head; heads of hamlets
fukun bot	the chief *fukun*
fukun ferik	female *fukun*
fukun ferik hat katuas hat	assembly of the four old women and the four old men
fukun katuas	male *fukun*; head of the clan

funan	'flowers' (girls) of the house; 'flowers' (literal meaning); 'daughters' (metaphorical meaning)
ha'i matan	the hearth
ha'i mate	the fire will die (Wehali discourse, without female children the kinship group will perish)
haa batar nurak	to eat baby maize
habasak we	throwing of water
haju'ut (noun)	derives from the root verb *fu'ut* meaning 'to twist' (verb); man's shoulder cloth (noun) (Indonesian, *selendang*)
hafu'ut kabala	division of property; to divide the man's belongings into two halves (one half for the wife's kin and the other half for the husband's kin)
hahaan biti ulun	feed the mat
hahaan rai	to feed the earth
hahaan troman	feed the centre of the garden
hahaek	woman's laugh (laughter, a typical woman's laugh)
hahida bua baa oan feto no oan mane sia kabinan, sia kakaluk	to lay betel-nut in the female child's basket and in the male child's pouch
hahori	alive (derives from *moris*)
hahoris	give life (function of a midwife) to a pregnant woman; *halo* = to make, *moris* = life (Tetun word)
hahoris batar	to make the maize alive
hahoris oan	to make the child alive
hahulu	to acknowledge someone as a leader
hahuuk kmurak ida	a valuable blow pipe
hakane rai	to wound the earth (in the context of house construction)
hakneter haktaek oa feto	to respect and to praise the woman (bridewealth)
hakneter malu, hakmoe malu	mutually respect and honour each other
haknotak	to sleep; to stretch one's body
hakraik	lower oneself down from the raised verandah to the lower ground
hakse hawak	a greetings (to salute//to counsel)

haksee	call up event
haksera mama	betel-nut offerings to the ancestors
hakur biti kluni	to cross mat and pillow (incest, south Tetun)
hakur kotan	crossing the beam (phrase to denote misconduct)
halanu	intoxicate
halirin	cooled (seeds to be); to make cool
halirin rai	cooling down the earth
halo mama	betel-nut (woman to prepare) offering
hamaan	to walk as to enlighten one self
Haman mai ti'an?	Are you making light your steps here?
hamana	to make hot
hamanas (hikar) ukun badu	to re-heat the *adat* law
hamanas kakaluk hatuda	to make heated the war pouch
hamenon	reminder
hamiis	make the fruits edible; to make fresh or to cool
hana'in	to acknowledge someone as a ruler, homage
hananu	to sing (verb)
hanasa	man's laugh
hanawa	to rest
hane matan	pyramidal-shaped palm leaf basket
hanematan	pyramid-shaped plaited basket
hanematan loro	gifts for 'ruler', which are offered in baskets
hanematan lulik	family's forbidden pyramidshaped plaited basket
hanimak	'to play around' and 'to stop for a while' (period of courtship); young man who courts a young woman
hare ekero	type of rice
hare kake	cockatoo rice
hare leten	dry upland rice
hasa'e	ascended
hasa'e horak	lift the prohibition
hasa'e kakaluk hatuda	to ascend the war pouch

hasai naran	reborn in the community (birth rite)
hasan	junction (top end of the female pillar is cut in a V-shape)
hasee hawaka	to greet, to counsel (form of ritual speech)
hasori dalan	cleaning the path (of the coming baby)
hatalin	linking
hatama baa Wehali	taken into Wehali
hatama batar fulin hitu	delivering the seven cobs of maize (Wehali, annual agricultural ritual)
hatama batar mana'i	delivering the maize of homage; the bringing in of maize of homage (Wehali agricultural ritual)
hatama batar ulun	delivering the head maize
hatama liurai lamak	sending the food of Liurai
hatodan	to sit as to make oneself heavy
hatuda Manufahi	battle of Manufahi
hatuka ha'i	heating the body after giving birth; new mother has to 'roast' her back over the fire (ritual in childbirth)
He'e. Fajudi hein tian?	Yes. Are you waiting while chatting?
heli	to conceal, to cover up
hisik fini	'give life' to the seeds; 'sprinkling the seeds' (agricultural rite)
Ho'ar Makbalin, Balin Liurai	Ho'ar the Liurai adviser
hoku fatik	muddy place where buffaloes lie down in the heat of the day
hola malu	*hola* = to take; *malu* = to reciprocate
hola tehen	to take the roof off the house
hudi baen	the oldest fruit in a banana bunch
hudi ulun	'banana head' (returning of the; repayment in the form of another woman returned to them; returned woman)
hun	'source', 'trunk' 'origin'; 'trunk of tree'; source, trunk, origin (botanical terms)
hun	(Tetun) origin, derivation (Indonesian, *asal usul*)
hun beli meti	to tie the trunks together

husar binan	umbilical cord
husar oan (*binan*)	types of marriage
hutun no renu	commoners
hutun rai hat	the four tribes
ikun	tail; last born; youngest
ikus	last
imperator	supreme ruler
ina	mother; addressing ego's mother and ego's MZ
ina fetok	girl's MBW; man's MBW; MBW, FZ (potentially one's parents-in-law); WM, HM
ina no ama	mother and father
ina no ama Wehali	the mother and father of Wehali (immediate protectors)
inak	hole that joined *amak* with the ridge pole
inan	mother
inan bi alin	'mother elder-younger sister' (bond); 'mothers are sisters'; mother, elder and younger sisters' group
inan ten	biological mother (children refer to their)
isin	content; inwards
iskoma	type of bean
izin mengadakan keramaian	permission for conducting festivity
ka'a	WZ (term of address for)
ka'an	'placenta' or the 'umbilical cord'
ka'an and/or *alin*	younger brother/sister; umbilical cord
ka'an or *ka'a*	'*ka'an, ka'an*, sister-in-law, a name that indicates that the sisters-in-law are regarded as sisters, cf. *rian*; *ka'an mane* or *ka'an feto*—male or female placenta, also known as *mane malun* or *feto malun*'
kabala	wrapping cloth used by men (Indonesian: *sarong*) or a loin cloth (Indonesian: *sabuk*)
kabas lahan	a length of cotton thread
kabir inan	betel-nut container
kabonan	mother's sarong
kabupaten	regency

kacang-kacangan	beans
kadain	a kind of net sack
kadain talin	'chain marriage' (continuation of marriage links)
kahak rae	female attic (above the hearth)
kakaluk	pouch
kakaluk lulik	sacred pouches
kakuluk	grand post (Tetun Indonesian-speakers *tiang agung*)
kakuluk feto	female pillar
kakuluk ha'i	fire post
kakuluk lor	front half of the house, which is conceptually oriented toward the seaside; front male pillar
kakuluk mane	male pillar
kakuluk mesak	the only pillar
kakuluk rae	pillar oriented toward the high place in the mountain
kalalak	shouting men
kaledik	small pointed stick erected in front of the mat
kanoea (*knua*) or *kotta* (*kota*)	village
karas	chest; front half of the house (chest)
kasu	to dismiss or to acquit
kasu ai knaer	to untie the string (rite held for particular purposes: namely, to arrange the movements of the foetus, to secure a healthier pregnancy and to ensure a successful delivery)
kasu horak	dismiss the prohibition (in marriage)
kasu kakaluk hatuda	to descend the war pouch
katan	to sew or to close
katuas	male guardian; old man (of the house)
katuas makaer lulik	'the old man who guards the forbidden objects'
kawen	marriage (probably originated from the Proto-Polynesian *qa(a)wana* meaning 'marriage')
kawen tama	'entering marriage' (Wehali; translation from Indonesian *kawin masuk*)
kawin syah	legal marriage (Tetun Indonesian-speakers translation of)

kawin tak syah	illegal marriage (Tetun Indonesian-speakers translation of)
kbabukar	passing of a rope of command (from the centre to the periphery); rope with knots
kbelak	golden chest plate (worn by men)
kbonan	upper part of her sarong
ke'e rai	to dig the ground (to cut the earth)
kecamatan	administrative districts
kelek ksoik ida	one chicken drumstick
kelen kwana	right leg
kena'ian	amalgam of four domains
Keser	king (colonial title)
ki'i	WeZ (term of address for)
kidun	back half of the house called (buttock); buttock
kilat	traditional guns
kilat inan liurai	the cannon of Liurai
kilat rahun	gunpowder
kla'ok (root word)	(= *klala'ok*) is *la'o* mea ning 'to walk'; adjective, *klala'ok* means 'behaviour' or 'conduct'
kladik	'border' (limit or border of one's own garden)
klalak	shouting
klaran	interior, inner side, centre; middle
klaut	fruits (literal meaning); 'sons' (metaphorical meaning)
kleik	type of shrub
kleni	wall screen
kleni feto	female mats
kleni mane	male mat
klosan	male servant; young men
klot	narrow
kmaan	light
kmalar	spirits of the ancestors
kmii	candle-nut
kmurak	silver coin
kmusan	betel-quids

knaban	palm leaf basket
knanuk	oral poetry; short poem
knar batar tasi	blossom of the sorghum
knaras	big pot used for water storage
knase	fish (mullet)
knaivar	work (north Tetun verb)
knete	a small ladder erected at the front gate of a garden used as access to the garden
knua	as high sheath
knua kraik	low sheath
knua or *kota*	a conglomeration of six to twenty households
knua(n)	rind or sheath
ko'us	to carry in the arms (polite terms used to describe pregnancies)
koba	square palm-leaf container (categorically female, because it is a woman's betel-nut container)
koba lulik	baskets
kona lia	person engaged in a court case (in colloquial Indonesian: *kena perkara*)
kopiah	hat (Indonesian)
korut batar ai naruk	to strip sorghum
kose	to rub
kota	fortress (Portuguese loan word); city (Tetun)
kota or *knua*	a conglomeration of six to twenty households
kotan	floor beam
kotan	for cross-beam (outside)
koto batar etu kukun	harvesting the sorghum
krade malae oan	a small wild duck
ksa'e(s)	rafter supporter posts
ksadan	ritual centre; sacred jungle
ksahat lulik	sacrificial baskets
kso'(e)	fruit shell (scoop)
ktuik	type of shrub
ku'u hare	to harvest (pinch) rice paddy

kuda	to plant
kukun	ancestral spirits, dark
kwa'ik	eldest
la'e tua	'the respected husband' (head of a particular lineage within the clan)
la'en	husband; huts
la'o sala dalan	walking the wrong path; walks the wrong path (person who has committed incest)
labis	platform (house symbolism)
labis klaran	middle platform
labis kraik	lower level platform
labis leten	higher level platform
labis na'in	platform masters
laen	garden hut; huts
lahan	a block of land used for cultivation; threads
laho dalan	path of rats
lain	tips of a tree as a whole
lakateu sina oan	a small Chinese dove
Lakuleik beik	the foolish Lakuleik
Lalaan	warmly protected
lalawar	garden in spector (North Tetun call this official *makle'at*)
lale'an	sky
lali'an	cooking stones
lamak	plates made of banana leaves; also a polite word to denote food as nourishment for nobles
lamak kukun	dark food
lanan	inside, interior
Larantuqueiros	Black Portuguese (whom the Dutch called)
le'un	a small section of narrow inhabited plain; sub-clans of hamlet
Le'un Has	four clans
le'un Loro Monu	the sunset *le'un*
le'un moris fatik	the birth place
le'un lelang	to rob

lena	sesame
leno aten	reading the liver
leo	hamlet; clan; origin unit
leo ain tasi	hamlets at the foot of the sea
leo feta	female hamlets
leo foho hun	hamlets on the trunk of the hill
leo klaran	middle clan or hamlet
leo laran	inner hamlets (female)
leo Liurai	hamlet of the Liurai
leo mane	male hamlets
leo molin	outer hamlets (male)
leo tasi tehen	hamlets at the edge of the sea
leon	the shade of a tree
leon feta	female shade
leon mane	male shade
let	gap; time
lia	language; also means word, phrase or news; can also denote some serious business
lia fuan	a definite conversation, a message or a mandate
lia hatuda	battle stories
lia hun	the trunk language
lia na'in	the source of all languages; elevated language/speech; the noble language
lia riik	'honour language'; greetings (the stand up language)
lia sasaluk	'disguised language'; language that wraps up or enfolds (translated into Indonesian as *bahasa bungkus*)
lia tasi	language of the sea
lia tebes	a true tale; true story
lia tuan	an old, highly valued story
likurai	dancing with snake-like movements
likusaen	python
Liurai	derives from *Liu* = to surpass and *rai* = land; above the earth; executive ruler (in Wehali system of government)

Liurai feto	female Liurai; a man who is ritually regarded as female *Liurai*
Liurai loro sa'e	ruler of Wehali's domains toward the sunrise
Liurai mane	male Liurai
loka laran	temporary compartment within the house for adolescent girl as her sleeping space
loloran	rolling waves
lor	horizon; low-lying ground, the tidal regions, seaside; south
loro	sun; male ruler (second rank of nobility in the structure of the Liurai's government); rulers
loro laran	the inside rulers
loro molin	outside or peripheral rulers
loro sa'en	the rising sun
loro toba	the sunset
lulik	forbidden; sacred; holy, taboo, prohibited
Madre de Deus	Mother of God (church)
mainikin	coolness
makaer kmi	holder of candle-nut (midwife)
makdakar	guardians; to look after; protectors
makerek	knowledgeable person (female category)
mako'an adat	historian; the one who cuts (*ko'a*) the words
maktane	supporters
maktukun	an inedible fruit (invalid wife)
malae	Malay (can be translated as foreign)
Malaka *foun*	new Malaka (the present district of Malaka)
Malaka *tuan*	old Malaka (on the Malay peninsula)
malirin	cool
mama lulik	forbidden betel-nut (offerings); obligatory gifts
manas	heat; hot (*menas* is probably a disguised form of *manas*)
manas hun	the source of heat
mane aa tur ti'an iha uma nabaa	the man is married to a woman in that house (the man sits in that house)

mane foun	new man (status raised in the final stage of the marriage process, bridegroom)
mane lais	rest of the in-married men, who are standing and sitting on the ground (addressed as quick men, helpers)
mane liman	men's arms
mane lor	the man of the wave
mane maksai uma	men who leave the house (term to refer to wife's brothers)
mane maktama uma	man who enters the house (married-in men); son-in-law
mane sanulu	group of ten men
mane talain	male cross-cousin
mantarun	money received from cockfight gambling; derives from *manu* (rooster) and *tarun* (to bet). In Tetun it means 'king's property'
manu do'u	a wild pigeon bird (Indonesian *burung dara*)
manu ida	one chicken
manu lamak oan ida	small nourishment of chicken (ritual language)
maran hun	dry land
maran ikus	last to dry
maran uluk	first to dry
marii lia	to erect words, the house that has the authority to decide *adat* matters
ma-roma-k	derives from *roman* or *kroman* meaning 'bright' while *oan* means 'small' and 'child'
maromak oan	'the small bright one, luminous one'
masin	cooked and salty
mata musan	'giving back a seed' (bilateral cross-cousin marriage); 'source seed'; 'the pupil of the eye' (translated into Indonesian as *biji* mata, which means the '(father's) beloved'); ideology and practice of returning a woman to her father's natal house upon the death of her father
mata(n)	eye, any eye-like feature, focus, centre, orifice, spring, origin and source
matak	raw (translation of Christian notion of 'blessing')

matak no let	types of marriage
matak no malirin	raw and cool
matan	notions of primacy
matdok	consists of two words: *mata* = eye; *dok* = far, distant; a shaman is 'one who
	can see 'far' into the future and 'far' into current inauspicious happenings'; shaman
matenek	cleverness, tricks, out-smarting
maun	elder brother; term of address for eB
maun alin ten	brothers who were born from the same womb (express their consanguinity as *mane malun*)
maun uma kain	person 's MZeS and FBeS
mengakali	out-smart
meo	hero (term used by wife's elder brother)
meo ana	small cats
meo naek	great cat
miis	plain taste; unsalted, tasteless or fresh (in *hamiis*)
molin	outside, periphery (general habitation symbolism); cultivation space; peripheral ('outside' the residential space); space outside a house, village or domain
monas	strength and invulnerability
mons	alive
moris ikus	last born
moris uluk	first born
mota dikin	tips of a river
murak tomak ida	silver coin
muti mo	clean white
na'an knase	fish
na'i	love (term grandparents address their grandchildren)
Na'i Lulik	priest, master of the forbidden
naan	sisters refer to their brothers and parallel cousins of the opposite sex
nababan	married-in man and persons in his generation
nahoris oan	to make the baby come alive

nakdohos	crawling like a baby (house idiom, polite way of moving down the levels)
nanaan	brothers; tongue
naran babaur	nickname
naran mata bian	ancestral names
nasai oan	to take the baby out
natar	a rice paddy field (east Tetun)
nato'o oan	to cause the baby to arrive
natoni	type of greeting (Dawan)
ne'e be rai ne'e no nikar ulun	so the land could have rulers
nea ksuik ida	a long boar's rusk
netan	begot (polite terms used to describe pregnancies)
nia nasa'e nikar niakan naan mane nen sia nalo ba ulun	she promoted the six brothers to become heads of the regions
nikah adat	*adat* marriage
nu mea	red coconut
nu modo	green coconut
nu'u mane la no fen, feto la no la'en	like a man without wife or a woman without husband
nuu kalabuk	young, unformed coconut
oa la'en	child husband (bridegroom)
oan	sons
oan feto	female child
oan klakar	phrase used for children of an invalid marriage
oan la'en	daughter's husband
oan mane	male child
oda matan	door
oda matan la sa'en	the unclimbed door; door facing the sunrise
oda matan lor	the male door (house symbolism)
oda matan loro sa'en	door of the rising sun
oda matan rae	door facing the sunset
odan	branches of bamboo (can also be translated as ladder)

oe mean	golden staff
omas	container used for boiling water
onderafdeeling	subdivisions (Durch)
pendatang	newcomers (Indonesian)
Perarakan Bunda Maria	the procession of Mother Mary (Indonesian)
pohon buah tinta	kind of shrub is known in Indonesian because the liquid of its berries is like the colour of ink
rae	a living space in the mountains, high regions on the mountains; associated with mountain, high (place)
rahaman	recently married couple (husband addressed as)
rahinan	recently married couple (wife addressed as)
rahuk	body hair
rai	earth, island, land, region, domain and dirt
rai bot	the great land
rai feto	land of women
rai hun	trunk land (centre of the universe); the original land
rai husar binan	navel of the earth
rai ikun	tail land
rai klaran	the middle, inside world, earth
rai leten	the above world, heaven
rai lian	language of the earth
rai lidun hat	the four-corner land
rai loro monu	land of the falling sun
rai loro sa'e	'the sunrise land'
rai loro toba	land of the setting sun
rai lulik	sacred land or domain
rai maran	dry land
rai na'in	owners of the land
rai saun	secular land or domain
rai sei we	land still covered with water
rai Timor	the island of Timor
rai ulun	the head land
rai Wehali	the domain of Wehali

ramas abut	to water the root
rate kukun and *fatu taman rik*	dark burial grounds
reinos	domains (Portuguese)
ri(n) lidun hat	four corner posts
riin	post
rin kiak	orphan posts (that support the rafters at the periphery)
rin lidun hat	four corner posts
ro'a	outstretched arms
roman	living human beings, bright
rumah adat	*adat* house
rumah sehat	healthier house (Indonesian)
rumah tidak seha	unhealthy house (Indonesian)
sadan	receive advice
sahit tabako	to pick tobacco leaves
sasadin	trying out period (before marriage)
sasaluk	a shroud obscuring or disguising the conditions of something
sasere	rhythm
sasi'an	a counsellor (noun)
sasolok	gifts
sasolok hohela feto foun	gifts that accompany the new woman (bridewealth)
sau nuu	to pick up coconut
saun	secular
sera mama	betel-nut offering
silu batar	to break off maize cobs
Sina mutin Malaka	the white Chinese of Malaka
sistem pemerintahan asli di Belu	a system of government native to Belu (Indonesian)
sorin balu	ribs
surik	liver milt; sword
surik lulik Liurai	swords
surik samara	swords with a long curved shield

swapraja	self-governing domains (Indonesian)
taa hudi	to cut banana
taek	a small step in front of a house that provides access to the verandah
tafatik	palace (derives from two words: *tur* = to sit; *fatik* = place); place to sit (translated into Indonesian as '*istana*')
taha tur	weeding equipment (gifts in terms of money)
tais at	old used sarongs (ugly sarongs)
tais hahoris	birth sarong (black handmade sarong used only for parturition)
tais lima rasan	woven cloth made of local cotton
tak punya adat	someone as without *adat* (serious insult or even a curse) (Indonesian)
tala etu	royal gongs
talain	FZS; marriageable cousin
talain besik	true cross-cousin; true cousins (MBC and FZC)
talain uma kain	classificatory cross-cousins; person's MMBSC and FFZSC
talin	rope, cord or string
taman	to plant (Wehali)
tan lia ne'e, rai ne'e foin halo no ukur	we now have government in our land
tan rai ne'e moris uluk iha ne'e	because the earth was first born here
tanasak	baskets for storing goods (associated with women)
tane	to face, to hold up from underneath, to support
tara horak	to hang up the prohibition; announces an annual 'ban' (*badu*) on harvesting coconuts for a certain period of time
tara kakaluk	to hang up the pouch
tasak	cooked; ripe
tasi	sea
tasi feto	female sea
tasi mane	male sea
tasi sere	the beating of surf on the beach

tatakan	lid
tatane	a woven serving tray (noun)
tate rai halo we	making the canal to drive water
tehen	edge
ten	intestine
tetek	ladder; step
to'os etu kukun	the royal dark garden
tora	foxtail millet
toro uman	the centre of the garden (north Tetun spell *troman* as *toro uman*)
troman	first spot in the garden that was 'cleared off' (*ta*) from shrubs when the garden was founded; sacrificial pillars in the middle of each garden
tua	palm juice; WyZ (term of address for)
tua botir ida	bottle of palm gin
tua kusi ida	one jar of palm gin
tua na'i	the most respected person; father's sister's husband (also addressed as *tuak*); girl's mother's brother (MB); mother's brothers; term for MB; MB, FZH (potentially one's parents-in-law); woman's mother's brother
tua na'i ama etuk	most respected elder of the house
tua sangkir ida	a cup of palm gin (referring to several bottles of palm gin)
tua(n)	old and respected (Tetun)
tuak	(MB) of his sister's children; 'the respected one'; the most 'respected' figure in the house (term of address for mother's brother); variety of palm tree (Borassus Sundaica)
tuan	notions of primacy
tubu	grew
tudak musan	sexual intercourse between nobles
tudik	knife
tukek	bamboo container (Dawan)
tunama	compound word of *tunu* (to roast) and *ama* (father)
tunu	roasted

tur	to sit (idiom to denote 'marriage'); reside
tuur fati	a sitting place (palace)
tuur lia	actual court or *adat* meeting (colloquial Indonesian: *duduk perkara*)
ubi-ubian	tuber plants; classified as root crops (in Indonesian)
udan baur	drizzle that sets in together with the appearance of a rainbow
udan fahi	the pig's rain
udan kakait	drizzle
udan lor	rain that sets in from the seaside
udan menas	unexpected rain
udan namate ahu kresan	rain that kills the hot ashes
udan narodan ai tahan	rain to shed leaves
udan tinan	annual rain; west monsoon
udan we toluk	type of rain is said only to last for three days
uem	house (pronounced as *uim* by the Tetun) is a metathesis from *ume*
uhi	native tubers
ukun badu	a rule of prohibition
ukun rai	rule of the earth
ukur	cords or threads that link the edges of a rectangular loom (noun); notions of both rites and ceremony
ulu	first born (adjective)
uluk	before, former or simply first in time (adverb)
uma	residential house
uma ai	as the high post house
uma amanas	heat house
uma at ida	an ugly house
uma ferik	the house of the respectable woman
uma feto	female house; the house where the husband resides
uma fukun	house of clan head
uma hanawa kosar	house to dry one's sweat
uma hun	the origin house; the trunk house
uma inan bin alin	mother elder sister, younger sister houses

uma kain	stalk of the house (signifies that the people concerned were not born in the same house but are related collaterally); born from a different womb
uma kakaluk	amulet house (popularly known as 'the medicine house')
uma katuas	the house of the respectable man
uma kre'is	closest house uma kukun dark house
uma laran	inner house
uma lidun hat	rectangular house; the four corner house
uma lulik	the forbidden house; sacred house
uma maho naran	named house
uma maho naran ha'i	unnamed house
uma maksian maktane	the up-holding, the supporting house
uma malae	foreign house
uma mane	male-house; patrilineal descent groups (wife-giving house)
uma metan	sacred black house
uma moris fatik	the birth place house
uma na'in	house masters; owner of the house; the lord of the house (term that refers to a man's wife)
uma rai lale'an	the house of Earth-Sky
uma ro malae	the foreign ship house
uma sasi'an tatane	supporting house
uma tasi	the sea house
uma tur fatik	the sitting place house
uma tur hanaiva kosar	the house to rest one's sweat
usan	navel
ut	powder, residue, waste
Vaiquenos	designates both the people and the language of the Dawan (term used widely in East Timor)
wakil camat	deputy head (Indonesian)
we klot	space inside a house to store water
we knuk	well
we matan Maromak	spring of Maromak
we miis	fresh water

Ritual Language Pairs

adomi malu//hatias malu	show love to each other//show affection to each other
akar Insana rohan//maek Insana rohan	edge of the gebang palm of Insana, edge of the tuber of Insana
Ami mai fo hatene ba emi tan oa feto isin manas ulun moras	We come to let you know that your daughter-in-law suffers from fever and headache (to convey condolences to the husband's kin)
asu mata balada oin baiada, asu besin, asu kai sa	following the track of a dog
banin Wehali//satan Wehali	the border of Wehali, the enclosure of Wehali
besi Wehali, baki Wehali	the stronghold of Wehali, the fortress of Wehali
dakar bua kau Wehali//takan kau Wehali	looking after the young areca nuts of Wehali, the young betel leaves of Wehali
deku na'in baa nia, dare na'in baa nia	place to knock, place to tap
ema matak no let	the raw and gap people, 'stranger'
ferik ain tasi//katuas ain tasi	'the old women of the leg of the sea//the old men of the leg of the sea'
ferik foho hun, katuas foho hun	'the old women of the trunk of the mountain, the old men of the trunk of the mountain'
ferik hat, katuas hat	the four old men, the four old women (origin group of the four-corner land council)
ferik tasi tehen, katuas tasi tehen	the old women of the edge of the sea, the old men of the edge of the sea
foho hun ain tasi	'the trunk of the mountain and the tips (instead of foot) of the sea'
fuik hitu, bua hitu	the seven betel leaves, the seven areca nuts

futk let//bua let	the empty (literally, 'gap') betel leaves, the empty areca nut
fuik maho naran//bua maho naran	named betel leaves, named areca nuts
fuik tebes, bua tebes	the true betel leaves, the true areca nut
fuik tolu, bua tolu	the three betel leaves, the three areca nuts
haa matak, hemu matak	the raw food, the raw drink
haa tasan, hemu tasan	the cooked food, the cooked drink
hakro'an hakmasin	'to plead and to make oneself salty'; action of praying
halon hakmasin bodik uma kain foun ha'i kain foun	to bow and to salinise for the new house and the new fire
haloon//hakmasin	to make straight//to salinise
hatetu harani	'gifts' and 'offerings'; literally *hatetu* means 'to lay s.t. on the ground' while *harani* means 'to lay s.t. above', 'to perch'
hatodan fatik//habesi fatik	the place to sit, the place to strengthen oneself
hoku fatik//natar fatik	the place to lie down, the place to dwell
iha kukun//kalan	in the dark//in the night (ancestors who are living)
inuk tuan, dalan tuan	the old path, the old track
kabas no fahan	rite or ceremony
klobor na'in//laen na'in	the lord of granaries, the lord of huts
knokar Liurai, inuk Liurai	stables of Liurai, the paths of Liurai
knua Wesei, knua Wehali	the sheath of Wesei, the sheath of Wehali
knuba hun//tetek hun	the trunk of the hip//the trunk of the ladder
koto lamak hatetu, lamak harani	providing food as offering, food as gifts
labis no na'in ti'an	the platform already has its occupant
lamak hatetu, lamak harani	sacrificial meat that consists of roasted bird
liman lais ain kmaan	fast arms, light feet (the helpers)
loro foho feten//loro tauk dikin	sun mountain peak//sun rock edge
mahaa rik//mahemu rik	eat while standing, drink while standing
mahaa toba//mahemu toba	the one who eats reclining, drink reclining
mahaa tur//mahemu tur	eat while sitting, drink while sitting

makaer lulik bot//makaer manas bot	holder of the great taboo, holder of the mighty heat
makdakar knokar Liurai	guardian of Liurai's stable
makdakar knokar Wehali	the guardians of the stable of Wehali
malaka na'in//amanas na'in	the owner of fire, the owner of heat
manas ha'in//klak ha'in	the only heat, the only burning charcoal
manas bun//lulik hun	the origin of heat and origin of sacredness
manas lulik wa'ik, klak lulik wa'ik	the great sacred heat, the great sacred of burning charcoal
mota fa hefe slfi sa'e	water never flows upstream
nalaka ha'i, hamanas we	to light the fire, boil the water in their house
namon matan//namon tuan	main harbour//old harbour
nanaet tasi kre'is, nanaet foho kre'is	to demarcate mount ain, to demarcate sea
nanan (inner)/ *mone* (outer)	superior/inferior relations
no'i nafofek onan//no'i naknanik onan	is rowing (toward here)//is swimming (toward here)
oa natar hat//oa lalu'an hat	the children of the four enclosures//the children of the four stables
rai husar//rai binan	the navel land//the umbilical cord land
rai lidun hat, rai sikun hat	the four-corner land, the four-elbow land
rai loro lakan//rai loro len	the land of the flaming sun, the land of the glowing sun
rai manu matan, rai bua klaras	the land as a chicken's eye, the land as a slice of areca nut
riin besi hat//riin kmurak hat	the strong posts, the valuable posts
riin makerek//riin mean	the engraved post, the golden post
sadan uma kain foun, ha'i kain foun	to make a place for the new stalk of the house, the new hearth of the house
sasi'an//tatane	facing (uphold//support, Tetun)
simu kmusan, simu matak no malirin	acquiring betel-chew, acquiring raw and cool
su kanufoun, baki foun	to dig a new ditch, a new canal
tama soi//sai seti	easy to put in, but hard to take out

411

tanasak talin//kadain talin	links that connect the plaited baskets (Wehali ritual language)
tetek hun//knuba hun	'trunk of the house step//trunk of the garden ladder'
to'os ai fatik//tua ai fatik	the first garden, the first palm tree
tuir dalan tuan//tuir inuk tuan	tracing the old path, the old crack
uma metan//uma lulik	the black house//the sacred house

Acknowledgements

In the course of my study, fieldwork and the writing of this book I have built up relations with numerous people who have assisted me in many sorts of ways. Here I acknowledge my appreciation, and at the same time reveal the relationship. My period of study in Canberra was made possible through an award under the Equity and Merit Scholarship Scheme sponsored by the Australian International Development Assistance Bureau (the present AusAid). Subsidy for my field research was granted by the Department of Anthropology, Research School of Pacific and Asian Studies, The Australian National University. I extend my appreciation for their role in this matter. I am indebted to many members of staff under the leadership of the late Professor Anthony Forge in the Department of Prehistory and Anthropology (the Faculties), and Professor James Fox, currently Director of the Research School of Pacific and Asian Studies, who moulded me as an anthropologist. Courses led by Dr Ian Keen, Dr Chris Gregory and Dr Don Gardner; an 18-month study group on Austronesian ethnographics under Professor James Fox's auspices; and the many hours of discussion with Dr Penny Graham stimulated my curiosity to know more. To Jim Fox I owe a great debt for his critical comments from the earliest stages of my work. His extensive knowledge and persistent interest in the region have become the source of my knowledge. His strategy 'to read things that are not in the text' challenged me to understand more of what I have been writing. I owe a great debt to Penny Graham who meticulously corrected many drafts of my chapters, clearly pointed out the weaknesses and strengths of the arguments and suggested alternative solutions. To Dr B.D. Grimes and Dr C.E. Grimes I owe thanks for their willingness to suggest valuable comments on various parts of the book. I thank Professor David Hicks for his kind support and his willingness to assist me with a number of books and articles.

I owe thanks to the general staff and research assistants in the department: Susan Toscan, Ann Buller, Ria van de Zandt and Dr Barbara Holloway, Dr Amanda Scott, Ian Heyward from the Cartography Laboratory, and Emily Brissenden from Pandanus Books for their excellent services. I want to acknowledge the value of companionship from former fellow students: Andrea Molnar, Yunita Winarto, Eriko Nakagawa, Nils Bubandt, Philip Taylor, Abdul Muhaimin, Ma'ruf Jamhari, I Gde Pitana, Dedi Adhuri, Catharina van Klinken, and Father Philip Tule. I am particularly indebted to Nontje Pellu for her time in organising the final draft of the book.

My acknowledgment is also extended to members of staff in the Artha Wacana Christian University and my colleagues in the Faculty of Theology. Their constant encouragement to accomplish this study has been a benefit of our solidarity. My gratitude in particular goes to Dr Ayub Ranoh and the Rev. D.J. Mauboi, MTh., who spent much time writing letters of encouragement during my period of study.

In Atambua I owe thanks to Mgr Pain Ratu, Bishop of the Diocese of Atambua and Father Justus Asa, *Provinsial* of the Divine Word of the *Societas Verbi Divini* of Timor Province, who allowed me to search for unpublished documents on the regency of Belu from the SVD's library; to Mr B.J. Manek who kindly gave permission to access his personal archives on *adat* court cases in Wehali; and to Mr Anthon Adi who allowed me to reproduce old photos of the crowning of Seran Nahak as the first *Keser* of the kingdom of Belu.

My greatest debt, however, rests with the many villagers in south Tetun who shared not only their stories but also their shelters and food with me. Their friendship, hospitality and generosity are immeasurable in words and therefore remain always in my heart. I especially thank *mama* and *bapa* Fuah who received me with open arms as the 'returned son' in their house and provided me with basic needs and most of all their love. Thanks also to my brothers and sisters, Suryadi and Roos, June and Mias, Mona, Mea and Min Usifa and Semy and Hanna Hauteas, who were always ready to take me wherever I went and introduced me to many villagers, which opened up the way for me in my early days in the field. To the whole house of Umanen, particularly *ina* Fouk, *mama* Funan, *ina* Bete, *tante* Bui and *ama* Frans Klau Nahak, Na'i Makde'an Rai and *om* Muti, who contributed so much to the knowledge I gained, I would also like to offer my gratitude.

I would like also to thank Luis Sanaka Tei Seran, the Liurai of Malaka, Agustinus Nahak Seran of Haitimuk, the Maromak Oan of Haitimuk and Agustinus Klau, the disputed Maromak Oan of Laran for their time in sharing their ideas on Wehali's political structure; and *adat* historians (*mako'an*) and many elders in Wehali, Wewiku and Fatuaruin, who tirelessly narrated 'the path of ancestors'. In this regard, my heartfelt appreciation goes to Piet Tahu Nahak, Bau Fahik La Rosi, Paulus Dini Sonbai, Cornelis Mau Nehi, Benedictus Bere Seran, Albertus Berek, Katuas Seran Teti and Yohannes Seran Kehik. There are also many friends whom I think of as field tutors in ritual language. Specific acknowledgment is due to the Rev. Gabriel Bria and Fini's *maman*, Ferdy Seran and Ibu Brigitta, *ama* Bo'uk and all members of the Uma Katuas (Umakatahan), Sam Kehik Seran, Salomon Tahu Berek, Bei Manek, Nikolas Teti, Silverius Bria, Alfonsius Klau, the late Bei Lulik, *ama* Dato Fatisin and Felix Bere Sou Rai.

During my stay in Betun, many people in the hamlet of Laran showed generosity and friendship I will long remember. My enjoyable months staying in this hamlet are related to their kind acceptance of a 'foreigner' in their midst. My deepest gratitude rests with Na'i Niis (Theresia Telik Seran), Na'i Mea (Welhelmina Ho'ar Seran), Na'i Man (Marianus Man), Na'i Nona (Yasinta Nona), Na'i Kloit (Dominikus Tei Seran), Na'i Nona (Hoa'r Nahak), Na'i Bo'uk and guardians of Uma Bei Nufa and Uma Ai Tou.

Finally, I thank my family, Dee, Rani and Lia. During my fieldwork in Timor, they had to live alone in Canberra. At the final stage of writing, they were in Kupang. To them I dedicate this study as a token of my indebtedness, love and acknowledgment of their patience and support.

www.ingramcontent.com/pod-product-compliance
Lightning Source LLC
Chambersburg PA
CBHW051441270326
41932CB00025B/3388